# CONTENTS

# LIST OF BIBLE INFORMATION CHARTS

# AN ALL-IN-ONE READING GUIDE

Most people read the Bible from time to time. But how many read it regularly enough to become really familiar with its teaching? The aim of this book is to help the reader establish a regular pattern of planned and coherent reading over a period of a year.

The readings are undated, so the book can be started at any time. But it is best to start on a Sunday, because the readings have been selected by weekly theme.

Each day's reading is quite brief, and can easily be read in five minutes—though the reader may want to pause and ponder the meaning for longer. Five major translations have been used, as best suits each reading: New International Version (NIV), Revised Standard Version (RSV), Revised English Bible (REB), New Jerusalem Bible (NJB) and Authorised Version (AV)—the old King James.

But in addition to the readings, each week offers an introduction and an explanatory feature. The introduction explains how each day's reading contributes to understanding that week's theme. And the explanatory feature unpacks the whole Bible teaching about that theme, so as to show how it affects our lives.

Take week one, which is all about creation, as an example. On page 9 comes the introduction: *The Infinite Designer.* The explanatory feature, *God the Creator,* can be found on page 10. On the following few pages the readings are printed for Sunday through to Saturday.

Many readers may like to give a little extra time on a Sunday to reading the introduction and explanatory feature, as well as the reading for that day. Then on the busier Monday to Saturday only the Bible passage need be read.

One other feature of this book will be an important aid to understanding: the twelve graphic information spreads (see the list on page 7). These give information on the different types of Bible book. Reading a psalm, for instance, is very different from reading a chapter from a New Testament letter, or from an Old Testament history book. These information spreads will help readers to read the various kinds of literature with understanding, and to bring the appropriate background of ideas to each day's passage. Perhaps you might want to turn to the relevant spread the first time you find the background of a passage hard to follow.

Generally speaking, it will be best to follow the sequence of themes as set. The exceptions are the major Christian festivals, as it will obviously be best to read about the first Christmas at Christmas-time and the first Easter at Easter-time! Our suggestions here are these:

*For Christmas week: week 18*
*For holy week (before Easter Day): week 21*
*For the week beginning on Easter Day: week 26*
*For the week beginning on Whitsunday: week 3*
*For the week in which Ash Wednesday falls: week 44*

Each reader will of course find his or her own preferred way of using this book. But we hope the one common feature will be regularity. Try to read from it *every day* for a year—or as near as possible.

Above all, read with enjoyment. The Bible is a fascinating book. Many have found their time of daily reading to be the highpoint of each day—something eagerly looked forward to. May this book of readings be the launching pad from which many embark on a lifetime's appreciation of the book of books.

# THE INFINITE DESIGNER

Belief in God the creator is easily taken for granted—until it is taken away. Notions of many creators, or no creator, or creation by remorseless fate or random accidents—all of these are common. But none has the grandeur of the Bible's consistent picture of God the sole maker, who plans and creates all that is.

The incomparably majestic opening words in Genesis (Sunday) set the scene for all that follows: the book of Job, too, though pursuing its own drama of suffering, touches at many points on the splendour of what God has made—whether we look wonderingly at the stars or warily at the hippo (or could 'behemoth' be the crocodile?—Monday).

The Psalms are for singing, with creation as their backcloth; there is much more to say about God, but worship often starts here (Tuesday). And among the earlier prophets, Amos punctuates his trenchant message with reminders of the all-creating Lord in whose name he dares to speak (Thursday). Isaiah ridicules the idolatries of his day in similar fashion (Wednesday).

In the New Testament we glimpse its leading missionary-apostle asserting, in the face of the Athenians' cultured confusion, both 'one world' and one redeemer (Friday). And the Bible's final pages ring out with songs in praise of the Creator (Saturday).

WEEK 1

# The Creator

The first thing we learn about God in the Bible is that he is the Creator who brought everything into being.

The Bible is clear that God created the universe because he loves. Creation flows from his desire to enter into a relationship of love with us all. Just as in a family our children are born from love and into love, so God's act of creation springs from his love which brings everything into existence.

In the first creation account (Genesis 1:1–2:4) the accent is on the creation of all things: 'In the beginning God created the heavens and the earth.' In the next verses there follows an ascending order of creation from the most primitive creatures to God's most perfect creation—humanity. And God was satisfied with his workmanship: 'God looked at everything he had made, and he was very pleased.'

In the second account (Genesis 2:5–25) the emphasis falls on this world and on relationships between men and women. This passage develops further the high place humanity holds in creation—to 'rule' the earth as God's stewards and to have responsibility over all life.

The rest of the Bible confirms the teaching found in Genesis and develops it in four ways:

◆ **God is at work in his creation.** He did not wind up the universe like a clock and leave it to tick away unattended.

◆ He is still at work in the universe, caring for it and giving it direction and purpose.

◆ **God providentially cares for everything.** A greatly neglected teaching these days is the doctrine of providence. This belief means that God is intimately interested in every aspect of his creation and our welfare is his delight.

◆ **We live in a sin-shot world.** This world has been spoiled through sin. God created all things well but his creation has been marred and spoiled through humanity's rebellion against God. Because we are part of this sin-shot creation we, too, carry within us the signs of its disintegration—weakness, sickness and death.

◆ **God is in control, however serious the plight facing humanity.**

The Bible's teaching about creation challenges much of current thinking. It reminds us that this world has meaning; if the universe came into being by chance then of course there is no basic purpose behind it, but if God created it then it has a meaning which affects all our lives.

It reminds us too that God's creation is to be enjoyed. God has given it to us to take pleasure in it, to admire it and use it enthusiastically without abusing it.

# SUNDAY

GENESIS 1:1–5 (AV)

In the beginning God created the heaven and the earth. And the earth was without form, and void; and darkness was upon the face of the deep. And the Spirit of God moved upon the face of the waters. And God said, Let there be light: and there was light. And God saw the light, that it was good: and God divided the light from the darkness. And God called the light Day, and the darkness he called Night. And the evening and the morning were the first day.

# MONDAY

JOB 9:4–12, 40:15–24 (NIV)

His wisdom is profound, his power is vast.
Who has resisted him and come out unscathed?
He moves mountains without their knowing it
and overturns them in his anger.
He shakes the earth from its place
and makes its pillars tremble.
He speaks to the sun and it does not shine;
he seals off the light of the stars.
He alone stretches out the heavens
and treads on the waves of the sea.
He is the Maker of the Bear and Orion,
the Pleiades and the constellations of the south.
He performs wonders that cannot be fathomed,
miracles that cannot be counted.
When he passes me, I cannot see him;
when he goes by, I cannot perceive him.
If he snatches away, who can stop him?
Who can say to him, 'What are you doing?'

The Lord said 'Look at the behemoth,
which I made along with you
and which feeds on grass like an ox.
What strength he has in his loins,
what power in the muscles of his belly!
His tail sways like a cedar;
the sinews of his thighs are close-knit.
His bones are tubes of bronze,
his limbs like rods of iron.
He ranks first among the works of God,
yet his Maker can approach him with his sword.
The hills bring him their produce,
and all the wild animals play nearby.
Under the lotus plant he lies,
hidden among the reeds in the marsh.
The lotuses conceal him in their shadow;
the poplars by the stream surround him.
When the river rages, he is not alarmed;
he is secure, though the Jordan should surge against his mouth.
Can anyone capture him by the eyes,
or trap him and pierce his nose?'

## TUESDAY

PSALMS 95, 100 (RSV)

O come, let us sing to the Lord;
  let us make a joyful noise to the rock of our salvation!
Let us come into his presence with thanksgiving;
  let us make a joyful noise to him with songs of praise!
For the Lord is a great God,
  and a great King above all gods.
In his hand are the depths of the earth;
  the heights of the mountains are his also.
The sea is his, for he made it;
  for his hands formed the dry land.

O come, let us worship and bow down,
  let us kneel before the Lord, our Maker!
For he is our God,
  and we are the people of his pasture,
  and the sheep of his hand.

O that today you would hearken to his voice!
  Harden not your hearts, as at Meribah,
  as on the day at Massah in the wilderness,
when your fathers tested me,
  and put me to the proof, though they had seen my work.
For forty years I loathed that generation
  and said, 'They are a people who err in heart,
  and they do not regard my ways.'
Therefore I swore in my anger
  that they should not enter my rest.

Make a joyful noise to the Lord, all the lands!
Serve the Lord with gladness!
Come into his presence with singing!

Know that the Lord is God!
  It is he that made us, and we are his;
  we are his people, and the sheep of his pasture.

Enter his gates with thanksgiving,
  and his courts with praise!
  Give thanks to him, bless his name!

For the Lord is good;
  his steadfast love endures for ever,
  and his faithfulness to all generations.

## WEDNESDAY

ISAIAH 45:5–12, 18–22 (REB)

I am the Lord, and there is none other;
  apart from me there is no god.
Though you have not known me I shall strengthen you,
  so that from east to west
  all may know there is none besides me:
I am the Lord, and there is none other;
I make the light, I create the darkness;
  author alike of wellbeing and woe,
I, the Lord, do all these things.

Rain righteousness, you heavens,
  let the skies above pour it down,

let the earth open for it
that salvation may flourish
with righteousness growing beside it.
I, the Lord, have created this.

Will the pot contend with the potter,
or the earthenware with the hand that shapes it?
Will the clay ask the potter what he is making
or his handiwork say to him,
'You have no skill'?
Will the child say to his father,
'What are you begetting?'
or to his mother, 'What are you bringing to birth?'
Thus says the Lord, Israel's Holy One, his Maker:
Would you dare question me concerning my children,
or instruct me in my handiwork?
I alone made the earth
and created mankind upon it.
With my own hands I stretched out the heavens
and directed all their host.

Thus says the Lord, the Creator of the heavens,
he who is God,
who made the earth and fashioned it
and by himself fixed it firmly,
who created it not as a formless waste
but as a place to be lived in:
I am the Lord, and there is none other.
I did not speak in secret, in realms of darkness;
I did not say to Jacob's people,
'Look for me in the formless waste.'
I the Lord speak what is right, I
declare what is just.

Gather together, come, draw near,
you survivors of the nations,
who in ignorance carry wooden idols in procession,
praying to a god that cannot save.
Come forward and urge your case,
consult together:
who foretold this in days of old,
who stated it long ago?
Was it not I, the Lord?
There is no god but me,
none other than I, victorious and able to save.

From every corner of the earth
turn to me and be saved;
for I am God, there is none other.

## THURSDAY

AMOS 4:12–13, 5:8–9, 9:5–6 (NIV)

'Therefore this is what I will do to you, Israel,
and because I will do this to you,
prepare to meet your God, O Israel.'
He who forms the mountains, creates the wind,
and reveals his thoughts to man,
he who turns dawn to darkness,
and treads the high places of the earth—
the Lord God Almighty is his name.

(He who made the Pleiades and Orion,
who turns blackness into dawn
and darkens day into night,
who calls for the waters of the sea

and pours them out over the face of the land—
the Lord is his name—
he flashes destruction on the stronghold
and brings the fortified city to ruin.)

The Lord, the Lord Almighty,
he who touches the earth and it melts,
and all who live in it mourn—
the whole land rises like the Nile,
then sinks like the river of Egypt—
he who builds his lofty palace in the heavens
and sets its foundation on the earth,
who calls for the waters of the sea
and pours them out over the face of the land—
the Lord is his name.

## FRIDAY

ACTS 17:22–31 (RSV)

So Paul, standing in the middle of the Areopagus, said: 'Men of Athens, I perceive that in every way you are very religious. For as I passed along, and observed the objects of your worship, I found also an altar with this inscription, "To an unknown god". What therefore you worship as unknown, this I proclaim to you. The God who made the world and everything in it, being Lord of heaven and earth, does not live in shrines made by man, nor is he served by human hands, as though he needed anything, since he himself gives to all men life and breath and everything. And he made from one every nation of men to live on all the face of the earth, having determined allotted periods and the boundaries of their habitation, that they should seek God, in the hope that they might feel after him and find him. Yet he is not far from each one of us, for
"In him we live and move and have our being";
as even some of your poets have said,
"For we are indeed his offspring".
Being then God's offspring, we ought not to think that the Deity is like gold, or silver, or stone, a representation by the art and imagination of man. The times of ignorance God overlooked, but now he commands all men everywhere to repent, because he has fixed a day on which he will judge the world in righteousness by a man whom he has appointed, and of this he has given assurance to all men by raising him from the dead.'

## SATURDAY

REVELATION 4:1–11 (NJB)

Then, in my vision, I saw a door open in heaven and heard the same voice speaking to me, the voice like a trumpet, saying, 'Come up here: I will show you what is to take place in the future.' With that, I fell into ecstasy and I saw a throne standing in heaven, and the One who was sitting on the throne, and the One sitting there looked like a diamond and a ruby. There was a rainbow encircling the throne, and this looked like an emerald. Round the throne in a circle were

twenty-four thrones, and on them twenty-four elders sitting, dressed in white robes with golden crowns on their heads. Flashes of lightning were coming from the throne, and the sound of peals of thunder, and in front of the throne there were seven lamps burning, the seven Spirits of God. In front of the throne was a sea as transparent as crystal. In the middle of the throne and around it, were four living creatures all studded with eyes, in front and behind. The first living creature was like a lion, the second like a bull, the third living creature had a human face, and the fourth living creature was like a flying eagle. Each of the four living creatures had six wings and was studded with eyes all the way round as well as inside; and day and night they never stopped singing'Holy, holy, holy is the Lord God, the Almighty;
who was, and is and is to come.'
Every time the living creatures glorified and honoured and gave thanks to the One sitting on the throne, who lives for ever and ever, the twenty-four elders prostrated themselves before him to worship the One who lives for ever and ever, and threw down their crowns in front of the throne, saying:

You are worthy, our Lord and God,
to receive glory and honour and
power,
for you made the whole universe;
by your will, when it did not exist, it
was created.

WEEK 2

# THE AUTHENTIC VOICE

The search for meaning was not invented by the twentieth century. It has surfaced in many ways down the ages. Christians believe that our search was anticipated and met by God's revelation. The New Testament letter to the Hebrews says 'he has spoken to us', uniquely and decisively, in Jesus Christ (Thursday)—not to be confused with any other prophet, king or angel, but specially designated 'the Word' (Monday). Words are heavily under attack today, but they remain our chief mode of communication. Christ himself is God's way of communicating with us.

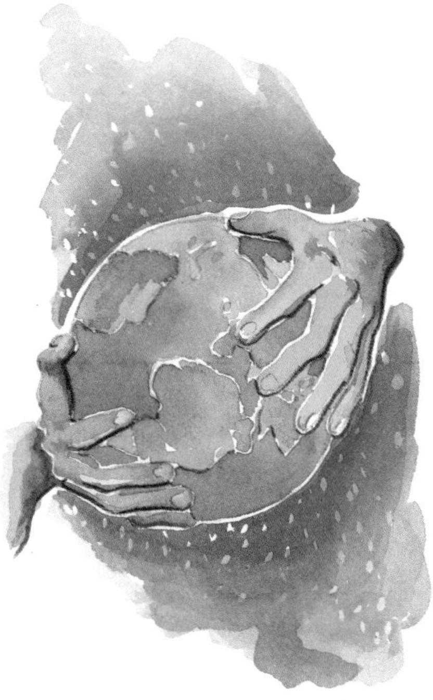

The first reading this week prepares the ground for this idea as 'Wisdom' personified addresses us in the book of Proverbs (Sunday). The point of the two stories from Mark (Tuesday) can easily be missed if we forget how the Bible begins. To ask 'Who then is this?' is a fair question about one whose voice shows God-like authority over creation: to say 'He has done all things well' is to echo the phrase in Genesis asserting that God's creative voice makes everything very good.

The apostle Paul spells out this high doctrine of Christ as he writes to the Christians at Colossae (Wednesday). John 'the elder' insists on this truth being taught and received (Friday). And in the last of seven 'letters to the churches' in Revelation (Saturday), the word from Jesus the faithful and true witness is again decisive—in perfect unity with the Father and the Spirit.

# Jesus the Word

The 'Word' is a title for Jesus found almost exclusively in John's Gospel. It was a term with a rich set of associations for both Jew and Greek. In fact John's decision to call Jesus the Word was a brilliant attempt to communicate the truth about Christ in language that would ring bells in both worlds at once.

◆ **For the Jew, the 'Word' could only mean the 'Word of the Lord' in the Old Testament**. It was by his Word that God made the world. When he said, 'Let there be . . .' something new came into existence. The Word, then, was the communication of what God had in mind. God acted powerfully through it. He had even made the world by it. To receive God's Word and live by it was the way to find life.

◆ **In the world of Greek thought, the Word (Logos in Greek) was one of the taken-for-granted ideas**. The Stoics, for example, said that the universe was not the result of random forces. It was not a chaos, a mess or a disorder. It had a logic to it. This hidden blueprint ensured that nature followed a regular pattern, that the grass grew, the beasts had their seasons and the stars did not fall from the sky. The reason why things were as they were, the Stoics called Logos. Logos was both the invisible programming and the examples of it in the print out.

About the time of Jesus a Jew called Philo, himself immersed in Greek ideas, took the bold step of connecting the Greek Logos with the Old Testament Word.

◆ **This process is not difficult for us to appreciate, since we use words in much the same way**. 'What do you have in mind?' we ask people. And they reply by putting their thoughts into words. We use words to plan our projects, to get things done, to communicate and explain ourselves to others. In one way we can look on our words as separate entities. And yet, of course, they could hardly be more closely related to us. Unless I'm putting on an act, who I am, what I think and what I say are all the same thing.

We can see how brilliantly John built a bridge between two worlds by calling Jesus the Logos/Word. But he was not just using a familiar term. There was one enormous leap forward. John made the incredible claim that the Word of God had become a particular human being: 'the Word became flesh.' 'Flesh' is what humans are made of; it is the stuff that bleeds. So the living, breathing, walking Jesus of Nazareth is the mind of God, God's thought-processes embodied. Jesus is the means by which God made the universe; he is the working-out of the blueprint.

If someone were to say, on a bleak Monday morning, 'What is life all about?' John would reply, 'Look at Jesus and you'll see what the universe means.' The way God is and the way God works is fleshed out in him. To receive Jesus is to tune in to the universe, to live the way you were designed to live. It is like running *with* the escalator and not against it.

WEEK 2

## SUNDAY

PROVERBS 8:22–31 (AV)

The Lord possessed me in the
beginning of his way,
before his works of old.
I was set up from everlasting,
from the beginning, or ever the
earth was.
When there were no depths, I was
brought forth;
when there were no fountains
abounding with water.
Before the mountains were settled,
before the hills was I brought
forth:
While as yet he had not made the
earth, nor the fields,
nor the highest part of the dust of
the world.
When he prepared the heavens, I
was there:
when he set a compass up on the
face of the depth:
When he gave to the sea his decree,
that the waters should not pass
his commandment:
when he appointed the foundations
of the earth:
Then I was by him, as one
brought up with him;
and I was daily his delight, rejoicing
always before him;
Rejoicing in the habitable part of his
earth;
and my delights were with the
sons of men.

## MONDAY

JOHN 1:1–14 (NJB)

In the beginning was the Word: the Word was with God and the Word was God. He was with God in the beginning. Through him all things came into being, not one thing came into being except through him. What has come into being in him was life, life that was the light of men; and light shines in darkness, and darkness could not overpower it.

A man came, sent by God. His name was John. He came as a witness, to bear witness to the light, so that everyone might believe through him. He was not the light, he was to bear witness to the light.

The Word was the real light that gives light to everyone; he was coming into the world. He was in the world that had come into being through him, and the world did not recognize him. He came to his own and his own people did not accept him. But to those who did accept him he gave power to become children of God, to those who believed in his name who were born not from human stock or human desire or human will but from God himself. The Word became flesh, he lived among us, and we saw his glory, the glory that he has from the Father as only Son of the Father, full of grace and truth.

## TUESDAY

MARK 4:35–41, 7:32–37 (RSV)

On that day, when evening had come, Jesus said to them, 'Let us go across to the other side.' And leaving the crowd, they took him with them in the boat, just as he was. And other boats were with him. And a great storm of wind arose, and the waves beat into the boat, so that the boat was already filling. But he was in the stern, asleep on the cushion; and they woke him and said to him, 'Teacher, do you not care if we perish?' And he awoke and rebuked the wind, and said to the sea, 'Peace! Be still!' And the wind ceased, and there was a great calm. He said to them, 'Why are you afraid? Have you no faith?' And they were filled with awe, and said to one another, 'Who then is this, that even wind and sea obey him?'

And they brought to Jesus a man who was deaf and had an impediment in his speech; and they besought him to lay his hand upon him. And taking him aside from the multitude privately, he put his fingers into his ears, and he spat and touched his tongue; and looking up to heaven, he sighed, and said to him, 'Ephphatha,' that is, 'Be opened.' And his ears were opened, his tongue was released, and he spoke plainly. And he charged them to tell no one; but the more he charged them, the more zealously they proclaimed it. And they were astonished beyond measure, saying, 'He has done all things well; he even makes the deaf hear and the dumb speak.'

## WEDNESDAY

COLOSSIANS 1:15–20 (NIV)

He is the image of the invisible God, the firstborn over all creation. For by him all things were created: things in heaven and on earth, visible and invisible, whether thrones or powers or rulers or authorities; all things were created by him and for him. He is before all things, and in him all things hold together. And he is the head of the body, the church; he is the beginning and the firstborn from among the dead, so that in everything he might have the supremacy. For God was pleased to have all his fullness dwell in him, and through him to reconcile to himself all things, whether things on earth or things in heaven, by making peace through his blood, shed on the cross.

## THURSDAY

HEBREWS 1:1–12 (RSV)

In many and various ways God spoke of old to our fathers by the prophets; but in these last days he has spoken to us by a Son, whom he appointed the heir of all things, through whom also he created the world. He reflects the glory of God and bears the very stamp of his nature, upholding the universe by his word of power. When he had made purification for sins, he sat down at the right hand of the Majesty on high, having become as much superior to angels as the name he has obtained is more excellent than theirs.

For to what angel did God ever say,

'Thou art my Son, today I have
begotten thee'?

Or again,

'I will be to him a father, and he
shall be to me a son'?

And again, when he brings the first born into the world, he says,

'Let all God's angels worship him.'

Of the angels he says,

'Who makes his angels winds, and
his servants flames of fire.'
But of the Son he says,
'Thy throne, O God, is for ever and
ever,
the righteous sceptre is the
sceptre of thy kingdom.
Thou hast loved righteousness and
hated lawlessness;
therefore God, thy God, has anointed thee
with the oil of gladness beyond
thy comrades.'
And,
'Thou, Lord, didst found the earth in
the beginning,
and the heavens are the work of
thy hands;
they will perish, but thou remainest;
they will all grow old like a
garment,
like a mantle thou wilt roll them up,
and they will be changed.
But thou art the same,
and thy years will never end.'

## FRIDAY

2 JOHN 1–11 (NIV)

The elder,

To the chosen lady and her children, whom I love in the truth—and not I only, but also all who know the truth—because of the truth, which lives in us and will be with us for ever:

Grace, mercy and peace from God the Father and from Jesus Christ, the Father's Son, will be with us in truth and love.

It has given me great joy to find some of your children walking in the truth, just as the Father commanded us. And now, dear lady, I am not writing you a new command but one we have had from the beginning. I ask that we love one another. And this is love: that we walk in obedience to his commands. As you have heard from the beginning, his command is that you walk in love.

Many deceivers, who do not acknowledge Jesus Christ as coming in the flesh, have gone out into the world. Any such person is the deceiver and the antichrist. Watch out that you do not lose what you have worked for, but that you may be rewarded fully. Anyone who runs ahead and does not continue in the teaching of Christ does not have God; whoever continues in the teaching has both the Father and the Son. If anyone comes to you and does not bring this teaching, do not take him into your house or welcome him. Anyone who welcomes him shares in his wicked work.

## SATURDAY

REVELATION 3:14–22 (REB)

To the angel of the church at Laodicea write:

'These are the words of the Amen, the faithful and true witness, the source of God's creation: I know what you are doing; you are neither cold or hot. How I wish you were either hot or cold! Because you are neither one nor the other, but just lukewarm, I will spit you out of my mouth. You say, "How rich I am! What a fortune I have made! I have everything I want." In fact, though you do not realize it, you are a pitiful wretch, poor, blind, and naked. I advise you to buy from me gold refined in the fire to make you truly rich, and white robes to put on to hide the shame of your nakedness, and ointment for your eyes so that you may see. All whom I love I reprove and discipline. Be wholehearted therefore in your repentance. Here I stand knocking at the door; if anyone hears my voice and opens the door, I will come in and he and I will eat together.

To anyone who is victorious I will grant a place beside me on my throne, as I myself was victorious and sat down with my Father on his throne. You have ears, so hear what the Spirit says to the churches!'

## THE FIRST FIVE BOOKS

These great opening books of the Bible tell one of the world's great stories—of how Israel, the people of God, began its national life. Two of the Bible's great characters, Abraham and Moses, appear in these stories, which end with Israel on the border of 'the promised land'.

Along with the stories is found much writing about laws for religion and society, and regulations about worship and about great festivals. It is as if the character of their life once the land was settled was being set out in the days before they entered it.

But first comes the great story of creation...

GENESIS

### GENESIS

The creation of the world and the beginning of human history 1—11

Abraham 12—23

Isaac, Esau and Jacob 24—36

Joseph and his brothers 37—45

Israel comes to Egypt 46—50

### EXODUS

The Israelites delivered from slavery in Egypt 1—15

The journey to Mount Sinai 16—18

The covenant is made and laws are given 19—24

The tent (tabernacle) for worship, and laws for worship 25—40

### LEVITICUS

Laws about sacrifices 1—7

Laws for priests 8—10

Food laws, and rules about health 11—15

The Day of Atonement 16

Life, worship and the festivals 17—27 (includes the great 'holiness code'—19)

### NUMBERS

Getting ready to leave Mount Sinai 1—9

The journey begins, and disaster strikes 10—21

Events during the wanderings 22—32

Summary of the journey 33—36

## THE LAWS

The Jews call the whole five books 'the Book of the Law'. But in fact there are four great central points where the laws can be found. **The Ten Commandments** (Exodus 20:1-17 and Deuteronomy 5:6-22); **the Book of the Covenant** (Exodus 21—23), a whole code of laws given at the time when God made a covenant with Israel at Mount Sinai; **the Levitical Law** which occupies that whole book; **the Deuteronomic Law** (Deuteronomy 12—26).

There are many different kinds of laws, but among them are these: **criminal laws, civil laws**, concerned with disputes between citizens, **family laws**, designed to protect and guide the clans of which Israel was made up, **laws for worship**, and **charitable laws**, particularly about justice for the poor.

Our circumstances today are very different, so we are not looking to observe all these Old Testament regulations. We need to look for the great moral principles which lie behind them, valid for all time.

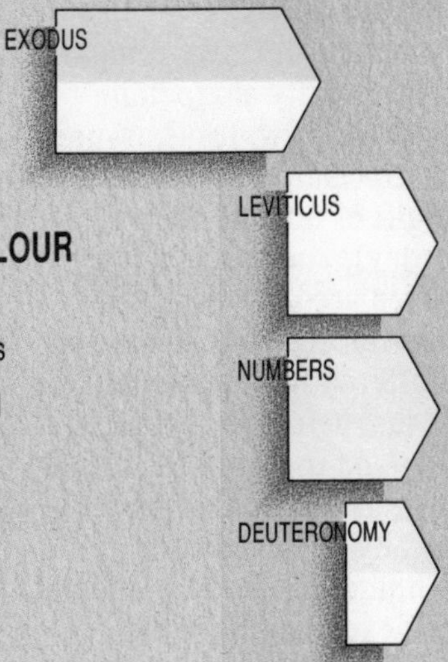

EXODUS

LEVITICUS

NUMBERS

DEUTERONOMY

## DEUTERONOMY

The lessons of the journey 1—4

God's laws and the blessings of obeying them 5—26

The covenant renewed 27—30

Moses hands over the leadership 31—34

## KEY TO COLOUR GRADING

The great stories

Laws for life and religion

WEEK 3

# THE BREATH OF LIFE

We return to Genesis (Sunday) for our introduction to the Spirit of God—his life-giving 'breath' or 'wind', active in creation.

Isaiah begins to unfold his character as the 'Holy Spirit' among God's people, while to Ezekiel, prophet of the exile, we owe the dramatic vision of new life for a nation who on their own estimation were worse than dead (Monday).

But these Old Testament texts remain shadowy compared with the rapidly-sharpening focus of the New. Jesus assures his disciples that the Spirit is the good gift of God his Father (Tuesday), and John's more extended account records the promise of 'the Counsellor' (or Comforter/Advocate/Helper) made just before the death of Jesus—and the work he will do after Jesus has gone from them physically (Wednesday).

Thursday's reading sets out Peter's explanation of the spectacular descent of the Spirit on the day of Pentecost, quoting from Joel's Old Testament prophecy. Two extracts from Paul's letters complete the week.

To the Romans he unfolds what it means to 'live according to the Spirit' (Friday), and to the Galatians, how the fruit or harvest of the Spirit (and their opposites) are evident (Saturday).

# The Holy Spirit

'I will not leave you comfortless. I will send to you another Comforter, who will be with you for ever.' These words of Jesus, spoken just before he died, are a fitting introduction to that divine being we call the Spirit. He comes to us through Jesus Christ, and he indwells us for ever.

Before the coming of Jesus there was no clear expression of the Spirit. The favourite Old Testament word for the Spirit is 'breath', which probably stands for the powerful energy of God in the world. As 'breath' of God he creates, inspires, gives leadership, empowers, reveals God's word and gives creative ability. The prophets herald the coming of the Messiah who will be anointed with God's Spirit, in an age when all of God's people will be visited with the Spirit of God. But throughout the Old Testament the Spirit came on people for specific tasks and for temporary periods. He did not indwell them permanently.

During the ministry of Jesus the Spirit acted in great power. The Spirit indwelt Jesus fully, and the gifts and graces in their very best were to be seen in his life. But the 'age of the Spirit' properly began when Jesus' work had been completed with his death, resurrection and ascension. Jesus, Spirit-filled, then became the giver of the Spirit. He told his disciples that he would not be leaving them alone: 'I will send to you another Comforter, who will be with you for ever.' The Spirit came in power on the day of Pentecost, inspiring the church to proclaim the good news of the kingdom.

There are four very important truths about the Holy Spirit:

- **He is the Spirit of Jesus.** Although the Spirit has a distinctive personality, his role is never to proclaim himself but to glorify Christ and 'floodlight' the work of Jesus. The Spirit is only satisfied when the beauty and glory of Jesus are lit up by his light. It is not surprising, then, that in the New Testament there is some overlap between the work of the Spirit and the Son—Jesus is said to indwell the Christian but so does the Spirit. This overlap, however, merely emphasizes our central point—the Spirit wants to make us more like Christ.
- **He is the Spirit of mission.** In the Acts of the Apostles we constantly see the Holy Spirit in action guiding the church, coming in power on the apostles and indwelling all believers. He is interested in enlarging the boundaries of the Christian family and making disciples. He continues to apply the work of Jesus Christ to every new situation and every age.
- **He is the Spirit of the church.** Without the Spirit there is no church. He who was the distinctive mark of the ministry of Jesus now fills the community of Jesus. No one can be born into God's family without him. He indwells all Christian people and he is the centre of the church's unity and the mainspring of its life.
- **He is the Spirit of power.** The word often used of the Spirit in the New

Testament gives us our word 'dynamite'. That explosive power of God is seen in the Acts of the Apostles as the apostles witness boldly to the resurrection of Christ. That self-same power is expressed through the gifts of the Spirit given to his people.

So where has that power gone today? There is, in fact, plenty of evidence throughout the world today of astonishing growth as the Spirit works among his people. Yet there are also many weak churches and powerless Christians. Two key things should be borne in mind. First, the Spirit can be grieved by hardness of heart, by unbelief and opposition and his work may be quenched or restrained. When the church tries to operate in its own power, that is when it is most weak. Second, remember that the incarnation and the cross of Christ were apparently very weak. The Spirit does not always take us along the pathways of blessing and power. Sometimes he takes us through the valleys of suffering, opposition and struggle. We should remember that Calvary was as much a sign of power as was Pentecost.

Although no clear teaching about the person of the Spirit can be found in the Old Testament, in the New Testament he is clearly portrayed as a separate person within the Godhead. In the Acts of the Apostles the Spirit leads the church. He may be lied to, he speaks, he takes direct action. But it is in John's Gospel that the personality of the Spirit reaches its peak when he is spoken of as the one who proceeds from the Father, sent in the name of the Son. The special name John gives to the Spirit is 'Paraclete', which comes from the root 'one who gives encouragement and comfort'. This sums up his nature very well.

We should never ignore the Spirit. A Spirit-less church is worse than powerless—it is dead. On the other hand, we should never exaggerate his importance so that he overshadows the Father and the Son. The Spirit exists to give glory to the Son and it follows that a balanced Christian faith will want to rest on the whole Trinity. But we certainly need to allow the Spirit room in our lives to make us more Christ-like, and allow the Spirit room in our churches to bring new life, change and development. Clinging to church tradition is sometimes the enemy of the Holy Spirit. He is always on the move and we should not be afraid to travel light.

## SUNDAY

GENESIS 1:1–2 (AV)

In the beginning God created the heaven and the earth. And the earth was without form, and void; and darkness was upon the face of the deep. And the Spirit of God moved upon the face of the waters.

ISAIAH 63:7–14 (AV)

I will mention the lovingkindnesses of the Lord, and the praises of the Lord, according to all that the Lord hath bestowed on us, and the great goodness toward the house of Israel, which he hath bestowed on them according to his mercies, and according to the multitude of his lovingkindnesses. For he said, Surely they are my people, children that will not lie: so he was their Saviour. In all their affliction he was afflicted, and the angel of his presence saved them: in his love and in his pity he redeemed them; and he bare them, and carried them all the days of old.

But they rebelled, and vexed his holy Spirit: therefore he was turned to be their enemy, and he fought against them. Then he remembered the days of old, Moses, and his people, saying, Where is he that brought them up out of the sea with the shepherd of his flock? where is he that put his holy Spirit within him? That led them by the right hand of Moses with his glorious arm, dividing the water before them, to make himself an everlasting name? That led them through the deep, as an horse in the wilderness, that they should not stumble? As a beast goeth down into the valley, the Spirit of the Lord caused him to rest: so didst thou lead thy people, to make thyself a glorious name.

## MONDAY

EZEKIEL 37:1–14 (NIV)

The hand of the Lord was upon me, and he brought me out by the Spirit of the Lord and set me in the middle of a valley; it was full of bones. He led me to and fro among them, and I saw a great many bones on the floor of the valley, bones that were very dry. He asked me, 'Son of man, can these bones live?'

I said, 'O Sovereign Lord, you alone know.'

Then he said to me, 'Prophesy to these bones and say to them, "Dry bones, hear the word of the Lord! This is what the Sovereign Lord says to these bones: I will make breath enter you, and you will come to life. I will attach tendons to you and make flesh come upon you and cover you with skin; I will put breath in you, and you will come to life. Then you will know that I am the Lord." '

So I prophesied as I was commanded. And as I was prophesying, there was a noise, a rattling sound, and the bones came together, bone to bone. I looked, and tendons and flesh appeared on them, but there was no breath in them.

Then he said to me, 'Prophesy to the breath; prophesy, son of man, and say to it, "This is what the Sovereign Lord says: Come from the four winds, O breath, and breathe into these slain, that they may live." ' So I prophesied as he commanded me, and breath entered them; they came to life and stood up on their feet—a vast army.

Then he said to me: 'Son of man, these bones are the whole house of Israel. They say, "Our bones are dried up and our hope is gone; we are cut off." Therefore prophesy and say to them: "This is what the Sovereign Lord says: O my people, I am going to open your graves and bring you back from them; I will bring you back to the land of Israel. Then you, my people will know that I am the Lord, when I open your graves and bring you up from them. I will put my Spirit in you and you will live, and I will settle you in your own land. Then you will know that I the Lord have spoken, and I have done it, declares the Lord." '

## TUESDAY

LUKE 11:9–13 (NJB)

Jesus said 'So I say to you: Ask, and it will be given to you; search, and you will find; knock, and the door will be opened to you. For everyone who asks receives; everyone who searches finds; everyone who knocks will have the door opened. What father among you, if his son asked for a fish, would hand him a snake? Or if he asked for an egg, hand him a scorpion? If you then, evil as you are, know how to give your children what is good, how much more will the heavenly Father give the Holy Spirit to those who ask him!'

## WEDNESDAY

JOHN 16:5–15 (RSV)

Jesus said 'Now I am going to him who sent me; yet none of you asks me, "Where are you going?" But because I have said these things to you, sorrow has filled your hearts. Nevertheless I tell you the truth: it is to your advantage that I go away, for if I do not go away, the Counsellor will not come to you; but if I go, I will send him to you. And when he comes, he will convince the world concerning sin and righteousness and judgment: concerning sin, because they do not believe in me; concerning righteousness, because I go to the Father, and you will see me no more; concerning judgment, because the ruler of this world is judged.

'I have yet many things to say to you, but you cannot bear them now. When the Spirit of truth comes, he will guide you into all the truth; for he will not speak on his own authority, but whatever he hears he will speak, and he will declare to you the things that are to come. He will glorify me, for he will take what is mine and declare it to you. All that the Father has is mine; therefore I said that he will take what is mine and declare it to you.'

## THURSDAY

ACTS 2:14–24 (NIV)

Then Peter stood up with the Eleven, raised his voice and addressed the crowd: 'Fellow Jews and all of you who live in Jerusalem, let me explain this to you; listen carefully to what I say. These men are not drunk, as you suppose. It's only nine in the morning! No, this is what was spoken by the prophet Joel:

"In the last days, God says,
I will pour out my Spirit on all people.
Your sons and daughters will prophesy,
your young men will see visions,
your old men will dream dreams.
Even on my servants, both men and women,
I will pour out my Spirit in those days,
and they will prophesy.
I will show wonders in the heaven above
and signs on the earth below,
blood and fire and billows of smoke.
The sun will be turned to darkness
and the moon to blood
before the coming of the great
and glorious day of the Lord.
And everyone who calls on the
name of the Lord will be saved."

Men of Israel, listen to this: Jesus of Nazareth was a man accredited by God to you by miracles, wonders and signs, which God did among you through him, as you yourselves know. This man was handed over to you by God's set purpose and foreknowledge; and you, with the help of wicked men, put him to death by nailing him to the cross. But God raised him from the dead, freeing him from the agony of death, because it was impossible for death to keep its hold on him.'

# FRIDAY

ROMANS 8:1–11 (RSV)

There is therefore now no condemnation for those who are in Christ Jesus. For the law of the Spirit of life in Christ Jesus has set me free from the law of sin and death. For God has done what the law, weakened by the flesh, could not do: sending his own Son in the likeness of sinful flesh and for sin, he condemned sin in the flesh, in order that the just requirement of the law might be fulfilled in us, who walk not according to the flesh, but according to the Spirit. For those who live according to the flesh set their minds on the things of the flesh, but those who live according to the Spirit set their minds on the things of the Spirit. To set the mind on the flesh is death, but to set the mind on the Spirit is life and peace. For the mind that is set on the flesh is hostile to God; it does not submit to God's law, indeed it cannot; and those who are in the flesh cannot please God.

But you are not in the flesh, you are in the Spirit, if in fact the Spirit of God dwells in you. Any one who does not have the Spirit of Christ does not belong to him. But if Christ is in you, although your bodies are dead because of sin, your spirits are alive because of righteousness. If the Spirit of him who raised Jesus from the dead dwells in you, he who raised Christ Jesus from the dead will give life to your mortal bodies also through his Spirit which dwells in you.

# SATURDAY

GALATIANS 5:16–25 (REB)

What I mean is this: be guided by the Spirit and you will not gratify the desires of your unspiritual nature. That nature sets its desires against the Spirit, while the Spirit fights against it. They are in conflict with one another so that you cannot do what you want. But if you are led by the Spirit, you are not subject to law.

Anyone can see the behaviour that belongs to the unspiritual nature: fornication, indecency, and debauchery; idolatry and sorcery; quarrels, a contentious temper, envy, fits of rage, selfish ambitions, dissensions, party intrigues, and jealousies; drinking bouts, orgies, and the like. I warn you, as I warned you before, that no one who behaves like that will ever inherit the kingdom of God.

But the harvest of the Spirit is love, joy, peace, patience, kindness, goodness, fidelity, gentleness, and self-control. Against such things there is no law. Those who belong to Christ Jesus have crucified the old nature with its passions and desires. If the Spirit is the source of our life, let the Spirit also direct its course.

# DIVINE LOOKALIKE

Human beings are neither animals nor machines—nor are they gods and goddesses. We occupy a place unique in creation, stamped with the image and likeness of God and endowed with qualities which reflect those of our maker (Sunday). The second part of this first reading shows that we also inherit the more mixed blessing of likeness to our human parents!

The Psalms are among the many meditations voiced throughout history which pause to wonder at our place in the scheme of things. Human beings are unique in all creation, yet so insignificant in the universe (Monday). But there is not just the secular question: 'What is man?'; there is also the religious one: 'What is man that you are mindful of him?'. Tuesday's psalm is among the most haunting and humbling as it probes the relationships between individual and creator, 'I' and 'You'.

Against this Jewish background the apostle Paul urges his friends at Corinth (Thursday and Friday's reading) that through Christ there is yet a far brighter image to be restored to us. Father, Son and Holy Spirit are all involved.

The letter to the Hebrews (Friday) also holds human beings in high esteem, since Christ is the sum of humanity as well as the unique Son of God. Finally, in his letter, James is practical as he urges us to examine the way we use our tongues and express our emotions.

WEEK
4

# The Image of God

'Isn't she like her mother!' 'Doesn't he look like his father!' And the new parent glows with pleasure that other people notice the family likeness. Similarly, it was God's intention from the beginning that we should bear the likeness of our heavenly Father. At the beginning of Genesis God declares: 'Let us make man in our image, after our likeness.' The narrative continues: 'So God created man in his own image, in the image of God he created him; male and female he created them.'

But what does it mean to be made in the image of God? Over this phrase oceans of ink have been spilt. Does it refer to our rational faculties, our moral responsibilities, our spiritual nature? Sensible as each suggestion is, none is really adequate on its own if our relationship to God is left out. This is probably the central idea, that God intended our relationship to him to remain unbroken and that we would grow up within the 'family', to bear the imprint of his nature in all its diversity and breadth.

Two illustrations may help us understand the biblical notion of the image of God:

- **An image is a stamp of ownership.** Just as a coin might bear the likeness of the Sovereign or President so it was God's desire that the family character of beauty, love and holiness might mark our lives. Although humanity's fall has defaced the image of God in us, it is not obscured totally. Even in the most evil and perverse of people God's image is present and marks that person as really belonging to him.
- **An image is seen in a mirror.** A mirror remains a mirror even though no one has used it for years but, of course, its nature and destiny are not fulfilled until it is used. Paul appears to draw on this idea: 'We who . . . all reflect the Word's glory, are being transformed into his likeness.' That is, those who are in Christ are like mirrors before him, reflecting in our lives the spiritual and moral unity between Creator and creature. Jesus Christ is the only true 'image of the invisible God'. In his likeness we are being shaped, and one day we will be fully like him.

The implications of this teaching are very great and have personal, social and political significance. To us as persons God declares his love and his estimate of our worth. We might sometimes despair of ourselves and might even wallow in terrifying seas of self-loathing. But how can we deny God's regard for us? We are made in his image and that means that he likes and loves us as we essentially are. The idea is very important for social and political thought as well. Here is the basis for Christian concern and action. If we are made in the image of God, then we are equal in God's sight and ought to have equal opportunities for a full, dignified human existence. This is the Christian charter for humanity, and because of it we should fight against all forces of oppression, poverty and ignorance which dehumanize people today.

## SUNDAY

GENESIS 1:26–28, 5:1–5 (REB)

Then God said, 'Let us make human beings in our image, after our likeness, to have dominion over the fish in the sea, the birds of the air, the cattle, all wild animals on land, and everything that creeps on the earth.'
God created human beings in his
    own image;
    in the image of God he created
    them;
    male and female he created them.
God blessed them and said to them, 'Be fruitful and increase, fill the earth and subdue it, have dominion over the fish in the sea, the birds of the air, and every living thing that moves on the earth.'

This is the list of Adam's descendants. On the day when God created human beings he made them in his own likeness. He created them male and female, and on the day when he created them, he blessed them and called them man.

Adam was one hundred and thirty years old when he begot a son in his likeness and image, and named him Seth. After the birth of Seth he lived eight hundred years, and had other sons and daughters. He lived nine hundred and thirty years, and then he died.

## MONDAY

PSALM 8 (NIV)

O Lord, our Lord,
    how majestic is your name in all
    the earth!
You have set your glory
    above the heavens.
From the lips of children and infants
    you have ordained praise
because of your enemies,
    to silence the foe and the
    avenger.

When I consider your heavens,
    the work of your fingers,
the moon and the stars,
    which you have set in place,
what is man that you are mindful of
    him,
    the son of man that you care for
    him?
You made him a little lower than the
    heavenly beings
    and crowned him with glory and
    honour.

You made him ruler over the works
    of your hands;
    you put everything under his
    feet:
all flocks and herds,
    and the beasts of the field,
the birds of the air,
    and the fish of the sea,
    all that swim the paths of the
    seas.
O Lord, our Lord,
    how majestic is your name in all
    the earth!

## TUESDAY

PSALM 139 (NIV)

O Lord, you have searched me
    and you know me.
You know when I sit and when I
    rise;

you perceive my thoughts from
afar.
You discern my going out and my
lying down;
you are familiar with all my
ways.
Before a word is on my tongue
you know it completely, O Lord.

You hem me in—behind and before;
you have laid your hand upon
me.
Such knowledge is too wonderful
for me,
too lofty for me to attain.

Where can I go from your Spirit?
Where can I flee from your presence?
If I go up to the heavens, you are
there;
if I make my bed in the depths,
you are there.
If I rise on the wings of the dawn,
if I settle on the far side of the
sea,
even there your hand will guide me,
your right hand will hold me fast.

If I say, 'Surely the darkness will
hide me
and the light become night
around me,'
even the darkness will not be dark
to you;
the night will shine like the day,
for darkness is as light to you.

For you created my inmost being;
you knit me together in my mother's womb.
I praise you because I am fearfully
and wonderfully made;
your works are wonderful,
I know that full well.
My frame was not hidden from you
when I was made in the secret
place.
When I was woven together in the
depths of the earth,
your eyes saw my unformed
body.
All the days ordained for me
were written in your book
before one of them came to be.

How precious to me are your
thoughts, O God!
How vast is the sum of them!
Were I to count them,
they would outnumber the grains
of sand.
When I awake,
I am still with you.

If only you would slay the wicked, O
God!
Away from me, you bloodthirsty
men!
They speak of you with evil intent;
your adversaries misuse your
name.
Do I not hate those who hate you, O
Lord,
and abhor those who rise up
against you?
I have nothing but hatred for them;
I count them my enemies.

Search me, O God, and know my
heart;
test me and know my anxious
thoughts.
See if there is any offensive way in
me,
and lead me in the way everlasting.

## WEDNESDAY

1 CORINTHIANS 3:16–23 (AV)

Know ye not that ye are the temple of God, and that the Spirit of God dwelleth in you? If any man defile the temple of God, him shall God destroy; for the temple of God is holy, which temple ye are. Let no man deceive himself. If any man among you seemeth to be wise in this world, let him become a fool, that he may be wise. For the wisdom of this world is foolishness with God. For it is written, He taketh the wise in their own craftiness. And again, the Lord knoweth the thoughts of the wise, that they are vain. Therefore let no man glory in men. For all things are yours; whether Paul, or Apollos, or Cephas, or the world, or life, or death, or things present, or things to come; all are yours; and ye are Christ's; and Christ is God's.

## THURSDAY

2 CORINTHIANS 3:12–4:6 (REB)

With such a hope as this we speak out boldly; it is not for us to do as Moses did: he put a veil over his face to keep the Israelites from gazing at the end of what was fading away. In any case their minds had become closed, for that same veil is there to this very day when the lesson is read from the old covenant; and it is never lifted, because only in Christ is it taken away. Indeed to this very day, every time the law of Moses is read, a veil lies over the mind of the hearer. But (as the scripture says) 'Whenever he turns to the Lord the veil is removed.' Now the Lord of whom this passage speaks is the Spirit; and where the Spirit of the Lord is, there is liberty. And because for us there is no veil over the face, we all see as in a mirror the glory of the Lord, and we are being transformed into his likeness with ever-increasing glory, through the power of the Lord who is the Spirit.

Since God in his mercy has given us this ministry, we never lose heart. We have renounced the deeds that people hide for very shame; we do not practise cunning or distort the word of God. It is by declaring the truth openly that we recommend ourselves to the conscience of our fellow-men in the sight of God. If our gospel is veiled at all, it is veiled only for those on the way to destruction; their unbelieving minds are so blinded by the god of this passing age that the gospel of the glory of Christ, who is the image of God, cannot dawn upon them and bring them light. It is not ourselves that we proclaim; we proclaim Christ Jesus as Lord, and ourselves as your servants for Jesus's sake. For the God who said, 'Out of darkness light shall shine,' has caused his light to shine in our hearts, the light which is knowledge of the glory of God in the face of Jesus Christ.

## FRIDAY

HEBREWS 2:10–18 (RSV)

For it was fitting that he, for whom and by whom all things exist, in bringing many sons to glory, should make the pioneer of their salvation perfect through suffering. For he who sanctifies and those who are sanctified have all one origin. That is why he is not ashamed to call them brethren, saying,

'I will proclaim thy name to my
brethren,
in the midst of the congregation I
will praise thee.'

And again,

'I will put my trust in him.'

And again,

'Here am I, and the children God has
given me.'

Since therefore the children share in flesh and blood, he himself likewise partook of the same nature, that through death he might destroy him who has the power of death, that is, the devil, and deliver all those who through fear of death were subject to lifelong bondage. For surely it is not with angels that he is concerned but with the descendants of Abraham. Therefore he had to be made like his brethren in every respect, so that he might become a merciful and faithful high priest in the service of God, to make expiation for the sins of the people. For because he himself has suffered and been tempted, he is able to help those who are tempted.

## SATURDAY

JAMES 3:7–18 (NJB)

Wild animals and birds, reptiles and fish of every kind can all be tamed, and have been tamed, by humans; but nobody can tame the tongue—it is a pest that will not keep still, full of deadly poison. We use it to bless the Lord and Father, but we also use it to curse people who are made in God's image: the blessing and curse come out of the same mouth. My brothers, this must be wrong—does any water supply give a flow of fresh water and salt water out of the same pipe? Can a fig tree yield olives, my brothers, or a vine yield figs? No more can sea water yield fresh water.

Anyone who is wise or understanding among you should from a good life give evidence of deeds done in the gentleness of wisdom. But if at heart you have the bitterness of jealousy, or selfish ambition, do not be boastful or hide the truth with lies; this is not the wisdom that comes from above, but earthly, human and devilish. Wherever there are jealousy and ambition, there are also disharmony and wickedness of every kind; whereas the wisdom that comes down from above is essentially something pure; it is also peaceable, kindly and considerate; it is full of mercy and shows itself by doing good; nor is there any trace of partiality or hypocrisy in it. The peace sown by peacemakers brings a harvest of justice.

# THE SPARK OF DELIGHT

This week's readings dip into the wealth of creativity explored within the Bible—itself a fusion of creativity of the highest order involving many disciplines, but originating with the 'spark' from God himself.

Sunday's reading touches some of the shadowy figures of pre-history, whose names are hardly known beyond these ancient texts. But the precious traditions of music and craftsmanship from Jubal and Tubalcain were well-guarded and lovingly recorded.

In fuller detail, Exodus shows us the varied talents of Bezalel and Oholiab, springing from the Spirit of God, for constructing 'the tabernacle', the tent for worship in the desert, as God had instructed. Music is heard again, and more names in the books of Chronicles with their close attention to worship (Tuesday). And music features explicitly in many of the Psalms, including the climactic 150th (Thursday).

Creativity includes construction, repairs—and leadership. Along with Nehemiah, some intriguing teams of non-professionals are pressed into service to rebuild the walls of Jerusalem (Wednesday). When a new temple is needed, Haggai's vision (Friday) reaches beyond stone and timber to see the treasures of all nations—a theme taken up on Saturday by the book of Revelation. The wheel comes full circle, returning to the creativity of God, which we first encountered in Genesis. From first book to last, the Bible opens a chain reaction of diverse creative gifts, originating with the 'spark' of God himself.

WEEK

5

# Creativity

Strictly speaking, only God can create, since creation is to bring something out of nothing. But the story of God's act of creation does shed some light on the nature of human creativity.

- ◆ **Creation involves a product—something 'new' comes into existence**.
- ◆ **It results in order and structure in place of what was chaotic and formless**.
- ◆ **It ought to issue in something 'good', which in the widest sense is made in praise of God**.
- ◆ **There can be no creativity, as the Bible sees it, which is not inspired by the Spirit of God**, whether he is directly acknowledged or not.

On this reckoning the truly creative man is Jesus Christ. In his mighty works people could see the creative power of God. His teaching was heard as a new doctrine because of its originality and freshness. People were born again when they encountered him. In his life, death and resurrection, as Paul saw clearly, a new creation came into existence.

Every true act of creation is a sign of that promise and possibility. In the story of Adam naming the animals we can see mankind ordering his environment, creatively giving it shape and meaning and making a 'cosmos' out of chaos. He has this power under God, as his vice-regent on earth. Creativity is also apparent in Proverbs, in the careful and systematic classification of human behaviour. Here is the early social scientist at work, bringing pattern and order into confusion, helping people to 'see' and understand the world in a new way. Psalm 150 points to the creative gifts of musicians who praise God on a variety of instruments. Exodus chapter 31 gives high prominence to a creative designer named Bezalel, a man 'filled with the Spirit of God', along with other craftsmen who used their powers to create and make beautiful the tent of meeting. The accounts of the building of the temple also show the value given to the skilled workman in Israel. Though the Bible says little directly about the artist in words, yet Jesus' own teaching methods show that he valued the world of verbal images and pictures.

Creativity is about more than simply the arts. The worship of the church can be a creative act. Where the Spirit is at work and where there is love and freedom within order and structure, the whole body of worshipping believers can offer a new sacrifice of praise to their Redeemer. Phrases like 'a living temple', 'the multi-coloured grace of God', 'varieties of gifts but the one Spirit', all point in this direction.

Sadly, the creative gift can be buried out of sight and never used to bring glory to the giver, or it can be employed destructively. Wisdom can degenerate into the cleverness that 'puffs up'; the gift of speech can be used for effect rather than for communication. People can build a tower of Babel as easily as a temple. But God calls us to use our creative gifts to the full, with the richness that he brought to creation.

## SUNDAY

GENESIS 4:17–22 (AV)

And Cain knew his wife; and she conceived, and bare Enoch: and he builded a city, and called the name of the city, after the name of his son Enoch. And unto Enoch was born Irad: and Irad begat Mehujael: and Mehujael begat Methusael: and Methusael begat Lamech.

And Lamech took unto him two wives: the name of the one was Adah, and the name of the other Zillah. And Adah bare Jabal: he was the father of such as dwell in tents, and of such as have cattle. And his brother's name was Jubal: he was the father of all such as handle the harp and organ. And Zillah, she also bare Tubal-cain, an instructer of every artificer in brass and iron: and the sister of Tubal-cain was Naamah.

## MONDAY

EXODUS 35:30–36:3, 36:8–13 (RSV)

And Moses said to the people of Israel, 'See the Lord has called by name Bezalel the son of Uri, son of Hur, of the tribe of Judah; and he has filled him with the Spirit of God, with ability, with intelligence, with knowledge, and with all craftsmanship, to devise artistic designs, to work in gold and silver and bronze, in cutting stones for setting, and in carving wood, for work in every skilled craft. And he has inspired him to teach, both him and Oholiab the son of Ahisamach of the tribe of Dan. He has filled them with ability to do every sort of work done by a craftsman or by a designer or by an embroiderer in blue and purple and scarlet stuff and fine twined linen, or by a weaver—by any sort of workman or skilled designer. Bezalel and Oholiab and every able man in whom the Lord has put ability and intelligence to know how to do any work in the construction of the sanctuary shall work in accordance with all that the Lord has commanded.'

And Moses called Bezalel and Oholiab and every able man in whose mind the Lord had put ability, every one whose heart stirred him up to come to do the work; and they received from Moses all the freewill offering which the people of Israel had brought for doing the work on the sanctuary.

And all the able men among the workmen made the tabernacle with ten curtains; they were made of fine twined linen and blue and purple and scarlet stuff, with cherubim skilfully worked. The length of each curtain was twenty-eight cubits, and the breadth of each curtain four cubits; all the curtains had the same measure.

And he coupled five curtains to one another, and the other five curtains he coupled to one another. And he made loops of blue on the edge of the outmost curtain of the first set; likewise he made them on the edge of the outmost curtain of the second set; he made fifty loops on the one curtain, and he made fifty loops on the edge of the curtain that was in the second set; the loops were opposite one another. And he made fifty clasps of gold, and coupled the curtains one to the other with clasps; so the tabernacle was one whole.

## TUESDAY

1 CHRONICLES 15:16–22, 25:1–3 (NIV)

David told the leaders of the Levites to appoint their brothers as singers to sing joyful songs, accompanied by musical instruments: lyres, harps and cymbals.

So the Levites appointed Heman son of Joel; from his brothers, Asaph son of Berekiah; and from their brothers the Merarites, Ethan son of Kushaiah; and with them their brothers next in rank: Zechariah, Jaaziel, Shemiramoth, Jehiel, Unni, Eliab, Benaiah, Maaseiah, Mattithiah, Eliphelehu, Mikneiah, Obed-Edom and Jeiel, the gatekeepers.

The musicians Heman, Asaph and Ethan were to sound the bronze cymbals; Zechariah, Aziel, Shemiramoth, Jehiel, Unni, Eliab, Maaseiah and Benaiah were to play the lyres according to *alamoth*, and Mattithiah, Eliphelehu, Mikneiah, Obed-Edom, Jeiel and Azaziah were to play the harps, directing according to *sheminith*. Kenaniah the head Levite was in charge of the singing; that was his responsibility because he was skilful at it.

David, together with the commanders of the army, set apart some of the sons of Asaph, Heman and Jeduthun for the ministry of prophesying, accompanied by harps, lyres and cymbals. Here is the list of the men who performed this service: From the sons of Asaph: Zaccur, Joseph, Nethaniah and Asarelah. The sons of Asaph were under the supervision of Asaph, who prophesied under the king's supervision. As for Jeduthun, from his sons: Gedaliah, Zeri, Jeshaiah, Shimei, Hashabiah and Mattithiah, six in all, under the supervision of their father Jeduthun, who prophesied, using the harp in thanking and praising the Lord.

## WEDNESDAY

NEHEMIAH 2:17–18, 3:1–3, 3:12, 4:6, 6:15–7:2 (REB)

Then I said to them, 'You see what trouble we are in: Jerusalem lies in ruins, its gates destroyed by fire. Come, let us rebuild the wall of Jerusalem and suffer derision no more. I told them also how the gracious hand of my God had been upon me and also what the king had said to me. They replied, 'Let us start the rebuilding,' and they set about the work vigorously and to good purpose.

Eliashib the high priest and his fellow-priests set to work and rebuilt the Sheep Gate. They laid its beams and put its doors in place; they carried the work as far as the Tower of the Hundred and the Tower of Hananel, and consecrated it. The men of Jericho worked next to Eliashib; and next to them Zaccur son of Imri.

The Fish Gate was built by the sons of Hassenaah; they laid its tie-beams and put its doors in place with their bolts and bars.

Next to them Shallum son of Hallohesh, ruler of half the district of Jerusalem, did the repairs with the help of his daughters.

We built up the wall until it was continuous all round up to half its height; and the people worked with a will.

On the twenty-fifth day of the month of Elul the wall was finished; it had taken fifty-two days. When all our enemies heard of it, and all the surrounding nations saw it, they thought it a very wonderful achievement, and recognized it was by the help of our God that this work had been accomplished.

In those days the nobles in Judah kept sending letters to Tobiah, and receiving replies from him, for many in Judah were in league with him, because he was a son-in-law of Shecaniah son of Arah, and his son Jehohanan had married a daughter of Meshullam son of Berechiah. They were always praising him in my presence and repeating to him what I said. Tobiah also wrote to me to intimidate me.

When the wall had been rebuilt, and I had put the gates in place and the gate-keepers had been appointed, I gave the charge of Jerusalem to my brother Hanani and to Hananiah, the governor of the citadel, for he was trustworthy and godfearing above other men.

## THURSDAY

PSALM 150 (AV)

Praise ye the Lord.
Praise God in his sanctuary:
praise him in the firmament of his power.
Praise him for his mighty acts:
praise him according to his excellent greatness.
Praise him with the sound of the trumpet:
praise him with the psaltery and harp.
Praise him with the timbrel and dance:
praise him with stringed instruments and organs.
Praise him upon the loud cymbals:
praise him upon the high sounding cymbals.
Let everything that hath breath praise the Lord.
Praise ye the Lord.

## FRIDAY

HAGGAI 1:13–2:9 (REB)

So Haggai the Lord's messenger, as the Lord had commissioned him, said to the people: 'I am with you, says the Lord.' Then the Lord stirred up the spirit of the governor of Judah Zerubbabel son of Shealtiel, of the high priest Joshua son of Jehozadak, and of the rest of the people, so that they went and set to work on the house of the Lord of Hosts their God on the twenty-fourth day of the sixth month.

In the second year of King Darius, on the twenty-first day of the seventh month, these words came from the Lord through the prophet Haggai: 'Say to the governor of Judah Zerubbabel son of Shealtiel, to the high priest Joshua son of Jehozadak, and to the rest of the people: Is there anyone still among you who saw this house in its former glory? How does it appear to you now? To you does it not seem as if it were not there? But now, Zerubbabel, take heart, says the Lord; take heart, Joshua son of Jehozadak, high priest; take heart, all you people, says the Lord. Begin the work, for I am with you, says the Lord of Hosts, and my spirit remains among you. Do not be afraid.

'For these are the words of the Lord of Hosts: In a little while from now I shall shake the heavens and the earth, the sea and the dry land. I shall shake all the nations, and the treasure of all nations will come here; and I shall fill this house with splendour, says the Lord of Hosts. Mine is the silver and mine the gold, says the Lord of Hosts, and the splendour of this latter house will surpass the splendour of the former, says the Lord of Hosts. In this place, I shall grant prosperity and peace. This is the word of the Lord of Hosts.'

## SATURDAY

REVELATION 21:15–27 (NJB)

The angel that was speaking to me was carrying a gold measuring rod to measure the city and its gates and wall. The plan of the city is perfectly square, its length the same as its breadth. He measured the city with his rod and it was twelve thousand furlongs, equal in length and in breadth, and equal in height. He measured its wall, and this was a hundred and forty-four cubits high—by human measurements. The wall was built of diamond, and the city of pure gold, like clear glass. The foundations of the city wall were faced with all kinds of precious stone: the first with diamond, the second lapis lazuli, the third turquoise, the forth crystal, the fifth agate, the sixth ruby, the seventh gold quartz, the eighth malachite, the ninth topaz, the tenth emerald, the eleventh sapphire and the twelfth amethyst. The twelve gates were twelve pearls, each gate being made of a single pearl, and the main street of the city was pure gold, transparent as glass. I could not see any temple in the city since the Lord God Almighty and the Lamb were themselves the temple, and the city did not need the sun or the moon for light, since it was lit by the radiant glory of God, and the Lamb was a lighted torch for it. The nations will come to its light and the kings of the earth will bring it their treasures. Its gates will never be closed by day—and there will be no night there—and the nations will come, bringing their treasure and their wealth. Nothing unclean may come into it: no one who does what is loathsome or false, but only those who are listed in the Lamb's book of life.

# THUS SAITH THE LORD

WEEK 6

The idea of a God who speaks is fundamental to the Bible's account of God. But it can be a problem for some people, both ancient and modern. Even those who hear his voice are not immune to the problems!

With this week's first reading we are at a famous turning-point in the history of God's people. The issue is not the genius of Moses, but that a long-silent God is choosing the moment to reveal himself.

Jeremiah and Ezekiel (Monday and Tuesday) are two from the Old Testament who were personally summoned to take God's words to other people. They did not find it easy. By contrast, Ezra's task is to teach from given documents, the 'law of the Lord' (Wednesday). The writings need to be explained and applied to our needs today.

For Thursday, the lyrical Psalm 19 compares the twin revelations in God's works and words. Early in the Sermon on the Mount, Jesus quickly ends any speculation that he aimed to overthrow the Scriptures (Friday). If anything, he pushed their demands further.

Finally, in Saturday's reading, the apostle Paul provides a classic summary of the practical value and divine origin of the scriptures. Here is a man like Moses, whose confidence in what God says is put to some extreme tests of endurance on his many travels.

WEEK 6

# God's Revelation

Any important discovery about another person may be called 'revelation'. Think of human love or friendship and you will know that from intimacy springs revelation. It is the nature of love to reveal itself.

This is true of God's revelation except that, because he is the 'unknown' God, we cannot discover him at all without his help. Unless he reveals himself we cannot find him. This he does in four ways: through **creation**, through the **prophets**, through the whole **Bible** and, above all, through **Jesus Christ**. Putting it another way: through the seen Word, through the spoken Word, through the written Word and through the incarnate Word.

- **Revelation which comes to us through creation is often spoken of as 'general revelation'.** This means that God has revealed himself in human history, through the beauty and order of creation, and in our own moral sense. This note is certainly there in the Bible. But we have to realize that such revelation is seriously affected by mankind's sin, so that instead of creation revealing God clearly, we have a distorted and incomplete vision of him.

- **Revelation through prophets, through the Bible and through Jesus Christ is called 'special revelation'.** Because of our rebellion against him, God in his love and mercy has sent to us special messengers and prophets to call us back to him. The prophets through the Holy Spirit claimed to bring God's word to his people. Time and again they came crying, 'Thus says the Lord!' In time, the somewhat elusive words of the prophets gave way to the full and final revelation given in Jesus Christ—the incarnate Word, the Word made flesh. The letter to the Hebrews puts it this way: 'In the past God spoke to our forefathers through the prophets... but in these last days he has spoken to us by his Son.'

It is the testimony of the Bible and the Christian church that God has revealed himself perfectly and clearly through Jesus Christ. What is the essence of that revelation? That he is our Father and Deliverer and that his Son is the only way to him. The very heart of God's revelation, therefore, is the good news brought to us through Jesus Christ.

A very difficult problem relating to revelation is the place of the Bible. There are those scholars who argue that the Bible is not itself revelation but rather a record of God's revelation. It points to him. The moment we make the Bible to be itself revelation, they say, we end up worshipping a book instead of a living Lord. While we must acknowledge that this is a danger to be guarded against, it is extremely difficult to separate a record from the revelation it is witnessing to. How can we know the revelation except through its teaching and witness? The Bible is a faithful record and for that reason the Christian church from the very beginning has spoken of it as God's word, through which God's revelation in Christ has been conveyed to us.

## SUNDAY

EXODUS 3:1–14 (NIV)

Now Moses was tending the flock of Jethro his father-in-law, the priest of Midian, and he led the flock to the far side of the desert and came to Horeb, the mountain of God. There the angel of the Lord appeared to him in flames of fire from within a bush. Moses saw that though the bush was on fire it did not burn up. So Moses thought, 'I will go over and see this strange sight—why the bush does not burn up.'

When the Lord saw that he had gone over to look, God called to him from within the bush, 'Moses, Moses!'

And Moses said, 'Here I am.'

'Do not come any closer,' God said. 'Take off your sandals, for the place where you are standing is holy ground.' Then he said, 'I am the God of your father, the God of Abraham, the God of Isaac and the God of Jacob.' At this, Moses hid his face, because he was afraid to look at God.

The Lord said, 'I have indeed seen the misery of my people in Egypt. I have heard them crying out because of their slave drivers, and I am concerned about their suffering. So I have come down to rescue them from the hand of the Egyptians and to bring them up out of that land into a good and spacious land, a land flowing with milk and honey—the home of the Canaanites, Hittites, Amorites, Perizzites, Hivites and Jebusites. And now the cry of the Israelites has reached me, and I have seen the way the Egyptians are oppressing them. So now, go. I am sending you to Pharaoh to bring my people the Israelites out of Egypt.'

But Moses said to God, 'Who am I, that I should go to Pharaoh and bring the Israelites out of Egypt.'

And God said, 'I will be with you. And this will be the sign to you that it is I who have sent you: When you have brought the people out of Egypt, you will worship God on this mountain.'

Moses said to God, 'Suppose I go to the Israelites and say to them, "The God of your fathers has sent me to you," and they ask me, "What is his name?" Then what shall I tell them?'

God said to Moses, 'I AM WHO I AM. This is what you are to say to the Israelites: "I AM has sent me to you." '

## MONDAY

JEREMIAH 1:4–12, 23:25–29 (RSV)

Now the word of the Lord came to me saying, 'Before I formed you in the womb I knew you, and before you were born I consecrated you; I appointed you a prophet to the nations.'

Then I said, 'Ah, Lord God! Behold, I do not know how to speak, for I am only a youth.'

But the Lord said to me, 'Do not say, "I am only a youth"; for to all to whom I send you you shall go, and whatever I command you you shall speak. Be not afraid of them, for I am with you to deliver you, says the Lord.'

Then the Lord put forth his hand and touched my mouth; and the Lord said to me, 'Behold I have put my words in your mouth. See, I have set you this day over nations and over kingdoms, to pluck up and to break down, to destroy and to overthrow, to build and to plant.'

And the word of the Lord came to me, saying, 'Jeremiah, what do you see?' And I said, 'I see a rod of almond.' Then the Lord said to me, 'you have seen well, for I am watching over my word to perform it.'

The Lord says 'I have heard what the prophets have said who prophesy lies in my name, saying, "I have dreamed, I have dreamed!" How long shall there be lies in the heart of the prophets who prophesy lies, and who prophesy the deceit of their own heart, who think to make my people forget my name by their dreams which they tell one another, even as their fathers forgot my name for Baal? Let the prophet who has a dream tell the dream, but let him who has my word speak my word faithfully. What has straw in common with wheat? says the Lord. Is not my word like fire, says the Lord, and like a hammer which breaks the rock in pieces?

## TUESDAY

EZEKIEL 3:1–8 (AV)

Moreover he said unto me, Son of man, eat that thou findest; eat this roll, and go speak unto the house of Israel. So I opened my mouth, and he caused me to eat that roll. And he said unto me, Son of man, cause thy belly to eat, and fill thy bowels with this roll that I give thee. Then did I eat it; and it was in my mouth as honey for sweetness.

And he said unto me, Son of man, go, get thee unto the house of Israel, and speak with my words unto them. For thou art not sent to a people of a strange speech and of an hard language, but to the house of Israel; Not to many people of a strange speech and of an hard language, whose words thou canst not understand. Surely, had I sent thee to them, they would have hearkened unto thee. But the house of Israel will not hearken unto thee; for they will not hearken unto me: for all the house of Israel are impudent and hardhearted. Behold, I have made thy face strong against their faces, and thy forehead strong against their foreheads.

## WEDNESDAY

EZRA 7:6–10 (REB)

Ezra had come up from Babylon; he was a scribe, expert in the law of Moses which the Lord the God of Israel had given them. The king granted him everything he requested, for the favour of the Lord his God was with him. He was accompanied to Jerusalem by some Israelites, priests, Levites, temple singers, door-keepers, and temple servitors in the seventh year of King Artaxerxes. They reached Jerusalem in the fifth month, in the seventh year of the king. On the first day of the first month Ezra fixed the day for departure from Babylon, and on the first day of the fifth month he arrived in Jerusalem; the favour of God was with him, for he had devoted himself to the study and observance of the law of the Lord and to teaching statute and ordinance in Israel.

NEHEMIAH 8:1–10 (REB)

All the people assembled with one accord in the broad space in front of the Water Gate, and requested Ezra the scribe to bring the book of the law of Moses, which the Lord had enjoined upon Israel. On the first day of the seventh month, Ezra the priest brought the law before the whole assembly, both men and women, and all who were capable of understanding what they heard. From early morning till noon he read aloud from it, facing the square in front of the Water Gate, in the presence of the men and the women, and those who could understand; the people all listened attentively to the book of the law.

Ezra the scribe stood on a wooden platform which had been made for this purpose; beside him stood Mattithiah, Shema, Anaiah, Uriah, Hilkiah, and Maaseiah on his right hand, and on his left Pedaiah, Mishael, Malchiah, Hashum, Hashbaddanah, Zechariah, and Meshullam. Then Ezra opened the book in the sight of all the people, for he was standing above them; and when he opened it, they all stood. Ezra blessed the Lord, the great God, and all the people raised their hands and responded, 'Amen, Amen'; then they bowed their heads and prostrated themselves before the Lord. Jeshua, Bani, Sherebiah, Jamin, Akkub, Shabbethai, Hodiah, Maaseiah, Kelita, Azariah, Jozabad, Hanan, and Pelaiah, the Levites, expounded the law to the people while the people remained in their places. They read from the book of the law of God clearly, made its sense plain, and gave instruction in what was read.

Then Nehemiah the governor and Ezra the priest and scribe, and the Levites who instructed the people, said to them all, 'This day is holy to the Lord your God; do not mourn or weep'; for the people had all been weeping while they listened to the words of the law. 'Go now,' he continued, 'feast yourselves on rich food and sweet drinks, and send a share to all who cannot provide for themselves, for the day is holy to our Lord. Let there be no sadness, for joy in the Lord is your strength.'

## THURSDAY

PSALM 19 (NIV)

The heavens declare the glory of God;
the skies proclaim the work of his hands.
Day after day they pour forth speech;
night after night they display knowledge.
There is no speech or language where their voice is not heard.
Their voice goes out into all the earth,
their words to the ends of the world.

In the heavens he has pitched a tent for the sun,
which is like a bridegroom coming forth from his pavilion,
like a champion rejoicing to run his course.
It rises at one end of the heavens
and makes its circuit to the other;

nothing is hidden from its heat.

The law of the Lord is perfect,
reviving the soul.
The statutes of the Lord are trustworthy,
making wise the simple.
The precepts of the Lord are right,
giving joy to the heart.
The commands of the Lord are radiant,
giving light to the eyes.
The fear of the Lord is pure,
enduring for ever.
The ordinances of the Lord are sure
and altogether righteous.
They are more precious than gold,
than much pure gold;
they are sweeter than honey,
than honey from the comb.
By them is your servant warned;
in keeping them there is great reward.

Who can discern his errors?
Forgive my hidden faults.
Keep your servant also from wilful sins;
may they not rule over me.
Then will I be blameless,
innocent of great transgression.

May the words of my mouth and the meditation of my heart
be pleasing in your sight,
O Lord, my Rock and my Redeemer.

## FRIDAY

MATTHEW 5:13–22 (NJB)

Jesus said 'You are salt for the earth. But if salt loses its taste, what can make it salty again? It is good for nothing, and can only be thrown out to be trampled under people's feet.

'You are light for the world. A city built on a hill-top cannot be hidden. No one lights a lamp to put it under a tub; they put it on the lamp-stand where it shines for everyone in the house. In the same way your light must shine in people's sight, so that, seeing your good works, they may give praise to your Father in heaven.

'Do not imagine that I have come to abolish the Law or the Prophets. I have come not to abolish but to complete them. In truth I tell you, till heaven and earth disappear, not one dot, not one little stroke, is to disappear from the Law until all its purpose is achieved. Therefore, anyone who infringes even one of the least of these commandments and teaches others to do the same will be considered the least in the kingdom of Heaven; but the person who keeps them and teaches them will be considered great in the kingdom of Heaven.

'For I tell you, if your uprightness does not surpass that of the scribes and Pharisees, you will never get into the kingdom of Heaven.

'You have heard how it was said to our ancestors, You shall not kill; and if anyone does kill he must answer for it before the court. But I say this to you, anyone who is angry with a brother will answer for it before the court; anyone who calls a brother "Fool" will answer for it before the Sanhedrin; and anyone who calls him "Traitor" will answer for it in hell fire.'

## SATURDAY

2 TIMOTHY 3:10–4:2 (NJB)

You, though, have followed my teaching, my way of life, my aims, my faith, my patience and my love, my perseverance and the persecutions and sufferings that came to me in places like Antioch, Iconium and Lystra—all the persecutions I have endured; and the Lord has rescued me from every one of them. But anybody who tries to live in devotion to Christ is certain to be persecuted; while these wicked imposters will go from bad to worse, deceiving others, and themselves deceived.

You must keep to what you have been taught and know to be true; remember who your teachers were, and how, ever since you were a child, you have known the holy scriptures—from these you can learn the wisdom that leads to salvation through faith in Christ Jesus. All scripture is inspired by God and useful for refuting error, for guiding people's lives and teaching them to be upright. This is how someone who is dedicated to God becomes fully equipped and ready for any good work.

Before God and before Christ Jesus who is to be judge of the living and the dead, I charge you, in the name of his appearing and of his kingdom: proclaim the message and, welcome or unwelcome, insist on it. Refute falsehood, correct error, give encouragement—but do all with patience and with care to instruct.

# FROM THE CONQUEST OF CANAAN TO THE FALL OF JERUSALEM

The big section of books from Joshua to Chronicles spans about 700 years of Jewish history—roughly 1200 to 500BC. They record what happened from the time the Israelites conquered and settled their land, on through the times of the judges and the kings, to their conquest by the great nations to the north and east, when they were taken into exile.

The writers had a special aim—to show how God's purpose was fulfilled in the nation's life. So they faithfully recorded the prosperity which followed obedience and the disasters which happened when kings and people did not heed God. The books were originally called the 'former prophets', and prophets appear frequently in the stories.

## JOSHUA

The story of the Israelite invasion of Canaan, the land God had promised. Led by Joshua, Moses' successor, they invade from the east, Jericho being the first city to fall.

## JUDGES

The stories of national heroes in the lawless times between the invasion of Canaan and the first kings. The picture is of a struggle between keeping faith in God and turning to the local gods.

## RUTH

A beautiful pastoral story from the time of the judges. Ruth was an ancestor of King David, and so of Jesus.

## 1 & 2 SAMUEL

From the last of the judges, through Saul's failure, to the final years of King David. Two of the Bible's great characters appear—Samuel and David. The theme develops of a kingly line that would last for ever, the line of David.

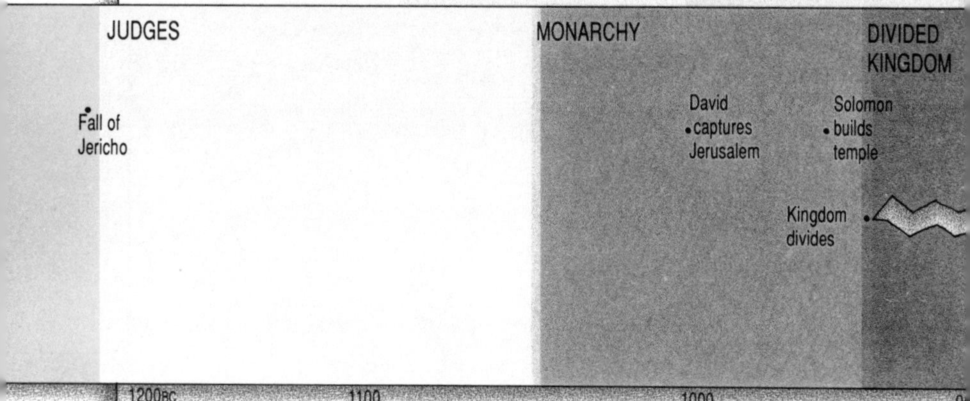

JUDGES

MONARCHY

DIVIDED KINGDOM

Fall of Jericho

David captures Jerusalem

Solomon builds temple

Kingdom divides

1200BC 1100 1000 9

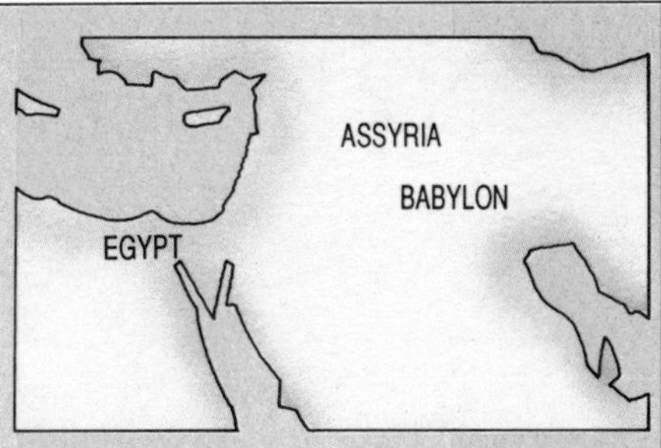


## 1 & 2 KINGS

From David's death, through Solomon's years of greatness, the division of the kingdom and the eventual fall of northern Israel to Assyria, to the years of beleaguered southern Judah and Jerusalem's fall to Babylon. Elijah and Elisha appear as great men of faith.

## 1 & 2 CHRONICLES

The period covered is the same as 2 Samuel and Kings. But because these books were intended for those who returned to Jerusalem from exile, the focus is on the southern kingdom of Judah. Despite all that has happened, the Jews are still God's people.

## THE TEMPLE

King David longed to build a temple in Jerusalem, to give permanent reality to the 'tabernacle', or worship tent, which had travelled with Israel in the wilderness years. But this project only took shape under David's son, Solomon.

From then on, the temple was the focus of Israel's devotion to God. This was one reason why the people's exile to Babylon was such a disaster. On their return, they began to rebuild the temple, which the Babylonians had destroyed. This building is known as 'the second temple'.

Finally, King Herod built a new temple, work on which was nearly complete in the days of Jesus. But this, too, met a violent end, when the Romans sacked Jerusalem in AD70. Only the east wall of Herod's temple remains.

Samaria falls to Assyrians

Fall of Nineveh, Assyrian capital

Babylonians take Jerusalem; exile begins

EXILE

800 700 600

WEEK 7

# UNBROKEN PROMISES

This week we look at some milestones on the journey of God's people in their 'covenant' with him. As far back as Noah we see the pattern which is repeated throughout the Bible —mercy in judgment, a promise, a sign, and the initiative taken by God (Sunday).

In the story of Abraham (Monday) God seems to narrow down his concern to focus on one man, but his purpose is that the world will eventually know him. This covenant God 'remembers' (brings back into action) for Moses (Tuesday).

In the last book of the Old Testament, Malachi looks forward to something even greater: a new messenger and a 'Sun of righteousness' (Wednesday). Indeed, the prophet Jeremiah's words, quoted in Saturday's first extract, foretold a new covenant better than the old.

Many generations later, the father of John the Baptist takes up this theme as John, the 'preparer or the way', is born (Thursday). And at the Last Supper every ear must have tingled as Jesus told his friends that the 'new covenant' was arriving, at the price of his own blood (Friday).

The letter to the Hebrews (Saturday) spells out both promise and fulfilment, pointing to Jesus as the 'mediator of a new covenant'—he is the one who brings reconciliation, fulfils all hopes and meets all needs, for those prepared to trust him.

# The Covenant

Covenant is the Bible's word for an 'agreement'. When we make agreements today—legal, social or personal ones—we seal them in a variety of ways with a legal document, a certificate, a wedding-ring, or even a kiss.

In the Bible four covenants with mankind are mentioned:

◆ **The covenant with Noah.** Following the great flood, God promised humanity that he would always be faithful. The rainbow was the sign of this covenant.

◆ **The covenant with Abraham.** Abraham's trusting faith, which made him risk everything on God's promise, was rewarded by God's covenant. God declared that he would make of Abraham's descendants a great nation. The sealing of this covenant was in the act of circumcision.

◆ **The covenant with Moses.** This covenant sprang from God delivering his people from Egypt. He led them out of captivity through Moses and revealed his name 'Yahweh' to them. In this covenant God declared: 'You are now my people and belong to me. You must be holy as I am holy.' At Mount Sinai the covenant was sealed on two sides. On God's side there came the gift of his law, given so that it might be the framework for life. 'Abide by these rules,' said Yahweh, 'keep them faithfully and you will honour me and be my delight.' On their part, the Israelites promised to keep these laws and to have no other gods but Yahweh.

◆ **The new covenant.** The tragedy of Israel was that they failed to keep God's covenant. In spite of God's many appeals through prophets and leaders, his agreement with Moses was repeatedly broken. The later prophets began to see that the sinfulness and weakness of humanity made it impossible for people to keep their end of the bargain. Through them God began to show that he would introduce a new and everlasting covenant: not an external but an internal one, that is, not written on stone tablets like the Ten Commandments, but on the very hearts of us all. More wonderfully still, it would no longer be limited to the Jews—it was to be for all people.

What the prophets awaited, Jesus fulfilled. His death was the sealing of this new agreement between God and humanity. At the very moment the lambs were being slaughtered in the temple for the Passover meal, Jesus the lamb of God sealed the new covenant with his own blood.

The covenants mentioned in the Bible show that they come from the gracious, free and generous act of God. He is utterly sure and dependable, and he longs for a people to enter fully into his love. Three aspects of his character emerge from the Bible's teaching about God's covenant. He is **Saviour**: he came to Israel's rescue through Moses, he came to our rescue through Jesus Christ. He is **Teacher**: he gave the Israelites guidelines for their relationship with him and he teaches us through his revelation in the Bible. He is **Lover**: he wants his people to love him as deeply as he loves us.

Still today God's new covenant gives meaning, hope and peace. It declares that God's everlasting agreement with us has been made and will not be broken. Whatever difficulty we face we can respond, 'God has expressed his faithfulness in the covenant and he will never let me go.' That faithfulness was sealed through the death of Jesus—such is the nature of God's love. But the covenant is also a covenant of *grace*. Salvation cannot be earned, it is a gift—God's eternal covenant is quite unmerited on our part. All we can do is to accept it gratefully through Christ and live it daily.

## SUNDAY

GENESIS 9:8–17 (REB)

God said to Noah and his sons: 'I am now establishing my covenant with you and with your descendants after you, and with every living creature that is with you, all birds and cattle, all the animals with you on earth, all that have come out of the ark. I shall sustain my covenant with you: never again will all living creatures be destroyed by the waters of a flood, never again will there be a flood to lay waste the earth.'

God said, 'For all generations to come, this is the sign which I am giving of the covenant between myself and you and all living creatures with you:
my bow I set in the clouds
  to be a sign of the covenant
  between myself and the earth.
When I bring clouds over the earth,
  the rainbow will appear in the
  clouds.
Then I shall remember the covenant which I have made with you and with all living creatures, and never again will the waters become a flood to destroy all creation. Whenever the bow appears in the cloud, I shall see it and remember the everlasting covenant between God and living creatures of every kind on earth.' So God said to Noah, 'This is the sign of the covenant which I have established with all that lives on earth.'

## MONDAY

GENESIS 17:1–9 (RSV)

When Abram was ninety-nine years old the Lord appeared to Abram, and said to him, 'I am God Almighty; walk before me, and be blameless. And I will make my covenant between me and you, and will multiply you exceedingly.' Then Abram fell on his face; and God said to him, 'Behold, my covenant is with you, and you shall be the father of a multitude of nations. No longer shall your name be Abram, but your name shall be Abraham; for I have made you the father of a multitude of nations. I will make you exceedingly fruitful; and I will make nations of you, and kings shall come forth from you. And I will establish my covenant between me and you and your descendants after you throughout their generations for an everlasting covenant, to be God to you and to your descendants after you. And I will give to you, and to your descendants after you, the land of your sojournings, all the land of Canaan, for an everlasting possession; and I will be their God.'

And God said to Abraham, 'As for you, you shall keep my covenant, you and your descendants after you throughout their generations.'

## TUESDAY

EXODUS 2:15–25 (NIV)

Moses fled from Pharaoh and went to live in Midian, where he sat down by a well. Now a priest of Midian had seven daughters, and they came to draw water and fill the troughs to water their father's flock. Some shepherds came along and drove them away, but Moses got up and came to their rescue and watered their flock.

When the girls returned to Reuel their father, he asked them, 'Why have you returned so early today?'

They answered, 'An Egyptian rescued us from the shepherds. He even drew water for us and watered the flock.'

'And where is he?' he asked his daughters. 'Why did you leave him? Invite him to have something to eat.'

Moses agreed to stay with the man, who gave his daughter Zipporah to Moses in marriage. Zipporah gave birth to a son and Moses named him Gershom, saying, 'I have become an alien in a foreign land.'

During that long period, the king of Egypt died. The Israelites groaned in their slavery and cried out, and their cry for help because of their slavery went up to God. God heard their groaning and he remembered his covenant with Abraham, with Isaac and with Jacob. So God looked on the Israelites and was concerned about them.

## WEDNESDAY

MALACHI 3:1–6, 4:1–6 (AV)

Behold, I will send my messenger, and he shall prepare the way before me: and the Lord, whom ye seek, shall suddenly come to his temple, even the messenger of the covenant, whom ye delight in: behold, he shall come, saith the Lord of hosts. But who may abide the day of his coming? and who shall stand when he appeareth? for he is like a refiner's fire, and like fullers' soap: And he shall sit as a refiner and purifier of silver: and he shall purify the sons of Levi, and purge them as gold and silver, that they may offer unto the Lord an offering in righteousness. Then shall the offering of Judah and Jerusalem be pleasant unto the Lord, as in the days of old, and as in former years. And I will come near to you to judgment; and I will be a swift witness against the sorcerers, and against the adulterers, and against false swearers, and against those that oppress the hireling in his wages, the widow, and the fatherless, and that turn aside the stranger from his right, and fear not me, saith the Lord of hosts. For I am the Lord, I change not; therefore ye sons of Jacob are not consumed.

For, behold, the day cometh, that shall burn as an oven; and all the proud, yea, and all that do wickedly, shall be stubble: and the day that cometh shall burn them up, saith the Lord of hosts, that it shall leave them neither root nor branch.

But unto you that fear my name shall the Sun of righteousness arise with healing in his wings; and ye shall go forth, and grow up as calves of the stall. And ye shall tread down the wicked; for they shall be ashes under the soles of your feet in the day that I shall do this, saith the Lord of hosts.

Remember ye the law of Moses my servant, which I commanded unto him in Horeb for all Israel, with the statutes and judgments.

Behold, I will send you Elijah the prophet before the coming of the great and dreadful day of the Lord: And he shall turn the heart of the fathers to the children, and the heart of the children to their fathers, lest I come and smite the earth with a curse.

## THURSDAY

LUKE 1:57, 67–79 (NIV)

When it was time for Elizabeth to have her baby, she gave birth to a son.

His father Zechariah was filled with the Holy Spirit and prophesied:

'Praise be to the Lord, the God of Israel,
because he has come and has redeemed his people.
He has raised up a horn of salvation for us
in the house of his servant David
(as he said through his holy prophets of long ago),
salvation from our enemies
and from the hand of all who hate us—
to show mercy to our fathers
and to remember his holy covenant,
the oath he swore to our father Abraham:
to rescue us from the hand of our enemies,
and to enable us to serve him without fear
in holiness and righteousness before him all our days.
And you, my child, will be called a prophet of the Most High;
for you will go on before the Lord to prepare the way for him,
to give his people the knowledge of salvation
through the forgiveness of their sins.
because of the tender mercy of our God,
by which the rising sun will come to us from heaven
to shine on those living in darkness and in the shadow of death,
to guide our feet into the path of peace.'

## FRIDAY

1 CORINTHIANS 11:23–26 (RSV)

For I received from the Lord what I also delivered to you, that the Lord Jesus on the night when he was betrayed took bread, and when he had given thanks, he broke it, and said, 'This is my body which is for you. Do this in remembrance of me.' In the same way also the cup, after supper, saying, 'This cup is the new covenant in my blood. Do this, as often as you drink it, in remembrance of me.' For as often as you eat this bread and drink the cup, you proclaim the Lord's death until he comes.

## SATURDAY

HEBREWS 8:6–13, 9:11–15 (NJB)

As it is, Christ has been given a ministry as far superior as is the covenant of which he is the mediator, which is founded on better promises. If that first covenant had been faultless, there would have been no room for a second one to replace it. And in fact God does find fault with them; he says:

Look, the days are coming, the Lord
declares,
when I will make a new covenant
with the House of Israel and the
House of Judah,
but not a covenant like the one I
made with their ancestors,
the day I took them by the hand
to bring them out of Egypt,
which covenant of mine they
broke,
and I too abandoned them, the
Lord declares.
No, this is the covenant I will make
with the House of Israel,
when those days have come, the
Lord declares:
In their minds I shall plant my laws
writing them on their hearts.
Then I shall be their God,
and they shall be my people.
There will be no further need for
each to teach his neighbour,
and each his brother, saying
'Learn to know the Lord!'
No, they will all know me,
from the least to the greatest,
since I shall forgive their guilt
and never more call their sins to
mind.

By speaking of a new covenant, he implies that the first one is old. And anything old and ageing is ready to disappear.

But now Christ has come, as the high priest of all the blessings which were to come. He has passed through the greater, the more perfect tent, not made by human hands, that is, not of this created order; and he has entered the sanctuary once and for all, taking with him not the blood of goats and bull calves, but his own blood, having won an eternal redemption. The blood of goats and bulls and the ashes of a heifer, sprinkled on those who have incurred defilement, may restore their bodily purity. How much more will the blood of Christ, who offered himself, blameless as he was, to God through the eternal Spirit, purify our conscience from dead actions so that we can worship the living God. This makes him the mediator of a new covenant, so that, now that a death has occurred to redeem the sins committed under an earlier covenant, those who have been called to an eternal inheritance may receive the promise.

# LEGIONS OF LIARS

In the third chapter of the first book of the Bible we find evil at work (Sunday). It arises unexplained from a source outside both God and humankind. And in the New Testament the existence of evil is portrayed in equally uncompromising terms.

Before Jesus began his work of teaching, he had to face such forces head on—explicitly personified by the devil or Satan, the enemy (Monday). In the gospel accounts the devil's agents or evil spirits are repeatedly roused as if in frenzied opposition to Jesus' presence (Tuesday). Indeed Jesus' teaching includes some forthright exposures of Satan's deceptions (Wednesday).

If there are things we cannot explain in all these accounts, that should not surprise us. Only God is greater than these malevolent forces. So when the early Christian leaders, Paul and Barnabas (Thursday) encounter direct opposition, they do not mince their words but rely on God's Holy Spirit to defeat the unholy ones. Later, in Ephesus new converts to Christianity, who had previously practised magic, burnt their books. There are few surer signs of a change of heart. Do our own bookshelves raise similar questions?

Friday's short extracts from the letters of Paul and Peter warn us of Satan's deceptions—he can appear as the 'angel of light' and the 'roaring lion'. His final doom, however, is portrayed most terribly by John in Revelation, the last book in the Bible (Saturday). The devil's deceits are finally exposed, and the truth and authority of Christ silence him.

WEEK 8

# The Powers of Evil

We live in a world where evil abounds on all sides and at times it seems to have the upper hand. In the Bible evil is regarded as a malevolent force which is personal in character. The Old Testament occasionally appears to regard evil as under God's control, but when we get into the clearer light of the New Testament it is seen as something quite distinct from Almighty God. Jesus speaks of this world as being under the tyranny of the Evil One whom he calls 'the Prince of this world'. Indeed, Jesus' ministry cannot be fully understood unless we take into account the very significant battle he had with the forces of evil from start to finish. He cast out demons, he spoke about the influence of Satan, and he looked on towards his death as the climax of his struggle with the powers of darkness.

This note is echoed in later New Testament writings. Paul, for example, adopts the language of his day and states that the Christian fights against 'the rulers, the authorities... evil in the heavenly realms'. The language suggests that behind the political powers of his day stood spiritual 'powers', controlling them just like a puppeteer with his strings. Nevertheless, Paul had no doubt that the cross of Jesus had shattered their power and influence. He uses a graphic image of the hosts of evil, broken and defeated, trailing behind a victorious Christ like beaten armies behind a triumphant Roman general. But the struggle with evil continues until God ushers in his kingdom; only then will come the end when Satan will be cast out for ever. In the meantime, the Christian fights against the desperate powers of evil and must put on the whole armour of God.

But is this language to be believed these days? There are some Christians who regard this kind of language as 'mythological' or pictorial expression, tied to the New Testament's world-view and not meaningful for us today. But it is hard to see how we can eradicate this element from the New Testament as it is so prominent there. Are we in danger of imagining that we know better than our Lord and the New Testament? A better alternative, perhaps, is to live with the tension that there is in the universe a force of evil which exists to frustrate the plans of a holy God and to plant the seeds of evil everywhere. The forces of good and evil are not equal, otherwise where is our Almighty God? But the battle is still on.

Some cautions are in order when we talk about the devil and the demonic.

- **Not everything that is bad is necessarily demonic**. Great harm is done to Christian witness by over-credulous Christians who have jumped to the conclusion that all pain, suffering, trouble and strife have demonic origins. We should not attribute responsibility to the devil unless there are real grounds for doing so.
- **No demon can ever inhabit a Christian**. The testimony of the Bible is against this unlikely idea. If the Holy Spirit of God indwells us the powers of evil cannot live alongside him.

## SUNDAY

GENESIS 3:1–5 (AV)

Now the serpent was more subtil than any beast of the field which the Lord God had made. And he said unto the woman, Yea, hath God said, Ye shall not eat of every tree of the garden? And the woman said unto the serpent, We may eat of the fruit of the trees of the garden: But of the fruit of the tree which is in the midst of the garden, God hath said, Ye shall not eat of it, neither shall ye touch it, lest ye die. And the serpant said unto the woman, Ye shall not surely die: For God doth know that in the day ye eat therof, then your eyes shall be opened, and ye shall be as gods, knowing good and evil.

## MONDAY

LUKE 4:1–13 (NJB)

Filled with the Holy Spirit, Jesus left the Jordan and was led by the Spirit into the desert, for forty days being put to the test by the devil. During that time he ate nothing and at the end he was hungry. Then the devil said to him, 'If you are Son of God, tell this stone to turn into a loaf.' But Jesus replied, 'Scripture says: "Human beings live not on bread alone." '

Then leading him to a height, the devil showed him in a moment of time all the kingdoms of the world and said to him, 'I will give you all this power and their splendour, for it has been handed over to me, for me to give it to anyone I choose. Do homage, then, to me, and it shall all be yours.' But Jesus answered him, 'Scripture says: "You must do homage to the Lord your God, him alone you must serve." '

Then he led him to Jerusalem and set him on the parapet of the Temple. 'If you are Son of God,' he said to him, 'throw yourself down from here, for scripture says: "He has given his angels orders about you, to guard you" and again: "They will carry you in their arms in case you trip over a stone." '

But Jesus answered him, 'Scripture says: "Do not put the Lord your God to the test." ' Having exhausted every way of putting him to the test, the devil left him, until the opportune moment.

## TUESDAY

MARK 5:2–20 (REB)

As Jesus stepped ashore, a man possessed by an unclean spirit came up to him from among the tombs where he had made his home. Nobody could control him any longer; even chains were useless, for he had often been fettered and chained up, but had snapped his chains and broken the fetters. No one was strong enough to master him. Unceasingly, night and day, he would cry aloud among the tombs and on the hillsides and gash himself with stones. When he saw Jesus in the distance, he ran up and flung himself down before him, shouting at the top of his voice, 'What do you want with me, Jesus, son of the Most High God? In God's name do not torment me.' For Jesus was already saying to him, 'Out unclean spirit, come out of the man!' Jesus asked him, 'What is your name?' 'My name is Legion,' he said, 'there are so many of us.' And he implored Jesus not to send them out of the district. There was a large herd of pigs nearby, feeding on the hillside, and the spirits begged him, 'Send us among the pigs; let us go into them.' He gave them leave; and the unclean spirits came out and went into the pigs; and the herd, of about two thousand, rushed over the edge into the lake and were drowned.

The men in charge of them took to their heels and carried the news to the town and countryside; and the people came out to see what had happened. When they came to Jesus and saw the madman who had been possessed by the legion of demons, sitting there clothed and in his right mind, they were afraid. When eyewitnesses told them what had happened to the madman and what had become of the pigs, they begged Jesus to leave the district. As he was getting into the boat, the man who had been possessed begged to go with him. But Jesus would not let him. 'Go home to your own people,' he said, 'and tell them what the Lord in his mercy has done for you.' The man went off and made known throughout the Decapolis what Jesus had done for him; and everyone was amazed.

## WEDNESDAY

JOHN 8:34–47 (NIV)

Jesus said, 'I tell you the truth, everyone who sins is a slave to sin. Now a slave has no permanent place in the family, but a son belongs to it for ever. So if the Son sets you free, you will be free indeed. I know you are Abraham's descendants. Yet you are ready to kill me, because you have no room for my word. I am telling you what I have seen in the Father's presence, and you do what you have heard from your father.'

'Abraham is our father,' they answered.

'If you were Abraham's children,' said Jesus, 'then you would do the things Abraham did. As it is, you are determined to kill me, a man who has told you the truth that I heard from God. Abraham did not do such things. You are doing the things your own father does.'

'We are not illegitimate children,' they protested. 'The only Father we have is God himself.'

Jesus said to them, 'If God were your Father, you would love me, for I came from God and now am here. I have not come on my own; but he sent me. Why is my language not clear to you? Because you are unable to hear what I say. You belong to your father, the devil, and you want to carry out your father's desire. He was a murderer from the beginning, not holding on to the truth, for there is no truth in him. When he lies, he speaks his native language, for he is a liar and the father of lies. Yet because I tell the truth, you do not believe me! Can any of you prove me guilty of sin? If I am telling the truth, why don't you believe me? He who belongs to God hears what God says. The reason you do not hear is that you do not belong to God.'

## THURSDAY

ACTS 13:6–12, 19:13–20 (REB)

Barnabas and Saul went through the whole island as far as Paphos, and there they came upon a sorcerer, a Jew who posed as a prophet, Barjesus by name. He was in the retinue of the governor, Sergius Paulus, a learned man, who had sent for Barnabas and Saul and wanted to hear the word of God. This Elymas the sorcerer (so his name may be translated) opposed them, trying to turn the governor away from the faith. But Saul, also known as Paul, filled with the Holy Spirit, fixed his eyes on him and said, 'You are a swindler, an out-and-out fraud! You son of the devil and enemy of all goodness, will you never stop perverting the straight ways of the Lord? Look now, the hand of the Lord strikes: you shall be blind, and for a time you shall not see the light of the sun.' At once a mist and darkness came over his eyes, and he groped about for someone to lead him by the hand. When the governor saw what had happened he became impressed by what he learnt about the Lord.

Some itinerant Jewish exorcists tried their hand at using the name of the Lord Jesus on those possessed by evil spirits; they would say, 'I adjure you by Jesus who Paul proclaims.' There were seven sons of Sceva, a Jewish chief priest, who were doing this, when the evil spirit responded, 'Jesus I recognize, Paul I know, but who are you? The man with the evil spirit flew at them, overpowered them all, and handled them with such violence that they ran out of the house battered and naked. Everybody in Ephesus, Jew and Gentile alike, got to know of it, and all were awestruck, while the name of the Lord Jesus gained in honour. Moreover many of those who had become believers came and openly confessed that they had been using magical spells. A good many of those who formerly practised magic collected their books and burnt them publicly, and when the total value was reckoned up it came to fifty thousand pieces of silver. In such ways the word of the Lord showed its power, spreading more and more widely and effectively.

## FRIDAY

2 CORINTHIANS 11:13–15 (REB)

Such people are sham apostles, confidence tricksters masquerading as apostles of Christ. And no wonder! Satan himself masquerades as an angel of light, so it is easy enough for his agents to masquerade as agents of good. But their fate will match their deeds.

1 PETER 5:6–11 (REB)

Humble yourselves, then, under God's mighty hand, and in due time he will lift you up. He cares for you, so cast all your anxiety on him.

Be on the alert! Wake up! Your enemy the devil, like a roaring lion, prowls around looking for someone to devour. Stand up to him, firm in your faith, and remember that your fellow-Christians in this world are going through the same kinds of suffering. After your brief suffering, the God of all grace, who called you to his eternal glory in Christ, will himself restore, establish, and strengthen you on a firm foundation. All power belongs to him for ever and ever! Amen.

## SATURDAY

REVELATION 12:7–12, 20:7–10 (RSV)

Now war arose in heaven, Michael and his angels fighting against the dragon; and the dragon and his angels fought, but they were defeated and there was no longer any place for them in heaven. And the great dragon was thrown down, that ancient serpent, who is called the Devil and Satan, the deceiver of the whole world—he was thrown down to the earth, and his angels were thrown down with him. And I heard a loud voice in heaven, saying, 'Now the salvation and power and the kingdom of our God and the authority of his Christ have come, for the accuser of our brethren has been thrown down, who accuses them day and night before our God. And they have conquered him by the blood of the Lamb and by the word of their testimony, for they loved not their lives even unto death. Rejoice then, O heaven and you that dwell therein! But woe to you, O earth and sea, for the devil has come down to you in great wrath, because he knows that his time is short!'

And when the thousand years are ended, Satan will be loosed from his prison and will come out to deceive the nations which are at the four corners of the earth, that is, Gog and Magog, to gather them for battle; their number is like the sand of the sea. And they marched up over the broad earth and surrounded the camp of the saints and the beloved city; but fire came down from heaven and consumed them, and the devil who had deceived them was thrown into the lake of fire and sulphur where the beast and the false prophet were, and they will be tormented day and night for ever and ever.

# THE LETHAL POISON

WEEK 9

The Bible faces the bad news that external evil soon becomes a chronic internal problem for the human race. The account given in the third chapter of Genesis (Sunday) has never been surpassed, both in its grand simplicity and in its telling detail.

In the next chapter further woes are soon to come (Monday). The first child, Cain, becomes the first human with murder in his heart and hand, and with resistance to accountability, which he has inherited.

Tuesday's extract, from Genesis chapter 6, shows the rapid growth of this evil. In David's penitential Psalm 51 this evil is given the name 'sin'—a term often misunderstood or falsely limited, but a fundamental aspect of the human condition. Here King David's part in sin, and his ensuing penitence and prayer, moves him to use language which speaks for us all, but ends in hope.

The words of Jesus (Thursday) cut the ground from under us when, for all sorts of reasons, we see sin as something outside ourselves. Later Paul quotes several other Psalms to prove his point: that 'no-one will be declared righteous' (Friday). Like Paul, the New Testament letter of John cannot speak of sin without also pointing to its remedy (Saturday).

WEEK 9

# Sin: Humanity's and Mine

'Sin,' declared G. K. Chesterton, 'is the most demonstrable of all Christian doctrines.' He meant that we do not need to prove the doctrine of original sin—the evidence is all around us.

The Bible teaches about sin on two different levels: original sin and individual sin.

◆ **Original sin** means that when Adam fell, his act of disobedience affected the whole human race. Of course there is disagreement about just how to understand the story at the beginning of Genesis. Is it describing the fall of a real couple called Adam and Eve? Or is it rather a great poetic drama about every person's sin and guilt before God? Either way the story of Adam and Eve is a profound account of humanity's greatest tragedy—our separation from a good and holy God.

The essence of sin is brought out clearly and is made up of two parts, unbelief and pride. First of all, God's word is denied. The tempter questions, 'Has God said?' God's clear command is brushed aside through the voice of doubt. Then comes the second element in sin—pride: 'When you eat (of the fruit of that tree) you will be like God . . .' Here, then, is the irony of mankind's revolt against God. We want to break free of God and his restrictions. But we end up falling into a real bondage, one which binds our wills, our hearts and our minds.

◆ **Individual sin** is the working out of this pattern in the lives of us all. Adam's sin is repeated in our own unbelief and pride. So we find ourselves daily living the tragedy of sin, wanting to be better people but failing to live up to our good intentions. First we say: 'It is so difficult to believe in God.' But what we mean most of the time is: 'I don't want to obey God's plain word to me to follow him.' Again we say: 'I don't want to be a slave to God and his out-of-date laws: I want to be free to be myself.' But we are by nature worshippers. Either we worship God or we worship false gods. Today's false gods include money, sex, prosperity and power. We extend their influence by creating pseudo-faiths such as Communism, totalitarianism and nationalism.

Such, then, are the chains of sin. They bind so tight that no one can break free by themselves. As Jesus himself pointed out, sin is not external to us so that it can be washed away; it arises from our hearts and minds. And Paul voiced the agony of many a human heart: 'What a wretched man I am! Who will rescue me from this body of death?'

Paul, of course, answers his own question firmly and triumphantly—Jesus Christ can and will rescue us. The death of Jesus is the only place where we can find forgiveness for our sin and strength to overcome it. Only the cross can penetrate the dark and twisted pathways of our nature and free us from the power of evil.

It is easy to forget that Christ's battle against sin, the world and the devil still continues, and that we are on the front line fighting with him in the power of the cross. We live in a sin-shot world, its beauty and goodness distorted by sin and sometimes made very ugly. Political and social structures too often display sin's cancerous presence. This fact will make the mature Christian into a realist. He or she will never disregard the existence of evil: it will never stop spoiling the best human beings can do. But also the Christian will never allow sin the last word. Jesus Christ has ultimately conquered sin in his death.

## SUNDAY

GENESIS 3:6–13 (AV)

And when the woman saw that the tree was good for food, and that it was pleasant to the eyes, and a tree to be desired to make one wise, she took of the fruit thereof, and did eat, and gave also unto her husband with her; and he did eat. And the eyes of them both were opened, and they knew that they were naked; and they sewed fig leaves together, and made themselves aprons.

And they heard the voice of the Lord God walking in the garden in the cool of the day: and Adam and his wife hid themselves from the presence of the Lord God amongst the trees of the garden. And the Lord God called unto Adam, and said unto him, Where art thou? And he said, I heard thy voice in the garden, and I was afraid, because I was naked: and I hid myself. And he said, Who told thee that thou wast naked? Hast thou eaten of the tree, whereof I commanded thee that thou shouldest not eat? And the man said, The woman whom thou gavest to be with me, she gave me of the tree, and I did eat. And the Lord God said unto the woman, What is this that thou hast done? And the woman said, The serpent beguiled me, and I did eat.

## MONDAY

GENESIS 4:1–10 (RSV)

Now Adam knew Eve his wife, and she conceived and bore Cain, saying, 'I have gotten a man with the help of the Lord.' And again, she bore his brother Abel. Now Abel was a keeper of sheep, and Cain a tiller of the ground. In the course of time Cain brought to the Lord an offering of the fruit of the ground, and Abel brought of the firstlings of his flock and of their fat portions. And the Lord had regard for Abel and his offering, but for Cain and his offering he had no regard. So Cain was very angry, and his countenance fell. The Lord said to Cain, 'Why are you angry, and why has your countenance fallen? If you do well, will you not be accepted? And if you do not do well, sin is couching at the door; its desire is for you, but you must master it.'

Cain said to Abel his brother, 'Let us go out to the field.' And when they were in the field, Cain rose up against his brother Abel, and killed him. Then the Lord said to Cain, 'Where is Abel your brother?' He said, 'I do not know; am I my brother's keeper?' And the Lord said, 'What have you done? The voice of your brother's blood is crying to me from the ground.'

## TUESDAY

GENESIS 6:5–13 (RSV)

The Lord saw that the wickedness of man was great in the earth, and that every imagination of the thoughts of his heart was only evil continually. And the Lord was sorry that he had made man on the earth, and it grieved him to his heart. So the Lord said, 'I will blot out man whom I have created from the face of the ground, man and beast and creeping things and birds of the air, for I am sorry that I have made them.' But Noah found favour in the eyes of the Lord.

These are the generations of Noah. Noah was a righteous man, blameless in his generation; Noah walked with God. And Noah had three sons, Shem, Ham and Japheth.

Now the earth was corrupt in God's sight, and the earth was filled with violence. And God saw the earth, and behold, it was corrupt; for all flesh had corrupted their way upon the earth. And God said to Noah, 'I have determined to make an end of all flesh; for the earth is filled with violence through them; behold, I will destroy them with the earth.'

## WEDNESDAY

PSALM 51:1–13 (REB)

God, be gracious to me in your
  faithful love;
  in the fullness of your mercy blot
  out my misdeeds.
Wash away all my iniquity
  and cleanse me from my sin.
For well I know my misdeeds,
  and my sins confront me all the
  time.
Against you only have I sinned
  and have done what displeases;
you are right when you accuse me
  and justified in passing sentence.
From my birth I have been evil,
  sinful from the time my mother
  conceived me.

You desire faithfulness in the inmost being,
  so teach me wisdom in my heart.
Sprinkle me with hyssop, so that I
  may be cleansed;
  wash me, and I shall be whiter
  than snow.
Let me hear the sound of joy and
  gladness;
  you have crushed me, but make
  me rejoice again.
Turn away your face from my sins
  and wipe out all my iniquity.

God, create a pure heart for me,
  and give me a new and steadfast
  spirit.
Do not drive me from your presence
  or take your holy spirit from me.
Restore to me the joy of your deliverance
  and grant me a willing spirit to
  uphold me.
I shall teach transgressors your
  ways,
  and sinners will return to you.

## THURSDAY

MARK 7:14–23 (NJB)

Jesus called the people to him again and said, 'Listen to me, all of you, and understand. Nothing that goes into someone from outside can make that person unclean; it is the things that come out of someone that make that person unclean. Anyone who has ears for listening should listen!'

When he had gone into the house, away from the crowd, his disciples questioned him about the parable. He said to them, 'Even you—don't you understand? Can't you see that nothing that goes into someone from outside can make a person unclean, because it goes not into the heart but into the stomach and passes into the sewer?' (Thus he pronounced all foods clean.) And he went on, 'It is what comes out of someone that makes that person unclean. For it is from within, from the heart, that evil intentions emerge: fornication, theft, murder, adultery, avarice, malice, deceit, indecency, envy, slander, pride, folly. All these evil things come from within and make a person unclean.'

## FRIDAY

ROMANS 3:9–20 (NIV)

What shall we conclude then? Are we any better? Not at all! We have already made the charge that Jews and Gentiles alike are all under sin. As it is written:

'There is no-one righteous, not even one;
there is no-one who understands,
no-one who seeks God.
All have turned away,
they have together become worthless;
there is no-one who does any good,
not even one.'
'Their throats are open graves;
their tongues practise deceit.'
'The poison of vipers is on their lips.'
'Their mouths are full of cursing and bitterness.'
'Their feet are swift to shed blood;
ruin and misery mark their ways,
and the way of peace they do not know.'
'There is no fear of God before their eyes.'

Now we know that whatever the law says, it says to those who are under the law, so that every mouth may be silenced and the whole world held accountable to God. Therefore no-one will be declared righteous in his sight by observing the law; rather, through the law we become conscious of sin.

## SATURDAY

1 JOHN 1:5–10 (NIV)

This is the message we have heard from him and declare to you: God is light; in him there is no darkness at all. If we claim to have fellowship with him yet walk in the darkness, we lie and do not live by the truth. But if we walk in the light, as he is in the light, we have fellowship with one another, and the blood of Jesus, his Son, purifies us from all sin. If we claim to be without sin, we deceive ourselves and the truth is not in us. If we confess our sins, he is faithful and just and will forgive us our sins and purify us from all unrighteousness. If we claim we have not sinned, we make him out to be a liar and his word has no place in our lives.

# UNBENDING RULES

WEEK 10

In the Old Testament, the Law (or Torah) was made up of much more than rules. Also included were a varied wealth of teaching, wisdom and love.

The first reading this week is also the most famous: known as the Ten Commandments, they were given to Moses for a people who were already redeemed. In the Bible'sp fifth book, Deuteronomy (Monday), comes that other command which Jesus himself named as the most important of all (Wednesday).

The extracts from Psalm 119 (Tuesday) are part of an elaborately composed celebration of God's law and teaching, which is lovingly lingered over line by line; Tuesday's extract gives its beginning and end, with two other sections.

Among the New Testament letter-writers, Paul and James treat the law rather differently. In the texts from Romans (Thursday and Friday) Paul first challenges the Jews on their own moral high ground, and then recounts his own painful experience of it.

James shares exactly the same goal: for readers not to deceive themselves with their own morality, but to come face to face with the demands of the living God.

WEEK 10

# The Law of God

Law is not a very popular word these days. In all societies law and order are under attack, and many seem to think that if we had complete freedom we would be better off.

Yet God is a great believer in law! In the Old Testament we see that, following the covenant he made with Moses, his Law (the *Torah*) was given to the people of Israel so that their lives might express that they were in fact the children of God.

It is important to remember that at the beginning the Torah was not intended to be simply a list of dos and don'ts. The Hebrew word *torah* means 'instruction' and it was intended to be a framework for life, a gift of grace so that Israel might become in conduct what they already were as the people of God. Unfortunately, such is human nature that we are apt to turn a benefit into a barrier and this happened with the Law. By the time of Jesus the Pharisees had hedged the covenant around with 613 laws which the Jews were expected to keep. Jesus condemned the legalists who had made a prison camp of God's Torah: 'The scribes and Pharisees sit on Moses' seat… (but) they bind heavy burdens, hard to bear, and lay them on men's shoulders.'

Jesus' attitude to the Law is interesting. On the one hand he was prepared to ignore and even criticize it. Yet, on the other hand, he commended it and obeyed it as having divine authority. This apparent contradiction is resolved when we understand that Jesus believed that he had come, not to condemn or abolish the Law, but to fulfil it.

Jesus fulfilled the Law firstly by showing that love is the fulfilling of the Law. Indeed, he declared the double command, to 'love the Lord your God with all your heart,… soul,… mind… and your neighbour as you love yourself,' to be the perfect summary of the entire Law.

And secondly Jesus showed, by his whole life of obedience to the Father from start to finish, that this was how the genuinely human life should be lived. His death on the cross ushered in the new covenant, so the way of salvation now is not by keeping laws but by receiving God's forgiveness through Christ. He and not the Law opens the way between the Father and us.

Is the Law relevant for us today?

- **The Law is fulfilled in Jesus Christ but this does not mean we can pass it by.** Its inadequacies are clear enough. It cannot lead a person to God, and because of its appeal to standards which are beyond us only increases our sinfulness. Nevertheless it still remains 'holy, just and good'. Although we are not bound by the 613 laws of the old Jewish tradition, and although the Old Testament ceremonial law is fulfilled in the new covenant, the essence of the moral law as expressed in the Ten Commandments must be kept by us all. We are not made Christian, of course, by keeping them. But we heed them because we *are* Christians and we want to live well for God.

◆ **The gospel cannot be properly understood as good news without the preaching of the Law.** Its standard of what God requires is the backcloth against which the gospel makes sense. The church fails when it neglects God's standards of holiness, justice and love

◆ **Paul writes of the 'natural' law written in our hearts.** He means by this that those who have had no chance of responding to the gospel in this life are not condemned automatically by God. Because he is the God of mercy and love, he judges such people by what they have made of the law of conscience within.

## SUNDAY

EXODUS 20:1–17 (NIV)

And God spoke all these words:

'I am the Lord your God, who brought you out of Egypt, out of the land of slavery.

'You shall have no other gods before me.

'You shall not make for yourself an idol in the form of anything in heaven above or on the earth beneath or in the waters below. You shall not bow down to them or worship them; for I, the Lord your God, am a jealous God, punishing the children for the sin of the fathers to the third and fourth generation of those who hate me, but showing love to thousands who love me and keep my commandments.

'You shall not misuse the name of the Lord your God, for the Lord will not hold anyone guiltless who misuses his name.

'Remember the Sabbath day by keeping it holy. Six days you shall labour and do all your work, but the seventh day is a Sabbath to the Lord your God. On it you shall not do any work, neither you, nor your son or daughter, nor your manservant or maidservant, nor your animals, nor the alien within your gates. For in six days the Lord made the heavens and the earth, the sea, and all that is in them, but he rested on the seventh day. Therefore the Lord blessed the Sabbath day and made it holy.

'Honour your father and your mother, so that you may live long in the land the Lord your God is giving you.

'You shall not murder.

'You shall not commit adultery.

'You shall not steal.

'You shall not give false testimony against your neighbour.

'You shall not covet your neighbour's house. You shall not covet your neighbour's wife, or his manservant or maidservant, his ox or donkey, or anything that belongs to your neighbour.'

## MONDAY

DEUTERONOMY 6:1–9 (RSV)

And Moses said: 'Now this is the commandment, the statutes and the ordinances which the Lord your God commanded me to teach you, that you may do them in the land to which you are going over, to possess it; that you may fear the Lord your God, you and your son and your son's son, by keeping all his statutes and his commandments, which I command you, all the days of your life; and that your days may be prolonged. Hear therefore, O Israel, and be careful to do them; that it may go well with you, and that you may multiply greatly, as the Lord, the God of your fathers, has promised you, in a land flowing with milk and honey.

Hear, O Israel: The Lord our God is one Lord; and you shall love the Lord your God with all your heart, and with all your soul, and with all your might. And these words which I command you this day shall be upon your heart; and you shall teach them diligently to your children, and shall talk of them when you sit in your house, and when you walk by the way, and when you lie down, and when you rise. And you shall bind them as a sign upon your hand, and they shall be as frontlets between your eyes. And you shall write them on the doorposts of your house and on your gates.'

## TUESDAY

PSALM 119:1–2, 33–40, 105–112, 175–176 (REB)

Happy are they whose way of life is
blameless,
who conform to the law of the
Lord.
Happy are they who obey his
instruction,
who set their heart on finding
him.

Teach me, Lord, the way of your
statutes,
and in keeping them I shall find
my reward.
Give me the insight to obey your law
and to keep it wholeheartedly.
Make me walk in the path of your
commandments,
for that is my desire.
Dispose my heart towards your instruction,
not towards love of gain;
turn my eyes away from all that is
futile;
grant me life by your word.
Fulfil your promise for your
servant,
the promise made to those who
fear you.
Turn away the taunts which I dread,
for your decrees are good.
How I long for your precepts!
By your righteousness grant me
life.

Your word is a lamp to my feet,
a light on my path;
I have bound myself by oath and
solemn vow
to keep your just decrees.
I am cruelly afflicted;
Lord, revive me as you have
promised.
Accept, Lord, the willing tribute of
my lips,
and teach me your decrees.
Every day I take my life in my
hands,
yet I never forget your law.
The wicked have set a trap for me,
but I do not stray from your
precepts.
Your instruction is my everlasting
heritage;
it is the joy of my heart.
I am resolved to fulfil your statutes;
they are a reward that never
fails.

Let me live to praise you;
let your decrees be my help.
I have strayed like a lost sheep;
come search for your servant,
for I have not forgotten your
commandments.

## WEDNESDAY

MARK 12:28–34 (AV)

And one of the scribes came, and having heard them reasoning together, and perceiving that he had answered them well, asked him, Which is the first commandment of all? And Jesus answered him, The first of all the commandments is, Hear, O Israel; The Lord our God is one Lord: And thou shalt love the Lord thy God with all thy heart, and with all thy soul, and with all thy mind, and with all thy strength: this is the first commandment. And the second is like, namely this, Thou shalt love thy neighbour as thyself. There is none other commandment greater than these. And the scribe said unto him, Well, Master, thou hast said the truth: for there is but one God; and there is none other but he: And to love him with all the heart, and with all the understanding, and with all the soul, and with all the strength, and to love his neighbour as himself, is more than all whole burnt offerings and sacrifices. And when Jesus saw that he answered discreetly, he said unto him, Thou art not far from the kingdom of God. And no man after that durst ask him any question.

## THURSDAY

ROMANS 2:12–24 (REB)

Those who have sinned outside the pale of the law of Moses will perish outside the law, and all who have sinned under that law will be judged by it. None will be justified before God by hearing the law, but by doing it. When Gentiles who do not possess the law carry out its precepts by the light of nature, then, although they have no law, they are their own law; they show that what the law requires is inscribed on their hearts, and to this their conscience gives supporting witness, since their own thoughts argue the case, sometimes against them, sometimes even for them. So it will be on the day when, according to my gospel, God will judge the secrets of human hearts through Christ Jesus.

But as for you who bear the name of Jew and rely on the law: you take pride in your God; you know his will; taught by the law, you know what really matters; you are confident that you are a guide to the blind, a light to those in darkness, an instructor of the foolish, and a teacher of the immature, because you possess in the law the embodiment of knowledge and truth. You teach others, then; do you not teach yourself? You proclaim, 'Do not steal'; but are you yourself a thief? You say, 'Do not commit adultery'; but are you an adulterer? You abominate false gods; but do you rob shrines? While you take pride in the law, you dishonour God by breaking it. As scripture says, 'Because of you the name of God is profaned among the Gentiles.'

## FRIDAY

ROMANS 7:7–13 (NJB)

What should we say then? That the Law itself is sin? Out of the question! All the same, if it had not been for the Law, I should not have known what sin was; for instance, I should not have known what it meant to covet if the Law had not said: *You are not to covet.* But once it found the opportunity through that commandment, sin produced in me all kinds of covetousness; as long as there is no Law, sin is dead.

Once, when there was no Law, I used to be alive; but when the commandment came, sin came to life and I died. The commandment was meant to bring life but I found it brought death, because sin; finding its opportunity by means of the commandment, beguiled me and, by means of it, killed me.

So then, the Law is holy, and what it commands is holy and upright and good. Does that mean that something good resulted in my dying? Out of the question! But sin, in order to be identified as sin, caused my death through that good thing, and so it is by means of the commandment that sin shows its unbounded sinful power.

## SATURDAY

JAMES 1:16–27 (NIV)

Don't be deceived, my dear brothers. Every good and perfect gift is from above, coming down from the Father of the heavenly lights, who does not change like shifting shadows. He chose to give us birth through the word of truth, that we might be a kind of firstfruits of all he created.

My dear brothers, take note of this: Everyone should be quick to listen, slow to speak and slow to become angry, for man's anger does not bring about the righteous life that God desires. Therefore, get rid of all moral filth and the evil that is so prevalent, and humbly accept the word planted in you, which can save you.

Do not merely listen to the word, and so deceive yourselves. Do what it says. Anyone who listens to the word but does not do what it says is like a man who looks at his face in a mirror and, after looking at himself, goes away and immediately forgets what he looks like. But the man who looks intently into the perfect law that gives freedom, and continues to do this, not forgetting what he has heard, but doing it—he will be blessed in what he does.

If anyone considers himself religious and yet does not keep a tight rein on his tongue, he deceives himself and his religion is worthless. Religion that God our Father accepts as pure and faultless is this: to look after orphans and widows in their distress and to keep oneself from being polluted by the world.

# EXILE AND RETURN

When the army of Nebuchadnezzar of Babylon overthrew Jerusalem in 586BC, the leaders and a great part of the citizenry were taken off to exile in Babylon. The city, its walls and its temple were left in ruins; only a dejected minority of people remained. Surely this was the end. Judah could not recover from this, any more than the northern kingdom had ever recovered after falling to Assyria a century and a half before.

But only a generation later, Babylon itself fell to Cyrus of Persia, whose policy was different. He allowed the Jewish captives to return, which gradually they did. They had no kings now, but they rebuilt the temple and the walls and in time the nation was re-established, as the greatest prophets had foretold.

## EZRA

Bit by bit the Jews return from Babylon to their homeland. Under Ezra's leadership they begin to observe the law in detail, and to live as a people apart.

## NEHEMIAH

Nehemiah leads a third group of returning Jews. The city walls are repaired. It is not easy to sort out how this story ties in with the book of Ezra.

## ESTHER

A story from the time when some Jews stayed on under Persian rule. A beautiful Jewish girl is made queen, and thwarts an anti-Jewish plot.

## HAGGAI

The last three Old Testament prophets wrote after the exiles had returned. Haggai urges the people to forget individual concerns and work together to rebuild the temple. Unlike all other prophets, his words were obeyed.

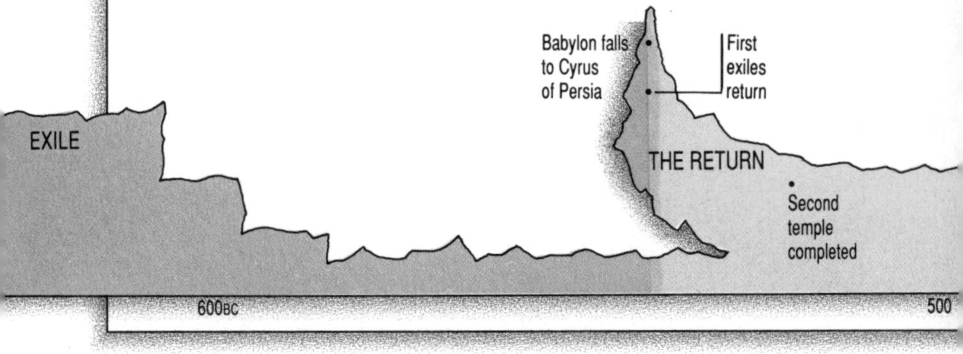

Babylon falls to Cyrus of Persia

First exiles return

EXILE

THE RETURN

Second temple completed

600BC

500

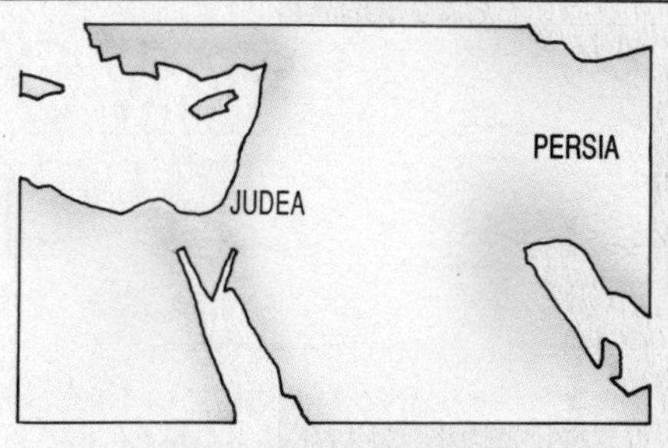


## ZECHARIAH

This visionary prophet worked alongside Haggai, though chapters 7 on are from some time later. His thought moves from the people's new beginnings to a future new age, not only for Jerusalem but for the whole world.

## MALACHI

These prophecies, from one whose name means 'messenger', may have been given around Nehemiah's time. He challenges the people to obey God wholeheartedly.

## RETURN OF THE EXILES

When Cyrus of Persia overthrew the Babylonian empire in 539BC, he issued an edict releasing captives to return to their homelands. Only two years later, the first group of Jews returned to Jerusalem with the temple treasures. They laid the foundations of the second temple.

Zerubbabel and Joshua led a second group, in 525BC. Under Haggai's urging, the temple was built. Nehemiah later led more Jews on a journey from Susa in Persia; he was appointed governor of Judah, and the city walls were repaired.

Ezra and another group returned home in 428BC. Probably other groups made the journey at other times. Life was very tough for some time, but gradually national and religious life took root again.

Nehemiah's group returns

WEEK 11

# UNAVOIDABLE CHECKOUT

The theme of judgment is explored throughout the Bible, starting with God's response to the first and fatal sin in the account of Adam and Eve (Sunday).

Then there is the catastrophe of the flood and Noah's story, not included here, followed by the calamity of the tower of Babel (Monday). Only in the New Testament is the fellowship of God, broken by these early acts of disobedience, fully restored.

Tuesday's reading presents the first exile of God's people as a punishment for constant rebellion and idolatry. And Wednesday's reading shows us Amos the farmer-prophet castigating the greed and oppression of Israel's ruling classes.

The New Testament extracts approach judgment, present and future, from different angles. Paul and Jude (Saturday and Sunday) both speak to their own generation, and to ours, as to those already condemned or at least in great danger, while the final words from Revelation (Saturday) show there is a point of no return. But the words of Jesus (Thursday) hold the key—in the end, he says it is his own word which will divide us. The process starts now, but 'the last day' reveals it.

# Judgment

Judgment is not a popular idea. It smacks too much of hell-fire preaching and vindictiveness. Yet it is impossible to detach the note of judgment from the Bible. In fact, it is difficult to know why any Christian would want to, because the Day of Judgment is when God will begin his reign, when good will finally overcome evil and we will see the triumph of both justice and grace.

In the Old Testament, belief in a 'Day of the Lord' was well established by the time of Amos. It was seen as a 'Good Time for all Israel' when God would see that his people were all right. But Amos turned this right round: the nation's sin would make it a day of darkness, not light. From then on it became commonplace for the prophets to preach God's judgment on a rebellious people. This judgment would come in national defeat and deportation, but the experience of exile would refine the people and create a purged remnant through whom God could work.

Alongside this theme lay the idea of a judgment on the nations which oppressed Israel. The literature which came from times of persecution developed this into a technicolour scenario, with God coming in the clouds, judging the living and the dead and bestowing a kingdom on the saints of the Most High. In this way those who were suffering comforted themselves with the thought that 'one day soon' their resistance would be recognized and their enemies vanquished.

And then Jesus came, throwing the whole question of a future judgment into the melting-pot. Because Jesus was God's last word. The end-time had arrived already. Up to a point all the 'future' things—eternal life, last judgment, second coming, resurrection of the dead—are now. As Jesus encountered people he created a crisis, a separation. They were for him or against him. Herod judged himself when he tried to murder Jesus; Pilate condemned himself when he dared to sit in judgment on him; and the cross was the ultimate judgment on the world's values. Paul presents judgment as a process where God allows people to live out the consequences of their own decisions.

And yet there is still a judgment to come. The Bible speaks of a time when the choices people have made will be confirmed. The eternal consequences of accepting or rejecting Jesus Christ will be made clear. God will judge the living and the dead. Judgment is guaranteed by the resurrection of Jesus. It follows his coming in glory. It will result in the overthrow of all that is evil and the triumphant reign of God.

Much of this is described in pictures, but it is important to take seriously the realities to which the pictures point. Jesus spoke of 'outer darkness', 'fire', 'weeping', 'a shut door', of people being 'lost'. Paul also wrote of the Christians' life-work (though built on a foundation which can never be touched) being 'tested by fire', so that they should be careful how they build. And the parable of the sheep and goats pictures the nations being judged by the way they treated Jesus when they met him unrecognized.

If judgment is a reality, then it is hard to go along with those who say everyone will be saved in the end, or there is a second chance after death. But many questions remain unanswered. Are we judged as soon as we die or do we await the Day of Judgment? Is punishment eternal or do only those in Christ survive? What about those who have never heard the gospel? The New Testament does give some clues but a good deal depends on what you make of the picture language.

In any case the Bible is not very concerned with the furniture of heaven and the temperature of hell. It concentrates on a positive truth. Christ has died, and so no one need be condemned. It speaks about being 'justified' by faith in Jesus, which is a picture of walking away from a law-court, free.

## SUNDAY

GENESIS 3:14–24 (AV)

And the Lord God said unto the serpent, Because thou hast done this, thou art cursed above all cattle, and above every beast of the field; upon thy belly shalt thou go, and dust shalt thou eat all the days of thy life: And I will put enmity between thee and the woman, and between thy seed and her seed; it shall bruise thy head, and thou shalt bruise his heel. Unto the woman he said, I will greatly multiply thy sorrow and thy conception; in sorrow thou shalt bring forth children; and thy desire shall be to thy husband, and he shall rule over thee. And unto Adam he said, Because thus hast hearkened unto the voice of thy wife, and hast eaten of the tree, of which I commanded thee, saying, Thou shalt not eat of it: cursed is the ground for thy sake; in sorrow shalt thou eat of it all the days of thy life; Thorns also and thistles shall it bring forth to thee; and thou shalt eat the herb of the field; In the sweat of thy face shalt thou eat bread, till thou return unto the ground; for out of it wast thou taken: for dust thou art, and unto dust shalt thou return. And Adam called his wife's name Eve; because she was the mother of all living. Unto Adam also and to his wife did the Lord God make coats of skins and clothed them.

And the Lord God said, Behold, the man is become as one of us, to know good and evil: and now, lest he put forth his hand, and take also of the tree of life, and eat, and live for ever: Therefore the Lord God sent him forth from the garden of Eden, to till the ground from whence he was taken. So he drove out the man; and he placed at the east of the garden of Eden Cherubims, and a flaming sword which turned every way, to keep the way of the tree of life.

## MONDAY

GENESIS 11:1–9 (RSV)

Now the whole earth had one language and few words. And as men migrated from the east, they found a plain in the land of Shinar and settled there. And they said to one another, 'Come, let us make bricks, and burn them thoroughly.' And they had brick for stone, and bitumen for mortar. Then they said, 'Come, let us build ourselves a city, and a tower with its top in the heavens, and let us make a name for ourselves, lest we be scattered abroad upon the face of the whole earth.' And the Lord came down to see the city and the tower, which the sons of men had built. And the Lord said, 'Behold, they are one people, and they have all one language; and this is only the beginning of what they will do; and nothing that they propose to do will now be impossible for them. Come, let us go down, and there confuse their language, that they may not understand one another's speech.' So the Lord scattered them abroad from there over the face of all the city. Therefore its name was called Babel, because there the Lord confused the language of all the earth; and from there the Lord scattered them abroad over the face of all the earth.

## TUESDAY

2 KINGS 17:5–15, 18–20 (REB)

The King of Assyria overran the whole country and, reaching Samaria, besieged it for three years. In the ninth year of Hoshea he captured Samaria and deported its people to Assyria, and settled them in Halah and on the Habor, the river of Gozan, and in the towns of Media.

All this came about because the Israelites had sinned against the Lord their God who brought them up from Egypt, from the despotic rule of Pharaoh king of Egypt; they paid homage to other gods and observed the laws and customs of the nations whom the Lord had dispossessed before them, and uttered blasphemies against the Lord their God; they built shrines for themselves in all their settlements, from watch-tower to fortified city; they set up for themselves sacred pillars and sacred poles on every high hill and under every spreading tree, and burnt offerings at all the shrines there, as the nations did whom the Lord had displaced before them. By this wickedness of theirs they provoked the Lord's anger. They worshipped idols, a thing which the Lord had forbidden them to do.

Still the Lord solemnly charged Israel and Judah by every prophet and seer, saying, 'Give up your evil ways; keep my commandments and statutes given in all the law which I enjoined on your forefathers and delivered to you through my servants the prophets.' They would not listen, however, but were as stubborn and rebellious as their forefathers had been, for they too refused to put their trust in the Lord their God. They rejected his statutes and the covenant which he had made with their forefathers and the solemn warnings which he had given to them. Following worthless idols they became worthless themselves and imitated the nations round about them, which the Lord had forbidden them to do.

Thus it was that the Lord was incensed against Israel and banished them from his presence; only the tribe of Judah was left. Even Judah did not keep the commandments of the Lord their God but followed the practices adopted by Israel; so the Lord rejected all the descendants of Israel and punished them and gave them over to plunderers and finally flung them out from his presence.

## WEDNESDAY

AMOS 7:7–9, 8:1–7 (NIV)

This is what he showed me: The Lord was standing by a wall that had been built true to plumb, with a plumb-line in his hand. And the Lord asked me, 'What do you see, Amos?'

'A plumb-line,' I replied.

Then the Lord said, 'Look, I am setting a plumb-line among my people Israel; I will spare them no longer.

'The high places of Isaac will be
destroyed
and the sanctuaries of Israel will be
ruined;
with my sword I will rise
against the house of Jeroboam.'

This is what the Sovereign Lord showed me: a basket of ripe fruit. 'What do you see, Amos?' he asked.

'A basket of ripe fruit,' I answered.

Then the Lord said to me, 'The time is ripe for my people of Israel; I will spare them no longer.'

'In that day,' declares the Sovereign Lord, 'the songs in the temple will turn to wailing. Many, many bodies—flung everywhere! Silence!'

Hear this, you who trample the
needy
and do away with the poor of the
land,
saying,
'When will the New Moon be over
that we may sell grain,
and the Sabbath be ended
that we may market wheat?—
skimping the measure,
boosting the price
and cheating with dishonest
scales,
buying the poor with silver
and the needy for a pair of
sandals,
selling even the sweepings with
the wheat.

The Lord has sworn by the Pride of Jacob: 'I will never forget anything they have done.'

## THURSDAY

JOHN 12:44–50 (NJB)

Jesus declared publicly: 'Whoever believes in me believes not in me but in the one who sent me, and whoever sees me, sees the one who sent me. I have come into the world as light, to prevent anyone who believes in me from staying in the dark any more. If anyone hears my words and does not keep them faithfully, it is not I who shall judge such a person, since I have come not to judge the world, but to save the world: anyone who rejects me and refuses my words has his judge already: the word itself that I have spoken will be his judge on the last day. For I have not spoken of my own accord; but the Father who sent me commanded me what to say and what to speak, and I know that his commands mean eternal life. And therefore what the Father has told me is what I speak.

## FRIDAY

ROMANS 1:18–25 (NJB)

The retribution of God from heaven is being revealed against the ungodliness and injustice of human beings who in their injustice hold back the truth. For what can be known about God is perfectly plain to them, since God has made it plain to them: ever since the creation of the world, the invisible existence of God and his everlasting power have been clearly seen by the mind's understanding of created things. And so these people have no excuse: they knew God and yet they did not honour him as God or give thanks to him, but their arguments became futile and their uncomprehending minds were darkened. While they claimed to be wise, in fact they were growing so stupid that they exchanged the glory of the immortal God for an imitation, for the image of a mortal human being, or of birds, or animals, or crawling things.

This is why God abandoned them in

their inmost cravings to filthy practices of dishonouring their own bodies—because they exchanged God's truth for a lie and have worshipped and served the creature instead of the Creator, who is blessed for ever. Amen.

## SATURDAY

JUDE 3–7 (REB)

My friends, I was fully intending to write to you about the salvation we share, when I found it necessary to take up my pen and urge you to join in the struggle for that faith which God entrusted to his people once for all. Certain individuals have wormed their way in, the very people whom scripture long ago marked down for the sentence they are now incurring. They are enemies of religion; they pervert the free favour of our God into licentiousness, disowning Jesus Christ, our only Master and Lord.

You already know all this, but let me remind you how the Lord, having once for all delivered his people out of Egypt, later destroyed those who did not believe. Remember too those angels who were not content to maintain the dominion assigned to them, but abandoned their proper dwelling place; God is holding them, bound in darkness with everlasting chains, for judgement on the great day. Remember Sodom and Gomorrah and the neighbouring towns; like the angels, they committed fornication and indulged in unnatural lusts; and in eternal fire they paid the penalty, a warning for all.

REVELATION 20:11–15 (REB)

I saw a great, white throne, and the One who sits upon it. From his presence earth and heaven fled away, and there was no room for them any more. I saw the dead, great and small, standing before the throne; and books were opened. Then another book, the book of life, was opened. The dead were judged by what they had done, as recorded in these books. The sea gave up the dead that were in it, and Death and Hades gave up the dead in their keeping. Everyone was judged on the record of his deeds. Then Death and Hades were flung into the lake of fire. This lake of fire is the second death; into it were flung any whose names were not to be found in the book of life.

# GIFT BEYOND WORDS

WEEK 12

Words are inadequate to express the wonder of Jesus, the Messiah long-awaited by God's people, the answer to a world's need, and God's eternal Son. Yet here are words which have been spoken, written, sung and prayed in his honour.

Psalm 110 (Sunday) is not an easy one, but Jesus clearly saw it as a prophecy of himself. The way it is used in Friday's passage from Acts repays study.

On Monday we see how the prophet Isaiah unveils the coming child—the prince, the branch, the Spirit-filled judge. And Micah, in another reading (Tuesday) familiar from Christmas carol services, points crucially to Bethlehem as the place of his arrival.

The Gospel according to Mark, bypassing Christmas altogether, plunges straight into the story of Jesus the adult—the beloved Son of God, preacher of the kingdom and the gospel, heralded by John the Baptist (Wednesday). Mark also describes Simon Peter leading the way in both daring faith when he recognizes Jesus as the Messiah and spectacular misunderstanding as he tries to prevent Jesus from carrying out his messianic purpose (Thursday).

It is the same Peter, now the first Christian preacher, who on the day of Pentecost declares the crucified and risen Jesus to be God's Messiah and the world's Lord (Friday). Two extracts from Paul's letter to Titus (Saturday) round off the week. Paul's words testify to the life-changing experience of believing in Jesus as Saviour.

WEEK 12

# Jesus the Messiah

The Hebrew word *Messiah* (with its Greek equivalent *Christ*) just means someone anointed by God. But in the Bible it usually means more: a God-sent rescuer who bursts into a crisis to sort things out.

A longing for a Messiah arises particularly when a people groan under a foreign oppressor, look back wistfully to past glories and yet cling to a creed which tells them they are God's special people. In the Old Testament, there were hints of the one who would come. But in the bitter days of Israel's occupation, first by the Greeks and then by the Romans, the cry for a deliverer became more desperate and insistent. Occasionally the 'coming one' was seen in spiritual terms but far more often he was a 'son of David' who would win military victories and expel the Romans. Literature produced in earlier persecutions liked to picture him in lurid colours, wielding supernatural weapons. It was this nerve which John the Baptist touched, with his message of one who was coming to thresh the people and baptize them in fire.

Certainly, Galilee was a breeding ground for messianic hotheads. In AD6, for example, Judas of Galilee raised the standard of rebellion in protest at the Roman-imposed census. We can imagine the effect on the boy Jesus as he watched the survivors of this ill-starred campaign limp home, wounded, demoralized, searching for bolt-holes to hide them from Rome's vengeance.

Jesus began his ministry in an atmosphere of intense messianic expectation, but in what sense can he be called the Messiah? Certainly, he displayed messianic qualities. He healed the sick, the lame, the deaf, the dumb and the blind. His sermon at Nazareth—given us in Luke chapter 4 verses 16–21—sounded like a manifesto for a new age. And his triumphal entry into Jerusalem and cleansing of the temple both suggested the actions of someone behaving 'as if he owned the place'.

People also drew messianic conclusions. In John's Gospel a number of individuals recognized Jesus as the Messiah and the crowd once tried to make him king. When the disciples were pressed by Jesus, 'Who do you say that I am?', Peter jumped to the shattering conclusion, 'You are the Christ.'

Yet Jesus disliked people calling him 'Messiah' publicly. He is reluctant to apply it to himself, too. His answer to the High Priest's question at his trial, 'Are you the Christ...?' is best taken as meaning, 'Yes, though that would not be my way of putting it.'

Why was he so reluctant to accept the title? Perhaps because a word is known by the company it keeps. 'Messiah' was too tied up with ideas of violence, military might and nationalism to do a useful job. So Jesus linked the term with suffering in an attempt to correct misconceptions. 'Yes,' he seems to be saying, 'I am the rescuer, but my way of delivering you involves dying on the cross.' To the average man, like Peter, this was impossible to understand.

After the resurrection the whole

world was changed. The glory, power and victory of the Messiah were now locked into Jesus' death on the cross. Christians could now understand what Jesus had hinted at before. They preached a suffering Messiah, a 'Christ crucified'.

Once the gospel moved out of its Jewish setting, of course, 'Christ' became a foreign word. It gradually lost its original meaning and was used, as it tends to be today, just as another name for Jesus. Which is a pity, because Jesus as the Messiah shows us that God always fulfils what he promises, even if the fulfilment is long delayed.

## SUNDAY

PSALM 110 (RSV)

The Lord says to my lord:
'Sit at my right hand,
till I make your enemies your footstool.'

The Lord sends forth from Zion
your mighty sceptre.
Rule in the midst of your foes!
Your people will offer themselves freely
on the day you lead your host
upon the holy mountains.
From the womb of the morning
like dew your youth will come to you.
The Lord has sworn
and will not change his mind,
'You are a priest for ever
after the order of Melchizedek.'

The Lord is at your right hand;
he will shatter kings on the day of his wrath.
He will execute judgment among the nations,
filling them with corpses;
he will shatter chiefs
over the wide earth.
He will drink from the brook by the way;
therefore he will lift up his head.

## MONDAY

ISAIAH 9:2–7, 11:1–4 (AV)

The people that walked in darkness have seen a great light: they that dwell in the land of the shadow of death, upon them hath the light shined. Thou hast multiplied the nation, and not increased the joy; they joy before thee according to the joy in harvest, and as men rejoice when they divide the spoil. For thou hast broken the yoke of his burden, and the staff of his shoulder, the rod of his oppressor, as in the day of Midian. For every battle of the warrior is with confused noise, and garments rolled in blood; but this shall be with burning and fuel of fire. For unto us a child is born, unto us a son is given: and the government shall be upon his shoulder: and his name shall be called Wonderful, Counseller, The mighty God, The everlasting Father, The Prince of Peace. Of the increase of his government and peace there shall be no end, upon the throne of David, and upon his kingdom, to order it, and to establish it with judgment and with justice from henceforth even for ever. The zeal of the Lord of hosts will perform this.

And there shall come forth a rod out of the stem of Jesse, and a Branch shall grow out of his roots: And the spirit of the Lord shall rest upon him, the spirit of wisdom and understanding, the spirit of counsel and might, the spirit of knowledge and of the fear of the Lord; And shall make him of quick understanding in the fear of the Lord: and he shall not judge after the sight of his eyes, neither reprove after the hearing of his ears: But with righteousness shall he judge the poor, and reprove with equity for the meek of the earth: and he shall smite the earth with the rod of his mouth, and with the breath of his lips shall he slay the wicked.

## TUESDAY

MICAH 5:2–5 (NIV)

'But you, Bethlehem Ephrathah,
    though you are small among the clans of Judah,
out of you will come for me
    one who will be ruler over Israel,
whose origins are from of old,
    from ancient times.

Therefore Israel will be abandoned
    until the time when she who is in labour gives birth
and the rest of his brothers return
    to join the Israelites.

He will stand and shepherd his flock
    in the strength of the Lord,
    in the majesty of the name of the Lord his God.
And they will live securely, for then his greatness
    will reach to the ends of the earth.
    And he will be their peace.

## WEDNESDAY

MARK 1:1–15 (REB)

The beginning of the gospel of Jesus Christ the Son of God.

In the prophet Isaiah it stands written:

I am sending my herald ahead of
    you;
    he will prepare your way.
A voice cries in the wilderness,
    'Prepare the way for the Lord;
    clear a straight path for him.'

John the Baptist appeared in the wilderness proclaiming a baptism in token of repentance, for the forgiveness of sins; and everyone flocked to him from the countryside of Judaea and the city of Jerusalem, and they were baptized by him in the river Jordan, confessing their sins. John was dressed in a rough coat of camel's hair, with a leather belt round his waist, and he fed on locusts and wild honey. He proclaimed: 'After me comes one mightier than I am, whose sandals I am not worthy to stoop down and unfasten. I have baptized you with water; he will baptize you with the Holy Spirit.'

It was at this time that Jesus came from Nazareth in Galilee and was baptized in the Jordan by John. As he was coming up out of the water, he saw the heavens break open and the Spirit descend on him, like a dove. And a voice came from heaven: 'You are my beloved Son; in you I take delight.'

At once the Spirit drove him out into the wilderness, and there he remained for forty days tempted by Satan. He was among the wild beasts; and angels attended to his needs.

After John had been arrested, Jesus came into Galilee proclaiming the gospel of God: 'The time has arrived; the kingdom of God is upon you. Repent, and believe the gospel.'

## THURSDAY

MARK 8:27–33 (REB)

Jesus and his disciples set out for the villages of Caesarea Philippi, and on the way he asked his disciples, 'Who do people say I am?' They answered, 'Some say John the Baptist, others Elijah, others one of the prophets.'

'And you,' he asked, 'who do you say I am?' Peter replied: 'You are the Messiah.' Then he gave them strict orders not to tell anyone about him; and he began to teach them that the Son of Man had to endure great suffering, and to be rejected by the elders, chief priests, and scribes; to be put to death, and to rise again three days afterwards. He spoke about it plainly. At this Peter took hold of him and began to rebuke him. But Jesus, turning and looking at his disciples, rebuked Peter. 'Out of my sight, Satan!' he said. 'You think as men think, not as God thinks.'

## FRIDAY

ACTS 2:25–36 (NJB)

David says of him:
I kept the Lord before my sight
always,
for with him at my right hand
nothing can shake me.
So my heart rejoiced
my tongue delighted;
my body too will rest secure,
for you will not abandon me to
Hades
or allow your holy one to see
corruption.
You have taught me the way of life,
you will fill me with joy in your
presence.

'Brothers, no one can deny that the patriarch David himself is dead and buried: his tomb is still with us. But since he was a prophet, and knew that God had sworn him an oath to make one of his descendants succeed him on the throne, he spoke with foreknowledge about the resurrection of the Christ: he is the one who was not abandoned to Hades, and whose body did not see corruption. God raised this man Jesus to life, and of that we are all witnesses. Now raised to the heights by God's right hand, he has received from the Father the Holy Spirit, who was promised, and what you see and hear is the outpouring of that Spirit. For David himself never went up to heaven, but yet he said:
The Lord declared to my Lord,
take your seat at my right hand,
till I have made your enemies
your footstool.

For this reason the whole House of Israel can be certain that the Lord and Christ whom God has made is this Jesus whom you crucified.'

## SATURDAY

TITUS 2:11–14, 3:3–7 (NIV)

For the grace of God that brings salvation has appeared to all men. It teaches us to say 'No' to ungodliness and worldly passions, and to live self-controlled, upright and godly lives in this present age, while we wait for the blessed hope—the glorious appearing of our great God and Saviour, Jesus Christ, who gave himself for us to redeem us from all wickedness and to purify for himself a people that are his very own, eager to do what is good.

At one time we too were foolish, disobedient, deceived and enslaved by all kinds of passions and pleasures. We lived in malice and envy, being hated and hating one another. But when the kindness and love of God our Saviour appeared, he saved us, not because of righteous things we had done, but because of his mercy. He saved us through the washing of rebirth and renewal by the Holy Spirit, whom he poured out on us generously through Jesus Christ our Saviour, so that, having been justified by his grace, we might become heirs having the hope of eternal life.

WEEK 13

# THE STRANGE COMMUNITY

The church is traditionally seen as a family-community on a journey, united by (among other things) the duty and the joy of worship. But when did the church, this motley yet glorious bunch of believers, really start? Some say it all began with Abram, with God's call to this Mesopotamian patriarch (Sunday).

In Monday's reading we see how Jesus gathers his embryonic community. The disciples are a mixed group of early leaders, one of whom, Judas, failed irretrievably. In the second part of the reading we see a much wider circle of people as the new 'family' of Jesus.

Or did the church as we know it begin with the coming of the Holy Spirit on the day of Pentecost? (Tuesday). Here is the 'birthday party' of the church with wind, fire, and telling in many tongues of God's wonderful works.

Wednesday's extract from Paul's letter to the early Christians in Corinth takes the lid off their church, revealing both its impressive strengths and its absurd deficiencies. On Thursday we can find real names of real people, united in love over the miles (for Paul the writer) and over the years (for us, who do not yet know them). In Friday's extract Paul, in another letter, speaks of the church as the 'bride' and the 'body', while Saturday's reading picks up that same church in Ephesus, maybe a generation later. The second extract looks ahead to the complete bride made perfect at last for her Lord.

# The Church

'For we are an Easter people and Hallelujah is our song,' said Pope John Paul II, and it is not a bad definition of what Jesus intended the church to be. Its bedrock is the resurrection and its message is one of joy.

Unfortunately, the church has not always expressed these things in its life. The established churches have often stood in the way of people reaching Jesus Christ. Yet at its best the church is something great. Four New Testament images give a clear picture of what God wants his people to be:

◆ **The church is the people of God.** Israel was originally chosen to be God's people and his witness to the nations. Then through Jesus a new way was opened up, and because of his life, death and resurrection all who follow him are now the 'people of God'. They are people of faith, trusting the promises of God.

But was it Jesus' intention to found a church? There can be little doubt that it was. He called twelve apostles around him, and sent them out to make disciples and to proclaim the message of the kingdom. His last act was to tell his followers to go and tell others. According to Matthew, Jesus said to Peter: 'You are Peter and on this rock I will build my church.' A new people was to grow from Jesus' ministry. Either Peter's confession or Peter himself was to be the starting-point of the people of God.

◆ **The church is the body of Christ.** Paul was the first to use this phrase of the church, and no one knows for certain where he got the idea from. It could have simply been taken from the notion of the human body with each limb and organ having its own function. If so, it is a beautiful picture of each person serving Christ joyfully, gladly and wholeheartedly. Whoever we are we matter to the body, which is the poorer for us not being there.

On the other hand, Paul may have taken the expression from Jesus' words at the Last Supper, 'This is my body.' If so, he is stressing the church's mission to continue the teaching and ministry of Jesus. It exists to be his body in the world; healing, helping, sharing and uniting. The two sacraments Jesus gave us express the meaning of the body, too. Through baptism we join it; through holy communion we are nourished in it.

◆ **The church is the temple of the Holy Spirit.** This rich description speaks of the presence of God's Spirit in and among his people. Each individual Christian is filled with God's Spirit and so is the whole body. He is given to us to make us 'holy' and powerful. Although it is possible to 'quench' the Spirit and 'grieve' him, the Spirit of God is active within the church and working through it. The growth of the church is a tribute to his work.

◆ **The church is the bride of Christ.** This metaphor, found in the writings of Paul and in Revelation, looks ahead to the future when at Christ's coming the church will be presented to the bridegroom as a glorious and pure bride. In that day all its imperfections will be removed and it will be a fitting partner for God himself. Wherever it is placed, God's church lives within the dynamic tension between what it is and what it ought to be. The **people of God** should live more like him, the **body** must continue to grow, the **temple** has still to be built and the **bride** awaits the call of the bride-groom.

Three dangers continue to dog the church's story. One such danger is exclusivism—that my church is the only true church. But the church belongs not to us but to Jesus Christ and those who confess him belong to it regardless of denominational tag. Another is tradition. Church tradition is often a great blessing but it may also silt up the channel of God's grace if it is valued above the message of the cross. And a third danger is organization. The church began as an 'organism', like a plant adapting to its environment and new situation. Inevitably, organization began to shape and direct the spontaneous ministries which sprang up. But when a church is over-organized the creative work of the Holy Spirit may be squeezed out and the gifts of God's people may not find expression. Only a church alive to the Holy Spirit will express the joy of the resurrection.

## SUNDAY

GENESIS 12:1–9 (RSV)

Now the Lord said to Abram, 'Go from your country and your kindred and your father's house to the land that I will show you. And I will make of you a great nation, and I will bless you, and make your name great, so that you will be a blessing. I will bless those who bless you, and him who curses you I will curse; and by you all the families of the earth shall bless themselves.'

So Abram went, as the Lord had told him; and Lot went with him. Abram was seventy-five years old when he departed from Haran. And Abram took Sarai his wife, and Lot his brother's son, and all their possessions which they had gathered, and the persons that they had gotten in Haran; and they set forth to go to the land of Canaan. When they had come to the land of Canaan, Abram passed through the land to the place at Shechem, to the oak of Moreh. At that time the Canaanites were in the land. Then the Lord appeared to Abram, and said, 'To your descendants I will give this land.' So he built there an altar to the Lord, who had appeared to him. Thence he removed to the mountain on the east of Bethel, and pitched his tent, with Bethel on the west and Ai on the east; and there he built an altar to the Lord and called on the name of the Lord. And Abram journeyed on, still going toward the Negeb.

## MONDAY

MARK 3:13–19, 31–35 (NIV)

Jesus went up on a mountainside and called to him those he wanted, and they came to him. He appointed twelve—designating them apostles—that they might be with him and that he might send them out to preach and to have authority to drive out demons. These are the twelve he appointed: Simon (to whom he gave the name Peter); James son of Zebedee, and his brother John (to them he gave the name Boanerges, which means Sons of Thunder); Andrew, Philip, Bartholomew, Matthew, Thomas, James son of Alphaeus, Thaddaeus, Simon the Zealot and Judas Iscariot, who betrayed him.

Then Jesus' mother and brothers arrived. Standing outside, they sent someone in to call him. A crowd was sitting around him, and they told him, 'Your mother and brothers are outside looking for you.'

'Who are my mother and my brothers?' he asked.

Then he looked at those seated in a circle around him and said, 'Here are my mother and my brothers! Whoever does God's will is my brother and sister and mother.'

## TUESDAY

ACTS 2:1–13 (AV)

And when the day of Pentecost was fully come, they were all with one accord in one place. And suddenly there came a sound from heaven as of a rushing mighty wind, and it filled all the house where they were sitting. And there appeared unto them cloven tongues like as of fire, and it sat upon each of them. And they were all filled with the Holy Ghost, and began to speak with other tongues, as the Spirit gave them utterance.

And there were dwelling at Jerusalem Jews, devout men, out of every nation under heaven. Now when this was noised abroad, the multitude came together, and were confounded, because that every man heard them speak in his own language. And they were all amazed and marvelled, saying one to another, Behold, are not all these which speak Galileans? And how hear we every man in our own tongue, wherein we were born? Parthians, and Medes and Elamites, and the dwellers in Mesopotamia, and in Judaea, and Cappadocia, in Pontus, and Asia, Phrygia, and Pamphylia, in Egypt, and in the parts of Libya about Cyrene, and strangers of Rome, Jews and proselytes. Cretes and Arabians, we do hear them speak in our tongues the wonderful works of God.

And they were all amazed, and were in doubt, saying to one another, What meaneth this? Others mocking said, These men are full of new wine.

## WEDNESDAY

1 CORINTHIANS 1:26–2:5, 3:6–9 (NIV)

Brothers think of what you were when you were called. Not many of you were wise by human standards; not many were influential; not many were of noble birth. But God chose the foolish things of the world to shame the wise; God chose the weak things of the world to shame the strong. He chose the lowly things of this world and the despised things—and the things that are not—to nullify the things that are, so that no-one may boast before him. It is because of him that you are in Christ Jesus, who has become for us wisdom from God—that is, our righteousness, holiness and redemption. Therefore, as it is written: 'Let him who boasts boast in the Lord.'

When I came to you, brothers, I did not come with eloquence or superior wisdom as I proclaimed to you the testimony about God. For I resolved to know nothing while I was with you except Jesus Christ and him crucified. I came to you in weakness and fear, and with much trembling. My message and my preaching were not with wise and persuasive words, but with a demonstration of the Spirit's power, so that your faith might not rest on men's wisdom, but on God's power.

I planted the seed, Apollos watered it, but God made it grow. So neither he who plants nor he who waters is anything, but only God, who makes things grow. The man who plants and the man who waters have one purpose, and each will be rewarded according to his own labour. For we are God's fellow-workers; you are God's field, God's building.

## THURSDAY

ROMANS 16:1–16 (NIV)

I commend to you our sister Phoebe, a servant of the church in Cenchreae. I ask you to receive her in the Lord in a way worthy of the saints and to give her any help she may need from you, for she has been a great help to many people, including me.

Greet Priscilla and Aquila, my fellow-workers in Christ Jesus. They risked their lives for me. Not only I but all the churches of the Gentiles are grateful to them. Greet also the church that meets at their house. Greet my dear friend Epenetus, who was the first convert to Christ in the province of Asia. Greet Mary, who worked very hard for you. Greet Andronicus and Junias, my relatives who have been in prison with me. They are outstanding among the apostles, and they were in Christ before I was. Greet Ampliatus, whom I love in the Lord. Greet Urbanus, our fellow-worker in Christ, and my dear friend Stachys. Greet Apeles, tested and approved in Christ. Greet those who belong to the household of Aristobulus. Greet Herodion, my relative. Greet those in the household of Narcissus who are in the Lord. Greet Tryphena and Tryphosa, those women who work hard in the Lord. Greet my dear friend Persis, another woman who has worked very hard in the Lord. Greet Rufus, chosen in the Lord, and his mother, who has been a mother to me, too. Greet Asyncritus, Phlegon, Hermes, Patrobas, Hermas and the brothers with them. Greet Philologus, Julia, Nereus and his sister, and Olympas and all the saints with them. Greet one another with a holy kiss. All the churches of Christ send greetings.

## FRIDAY

EPHESIANS 5:25–32 (REB)

Husbands, love your wives, as Christ loved the church and gave himself up for it, to consecrate and cleanse it by water and word, so that he might present the church to himself all glorious, with no stain or wrinkle or anything of the sort, but holy and without blemish. In the same way men ought to love their wives, as they love their own bodies. In loving his wife a man loves himself. For no one ever hated his own body; on the contrary, he keeps it nourished and warm, and that is how Christ treats the church, because it is his body, of which we are living parts. 'This is why' (in the words of scripture) 'a man shall leave his father and mother and be united to his wife, and the two shall become one flesh.' There is hidden here a great truth, which I take to refer to Christ and to the church.

## SATURDAY

REVELATION 2:1–7, 21:1–5 (RSV)

To the angel of the church in Ephesus write: 'The words of him who holds the seven stars in his right hand, who walks among the seven golden lampstands.

'I know your works, your toil and your patient endurance, and how you cannot bear evil men but have tested those who call themselves apostles but are not, and found them to be false; I know you are enduring patiently and bearing up for my name's sake, and you have not grown weary. But I have this against you, that you have abandoned the love you had first. Remember then from what you have fallen, repent and do the works you did at first. If not, I will come to you and remove your lampstand from its place, unless you repent. Yet this you have, you hate the works of the Nicolatians, which I also hate. He who has an ear, let him hear what the Spirit says to the churches. To him who conquers I will grant to eat of the tree of life, which is in the paradise of God.'

Then I saw a new heaven and a new earth; for the first heaven and the first earth had passed away, and the sea was no more. And I saw the holy city, new Jerusalem, coming down out of heaven from God, prepared as a bride adorned for her husband; and I heard a loud voice from the throne saying, 'Behold, the dwelling of God is with men. He will dwell with them, and they shall be his people, and God himself will be with them; he will wipe away every tear from their eyes, and death shall be no more, neither shall there be mourning nor crying nor pain any more, for the former things have passed away.'

And he who sat upon the throne said, 'Behold, I make all things new.' Also he said, 'Write this, for these words are trustworthy and true.'

# THE WAY OUT AND IN

This week starts with part of the account of 'the salvation of the Lord' when the people of Israel, led by Moses, crossed over the Red Sea. Here they find the Egyptians behind them and the sea in front. This 'salvation', or deliverance, followed the first-ever Passover night when God's people put their trust in him to free them from slavery in Egypt. The lyrical chapter from Isaiah (Monday) remembers this earlier rescue by God. Throughout the Bible, Israel's 'exodus' is the great picture of salvation. But however vividly this historical event was recalled, it failed to meet the deepest needs of this liberated nation as the centuries rolled on.

On Tuesday we hear how, at the dawn of the New Testament day, Simeon has the extraordinary faith to believe that the child in his arms embodies a greater salvation than even Moses knew—a rescue available for the world. The second part of Tuesday's reading shows the adult Jesus taking up Simeon's word (and the meaning of his own name, 'Saviour') to confirm what his coming would mean for those who welcomed him.

In the remaining extracts, Peter and Paul each point to the same reality of salvation through Jesus Christ: Peter testifies in spoken defence (Wednesday) and written letter (Saturday), while three of Paul's major writings describe Jesus Christ's death on the cross as the supreme saving moment (Friday and Saturday). Through God's achievement not ours, we find the way out of sin, rebellion and death, and into life, joy and heaven.

WEEK 14

# Salvation

Christians used often to talk about 'being saved', and others knew what they meant. Today 'salvation' has become a mainly religious word. To get a full idea of its meaning in the Bible let us use three other words instead—**deliverance, revolution, wholeness**.

- **Deliverance.** In the Old Testament the Passover Festival stood for God's deliverance of his people from bondage in Egypt. To this day the Passover for the Jew means 'freedom' because God saved them from a desperate plight when nothing else could have helped. Many times later Israel wandered away from its God and drifted into bondage. Then, too, the people cried out for freedom.

  In the time of Jesus the great longing was for deliverance from the might of Rome, and this was probably in the minds of the Jews when they greeted Jesus on Palm Sunday with the words: 'Hosanna' (meaning 'our God saves')! Blessed is he who comes in the name of the Lord!' No doubt many saw Jesus as the long-awaited deliverer of Israel in a political sense. Jesus rejected this interpretation because it was too narrow. He had come to set people free from everything that dehumanized them and kept them away from God.

- **Revolution.** Jesus came preaching 'repentance' and 'the kingdom of God'. 'Repentance' means 'turning around' or turning right away from yourself to head in a completely new direction. So Jesus' call was radical. He called his first disciples away from their houses, jobs and families. When Jesus said to Zacchaeus, 'Today salvation has come to your house', he did not mean an insipid change of lifestyle. He meant revolution. Zacchaeus' whole life was now turned upside down. From God's point of view it was now the right way up.

  Jesus still calls people to turn away from themselves to a lifelong discipleship in following a Lord who demands obedience and faithfulness. To say that he is 'Lord' means, in fact, that I am now his slave and anxious to please him. Christians are, therefore, 'turned-around people'. They are always undergoing conversion as they seek to follow their Lord Jesus, or, in other words, they are always entering more fully into their 'salvation'.

- **Wholeness.** The word 'to save' in the New Testament can also mean 'to heal'. So when people asked Jesus to heal them, they were actually crying out: 'Lord, I want to be made whole.' This is at the very heart of salvation. God is not only interested in our souls, he also wants us whole in body, mind and spirit—fully human, as we were created to be.

  Today many churches are rediscovering a healing ministry and praying positively for mental and bodily wholeness. But we have to recognize that even the most spectacular of modern 'healings' fall far short of the mighty works that marked the ministry of Jesus. It is important to bear in mind three things when we engage in the work of healing today. First, Jesus' healings were signs of the kingdom, to show that God has broken into this world through the work of Jesus. Modern healings cannot be signs in quite this unique way. Second, we must never separate medical from spiritual healing. Medicine and hospital care are part of God's plan for our wholeness. Third, a balanced understanding of the ministry of healing will bear in mind that salvation is never complete in this life. It looks forward to the future when God will usher in his kingdom and take up his reign. In the meantime we live in a fallen world in which sin, sickness and death are always present.

Applying these three great pictures—deliverance, revolution, wholeness—to life today we can see that 'salvation' should operate on many different levels of human experience. We get a warped idea if we limit it to just one area of life.

Salvation applies to our spiritual lives. It is deeply personal. When Jesus died and rose again, this great deliverance opened for us a new way with God. Many images of this are used in the New Testament: a person is 'born again', made a new being, made free, 'justified', or put right with God. All these rich descriptions reveal the deep change that has taken place in the life of the new Christian. According to the New Testament this salvation must be allowed to flood every area of my life through the work of the Holy Spirit so that I become a 'whole' person with a transformed mind and heart. This spiritual encounter with the living God is a revolution and should lead to 'turned-around' people.

But salvation applies to social and political life as well. Jesus preached a kingdom which was concerned with the poor, the oppressed and the despised. The good news of the gospel cannot be limited just to the individual or pushed into a future world. The Christian church striving for justice is preaching 'salvation'. The gospel cannot live happily with aspects of life which bind or grind people made in God's image.

Salvation, then, affects the whole of life. It comes from a great God whose love desires our total wholeness and complete freedom. It comes to us through Jesus, whose name means 'he who saves'.

## SUNDAY

EXODUS 14:10–22 (AV)

And when Pharaoh drew nigh, the children of Israel lifted up their eyes, and behold, the Egyptians marched after them; and they were sore afraid: and the children of Israel cried out unto the Lord. And they said unto Moses, Because there were no graves in Egypt, hast thou taken us away to die in the wilderness? wherefore hast thou dealt thus with us, to carry us forth out of Egypt? Is not this the word that we did tell thee in Egypt, saying, Let us alone, that we may serve the Egyptians? For it had been better for us to serve the Egyptians, than that we should die in the wilderness.

And Moses said unto the people, Fear ye not, stand still, and see the salvation of the Lord, which he will shew to you to day: for the Egyptians whom ye have seen to day, ye shall see them again no more for ever. The Lord shall fight for you, and ye shall hold your peace.

And the Lord said unto Moses, Wherefore criest thou unto me? speak unto the children of Israel, that they go forward: But lift thou up thy rod, and stretch out thine hand over the sea, and divide it: and the children of Israel shall go on dry ground through the midst of the sea. And I, behold, I will harden the hearts of the Egyptians, and they shall follow them: and I will get me honour upon Pharaoh, and upon all his host, upon his chariots, and upon his horsemen. And the Egyptians shall know that I am the Lord, when I have gotten me honour upon Pharaoh, upon his chariots, and upon his horsemen.

And the angel of God, which went before the camp of Israel, removed and went behind them; and the pillar of the cloud went from before their face, and stood behind them: And it came between the camp of the Egyptians and the camp of Israel; and it was a cloud and darkness to them, but it gave light by night to these: so that the one came not near the other all the night. And Moses stretched out his hand over the sea; and the Lord caused the sea to go back by a strong east wind all that night, and made the sea dry land, and the waters were divided. And the children of Israel went into the midst of the sea upon the dry ground: and the waters were a wall unto them on their right hand, and on their left.

## MONDAY

ISAIAH 12:1–6 (RSV)

You will say in that day:
'I will give thanks to thee, O Lord,
for though thou wast angry with me,
thy anger turned away,
and thou didst comfort me.

'Behold, God is my salvation;
I will trust, and will not be afraid;
for the Lord God is my strength and my song,
and he has become my salvation.'

With joy you will draw water from the wells of salvation. And you will say in that day:
'Give thanks to the Lord,
call upon his name;

make known his deeds among the
nations,
proclaim that his name is
exalted.

'Sing praises to the Lord, for he has
done gloriously;
let this be known in all the earth.
Shout, and sing for joy, O inhabitant
of Zion,
for great in your midst is the
Holy One of Israel.'

## TUESDAY

LUKE 2:25–32, 19:1–10 (NIV)

Now there was a man in Jerusalem called Simeon, who was righteous and devout. He was waiting for the consolation of Israel, and the Holy Spirit was upon him. It had been revealed to him by the Holy Spirit that he would not die before he had seen the Lord's Christ. Moved by the Spirit, he went into the temple courts. When the parents brought in the child Jesus to do for him what the custom of the Law required, Simeon took him in his arms and praised God, saying:

'Sovereign Lord, as you have
promised,
you now dismiss your servant in
peace.
For my eyes have seen your
salvation,
which you have prepared in the
sight of all people,
a light for revelation to the Gentiles
and for glory to your people
Israel.'

Jesus entered Jericho and was passing through. A man was there by the name of Zacchaeus; he was a chief tax collector and was wealthy. He wanted to see who Jesus was, but being a short man he could not, because of the crowd. So he ran ahead and climbed a sycamore-fig tree to see him, since Jesus was coming that way.

When Jesus reached the spot, he looked up and said to him, 'Zacchaeus, come down immediately. I must stay at your house today.' So he came down at once and welcomed him gladly.

All the people saw this and began to mutter, 'He has gone to be the guest of a "sinner".'

But Zacchaeus stood up and said to the Lord, 'Look, Lord! Here and now I give half of my possessions to the poor, and if I have cheated anybody out of anything, I will pay back four times the amount.'

Jesus said to him, 'Today salvation has come to this house, because this man, too, is a son of Abraham. For the Son of Man came to seek and to save what was lost.'

## WEDNESDAY

ACTS 4:1–12 (REB)

Peter and John were still addressing the people when the chief priests, together with the controller of the temple and the Sadducees, broke in on them, annoyed because they were proclaiming the resurrection from the dead by teaching the people about Jesus. They were arrested and, as it was already evening, put in prison for the night. But many of those who had heard the message became believers, bringing the number of men to about five thousand.

Next day the Jewish rulers, elders, and scribes met in Jerusalem. There were present Annas the high priest, Caiaphas, John, Alexander, and all who were of the high-priestly family. They brought the apostles before the court and began to interrogate them. 'By what power', they asked, 'or by what name have such men as you done this?' Then Peter, filled with the Holy Spirit, answered, 'Rulers of the people and elders, if it is about help given to a sick man that we are being questioned today, and the means by which he was cured, this is our answer to all of you and to all the people of Israel: it was by the name of Jesus Christ of Nazareth, whom you crucified, and whom God raised from the dead; through him this man stands here before you fit and well. This Jesus is the stone, rejected by you the builders, which has become the corner-stone. There is no salvation through anyone else; in all the world no other name has been granted to mankind by which we can be saved.'

## THURSDAY

ROMANS 3:21–26 (NIV)

But now, a righteousness from God, apart from law, has been made known, to which the Law and the Prophets testify. This righteousness from God comes through faith in Jesus Christ to all who believe. There is no difference, for all have sinned and fall short of the glory of God, and are justified freely by his grace through the redemption that came from Christ Jesus. God presented him as a sacrifice of atonement, through faith in his blood. He did this to demonstrate his justice, because in his forebearance he had left the sins committed beforehand unpunished—he did it to demonstrate his justice at the present time, so as to be just and the one who justifies the man who has faith in Jesus.

2 CORINTHIANS 5:17–6:2 (NIV)

Therefore, if anyone is in Christ, he is a new creation; the old has gone, the new has come! All this is from God, who reconciled us to himself through Christ and gave us the ministry of reconciliation: that God was reconciling the world to himself in Christ, not counting men's sins against them. And he has committed to us the message of reconciliation. We are therefore Christ's ambassadors, as though God were making his appeal through us. We implore you on Christ's behalf: Be reconciled to God. God made him who had no sin to be sin for us, so that in him we might become the righteousness of God.

As God's fellow workers we urge you not to receive God's grace in vain. For he says,

'At the time of my favour I heard
you,
and on the day of salvation I
helped you.'

I tell you, now is the time of God's favour, now is the day of salvation.

## FRIDAY

EPHESIANS 2:1–10 (NJB)

And you were dead, through the crimes and the sins which used to make up your way of life when you were living by the principles of this world, obeying the ruler who dominates the air, the spirit who is at work in those who rebel. We too were all among them once, living only by our natural inclinations, obeying the demands of human self-indulgence and our own whim; our nature made us no less liable to God's retribution than the rest of the world. But God, being rich in faithful love, through the great love with which he loved us, even when we were dead in our sins, brought us to life with Christ—it is through grace that you have been saved—and raised us up with him and gave us a place with him in heaven, in Christ Jesus.

This was to show for all ages to come, through his goodness towards us in Christ Jesus, how extraordinarily rich he is in grace. Because it is by grace that you have been saved, through faith; not by anything of your own, but by a gift from God; not by anything you have done, so that nobody can claim the credit. We are God's work of art, created in Christ Jesus for the good works which God has already designated to make up our way of life.

## SATURDAY

1 PETER 1:1–9 (NJB)

Peter, apostle of Jesus Christ, to all those living as aliens in the Dispersion of Pontus, Galatia, Cappadocia, Asia and Bithynia, who have been chosen, in the foresight of God the Father, to be made holy by the Spirit, obedient to Jesus Christ and sprinkled with his blood: Grace and peace be yours in abundance.

Blessed be God the Father of our Lord Jesus Christ, who in his great mercy has given us a new birth into a living hope through the resurrection of Jesus Christ from the dead and into a heritage that can never be spoilt or soiled and never fade away. It is reserved in heaven for you who are being kept safe by God's power through faith until the salvation which has been prepared is revealed at the final point of time.

This is a great joy to you, even though for a short time yet you must bear all sorts of trials; so that the worth of your faith, more valuable than gold, which is perishable even if it has been tested by fire, may be proved—to your praise and honour when Jesus Christ is revealed. You have not seen him, yet you love him; and still without seeing him you believe in him and so are already filled with a joy so glorious that it cannot be described; and you are sure of the goal of your faith, that is, the salvation of your souls.

# ISRAEL'S HYMNBOOK: THE PSALMS

The Psalms are a collection of 150 hymns, prayers and poems, expressing every kind of emotion. What unites them is deep faith in and love for God. After Israel had returned from exile, the Psalms became their hymnbook and prayerbook. Christians, too, still use them in this way.

Many psalms were used in temple worship. But others plainly stem from times of exile. Some express the faith of all Israel, while others are deeply personal.

Seventy-three psalms are traditionally linked to King David. Plainly his love of music and worship made him the first patron of Israel's psalms.

The range is tremendous—from the utmost joy to the deepest despair. The most searching

## REFUGE

The Israelites lived in a part of the world seldom free from war—then as now. Their towns were well-defended, with strong walls. And hill-top fortresses were a common feature. These places of refuge became an image of spiritual security in God. 'God is our refuge and strength.'

## WATER

The Israelites were not great seafarers. Wind, wave and flood appalled them. But equally, as shepherds they knew the value of still, refreshing pools and brooks. Both faces of water—the frightening and the peaceful—recur frequently in the psalms. Psalm 46 has both. 'Waters roar and foam...'; 'There is a river whose streams make glad the city of God.'

realism about human experience is joined to an unshakeable faith in God's love.

Some beautiful images haunt the Psalms, some of which are illustrated here. To feel the force of these images is to touch the psalmist's heart.

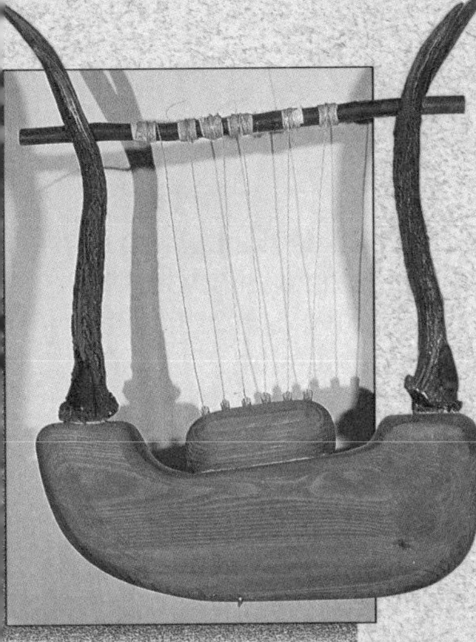

## MUSIC

Many psalms were written to be sung. So not surprisingly the beauty and excitement of music crops up frequently. 'Sing a new song'; 'make music to the Lord'. Singers and a whole range of instruments joined to worship God. And so flooded are the psalms with music that the whole of life becomes a song.

## LIGHT

In Old Testament times there was only one type of light, for the household or to show the way outside at night. Their lamps were simply pottery dishes with oil in them and a wick. But, in the absence of general lighting, the glow of a light in a window was a sign of welcome and of safety.

## HILLS

Much of Israel was hill-country. Jerusalem is ringed by hills, and hills are in sight nearly everywhere. The image of mountains and hills is more common than any other in the psalms, speaking of changelessness, of security and of the awe of God which mountains still bring. 'I will lift up my eyes to the hills.'

WEEK 15

# THE VITAL U-TURN

This week we see how 're-pentance' brought a turning-round in the lives of different characters in the Bible. And, of course, repentance is something we can all recognize. Such is our human condition that we need to change in attitude and action if we are to be in tune with God.

After the notorious moral disaster of King David's affair with Bathsheba and the subsequently arranged murder of her husband, David's reaction to Nathan's accusation seems brief enough (Sunday). But only God can know the depth of our confession.

Later, King Manasseh's change of heart (Monday) was even more dramatic, resulting in a reversal of public policies, while (like David) being unable to cancel the effects of the past.

Later still, the prophet Ezekiel (Tuesday) emphasizes personal accountability for this turn-about. We cannot hide behind inherited failings or claim credit from the past, in order to avoid God's demands.

All these Old Testament extracts form part of the background for the renewed call to repentance sounded by John the Baptist, Christ's forerunner (Wednesday). And in Thursday's pair of extracts from the two gospels, Jesus continues where John left off, showing that repentance is not optional. Jesus also insists that the newly-penitent are welcomed on earth, since heaven itself is overjoyed when the lost are found (Friday).

Finally, Paul the apostle gives his own testimony in court. He himself has made such a U-turn, and been given the job of urging others to do the same.

# Repentance



You do not always reap exactly what you sow. People are not locked into the mistakes and sins which they committed in the past. They are not trapped and programmed for disaster because it is possible to repent. And when people repent they prove that **the past need not determine the future**. The Bible even speaks of God himself 'repenting', changing his course of action, in response to a change of heart. Of course this is picture language, but it is a picture which brings hope and possibility into situations of despair.

To repent is, in essence, to turn around: to turn from our own ways and re-turn to God. It was one of the great cries of the prophets in Israel. As the people of God strayed from the right path, murmured against God and his representatives, went after strange gods, broke the covenant by oppressing the brother-Israelite, played power politics in defiance of their vocation and rebelled against the light, so prophet after prophet called them to turn back and return to the Lord.

Sometimes the repentance was slick and easy and the prophet agonized in God's name over the nation's superficiality. Sometimes it seemed as if they were unwilling to repent at all and the prophet thundered judgment. Sometimes the refusal to turn just seemed inexplicable, flying in the face of nature. But despite the elaborate system of sacrifices, it was true repentance that wiped the slate clean. There was no sacrifice for 'defiant' sin, but when the sinner acknowledged he had done wrong God himself would have mercy without sacrifice. In the period between the Old Testament and the New, this truth became a fundamental principle of Judaism.

Against this background John the Baptist called the nation back to God, baptizing penitents to prepare for the crisis of the Messiah's coming with fire. Repentance was also at the heart of Jesus' first preaching: 'The kingdom of heaven is at hand' (the same note of urgency and crisis), 'Repent and believe the gospel.' The prodigal son reaches rock bottom, 'comes to himself' and 'repents' when he turns for home and his father's house. The first Christian sermons called on their hearers to repent and put their faith in Christ.

Repentance must always be genuine. Paul distinguished between grief and godly grief, or remorse and repentance. True repentance shows itself when people change the way they live. Tax-collectors are told not to exact more than is right, soldiers not to be extortionate; Zacchaeus publicly offers to restore four times the amount by which he had cheated people.

It is here that the mystery of repentance is found. It may seem as if this is all a matter of human decision. But the Bible writers always recognized that no one has the power to turn unless God turns them. God must create the clean heart. It is God who takes the initiative, whether it is in the wholehearted and scandalous acceptance of despised tax-collector Zacchaeus or through the kind but searching questions put to disloyal disciple Peter. Paul writes, 'The goodness of God leads us to repentance.'

It is wrong to call people to repentance in a context of judgment, condemnation and fear. It is often the prodigal son remembering his father's house, the shepherd searching for the sheep, the look on the face of Christ when Peter had denied him, which break the heart and work the miracle.

## SUNDAY

2 SAMUEL 12:1–10, 13 (REB)

The Lord sent Nathan the prophet to David, and when he entered the king's presence, he said, 'In a certain town there lived two men, one rich, the other poor. The rich man had large flocks and herds; the poor man had nothing of his own except one little ewe lamb he had bought. He reared it, and it grew up in his home together with his children. It shared his food, drank from his cup, and nestled in his arms; it was like a daughter to him. One day a traveller came to the rich man's house, and he, too mean to take something from his own flock or herd to serve to his guest, took the poor man's lamb and served that up.'

David was very angry, and burst out, 'As the Lord lives, the man who did this deserves to die! He shall pay for the lamb four times over, because he has done this and shown no pity.'

Nathan said to David, 'You are the man! This is the word of the Lord the God of Israel to you: I anointed you king over Israel, I rescued you from the power of Saul, I gave you your master's daughter and his wives to be your own, I gave you the daughters of Israel and Judah; and had this not been enough, I would have added other favours as well. Why then have you flouted the Lord's word by doing what is wrong in my eyes? You have struck down Uriah the Hittite with the sword; the man himself you murdered by the sword of the Ammonites, and you have stolen his wife. Now, therefore, since you have despised me and taken the wife of Uriah the Hittite to be your own wife, your family will never again have rest from the sword.'

David said to Nathan, 'I have sinned against the Lord.' Nathan answered, 'The Lord has laid on another the consequences of your sin: you will not die.'

## MONDAY

2 CHRONICLES 33:9–16 (RSV)

Manasseh seduced Judah and the inhabitants of Jerusalem, so that they did more evil than the nations whom the Lord destroyed before the people of Israel. The Lord spoke to Manasseh and to his people, but they paid no heed. Therefore the Lord brought upon them the commanders of the army of the king of Assyria, who took Manasseh with hooks and bound him with fetters of bronze and brought him to Babylon. And when he was in distress he entreated the favour of the Lord his God and humbled himself greatly before the God of his fathers. He prayed to him, and God received his entreaty and heard his supplication and brought him again to Jerusalem into his kingdom. Then Manasseh knew that the Lord was God.

Afterwards he built an outer wall for the city of David west of Gihon, in the valley, and for the entrance into the Fish Gate, and carried it round Ophel, and raised it to a very great height; he also put commanders of the army in all the fortified cities in Judah. And he took away the foreign gods and the idol from the house of the Lord, and all the altars that he had built on the mountain of the house of the Lord and in Jerusalem, and he threw them outside of the city. He also restored the altar of the Lord and offered upon it sacrifices of peace offerings and of thanksgiving; and he commanded Judah to serve the Lord the God of Israel.

## TUESDAY

EZEKIEL 18:19–33 (AV)

Yet say ye, Why? doth not the son bear the iniquity of the father? When the son hath done that which is lawful and right, and hath kept all my statutes, and hath done them, he shall surely live. The soul that sinneth, it shall die. The son shall not bear the iniquity of the father, neither shall the father bear the iniquity of the son: the righteousness of the righteous shall be upon him, and the wickedness of the wicked shall be upon him. But if the wicked will turn from all his sins that he hath committed, and keep all my statutes, and do that which is lawful and right, he shall surely live, and he shall not die. All his transgressions that he hath committed, they shall not be mentioned unto him: in his righteousness that he hath done he shall live. Have I any pleasure at all that the wicked should die? saith the Lord God: and not that he should return from his ways, and live?

But when the righteous turneth away from his righteousness, and committeth iniquity, and doeth according to all the abominations that the wicked man doeth, shall he live? All his rightousness that he hath done shall not be mentioned: in his trespass that he hath trespassed, and in his sin that he hath sinned, in them shall he die.

Yet ye say, The way of the Lord is not equal. Hear now, O house of Israel; Is not my way equal? are not your ways unequal? When a righteous man turneth away from his righteousness, and committeth iniquity, and dieth in them; for his iniquity that he hath done shall he die. Again, when the wicked man turneth away from his wickedness that he hath committed, and doeth that which is lawful and right, he shall save his soul alive. Because he considereth, and turneth away from all his transgressions that he hath committed, he shall surely live, he shall not die. Yet saith the house of Israel, The way of the Lord is not equal. O house of Israel, are not my ways equal? are not your ways unequal? Therefore I will judge you, O house of Israel, every one according to his ways, saith the Lord God. Repent, and turn yourselves from all your transgressions; so iniquity shall not be your ruin.

Cast away from you all your transgressions, whereby ye have transgressed; and make you a new heart and a new spirit: for why will ye die, O house of Israel? For I have no pleasure in the death of him that dieth, saith the Lord God: wherefore turn yourselves, and live ye.

## WEDNESDAY

MATTHEW 3:1–12 (NIV)

In those days John the Baptist came,

preaching in the Desert of Judea and saying, 'Repent, for the kingdom of heaven is near.' This is he who was spoken of through the prophet Isaiah:
'A voice of one calling in the desert,
"Prepare the way for the Lord,
make straight paths for him." '
John's clothes were made of camel's hair, and he had a leather belt around his waist. His food was locusts and wild honey. People went out to him from Jerusalem and all Judea and the whole region of the Jordan. Confessing their sins, they were baptized by him in the Jordan River.

But when he saw many of the Pharisees and Sadducees coming to where he was baptising, he said to them: 'You brood of vipers! Who warned you to flee from the coming wrath? Produce fruit in keeping with repentance. And do not think you can say to yourselves, "We have Abraham as our Father." I tell you that out of these stones God can raise up children for Abraham. The axe is already at the root of the trees, and every tree that does not produce good fruit will be cut down and thrown into the fire.

I will baptize you with water for repentance. But after me will come one who is more powerful than I, whose sandals I am not fit to carry. He will baptize you with the Holy Spirit and with fire. His winnowing fork is in his hand, and he will clear his threshing floor, gathering wheat into his barn and burning up the chaff with unquenchable fire.'

# THURSDAY

MATTHEW 4:12–17 (NJB)

Hearing that John had been arrested Jesus withdrew to Galilee, and leaving Nazara he went and settled in Capernaum, beside the lake, on the borders of Zebulun and Naphtali. This was to fulfil what was spoken by the prophet Isaiah:
Land of Zebulun! Land of Naphtali!
Way of the sea beyond Jordan.
Galilee of the nations!
The people that lived in darkness
have seen a great light;
on those who lived in a country
of shadow dark as death a light
has dawned.
From then onwards Jesus began his proclamation with the message, 'Repent, for the kingdom of Heaven is close at hand.'

LUKE 13:1–5 (NJB)

Some people arrived and told Jesus about the Galileans whose blood Pilate had mingled with that of their sacrifices. At this he said to them, 'Do you suppose that these Galileans were worse sinners than any others, that this should have happened to them? They were not, I tell you. No; but unless you repent you will all perish as they did. Or those eighteen on whom the tower at Siloam fell, killing them all? Do you suppose that they were more guilty than all the other people living in Jerusalem? They were not, I tell you. No; but unless you repent you will all perish as they did.'

## FRIDAY

LUKE 15:1–10 (REB)

The tax-collectors and sinners were all crowding in to listen to Jesus; and the Pharisees and scribes began murmuring their disapproval: 'This fellow', they said, 'welcomes sinners and eats with them.' He answered them with this parable: 'If one of you has a hundred sheep and loses one of them, does he not leave the ninety-nine in the wilderness and go after the one that is missing until he finds it? And when he does, he lifts it joyfully on to his shoulders, and goes home to call his friends and neighbours together. "Rejoice with me!" he cries. "I have found my lost sheep." In the same way, I tell you, there will be greater joy in heaven over one sinner who repents than over ninety-nine righteous people who do not need to repent.

Or again, if a woman has ten silver coins and loses one of them, does she not light the lamp, sweep out the house, and look in every corner till she finds it? And when she does, she calls her friends and neighbours together, and says, "Rejoice with me! I have found the coin that I lost." In the same way, I tell you, there is joy among the angels of God over one sinner who repents.'

## SATURDAY

ACTS 26:9–18 (NIV)

Paul continued, 'I too was convinced that I ought to do all that was possible to oppose the name of Jesus of Nazareth. And that is just what I did in Jerusalem. On the authority of the chief priests I put many of the saints in prison, and when they were put to death, I cast my vote against them. Many a time I went from one synagogue to another to have them punished, and I tried to force them to blaspheme. In my obsession against them, I even went to foreign cities to persecute them.

On one of these journeys I was going to Damascus with the authority and commission of the chief priests. About noon, O king, as I was on the road, I say a light from heaven, brighter than the sun, blazing around me and my companions. We all fell to the ground, and I heard a voice saying to me in Aramaic, "Saul, Saul, why do you persecute me? It is hard for you to kick against the goads."

Then I asked, "Who are you, Lord?"

"I am Jesus, whom you are persecuting," the Lord replied. "Now get up and stand on your feet. I have appeared to you to appoint you as a servant and as a witness of what you have seen of me and what I will show you. I will rescue you from your own people and from the Gentiles. I am sending you to open their eyes and turn them from darkness to light, and from the power of Satan to God, so that they may receive forgiveness of sins and a place among those who are sanctified by faith in me." '

# JOURNEY INTO LIFE

WEEK 16

Faith starts with believing God's promises. And if like Abraham (Sunday) we really do believe, that is all we need—or rather, everything else follows!

One of Israel's little-known prophets was Habakkuk, some six centuries before Christ. In this extract (Monday) we see him reach a pinnacle of trust in God when everything else fell apart and there were no strings attached nor props provided.

So it was faith that strongly moved Jesus when he found it in surprising places, such as in a Roman centurion (Tuesday). Faith also proved the gateway to life in Jesus' night-time encounter (Wednesday). It is those who believe in the 'lifted up' Son of God who avoid the ultimate ruin and enjoy immediate light.

Faith is seen as crucial in the extracts from three New Testament letters for the next three days. These letters are in refreshing contrast to the vagueness which sometimes obscures the subject today. All three writers refer back (as Jesus had done) to Abraham, faith's father-figure.

Paul (Thursday) uses Abraham to undermine any idea of piling up our achievements (ritual, racial or moral) to impress God. The writer to the Hebrews (Friday) shows some of faith's risks and effects—impressive in success, even more outstanding in failure. And James (Saturday) attacks a dead faith that all too commonly never gets beyond a private mental assent.

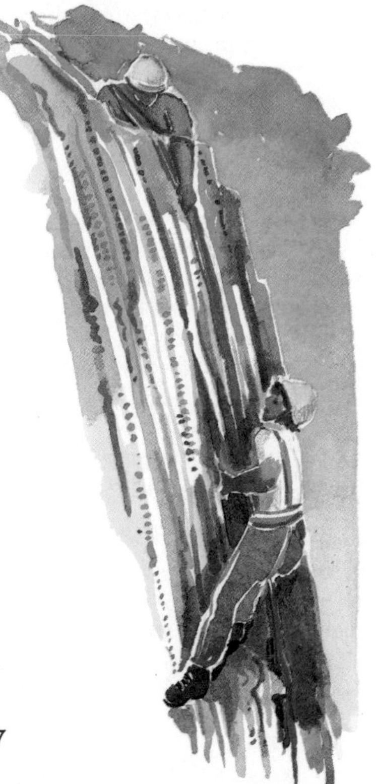

WEEK
16

# Faith

Biblical faith is never a matter of believing impossible things. It is responding to a God-given vision, as Abraham did, when he left his home city, not knowing where God would take him.

Faith means 'seeing' the world in a particular way, from an angle God has shown us. To those who refused to see, the miracles might appear just as wonders or even works of Satan. To the eye of faith they were 'signs'. The man born blind has faith in that he 'sees' who Jesus really is. The Jews, who have sight in a physical sense, are unable to perceive that they are in the presence of the Messiah. The centurion in Mark's passion story witnesses the bare facts of the crucifixion and yet sees through them to the deeper truth and so confesses his faith: 'This man was the Son of God.' At the empty tomb John 'sees' the graveclothes and 'believes'.

It is in the thought of Paul that faith is most fully worked out. For him, faith is the encounter of the whole person (not just intellect or feelings) with Jesus himself (not just a set of beliefs or doctrines). Faith in Christ is never just ticking off a list of things you believe. It is coming to the end of your resources and crying out to God to save you. It is staking your eternal destiny on his death on the cross. It is trusting him with your life, the 'yes' of your whole personality to Christ.

For Paul, such an act of commitment opens a person's life to all the blessings God has in store. Through faith we are acquitted of our sins and made right with God; we are given the Spirit to live within us. We are a new creation, with a new purpose, power and hope.

Paul's teaching about faith came under two different kinds of attack. The first emphasized the painstaking keeping of legal requirements in the hope of working one's way into God's good books. Such labour produced only a dismal catalogue of failure. God had already sent his Son to set mankind free from such slavery. The opposite position was as bad. This argued that, provided you believed, you could live how you liked because God's grace would cover all your misdeeds. This was a perversion of the gospel. Neither view had begun to grasp the truth that faith is not primarily our offering to God, but his gift to us.

It is left to James to hammer the point home in a passage which superficially seems to be contradicting Paul. Real faith shows its genuineness by the obedience which flows from it. It always leads to love in action. 'Faith' in the sense of mere intellectual assent or cold orthodoxy is a dead thing. A 'faith' which ignores the hungry, the poor, the widow or the orphan is just a word.

This is not to deny that faith will sometimes mean witnessing to a set of truths. The Christian believes that certain things are true: God sent his Son, Jesus is the Christ, God raised him from the dead... As these truths became organized, so 'the faith once delivered to the saints' emerged. Christians are called to contend for this body of truth. Yet, in the end, Christianity is not a set of beliefs or a creed. It is a living relationship with Christ.

## SUNDAY

GENESIS 15:1–6 (RSV)

After these things the word of the Lord came to Abram in a vision, 'Fear not, Abram, I am your shield; your reward shall be very great.' But Abram said, 'O Lord God, what wilt thou give me, for I continue childless, and the heir of my house is Eliezer of Damascus?' And Abram said, 'Behold, thou hast given me no offspring; and a slave born in my house will be my heir.' And behold, the word of the Lord came to him, 'This man shall not be your heir; your own son shall be your heir.' And he brought him outside and said, 'Look toward heaven, and number the stars, if you are able to number them.' Then he said to him, 'So shall your descendants be.' And he believed the Lord; and he reckoned it to him as righteousness.

## MONDAY

HABAKKUK 1:12–13, 2:1–4, 3:17–19 (NIV)

O Lord, are you not from everlasting?
My God, my Holy One, we will not die.
O Lord, you have appointed them to execute judgment;
O Rock, you have ordained them to punish.
Your eyes are too pure to look on evil;
you cannot tolerate wrong.
Why then do you tolerate the treacherous?
Why are you silent while the wicked
swallow up those more righteous than themselves?

I will stand at my watch
and station myself on the ramparts;
I will look to see what he will say to me,
and what answer I am to give to this complaint.
Then the Lord replied:
'Write down the revelation
and make it on plain tablets
so that a herald may run with it.
For the revelation awaits an appointed time;
it speaks of the end
and will not prove false.
Though it linger, wait for it;
it will certainly come and will not delay.
See, he is puffed up; his desires are not upright—
but the righteous will live by his faith.

Though the fig-tree does not bud
and there are no grapes on the vines,
though the olive crop fails
and the fields produce no food,
though there are no sheep in the pen
and no cattle in the stalls,
yet I will rejoice in the Lord,
I will be joyful in God my Saviour.

The Sovereign Lord is my strength;
he makes my feet like the feet of a deer,
he enables me to go on the heights.

## TUESDAY

LUKE 7:1–10 (REB)

When Jesus had finished addressing the people, he entered Capernaum. A centurion there had a servant whom he valued highly, but the servant was ill and near to death. Hearing about Jesus, he sent some Jewish elders to ask him to come and save his servant's life. They approached Jesus and made an urgent appeal to him: 'He deserves this favour from you,' they said, 'for he is a friend of our nation and it is he who built us our synagogue.' Jesus went with them; but when he was not far from the house, the centurion sent friends with this message: 'Do not trouble further, sir; I am not worthy to have you come under my roof, and that is why I did not presume to approach you in person. But say the word and my servant will be cured. I know, for I am myself under orders, with soldiers under me. I say to one, "Go," and he goes; to another, "come here," and he comes; and to my servant, "Do this," and he does it.' When Jesus heard this, he was astonished, and, turning to the crowd that was following him, he said, 'I tell you, not even in Israel have I found such faith.' When the messengers returned to the house, they found the servant in good health.

## WEDNESDAY

JOHN 3:14–21 (NJB)

Jesus said: 'As Moses lifted up the snake in the desert, so must the Son of man be lifted up so that everyone who believes may have eternal life in him. For this is how God loved the world: he gave his only Son, so that everyone who believes in him may not perish but may have eternal life. For God sent his Son into the world not to judge the world, but so that through him the world might be saved. No one who believes in him will be judged; but whoever does not believe in the Name of God's only Son. And the judgment is this: though the light has come into the world people have preferred darkness to the light because their deeds were evil. And indeed, everybody who does wrong hates the light and avoids it, to prevent his actions from being shown up; but whoever does the truth comes out into the light, so that what he is doing may plainly appear as done in God.'

## THURSDAY

GALATIANS 3:1–14 (NIV)

You foolish Galatians! Who has bewitched you? Before your very eyes Jesus Christ was clearly portrayed as crucified. I would like to learn just one thing from you: Did you receive the Spirit by observing the law, or by believing what you heard? Are you so foolish? After beginning with the Spirit, are you now trying to attain you goal by human effort? Have you suffered so much for nothing—if it really was for nothing? Does God give you his Spirit and work miracles among you because you observe the law, or because you believe what you heard?

Consider Abraham: 'He believed God, and it was credited to him as righteousness.' Understand, then, that those who believe are children of Abraham. The Scripture foresaw that God would justify the Gentiles by faith, and announced the gospel in advance to Abraham: 'All nations will be blessed through you.' So those who have faith are blessed along with Abraham, the man of faith.

All who rely on observing the law are under a curse, for it is written: 'Cursed is everyone who does not continue to do everything written in the Book of the Law.' Clearly no-one is justified before God by the law, because, 'The righteous will live by faith.' The law is not based on faith; on the contrary, 'The man who does these things will live by them.' Christ redeemed us from the curse of the law by becoming a curse for us, for it is written: 'Cursed is everyone who is hanged on a tree.' He redeemed us in order that the blessing given to Abraham might come to the Gentiles through Christ Jesus, so that by faith we might receive the promise of the Spirit.

## FRIDAY

HEBREWS 11:1–11, 32–40 (AV)

Now faith is the substance of things hoped for, the evidence of things not seen. For by it the elders obtained a good report. Through faith we understand that the worlds were framed by the word of God, so that things which are seen were not made of things which do appear. By faith Abel offered unto God a more excellent sacrifice than Cain, by which he obtained witness that he was righteous, God testifying of his gifts: and by it he being dead yet speaketh. By faith Enoch was translated that he should not see death; and was not found, because God had translated him: for before his translation he had this testimony, that he pleased God. But without faith it is impossible to please him: for he that cometh to God must believe that he is, and that he is a rewarder of them that diligently seek him. By faith Noah, being warned of God of things not seen as yet, moved with fear, prepared an ark to the saving of his house; by the which he condemned the world, and became heir of the righteousness which is by faith. By faith Abraham when he was called to go out into a place which he should after receive for an inheritance, obeyed; and he went out, not knowing whither he went. By faith he sojourned in the land of promise, as in a strange country, dwelling in tabernacles with Isaac and Jacob, the heirs with him of the same promise: For he looked for a city which hath foundations, whose builder and maker is God. Through faith also Sara herself received strength to conceive seed, and was delivered of a child when she was past age, because she judged him faithful who had promised.

And what shall I more say? for the time would fail me to tell of Gedeon and of Barak, and of Samson, and of Jephthae; of David also, and Samuel, and of the prophets: Who through faith subdued kingdoms, wrought righteousness, obtained promises, stopped the mouths of lions, quenched the violence of fire, escaped the edge of the sword, out of weakness were made strong, waxed valiant in fight, turned to flight the armies of the aliens. Women received their dead raised to life again: and others were tortured, not accepting deliverance; that they might obtain a better resurrection: And others had trial of cruel mockings and scourgings, yea, moreover of bonds and imprisonment: They were stoned, they were sawn asunder, were tempted, were slain with the sword: they wandered about in sheepskins and goatskins; being destitute, afflicted, tormented; (Of whom the world was not worthy:) they wandered in deserts, and in mountains, and in dens and caves of the earth. And these all, having obtained a good report through faith, received not the promise: God having provided some better thing for us, that they without us should not be made perfect.

## SATURDAY

JAMES 2:14–26 (REB)

What good is it, my friends, for someone to say he has faith when his actions do nothing to show it? Can that faith save him? Suppose a fellow-Christian, whether man or woman, is in rags with not enough food for the day, and one of you says, 'Goodbye, keep warm, and have a good meal,' but does nothing to supply their bodily needs, what good is that? So with faith; if it does not lead to action, it is by itself a lifeless thing.

But someone may say: 'One chooses faith, another action.' To which I reply: 'Show me this faith you speak of with no actions to prove it, while I by my actions will prove it, while I by my actions will prove to you my faith.' You have faith and believe that there is one God. Excellent! Even demons have faith like that, and it makes them tremble. Do you have to be told, you fool, that faith divorced from action is futile? Was it not by his action, in offering his son Isaac upon the altar, that our father Abraham was justified? Surely you can see faith was at work in his actions, and by these actions his faith was perfected? Here was fulfilment of the words of scripture: 'Abraham put his faith in God, and that faith was counted to him as righteousness,' and he was called 'God's friend'. You see then it is by action and not by faith alone that a man is justified. The same is true also of the prostitute Rahab. Was she not justified by her action in welcoming the messengers into her house and sending them away by a different route? As the body is dead when there is no breath left in it, so faith divorced from action is dead.

# THE CHRISTIAN'S NATIVE AIR

WEEK 17

Prayer in the Bible is a way of life. To pray is to communicate with God in many different ways. But prayer is also framed in actual words. After Abraham, Moses is always thought of as the next great 'man of prayer'. Sunday's readings show Moses pleading with God for the people he leads, and communing with God in a way that dazzles them.

There are many more Bible people who give us food for thought. On Monday we see how Elijah prays not so much for a dramatic miracle as that the people will know that the Lord is God.

Two readings from the gospels (Wednesday and Thursday) reveal Jesus the teacher and example, as he gives practical warnings and a 'model' prayer, and later prays himself at immeasurable cost.

On Thursday we eavesdrop on a very early Christian prayer-meeting in a crisis, recorded in Acts, and notice the Bible's place in their praying. Friday gathers some shorter extracts from Paul's letters, acknowledging how much he needs prayer—and gives it. Saturday's final 'letter-prayer' overflows with love for those on Paul's heart.

Our words and wisdom are limited. Prayer to the Father, through Christ, in the Spirit, tunes us in to the unlimited resources of God.

WEEK 17

# Prayer

Most people pray. Some, it is true, only pray when they are in trouble, but statistics show that many people consider prayer important.

For the Christian, prayer is more than a religious duty—it is his or her native air, a lifeline to God with whom he or she has a permanent relationship of love. This relationship is the start of real believing prayer. Paul tells us that it is the Spirit's job to spark off this prayer life in us: 'Because you are sons, God sent the Spirit of his Son into our hearts, the Spirit who calls out, "Abba, Father!"' Because of this new relationship of children to God our 'Father', we can always come into his presence, and we know that he cares intimately for us.

Prayer takes many different forms, of course. One helpful outline of the various forms of prayer is in the letters of the word ACTS—Adoration, Confession, Thanksgiving, Supplication (that is, asking).

But fundamental to prayer is conversation. Just as chatter, laughter, talking and asking is the life-blood of normal conversation in any family, so God is anxious for us to speak to him and for this conversation to be as natural as breathing. And God is not the slightest bit interested in the type of language we use when we talk to him. He does not demand liturgical or religious expressions, and he does not pick us up when we make grammatical errors! Because prayer is heart-to-heart sharing with someone we love, we should use language which comes naturally to us.

'Lord, teach us to pray,' asked the disciples. Jesus replied by reciting the Lord's Prayer, more or less implying, 'This should be your pattern.' This great prayer breaks down into seven petitions:

- ◆ **The first three are concerned with God's glory**—'hallowed be thy name...', 'thy kingdom come...', 'thy will be done...'
- ◆ **The next three are to do with our needs**—'give us...', 'forgive us...', 'protect us...'
- ◆ **Finally we come back to God's glory**—'thine is the kingdom...'

Here, then, is the Jesus dimension in prayer. It is all too easy to begin with ourselves and our needs, but Jesus commands us to begin with God and his honour. He who taught us to say 'Our Father' is the one who knows that we may rely on God with utter confidence.

But why do we pray? If God is a loving Father, why do we need to go to him with a begging bowl? Yet look at the example of Jesus. He told his disciples, 'Ask, seek, knock,' but just before he had said about human needs: 'Your Father in heaven knows that you need them.' He saw no contradiction between the two things, possibly because prayer is much more than asking God for help. In prayer we enter into his concerns for the world, for others as well as for ourselves. It is a dynamic engagement with the resources of God, not twisting the arm of a reluctant God, but joining in God's spiritual battle against all forces which oppose his kingdom. God will expect us, therefore, to go to him with all our burdens and needs because that is what it means to belong to a family.

And will he give us what we want? God will always hear our prayers—of that we can be sure. But his response will not always be in accord with what we want or when we want it. Because he is the sovereign Lord of all, we must leave him to respond 'according to his will'.

We have said that most people pray. But, to God's great sorrow, and our impoverishment, most of us are mere novices when it comes to prayer. We paddle in the shallows of a relationship with God, when he longs for us to enter into the depths of a vibrant and rich prayer fellowship with him. For that to happen we need to spend time in his presence, just resting, contemplating, questioning, seeking—and finding.

In this, as in any great enterprise, we shall need the help and advice of counsellors and spiritual giants who know more about depths of prayer than we do. These days there are many sources we can go to. Because prayer is power, God wants to raise up 'prayer warriors' so that they may join him in the spiritual battle against all that opposes his will.

WEEK 17

## SUNDAY

EXODUS 32:9–14, 30–34, 34:29–35 (RSV)

And the Lord said to Moses, 'I have seen this people, and behold, it is a stiff-necked people; now therefore let me alone, that my wrath may burn hot against them and I may consume them; but of you I will make a great nation.'

But Moses besought the Lord his God, and said, 'O Lord, why does thy wrath burn hot against thy people, whom thou hast brought forth out of the land of Egypt with great power and with a mighty hand? Why should the Egyptians say, "With evil intent did he bring them forth, to slay them in the mountains, and to consume them from the face of the earth"? Turn from thy fierce wrath, and repent of this evil against thy people. Remember Abraham, Isaac, and Israel, thy servants, to whom thou didst swear by thine own self, and didst say to them, "I will multiply your descendants as the stars of heaven, and all this land that I have promised I will give to your descendants, and they shall inherit it for ever." ' And the Lord repented of the evil which he thought to do to his people.

On the morrow Moses said to the people, 'You have sinned a great sin. And now I will go up to the Lord; perhaps I can make atonement for your sin.' So Moses returned to the Lord and said, 'Alas, this people have sinned a great sin; they have made for themselves gods of gold. But now, if thou wilt forgive their sin—and if not, blot me, I pray thee, out of thy book which thou hast written.' But the Lord said to Moses, 'Whoever has sinned against me, him will I blot out of my book. But now go, lead the people to the place of which I have spoken to you; behold, my angel shall go before you. Nevertheless, in the day when I visit, I will visit their sin upon them.'

When Moses came down from Mount Sinai, with the two table of the testimony in his hand as he came down from the mountain, Moses did not know that the skin of his face shone because he had been talking with God. And when Aaron and all the people of Israel saw Moses, behold, the skin of his face shone, and they were afraid to come near him. But Moses called to them; and Aaron and all the leaders of the congregation returned to him, and Moses talked with them. And afterward all the people of Israel came near, and he gave them in commandment all that the Lord had spoken with him in Mount Sinai. And when Moses had finished speaking with them, he put a veil on his face; but whenever Moses went in before the Lord to speak with him, he took the veil off, until he came out; and when he came out, and told the people of Israel what he was commanded, the people of Israel saw the face of Moses, that the skin of Moses' face shone; and Moses would put the veil upon his face again, until he went in to speak with him.

## MONDAY

1 KINGS 18:30–39 (REB)

Elijah said to the people, 'Come here to me,' and they all came to him. He repaired the altar of the Lord which had been torn down. He took twelve stones, one for each tribe of the sons of Jacob, him who was named Israel by the word of the Lord. With these stones he built an altar in the name of the Lord, and dug a trench round it big enough to hold two measures of seed; he arranged the wood, cut up the bull, and laid it on the wood. Then he said, 'Fill four jars with water and pour it on the whole-offering and on the wood.' They did so; he said, 'Do it again.' They did it again; he said, 'Do it a third time.' They did it a third time, and the water ran all round the altar and even filled the trench.

At the hour of the regular offering the prophet Elijah came forward and prayed, 'Lord God of Abraham, of Isaac, and of Israel, let it be known today that you are God in Israel and that I am your servant and have done all these things at your command. Answer me, Lord, answer me and let this people know that you, Lord, are God and that it is you who have brought them back to their allegiance.' The fire of the Lord fell, consuming the whole-offering, the wood, the stones, and the earth, and licking up the water in the trench. At the sight the people all bowed with their faces to the ground and cried, 'The Lord is God, the Lord is God.'

## TUESDAY

MATTHEW 6:5–15 (NIV)

Jesus said, 'When you pray, do not be like the hypocrites, for they love to pray standing in the synagogues and on the street corners to be seen by men. I tell you the truth, they have received their reward in full. When you pray, go into your room, close the door and pray to your Father, who is unseen. Then your Father, who sees what is done in secret, will reward you. And when you pray, do not keep on babbling like pagans, for they think they will be heard because of their many words. Do not be like them, for your Father knows what you need before you ask him.

This is how you should pray:

Our Father in heaven,
  hallowed be your name,
your kingdom come,
your will be done
  on earth as it is in heaven.
Give us this day our daily bread.
Forgive us our debts,
  as we also have forgiven our debtors.
And lead us not into temptation,
  but deliver us from the evil one.

For if you forgive men when they sin against you, your heavenly Father will also forgive you. But if you do not forgive men their sins, your Father will not forgive your sins.

## WEDNESDAY

MATTHEW 26:36–46 (REB)

Jesus then came with his disciples to a place called Gethsemane, and he said to them, 'Sit here while I go over there to pray.' He took with him Peter and the two sons of Zebedee. Distress and anguish overwhelmed him, and he said to them, 'My heart is ready to break with grief. Stop here, and stay awake with me.' Then he went on a little farther, threw himself down, and prayed, 'My Father, if it is not possible, let this cup pass me by. Yet not my will but yours.'

He came back to the disciples and found them asleep; and he said to Peter, 'What! Could none of you stay awake with me for one hour? Stay awake, and pray that you may be spared the test. The spirit is willing, but the flesh is weak.'

He went away a second time and prayed: 'My Father, if it is not possible for this cup to pass me by without my drinking it, your will be done.' He came again and found them asleep, for their eyes were heavy. So he left them and went away again and prayed a third time, using the same words as before.

Then he came to the disciples and said to them, 'Still asleep? Still resting? The hour has come! The Son of Man is betrayed into the hands of sinners. Up, let us go! The traitor is upon us.'

# THURSDAY

ACTS 4:23–31 (NIV)

On their release, Peter and John went back to their own people and reported all that the chief priests and elders had said to them. When they heard this, they raised their voices together in prayer to God. 'Sovereign Lord,' they said, 'you made the heaven and the earth and the sea, and everything in them. You spoke by the Holy Spirit through the mouth of your servant, our father David:

"Why do the nations rage
and the peoples plot in vain?
The kings of the earth take their stand
and the rulers gather together
against the Lord and against his Anointed One."

Indeed Herod and Pontius Pilate met together with the Gentiles and the people of Israel in this city to conspire against your holy servant Jesus, whom you anointed. They did what your power and will had decided beforehand should happen. Now, Lord, consider their threats and enable your servants to speak your word with great boldness. Stretch out your hand to heal and perform miraculous signs and wonders through the name of your holy servant Jesus.'

After they prayed, the place where they were meeting was shaken. And they were all filled with the Holy Spirit and spoke the word of God boldly.

# FRIDAY

ROMANS 8:26–27 (RSV)

Likewise the Spirit helps us in our weakness; for we do not know how to pray as we ought, but the Spirit himself intercedes for us with sighs too deep for words. And he who searches the hearts of men knows what is the mind of the Spirit, because the Spirit intercedes for the saints according to the will of God.

EPHESIANS 6:18–20 (RSV)

Pray at all times in the Spirit, with all prayer and supplication. To that end keep alert with all perseverance, making supplication for all the saints, and also for me, that utterance may be given me in opening my mouth boldly to proclaim the mystery of the gospel, for which I am an ambassador in chains; that I may declare it boldly, as I ought to speak.

PHILIPPIANS 1:3–6 (RSV)

I thank my God in all my remembrance of you, always in every prayer of mine for you all making my prayer with joy, thankful for your partnership in the gospel from the first day until now. And I am sure that he who began a good work in you will bring it to completion at the day of Jesus Christ.

COLOSSIANS 4:2–4 (RSV)

Continue steadfastly in prayer, being watchful in it with thanksgiving; and pray for us also, that God may open to us a door for the word, to declare the mystery of Christ, on account of which I am in prison, that I may make it clear, as I ought to speak.

## SATURDAY

EPHESIANS 3:14–21 (AV)

For this cause I bow my knees unto the Father of our Lord Jesus Christ, Of whom the whole family in heaven and earth is named, that he would grant you, according to the riches of his glory, to be strengthened with might by his Spirit in the inner man; That Christ may dwell in your hearts by faith; that ye, being rooted and grounded in love, may be able to comprehend with all saints what is the breadth, and length, and depth, and height; And to know the love of Christ, which passeth knowledge, that ye might be filled with all the fulness of God. Now unto him that is able to do exceeding abundantly above all that we ask or think, according to the power that worketh in us, unto him be glory in the church by Christ Jesus throughout all ages, world without end. Amen.

WEEK 18

# THE GRAND MIRACLE

This week we look at a theme which many people have tried to express—the mystery of God becoming man. Many of the stories and images have great value, but truly none can compare with the simple, yet profound, account we read in the Bible. C.S. Lewis, who himself used many analogies, called it 'the grand miracle'.

Our readings start by telling the story in the words of Matthew (Sunday and Wednesday) and Luke (Monday and Tuesday). These sources—the only two we have—are marvellously complementary. First we see through Joseph's eyes, then through Mary's. But even Luke, whose research provides the familiar 'Christmas' details, is far more reticent than the embroidery of subsequent traditions. God's arrival in this world is told with tantalizing conciseness! Both authors, though, are clear about the virginal conception and unique glory of this child, and about his divine origin and all-embracing destiny.

The magi or 'wise men' who arrive later in Matthew's account, balance the visiting shepherds in Luke; Jesus is recognized by a small but diverse company of rich and poor, near and far, Jew and Gentile.

Thursday's and Friday's twinned readings see the coming of Christ from the perspectives of John and Peter (Thursday) and of Paul (Friday).

Lastly, John's first letter (Saturday) sums up the truth about the coming of the eternal Son of God to our world, so that 'our joy may be complete.'

# God made Man

WEEK 18

Christian doctrine uses a beautiful word to describe the meaning of Jesus: 'incarnation'. It carries the sense that God in Jesus 'took flesh' and became a human person. This great claim of Christians finds abundant support in the Bible.

The Old Testament begins with God creating humanity in his own 'image'. That is, we were meant from the start to walk with God, grow like him and share his nature. But humanity's fall into sin wrecked this relationship and introduced guilt and death. It is the unspoken assumption of the Old Testament that God had to do something about this tragic parting of ways to bring us back to himself. It looks forward to the coming of God's 'Messiah' who would deliver his people from their sins. The New Testament sees Jesus fulfilling that expectation.

The New Testament takes Jesus' humanity for granted. Although his birth was exceptional, he grew as all children do in knowledge as well as physical growth; he experienced hunger and thirst; he knew what it was to feel tired; he learned from experience; there were times when he was ignorant; and he suffered a real death. The incarnation stresses the reality of the human Jesus. William Temple used to say, 'Christianity is the most materialistic of religions', because of its central message that God has revealed himself in the human life of Jesus Christ.

But equally firmly the New Testament is clear that Jesus was more than man. The total impression of this man's life, his teaching, mighty works, deliberate death and resurrection led the first Christians to preach with great excitement that this Jesus was the 'Christ', the 'Lord', the 'promised Saviour', and even 'the image of the invisible God'. The New Testament is compelled, therefore, by the impact of Jesus to make the most staggering claims for him, knowing that this would infuriate the Jews and send the learned Greek philosophers into peals of laughter.

But the reality of the incarnation was unquestioned by the apostles and as they preached the good news of God's salvation through Jesus Christ they saw its effectiveness in a confident, growing church. In the words of John's Gospel, they believed firmly that the 'Word took flesh and dwelt among us'.

Why did Jesus Christ become a human being?

- **Because humanity's need requires a saviour.** Christ did not come to us because we needed a social worker. Such was our predicament that he came 'to seek and to save the lost'. God's response to human sin was personally to intervene in our history.
- **Because God wanted to identify with human sorrows, joys and needs.** We should never present the Christian faith as though the last week of Jesus' life was the only period that really mattered. The death and resurrection of Jesus were the climax of a life given over for us. He *lived* the cross before he died it. Incarnation therefore means that Christ has now taken our

human nature into God's presence as a foretaste of the glory we shall share one day.

◆ **Because we need a model for Christian living.** Jesus reveals the beauty of human nature when it is lived for the glory of God. Just as a good teacher will hold up to his pupils a model of what he is trying to teach, so God declares to us through the incarnation: 'This is what is meant by the image of God. See my Son's holiness, his joy and goodness, his power and victory over sin. This was my intention for you from the beginning.' Although as far as this life is concerned we shall fall far short of the quality of Jesus' life, nevertheless we should not be afraid of following the practice of the early Christians who kept before them the inspiration of Christ's life as the way they ought to live.

## SUNDAY

MATTHEW 1:18–25 (RSV)

Now the birth of Jesus Christ took place in this way. When his mother Mary had been betrothed to Joseph, before they came together she was found to be with child of the Holy Spirit; and her husband Joseph, being a just man and unwilling to put her to shame, resolved to divorce her quietly. But as he considered this, behold, an angel of the Lord appeared to him in a dream, saying, 'Joseph, son of David, do not fear to take Mary your wife, for that which is conceived in her is of the Holy Spirit; she will bear a son, and you shall call his name Jesus, for he will save his people from their sins.' All this took place to fulfil what the Lord had spoken by the prophet:

'Behold, a virgin shall conceive and
bear a son,
and his name shall be called
Emmanuel'

(which means, God with us). When Joseph woke from sleep, he did as the angel of the Lord commanded him; he took his wife, but knew her not until she had borne a son; and he called his name Jesus.

## MONDAY

LUKE 1:26–38 (NIV)

In the sixth month, God sent the angel Gabriel to Nazareth, a town in Galilee, to a virgin pledged to be married to a man named Joseph, a descendant of David. The virgin's name was Mary. The angel went to her and said, 'Greetings, you who are highly favoured! The Lord is with you.'

Mary was greatly troubled at his words and wondered what kind of greeting this might be. But the angel said to her, 'Do not be afraid, Mary, you have found favour with God. You will be with child and give birth to a son, and you are to give him the name Jesus. He will be great and will be called the Son of the Most High. The Lord God will give him the throne of his father David, and he will reign over the house of Jacob for ever; his kingdom will never end.'

'How will this be,' Mary asked the angel, 'since I am a virgin?'

The angel answered, 'The Holy Spirit will come upon you, and the power of the Most High will overshadow you. So the holy one to be born will be called "the Son of God". Even Elizabeth your relative is going to have a child in her old age, and she who was said to be barren is in her sixth month. For nothing is impossible with God.'

'I am the Lord's servant,' Mary answered. 'May it be to me as you have said.' Then the angel left her.

## TUESDAY

LUKE 2:1–16 (AV)

And it came to pass in those days, that there went out a decree from Caesar Augustus, that all the world should be taxed. (And this taxing was first made when Cyrenius was governor of Syria.) And all went to be taxed, every one into his own city. And Joseph also went up from Galilee, out of the city of Nazareth, into Judaea, unto the city of David, which is called Bethlehem; (because he was of the house and lineage of David:) To be taxed with Mary his espoused wife, being great with child.

And so it was, that while they were there, the days were accomplished that she should be delivered. And she brought forth her firstborn son, and wrapped him in swaddling clothes, and laid him in a manger; because there was no room for them in the inn.

And there were in the same country shepherds abiding in the field, keeping watch over their flock by night. And, lo, the angel of the Lord came upon them, and the glory of the Lord shone round about them: and they were sore afraid. And the angel said unto them, Fear not: for, behold, I bring you good tidings of great joy, which shall be to all people. For unto you is born this day in the city of David a Saviour, which is Christ the Lord. And this shall be a sign unto you; Ye shall find the babe wrapped in swaddling clothes, lying in a manger. And suddenly there was with the angel a multitude of the heavenly host praising God, and saying, Glory to God in the highest, and on earth peace, good will toward men.

And it came to pass, as the angels were gone away from them into heaven, the shepherds said one to another, Let us now go even unto Bethlehem, and see this thing which is come to pass, which the Lord hath made known unto us.

## WEDNESDAY

MATTHEW 2:1–12 (NJB)

After Jesus had been born at Bethlehem in Judaea during the reign of King Herod, suddenly some wise men came to Jerusalem from the east asking, 'Where is the infant king of the Jews? We saw his star as it rose and have come to do him homage.' When King Herod heard this he was perturbed, and so was the whole of Jerusalem. He called together all the chief priests and the scribes of the people, and enquired of them where the Christ was to be born. They told him, 'At Bethlehem in Judaea, for this is what the prophet wrote:

And you Bethlehem, in the land of
  Judah,
  you are by no means the least
  among the leaders of Judah,
for from you will come a leader
  who will shepherd my people
  Israel.'

Then Herod summoned the wise men to see him privately. He asked them the exact date on which the star had appeared and sent them on to Bethlehem with the words, 'Go and find out all about the child, and when you have found him, let me know, so that I too may go and do him homage. Having listened to what the king had to say, they set out. And suddenly the star they had seen rising went forward and halted over the place where the child was. The sight of the star filled them with delight, and going into the house they saw the child with his mother Mary, and falling to their knees they did him homage. Then, opening their treasures, they offered him gifts of gold and frankincense and myrrh. But they were given a warning in a dream not to go back to Herod, and returned to their own country by a different way.

## THURSDAY

JOHN 1:14–18 (RSV)

And the Word became flesh and dwelt among us, full of grace and truth; we have beheld his glory, glory as of the only Son from the Father. (John bore witness to him, and cried, 'This was he of whom I said, "He who comes after me ranks before me, for he was before me." ') And from his fullness have we all received, grace upon grace. For the law was given through Moses; grace and truth came through Jesus Christ. No one has ever seen God; the only Son, who is in the bosom of the Father, he has made him known.

2 PETER 1:16–18 (RSV)

For we did not follow cleverly devised myths when we made known to you the power and coming of our Lord Jesus Christ, but we were eyewitnesses of his majesty. For when he received honour and glory from God the Father and the voice was borne to him by the Majestic Glory, 'This is my beloved son, with whom I am well pleased,' we heard this voice borne from heaven, for we were with him on the holy mountain.

## FRIDAY

PHILIPPIANS 2:5–11 (REB)

Take to heart among yourselves what you find in Christ Jesus: 'He was in the form of God; yet he laid no claim to equality with God, but made himself nothing, assuming the form of a slave. Bearing the human likeness, sharing the human lot, he humbled himself, and was obedient, even to the point of death, death on a cross! Therefore God raised him to the heights and bestowed on him the name above all names, that at the name of Jesus every knee should bow—in heaven, on earth, and in the depths—and every tongue acclaim, "Jesus Christ is Lord," to the glory of God the Father.'

1 TIMOTHY 3:14–16 (REB)

I am hoping to come to you before long, but I write this in case I am delayed, to let you know what is proper conduct in God's household, that is, the church of the living God, the pillar and bulwark of the truth. And great beyond all question is the mystery of our religion:

He was manifested in flesh,<br>
  vindicated in spirit,<br>
  seen by angels;<br>
he was proclaimed among the<br>
  nations,<br>
  believed in throughout the<br>
  world,<br>
  raised to heavenly glory.

## SATURDAY

1 JOHN 1:1–4, 5:18–21 (NIV)

That which was from the beginning, which we have heard, which we have seen with our eyes, which we have looked at and our hands have touched—this we proclaim concerning the Word of life. The life appeared; we have seen it and testify to it, and we proclaim to you eternal life, which was with the Father and has appeared to us. We proclaim to you what we have seen and heard, so that you also may have fellowship with us. And our fellowship is with the Father and with his Son, Jesus Christ. We write this to make our joy complete.

We know that anyone born of God does not continue to sin; the one who was born of God keeps him safe, and the evil one cannot harm him. We know that we are children of God, and that the whole world is under the control of the evil one. We know also that the Son of God has come and has given us understanding, so that we may know him who is true. And we are in him who is true—even in his Son Jesus Christ. He is the true God and eternal life.

Dear children, keep yourselves from idols.

WEEK 19

# THE AMAZING TEACHER

What was it like to be an early follower of Jesus the teacher? Amazement seems to have been the most common reaction to his words. Here was a thirty-year-old 'rabbi' who lacked the formal training normally qualifying a man for that title, and who made some outrageous and compelling statements.

The authority of his words appeared immediately. And this authority was confirmed by visible signs. Our first reading shows Jesus exorcizing evil and healing disorder (Sunday). Monday's story-plus-explanation, known as the parable of the sower, represents the challenge of hearing the life-giving word of God and responding to it.

Tuesday introduces the 'Sermon on the Mount' with its opening 'beatitudes' or blessings. Here, most conventional recipes for happiness are turned upside-down in a way which must have caused shock and alarm. On Wednesday and Thursday we continue and conclude the same body of teaching in which the underlying thread is 'my Father in heaven'.

Not long before his arrest, Jesus spent his last precious days in Jerusalem teaching in the temple area. Friday brings us two of several brisk confrontations with 'official' religious leaders, the Sadducees and the Pharisees. But Saturday shows Jesus, risen from the dead, still teaching the Scriptures, still the master of words and situations, still claiming extraordinary authority and now committing his followers to a lifetime of hair-raising service—and teaching.

WEEK
19

# Jesus the Teacher

If the Christian gospel can change people's lives for eternity, then we have a vital duty to get it across to others. But how is this to be done? Surely the example of Jesus the Teacher is the one to follow.

The rabbi in Jesus' day was held in high regard. He went through a taxing course of training, gathered his disciples (a little like a modern guru), and delivered weighty commentaries on the Old Testament and its application to everyday life. No wonder 'teacher' was an esteemed title.

Jesus was also called 'rabbi' and 'teacher'. He was recognized as one who explained the scriptures, debated them with other experts and gathered disciples. Yet there was a difference. He obviously had had no formal training; he was as happy to teach in the fields or from a boat as in the synagogues; he was not averse to setting aside the Law of Moses if the demands of the occasion required it or making it a hundred times *more* demanding by drawing out its deepest implications.

The typical teacher taught by making scrupulous and painstaking reference to the line of teachers who had gone before him. None would feel free to ignore the line of tradition. But Jesus astonished everyone by the freedom with which he handled the Law and by his personal authority. As a teacher he inspired awe, fear and confidence. On the road to Jerusalem no one dared to ask him any question who had caught a glimpse of his face set like a flint towards the cross. Yet he encouraged an openness to outcasts, taxmen, prostitutes, lepers and children which contrasted with the typically tight rabbinical circle of teacher with disciples. And perhaps most significantly, he called people to follow him as his personal disciples rather than just learn the Law. His authority as a teacher did not seem to hang on his learning, his training or his social status.

The ordinary people heard him with delight, which is not surprising when we look at his methods. Jesus revelled in the vivid image and the outrageous picture. He writes in the sand while the respectable demand punishment for an adulteress; he washes his followers' feet to make a point they will never forget. He sets the crowd buzzing with a startling paradox ('not peace but a sword'), a blistering turn of phrase ('whitewashed tombs') or a scandalous demand ('go the second mile'). They may have complained 'this is a hard saying', but they never found him boring.

Jesus was different in two other respects:

- **He put himself at the centre of his teaching** ('follow me'). This would have been distasteful on the lips of anyone else, but was not so on his.
- **He was not interested in information for its own sake**. To Nicodemus who begins promisingly—'Rabbi, we know you are a teacher come from God'—he replies with a statement which goes to the heart—'Unless a man be born again he cannot see the kingdom of God.' Jesus' questions are

never to be taken at their face value. His parables are never simple stories, despite all appearances. He hinted that since a parable's real meaning could only be 'lived', not mugged up, whether you understood it or not depended on the openness of your heart rather than your intellect or education. There were those who understood a parable well enough, but because of their hardness they were probably worse off after hearing it than before. None of his teaching, least of all the 'beautiful' Sermon on the Mount, was designed to entertain the intellect. As many have found since, his words are a revolutionary manifesto and a rock on which to build a life.

## SUNDAY

MARK 1:21–28 (NIV)

They went to Capernaum, and when the Sabbath came, Jesus went into the synagogue and began to teach. The people were amazed at his teaching, because he taught them as one who had authority, not as the teachers of the law. Just then a man in their synagogue who was possessed by an evil spirit cried out, 'What do you want with us, Jesus of Nazareth? Have you come to destroy us? I know who you are—the Holy One of God!'

'Be quiet!' said Jesus sternly. 'Come out of him!' The evil spirit shook the man violently and came out of him with a shriek.

The people were all so amazed that they asked each other, 'What is this? A new teaching—and with authority! He even gives orders to evil spirits and they obey him.' News about him spread quickly over the whole region of Galilee.

## MONDAY

MARK 4:3–20 (NJB)

Jesus said, 'Listen! Imagine a sower going out to sow. Now it happened that, as he sowed, some of the seed fell on the edge of the path, and the birds came and ate it up. Some seed fell on rocky ground where it found little soil and at once sprang up, because there was no depth of earth; and when the sun came up it was scorched and, not having any roots, it withered away. Some seed fell into thorns, and the thorns grew up and choked it, and it produced no crop. And some seeds fell into rich soil, grew tall and strong, and produced a good crop; the yield was thirty, sixty, even a hundredfold. And he said, 'Anyone who has ears for listening should listen!'

When he was alone, the Twelve, together with the others who formed his company, asked what the parables meant. He told them, 'To you is granted the secret of the kingdom of God, but to those who are outside everything comes in parables, so that they may look and look, but never perceive; listen and listen, but never understand; to avoid changing their ways and being healed.'

He said to them, 'Do you not understand this parable? Then how will you understand any of the parables? What the sower is sowing is the word. Those on the edge of the path where the word is sown are people who have no sooner heard it than Satan at once comes and carries away the word that was sown in them. Similarly, those who are sown on patches of rock are people who, when first they hear the word, welcome it at once with joy. But they have no root deep down and do not last; should some trial come, or some persecution on account of the word, at once they fall away. Then there are others who are sown in thorns. These have heard the word, but the worries of the world, the lure of riches and all the other passions come in to choke the word, and so it produces nothing. And there are those who have been sown in rich soil; they hear the word and accept it and yield a harvest, thirty and sixty and a hundredfold.'

## TUESDAY

MATTHEW 5:1–12 (AV)

Seeing the multitudes, he went up into a mountain: and when he was set, his disciples came unto him: And he opened his mouth, and taught them, saying, Blessed are the poor in spirit: for theirs is the kingdom of heaven. Blessed are they that mourn: for they shall be comforted. Blessed are the meek: for they shall inherit the earth. Blessed are they which do hunger and thirst after righteousness: for they shall be filled. Blessed are the merciful: for they shall obtain mercy. Blessed are the pure in heart: for they shall see God. Blessed are the peacemakers: for they shall be called the children of God. Blessed are they which are persecuted for righteousness' sake: for theirs is the kingdom of heaven. Blessed are ye, when men shall revile you, and persecute you, and shall say all manner of evil against you falsely, for my sake. Rejoice, and be exceeding glad: for great is your reward in heaven: for so persecuted they the prophets which were before you.

## WEDNESDAY

MATTHEW 6:25–34 (RSV)

'Therefore I tell you, do not be anxious about your life, what you shall eat or what you shall drink, nor about your body, what you shall put on. Is not life more than food, and the body more than clothing? Look at the birds of the air; they neither sow nor reap nor gather into barns, and yet your heavenly Father feeds them. Are you not of more value than they? And which of you by being anxious can add one cubit to his span of life? And why are you anxious about clothing? Consider the lilies of the field, how they grow; they neither toil nor spin; yet I tell you, even Solomon in all his glory was not arrayed like one of these. But if God so clothes the grass of the field, which today is alive and tomorrow is thrown into the oven, will he not much more clothe you, O men of little faith? Therefore do not be anxious, saying, "What shall we eat?" or "What shall we wear?" For the Gentiles seek all these things; and your heavenly Father knows that you need them all. But seek first his kingdom and his righteousness, and all these things shall be yours as well.

'Therefore do not be anxious about tomorrow, for tomorrow will be anxious for itself. Let the day's own trouble be sufficient for the day.'

## THURSDAY

MATTHEW 7:21–27 (NIV)

'Not everyone who says to me, "Lord, Lord," will enter the kingdom of heaven, but only he who does the will of my Father who is in heaven. Many will say to me on that day, "Lord, Lord, did we not prophesy in your name, and in your name drive out demons and perform many miracles?" Then I will tell them plainly, "I never knew you. Away from me, you evildoers!"

'Therefore everyone who hears these words of mine and puts them into practice is like a wise man who built his house on the rock. The rain came down, the streams rose, and the winds blew and beat against that house; yet it did not fall, because it had its foundation on the rock. But everyone who hears these words of mine and does not put them into practice is like a foolish man who built his house on sand. The rain came down, the streams rose, and the winds blew and beat against that house, and it fell with a great crash.'

## FRIDAY

MATTHEW 22:23–33, 41–46 (REB)

The same day Sadducees, who maintain that there is no resurrection, came to him and asked: 'Teacher, Moses said that if a man dies childless, his brother shall marry the widow and provide an heir for his brother. We know a case involving seven brothers. The first married and died, and as he was without issue his wife was left to his brother. The same thing happened with the second, and the third, and so on with all seven. Last of all the woman died. At the resurrection, then, whose wife will she be, since they had all married her?' Jesus answered: 'How far you are from the truth! You know neither the scriptures nor the power of God. In the resurrection men and women do not marry; they are like angels in heaven.

'As for the resurrection of the dead, have you never read what God himself said to you: "I am the God of Abraham, the God of Isaac, the God of Jacob"? God is not God of the dead but of the living.' When the crowds heard this, they were amazed at his teaching.

Turning to the assembled Pharisees Jesus asked them, 'What is your opinion about the Messiah? Whose son is he?' 'The son of David,' they replied. 'Then how is it', he asked, 'that David by inspiration calls him "Lord"? For he says, "The Lord said to my Lord, 'Sit at my right hand until I put your enemies under your feet.'" If then David calls him "Lord", how can he be David's son?' Nobody was able to give him an answer; and from that day no one dared to put any more questions to him.

## SATURDAY

LUKE 24:36–49 (NJB)

They were still talking about all this when Jesus himself stood among them and said to them, 'Peace be with you!' In a state of alarm and fright, they thought they were seeing a ghost. But he said, 'Why are you so agitated, and why are these doubts stirring in your hearts? See by my hands and my feet that it is I myself. Touch me and see for yourselves; a ghost has no flesh and bones as you can see I have.' And as he said this he showed them his hands and his feet. Their joy was so great that they still could not believe it, as they were dumbfounded; so he said to them, 'Have you anything to eat?' And they offered him a piece of grilled fish, which he took and ate before their eyes.

Then he told them, 'This is what I meant when I said, while I was still with you, that everything written about me in the Law of Moses, in the Prophets and in the Psalms, was destined to be fulfilled.' He then opened their minds to understand the scriptures, and he said to them, 'So it is written that the Christ would suffer and on the third day rise from the dead, and that, in his name, repentance for the forgiveness of sins would be preached to all nations, beginning from Jerusalem. You are witnesses to this.

'And now I am sending upon you what the Father has promised. Stay in the city, then, until you are clothed with the power from on high.'

## ISRAEL'S WISDOM

The books of Job, Proverbs and Ecclesiastes are collectively known as books of Wisdom. The same sort of writing appears elsewhere in the Old Testament, especially in some of the Psalms. It is found also in the literature of some of Israel's neighbours.

King Solomon had a great reputation for wisdom, and his name is linked to Proverbs and Ecclesiastes, much as King David's is to the poetry of the Psalms.

The three Wisdom books are very different from each other in tone and subject, but they have many features in common. Each is about behaviour and everyday life. God is the source of wisdom in all three. We find wisdom when we respect him and follow his laws.

The Song of Songs is often associated with the Wisdom books. But in fact it is unique.

### JOB
### Why suffering?

This wonderful dramatic poem tells of a good man, Job, who lost everything but still believed in God. Its origins are lost in antiquity.

Job's many disasters convince his friends that he must have done something wrong. But Job is persuaded this is not so.

**“The fear of the Lord—that is wisdom, and to shun evil is understanding.”**

At first he cannot find God, to argue his case before him. But at last God reveals himself to him, and Job is satisfied not by arguments but by meeting God himself in all his power and wisdom.

### PROVERBS
### How to live?

Unlike Job and Ecclesiastes, this is a basically optimistic book. It is a collection of sayings by Israel's wisdom teachers.

The important thing to find and follow God centred wisdom, and apply it to practical everyday living. The belief is that by following God's way a person will find blessing.

The setting is home and friendship, work and business, the life king and subject. And the topics are wisdom and folly, the righteou and the wicked, how t speak wisely, wealth and poverty, hopes ar fears, joys and sorrow anger, hard work and idleness.

The foundation of a wisdom is fear of (respect for) God.

**“In all your ways acknowledge th Lord, and he wi make your path straight.”**

## ECCLESIASTES What does it all mean?

e writer is called oheleth', the ilosopher. It is not own who he was, or at his connection h Solomon.

He is troubled by the seeming meaninglessness of life. However hard people strive for wisdom, success or justice, the results are always short-term and limited. To look for anything lasting in life is like 'chasing the wind'. The book reflects the poverty of a life limited to purely human concerns.

The presence of this book in the Bible shows that God has time for the person who finds faith difficult.

> **"Who knows what is good for a man in life, during the few nd meaningless ays he passes through like a shadow?"**

## THE SONG OF SONGS Six love songs

The six songs which form this beautiful book are a dialogue between a young man and his bride. The theme is their love for each other.

The songs are set against the background of the countryside in springtime, and many rural images are used to express their delight in each other.

Physical love is God-given, and it is entirely fitting that one Bible book should be given to this subject.

> **"Show me your face, let me hear your voice; for your voice is sweet and your face is lovely."**

WEEK 20

# THE NEW TEACHING

People could see that Jesus was different from the other rabbis of his time. One of the greatest changes he introduced to the world was in his relating to God as 'Abba'—'Father'. This was something rarely encountered in the Old Testament, but in Sunday's reading the prophets Isaiah and Malachi sow the seeds of what later came to full fruition. Here God is seen fleetingly as a Father, and the nation of Israel as the son.

When Jesus burst in on the Jewish scene with words of such confident intimacy between God and himself, these were very soon to cause offence, and worse. His sense of God's fatherhood is expressed thoughout his teaching, and the readings from John's gospel on Tuesday, Wednesday and Thursday show different aspects.

Even as Jesus was dying, his words show consistency to the end. While hanging in degrading public torture, he calls God his Father still—the same familiar name which appears in his first recorded words as a lad of twelve (Friday).

But what is even more breathtaking, this privilege is not to be his alone. He expects his followers to enjoy the same relationship with the Father (Monday). This understanding should inform our whole lives to the point of loving our enemies. Paul's letter to the Romans spells out further the wonder of being adopted as the sons and heirs of God (Saturday).

# God the Father

Words like 'mother', 'father', 'son' and 'daughter' stand for the richest relationships in human life. We are bound to our parents in a very special relationship of love. We owe them life, because without them we would not exist. But we can go much further than that: if they have been wise and good parents we can be grateful to them for bringing us up in a loving family which has helped us to develop into mature and whole people. It is against this background that we should try to understand what the Bible has to say about God being our 'Father'.

It is strange at first sight to discover that the Old Testament rarely talks about God as Father. It is the New Testament which develops this teaching and for this reason—God is only known as Father through Jesus the Son. It is a striking fact that Jesus came preaching the kingdom in which the king is a Father. Jesus spoke of his Father as 'Abba'. This is an intimate word, similar to but not the same as our word 'Daddy'. Even today in Israel you can hear small children calling out *Imma* (Mummy) and *Abba* (Daddy). By using this word Jesus was showing his own personal relationship with the Lord of all and showing that this God is not aloof and distant but close at hand. This must have seemed almost blasphemous to fellow-Jews who placed such an emphasis on God's distance from us. God's name was too sacred even to be uttered, so whenever they came upon the word 'Yahweh' in the Bible they used 'Lord'. But Jesus called him 'Father'—even 'my Abba'!

The first Christians continued this emphasis. Paul, for example, talked frequently about 'the God and Father of our Lord Jesus Christ'. It was also very natural for them to speak of God as 'Abba' because hadn't this been their Lord's practice? This awareness of God as Abba, they realized, came through lives opened by the Holy Spirit. So Paul writes: 'God has sent the Spirit of his Son into our hearts crying "Abba! Father!" '

Clearly, then, two events had to happen before God could be known as Father:

- **He had to come and show himself, not as a distant God, but as Father** of a man who was his very dear Son. Through the ministry of Jesus of Nazareth, God is revealed as Father.
- **Then it has to become personal to us.** We cannot enter God's family without his Holy Spirit entering our lives and starting the new creation within us. This is what Jesus meant when he said to the Jewish rabbi Nicodemus: 'Unless a man is born of water and the Spirit he cannot enter the kingdom of God.' 'Water' here stands for baptism, the outward symbol of belonging to the family, and 'Spirit' means the working of God in our lives bringing us to faith.

It is important to note that when we call God 'Father' we are not suggesting that he is masculine in our understanding of sexuality. God's nature embraces qualities which belong to both male and female natures and the Bible does not shrink from speaking of God's maternal care and love. What the term 'Father' means is that God looks after us as a real parent should. He provides for us, he defends us, he loves us. We should not hesitate to use such a term for God when it was so important to Jesus and handed on to us from him.

In our anonymous world where people are often fearful and insecure, the doctrine of God as Father is exciting and inexhaustible. Jesus lived life aware and confident that he could not drift from his Father's care and love. We must be careful not to pray 'Our Father' and live as though we are orphans.

# SUNDAY

ISAIAH 63:15–16 (RSV)

Look down from heaven and see,
  from thy holy and glorious
  habitation.
Where are thy zeal and thy might?
  The yearning of thy heart and
  thy compassion
  are withheld from me.
For thou art our Father,
  though Abraham does not know
  us
  and Israel does not acknowledge
  us;
thou, O Lord, art our Father,
  our Redeemer from of old is thy
  name.

MALACHI 1:1, 6–9 (RSV)

The oracle of the word of the Lord to Israel by Malachi.

'A son honours his father, and a servant his master. If then I am a father, where is my honour? And if I am a master, where is my fear? says the Lord of hosts to you, O priests, who despise my name. You say, 'How have we despised thy name?' By offering polluted food upon my altar. And you say, 'How have we polluted it?' By thinking that the Lord's table may be despised. When you offer blind animals in sacrifice, is that no evil? And when you offer those that are lame or sick, is that no evil? Present that to your governor; will he be pleased with you or show you favour? say the Lord of hosts. And now entreat the favour of God, that he may be gracious to us. With such a gift from your hand, will he show favour to any of you? says the Lord of hosts.'

# MONDAY

MATTHEW 5:43–48, 7:7–12 (AV)

Jesus said, 'Ye have heard that it hath been said, Thou shalt love thy neighbour, and hate thine enemy. But I say unto you, Love your enemies, bless them that curse you, do good to them that hate you, and pray for them which despitefully use you, and persecute you; That ye may be the children of your Father which is in heaven: for he maketh his sun to rise on the evil and on the good, and sendeth rain on the just and on the unjust. For if ye love them which love you, what reward have ye? do not even the publicans the same? And if ye salute your brethren only, what do ye more than others? do not even the publicans so? Be ye therefore perfect, even as your Father which is in heaven is perfect.'

'Ask, and it shall be given you; seek, and ye shall find; knock, and it shall be opened unto you: For every one that asketh receiveth; and he that seeketh findeth; and to him that knocketh it shall be opened. Or what man is there of you, whom if his son ask bread, will he give him a stone? Or if he ask a fish, will he give him a serpent? If ye then, being evil, know how to give good gifts unto your children, how much more shall your Father which is in heaven give good things to them that ask him? Therefore all things whatsoever ye would that men should do to you, do ye even so to them: for this is the law and the prophets.

## TUESDAY

JOHN 5:16–27 (NIV)

So, because Jesus was doing these things on the Sabbath, the Jews persecuted him. Jesus said to them, 'My Father is always at his work to this very day, and I, too, am working.' for this reason the Jews tried all the harder to kill him; not only was he breaking the Sabbath, but he was even calling God his own Father, making himself equal with God.

Jesus gave them this answer: 'I tell you the truth, the Son can do nothing by himself; he can do only what he sees his Father doing, because whatever the Father does the Son also does. For the Father loves the Son and shows him all he does. Yes, to your amazement he will show him even greater things than these. For just as the Father raises the dead and gives them life, even so the Son gives life to whom he is pleased to give it. Moreover, the Father judges no-one, but has entrusted all judgment to the Son, that all may honour the Son just as they honour the Father. He who does not honour the Son does not honour the Father, who sent him.

I tell you the truth, whoever hears my word and believes him who sent me has eternal life and will not be condemned; he has crossed over from death to life. I tell you the truth, a time is coming and has now come when the dead will hear the voice of the Son of God and those who hear will live. For as the Father has life in himself, so he has granted the Son to have life in himself. And he has given him authority to judge because he is the Son of Man.

## WEDNESDAY

JOHN 5:36–47 (NIV)

'I have testimony weightier than that of John. For the very work that the Father has given me to finish, and which I am doing, testifies that the Father has sent me. And the Father who sent me has himself testified concerning me. You have never heard his voice nor seen his form, nor does his word dwell in you, for you do not believe the one he sent. You diligently study the Scriptures because you think that by them you possess eternal life. These are the Scriptures that testify about me, yet you refuse to come to me to have life.

I do not accept praise from men, but I know you. I know that you do not have the love of God in your hearts. I have come in my Father's name, and you do not accept me; but if someone else comes in his own name, you will accept him. How can you believe if you accept praise from one another, yet make no effort to obtain the praise that comes from the only God?

But do not think I will accuse you before the Father. Your accuser is Moses, on whom your hopes are set. If you believed Moses, you would believe me, for he wrote about me. But since you do not believe what he wrote, how are you going to believe what I say?'

## THURSDAY

JOHN 17:1–11, 20–24 (NIV)

Jesus looked towards heaven and prayed: 'Father, the time has come. Glorify your Son, that your Son may glorify you. For you granted him authority over all people that he might give eternal life to all those you have given him. Now this is eternal life: that they may know you, the only true God, and Jesus Christ, whom you have sent. I have brought you glory on earth by completing the work you gave me to do. And now, Father, glorify me in your presence with the glory I had with you before the world began.

I have revealed you to those whom you gave me out of the world. They were yours; you gave them to me and they have obeyed your word. Now they know that everything you have given me comes from you. For I gave them the words you gave me and they accepted them. They knew with certainty that I came from you, and they believed that you sent me. I pray for them. I am not praying for the world, but for those you have given me, for they are yours. All I have is yours, and all you have is mine. And glory has come to me through them. I will remain in the world no longer, but they are still in the world, and I am coming to you. Holy Father, protect them by the power of your name—the name you gave me—so that they may be one as we are one.'

'My prayer is not for them alone. I pray also for those who will believe in me through their message, that all of them may be one, Father, just as you are in me and I am in you. May they also be in us so that the world may believe that you have sent me. I have given them the glory that you gave me, that they may be one as we are one: I in them and you in me. May they be brought to complete unity to let the world know that you sent me and have loved them even as you have loved me.

'Father, I want those you have given me to be with me where I am, and to see my glory, the glory you have given me because you loved me before the creation of the world.'

## FRIDAY

LUKE 2:41–50, 23:32–35, 44–46 (REB)

Now it was the practice of his parents to go to Jerusalem every year for the Passover festival; and when he was twelve, they made the pilgrimage as usual. When the festive season was over and they set off for home, the boy Jesus stayed behind in Jerusalem. His parents did not know of this; but supposing that he was with the party they travelled for a whole day, and only then did they begin looking for him among their friends and relations. When they could not find him they returned to Jerusalem to look for him; and after three days they found him sitting in the temple surrounded by the teachers, listening to them and putting questions; and all who heard him were amazed at his intelligence and the answers he gave. His parents were astonished to see him there, and his mother said to him, 'My son, why have you treated us like this? Your father and I have been anxiously searching for you.' 'Why did you search for me?' he said. 'Did you not know that I was bound to be in my father's house?' But they did not understand what he meant. Then he went back with them to Nazareth, and continued to be under their authority; his mother treasured up all these things in her heart. As Jesus grew he advanced in wisdom and in favour with God and men.

There were two others with Jesus, criminals who were being led out to execution; and when they reached the place called The Skull, they crucified him there, and the criminals with him, one on his right and the other on his left. Jesus said, 'Father, forgive them; they do not know what they are doing.'

They shared out his clothes by casting lots. The people stood looking on, and their rulers jeered at him: 'He saved others: now let him save himself, if this is God's Messiah, his Chosen.'

By now it was about midday and a darkness fell over the whole land, which lasted until three in the afternoon: the sun's light failed. And the curtain of the temple was torn in two. Then Jesus uttered a loud cry and said, 'Father, into your hands I commit my spirit'; and with these words he died.

## SATURDAY

ROMANS 8:12–17 (RSV)

So then, brethren, we are debtors, not to the flesh, to live according to the flesh—for if you live according to the flesh you will die, but if by the Spirit you put to death the deeds of the body you will live. For all who are led by the Spirit of God are sons of God. For you did not receive the spirit of slavery to fall back into fear, but you have received the spirit of sonship. When we cry, 'Abba! Father!' it is the Spirit himself bearing witness with our spirit that we are children of God, and if children, then heirs, heirs of God and fellow heirs with Christ, provided we suffer with him in order that we may also be glorified with him.

# THE CRUCIAL HOUR

WEEK 21

The Bible uses many terms to convey the meaning and power of the death of Christ: his hour, his glory, his cross, his blood, are some of them.

Jesus' disciples retained the references which Jesus himself made to his coming death and later applied the centuries-old prophecy in Isaiah (Sunday) to the events of Good Friday. Christians have long pondered the application of this portrait to Jesus, both because of the graphic details of his dying and the meaning given to his death here.

Monday's reading, the Parable of the Vineyard, is one of Jesus' final parables, told in Jerusalem and pointedly prophetic .

The following extracts come from three of the gospels, all of which describe the suffering of Jesus in far more detail than they give to any other episode of his life. John shows how Jesus prepared his friends for what was to come (Tuesday). Luke describes part of his trial (Wednesday). The paragraphs from Mark include the mocking, flogging, and finally the nailing of Jesus to the cross (Thursday), and we return to John for the final moments of Jesus' life and his burial (Friday).

It is left to the anonymous letter to the Hebrews to show the achievement of that day, that hour, in terms of love's sacrifice—made 'once for all' and eternal in its consequences (Saturday).

WEEK
21

# The Death of Jesus

The question 'Why the cross?' has haunted the Christian faith from the beginning. The crucifixion was a penalty reserved for criminals, and many non-Christian writers in the first few centuries thought it was a rather sick joke that the Christians preached a crucified saviour. But in spite of the offence of the cross the New Testament and the first Christians did not shrink from declaring proudly and firmly that Jesus' death was God's chosen way of salvation.

But was the cross an accident? At what point in his life was Jesus aware of the cross? We do not know for sure, but it was after Peter had given voice to his famous confession—'You are the Christ'—that Jesus began to talk less about the kingdom and more about his death. What we can say firmly is that according to the New Testament the cross was planned in the purposes of God. God prepared it as the 'highway' home to him.

'Why did the cross have to happen? Why couldn't God just forgive us and let "bygones be bygones"?' some people ask. But mankind's situation was far too tragic for such a trivial response from God. So terrible was humanity's burden of guilt and sin that only God could mend the broken relationship and heal the hearts of us all. The incarnation means that God identified with human need and suffering, and the cross declares that God took all the sin and shame and dealt with it once and for all in Jesus' death. Paul put it this way: 'God made him who had no sin to be sin for us, so that in him we might become the righteousness of God.'

We shall never fully understand the cross in this life; at the heart of it there is mystery. But God does not require us so much to understand it as to experience it, and that is to discover its benefits. We do know this, that it is God's way of salvation and it has changed the lives of millions.

Here are some of the many different ways people have understood the cross:

- **Jesus our Example.** For many people the death of Jesus has been an inspiring example of patient and quiet suffering in the face of overwhelming odds. We can take it as a pattern when we are suffering unjustly. In the New Testament writings Jesus' obedience, ending in his death, is marked out as an example of how Christians should react when persecuted or opposed.

- **Jesus our Liberator.** Although for us today we know Jesus to be someone who removed the sin of the world by his death, it clearly did not have this meaning for those occupying Roman soldiers who put him to death. They saw him as a political agitator. To the Jews he was a 'messianic upstart'. His claims about the coming of his kingdom appeared to challenge the law of Moses. His final entry into Jerusalem as the crowds waved palm branches and cried 'Blessed is he who comes in the name of the Lord' was laden with symbolic meaning. Today many who are fighting oppression, injustice and poverty have taken hold of the cross of Jesus as a model of someone who fought against the forces of evil and conquered.

- **Jesus our Representative.** A representative is someone we put into a position of power and influence to express our point of view. So this theory sees Jesus as the perfect man who stands before the Father on our behalf and represents us there. This idea is well caught in Newman's great hymn: 'A second Adam to the fight and to the rescue came.'

- **Jesus our Sin-bearer**. A dominant view in the New Testament is that Jesus died for our sin. Many have extended this to mean that Jesus died as 'my substitute'. That is, his death was a death I deserved to die; he took my guilt and sin and nailed it to the cross so that I might be forgiven and rise to new life through him.

In these ways and more the death of Jesus has been interpreted for our time. If the resurrection is the heartbeat of the Christian faith, it must be the case that the death of Jesus is its heart. A cross-less Christianity is a cost-less Christianity and will be anaemic and insipid. An effective gospel today must present the death of Jesus confidently and clearly. It is still the way of hope, peace and eternal life.

WEEK 21

# SUNDAY

ISAIAH 53:1–12 (NIV)

Who has believed our message
  and to whom has the arm
  of the Lord been revealed?
He grew up before him like a tender
  shoot,
  and like a root out of dry ground.
He had no beauty or majesty to
  attract us to him,
  nothing in his appearance that
  we should desire him.
He was despised and rejected by
  men,
  a man of sorrows, and familiar
  with suffering.
Like one from whom men hide their
  faces
  he was despised and we
  esteemed him not.

Surely he took up our infirmities
  and carried our sorrows,
yet we considered him stricken by
  God,
  smitten by him, and afflicted.
But he was pierced for our transgressions,
  he was crushed for our iniquities;
the punishment that brought us
  peace was upon him,
  and by his wounds we are
  healed.
We all, like sheep, have gone astray,
  each of us has turned to his own
  way;
and the Lord has laid on him the
  iniquity of us all.

He was oppressed and afflicted,
  yet he did not open his mouth;
he was led like a lamb to the
  slaughter,
  and as a sheep before her
  shearers is silent,
  so he did not open his mouth.
By oppression and judgment, he
  was taken away.
  And who can speak of his descendants?
For he was cut off from the land of
  the living;
  for the transgression of my people he was stricken.
He was assigned a grave with the
  wicked,
  and with the rich in his death,
though he had done no violence,
  nor was any deceit in his mouth.

Yet it was the Lord's will to crush
  him and cause him to suffer,
  and though the Lord makes his
  life a guilt offering,
he will see his offspring and prolong
  his days,
  and the will of the Lord will
  prosper in his hand.
After the suffering of his soul,
  he will see the light (of life) and
  be satisfied;
by his knowledge my righteous
  servant will justify many,
  and he will bear their iniquities.
Therefore I will give him a portion
  among the great,
  and he will divide the spoils with
  the strong,
because he poured out his life unto
  death,
  and was numbered with the
  transgressors.
For he bore the sin of many,
  and made intercession for the
  transgressors.

## MONDAY

MARK:12:1–12 (AV)

And Jesus began to speak unto them by parables.

A certain man planted a vineyard, and set an hedge about it, and digged a place for the winefat, and built a tower, and let it out to husbandmen, and went into a far country. And at the season he sent to the husbandmen a servant, that he might receive from the husbandmen of the fruit of the vineyard. And they caught him, and beat him, and sent him away empty. And again he sent unto them another servant; and at him they cast stones, and wounded him in the head, and sent him away shamefully handled. And again he sent another; and him they killed, and many others; beating some, and killing some. Having yet therefore one son, his wellbeloved, he sent him also last unto them, saying, They will reverence my son. But those husbandmen said among themselves, This is the heir; come, let us kill him, and the inheritance shall be ours. And they took him, and killed him, and cast him out of the vineyard. What shall therefore the lord of the vineyard do? he will come and destroy the husbandmen, and will give the vineyard unto others. And have ye not read this scripture; The stone which the builders rejected is become the head of the corner: This was the Lord's doing, and it is marvellous in our eyes?

And they sought to lay hold on him, but feared the people: for they knew that he had spoken the parable against them: and they left him, and went their way.

## TUESDAY

JOHN 13:1–2, 31–38 (REB)

It was before the Passover festival, and Jesus knew that his hour had come and that he must leave this world and go to the Father. He had always loved his own who were in the world, and he loved them to the end.

When Judas had gone out, Jesus said, 'Now the Son of Man is glorified, and in him God is glorified. If God is glorified in him, God will also glorify him in himself; and he will glorify him now. My children, I am to be with you for a little longer; then you will look for me, and, as I told the Jews, I tell you now: where I am going you cannot come. I give you a new commandment: love one another; as I have loved you, so you are to love one another. If there is love among you, then everyone will know that you are my disciples.'

Simon Peter said to him, 'Lord, where are you going?' Jesus replied, 'I am going where you cannot follow me now, but one day you will.' Peter said, 'Lord, why cannot I follow you now? I will lay down my life for you.' Jesus answered, 'Will you really lay down your life for me? In very truth I tell you, before the cock crows you will have denied me three times.'

## WEDNESDAY

LUKE 23:13–25 (NJB)

Pilate then summoned the chief priests and the leading men and the people. He said to them, 'You brought this man before me as a popular agitator. Now I have gone into the matter myself in your presence and found no grounds in the man for any of the charges you bring against him. Nor has Herod either, since he has sent him back to us. As you can see, the man has done nothing that deserves death, so I shall have him flogged and then let him go. But as one man they howled, 'Away with him! Give us Barabbas!' (This man had been thrown into prison because of a riot in the city and murder.)

In his desire to set Jesus free, Pilate addressed them again, but they shouted back, 'Crucify him! Crucify him!' And for the third time he spoke to them, 'But what harm has this man done? I have found no case against him that deserves death, so I shall have him flogged and then let him go.' But they kept on shouting at the top of their voices, demanding that he should be crucified. And their shouts kept growing louder.

Pilate then gave his verdict: their demand was to be granted. He released the man they asked for, who had been imprisoned because of rioting and murder, and handed Jesus over to them to deal with as they pleased.

## THURSDAY

MARK 15:16–32 (NJB)

The soldiers led him away to the inner part of the palace, that is, the Praetorium, and called the whole cohort together. They dressed him up in purple, twisted some thorns into a crown and put it on him. And they began saluting him, 'Hail king of the Jews!' They struck his head with a reed and spat on him; and they went down on their knees to do him homage. And when they had finished making fun of him, they took off the purple and dressed him in his own clothes.

They led him out to crucify him. They enlisted a passer-by, Simon of Cyrene, father of Alexander and Rufus, who was coming in from the country, to carry his cross. They brought Jesus to the place called Golgotha, which means the place of the skull. They offered him wine mixed with myrrh, but he refused it. Then they crucified him, and shared out his clothing, casting lots to decide what each should get. It was the third hour when they crucified him. The inscription giving the charge against him read, 'The King of the Jews'. And they crucified two bandits with him, one on his right and one on his left.

The passers-by jeered at him; they shook their heads and said, 'Aha! So you would destroy the Temple and rebuild it in three days! Then save yourself; come down from the cross!' The chief priests and the scribes mocked him among themselves in the same way with the words, 'He saved others, he cannot save himself. Let the Christ, the king of Israel, come down from the cross now, for us to see it and believe.' Even those who were crucified with him taunted him.

## FRIDAY

JOHN 19:28–42 (REB)

After this, Jesus, aware that all had

now come to its appointed end, said in fulfilment of scripture, 'I am thirsty.' A jar stood there full of sour wine; so they soaked a sponge with the wine, fixed it on hyssop, and held it to his lips. Having received the wine, he said, 'It is accomplished!' Then he bowed his head and gave up his spirit.

Because it was the eve of the sabbath, the Jews were anxious that the bodies should not remain on the crosses, since that sabbath was a day of great solemnity; so they requested Pilate to have the legs broken and the bodies taken down.

The soldiers accordingly came to the men crucified with Jesus and broke the legs of each in turn, but when they came to Jesus and found he was already dead, they did not break his legs. But one of the soldiers thrust a lance into his side, and at once there was a flow of blood and water. This is vouched for by an eyewitness, whose evidence is to be trusted. He knows that he speaks the truth, so that you too may believe; for this happened in fulfilment of the text of scripture: 'No bone of his body shall be broken.' And another text says, 'They shall look on him whom they pierced.'

After that Joseph of Arimathaea, a disciple of Jesus, but a secret disciple for fear of the Jews, asked Pilate for permission to remove the body of Jesus. He consented; so Joseph came and removed the body. He was joined by Nicodemus (the man who had visited Jesus by night), who brought with him a mixture of myrrh and aloes, more than half a hundredweight. They took the body of Jesus and following Jewish burial customs they wrapped it, with the spices, in strips of linen cloth. Near the place where he had been crucified there was a garden, and in the garden a new tomb, not yet used for burial; and there, since it was the eve of the Jewish sabbath and the tomb was near at hand, they laid Jesus.

## SATURDAY

HEBREWS 9:23–28 (RSV)

Thus it was necessary for the copies of the heavenly things to be purified with these rites, but the heavenly things themselves with better sacrifices than these. For Christ has entered, not into a sanctuary made with hands, a copy of the true one, but into heaven itself, now to appear in the presence of God on our behalf. Nor was it to offer himself repeatedly, as the high priest enters the Holy Place yearly with blood not his own; for then he would have had to suffer repeatedly since the foundation of the world. But as it is, he has appeared once for all at the end of the age to put away sin by the sacrifice of himself. And just as it is appointed for men to die once, and after that comes judgment, so Christ, having been offered once to bear the sins of many, will appear a second time, not to deal with sin but to save those who are eagerly waiting for him.

WEEK 22

# THE HEALING WELCOME

Forgiveness is in the very heart of God. Psalm 103, our first reading this week, illustrates the profound nature of God's forgiveness. But elsewhere in the Old Testament we find there are some categories of sin and some people excluded from forgiveness. Not all could be 'ransomed, healed, restored, forgiven'.

With Jesus it is different. Very early in his public career, forgiveness comes to the forefront—totally unexpected and even before it was asked for (Monday). Later, Matthew's hospitality towards Jesus and a great many other guests shows unmistakably that 'Welcome' must be more than a word.

When Peter asks 'how often?' we should forgive, Jesus patiently teaches that forgiveness is not measurable, and that the forgiven must forgive (Tuesday). We have yet more to learn with the scribes and Pharisees, and with the guilty woman they hustle into Jesus' presence (Wednesday).

It may seem scandalous to some that forgiveness can be available simply on application—when there are no guarantees of future conduct or simply no opportunity for restitution or amendment (Thursday). But by the time the church was born by the Holy Spirit, its apostles soon discovered how to preach free forgiveness (Friday) and to set it down in writing (Saturday). The final extract from Paul's shortest surviving letter shows how forgiveness begins to dissolve the fetters of both slaves and masters.

# Forgiveness

WEEK 22

'One day I'll get my own back'; 'I've got an old score to settle'; 'Now we're quits'. These sayings take us into the heart of the idea of forgiveness. Forgiveness always implies two people—the offender and the offended. When someone has wronged someone else the balance of the relationship is upset. It can be restored in one of two ways. Either the offended person can 'repay' the wrong with a fresh offence, or he or she can clear the account by letting the matter go, refusing to keep resentment alive and making a fresh start in the relationship.

The Bible is clear that God is a forgiving God. Though human beings constantly offend against his law, if they show any desire to repent and turn away from their sin, divine forgiveness is instantaneous. The elaborate sacrificial system of the Old Testament made this basic point. It was always possible to 'return' to God and find, according to the root meaning of the original Hebrew words, that he had 'covered' or 'set loose' or 'carried away' the offence.

The New Testament shows a new way to forgiveness: through Jesus. He scandalized the respectable by declaring that the sins of a paralyzed man and 'a woman of the city' were forgiven. He prayed that his executioners might be forgiven even as they were crucifying him. He told the unforgettable story of a father who was rejected by his son but who welcomed and restored the son to his original status as soon as he returned home. Jesus' death was seen by the early Christians as the way in which humanity's sins could be forgiven. And it was in his name that his followers were to declare that God forgives those who repent.

The New Testament actually says as much about the Christian's duty to forgive as about God's forgiveness. Peter once asked how many times he should forgive his offending brother. Jesus' answer, 'seventy times seven', really means 'stop counting'. One translation of Paul's great passage on love has, 'Love keeps no score of wrongs'. Christians are to 'forgive as the Lord forgave' them. Jesus severely condemned the man who was let off an enormous debt but refused to forget the paltry sum which a neighbour owed him. In fact the Lord's Prayer connects being forgiven with our willingness to forgive. You can't have one without the other. Those who will not forgive can hardly repent. People who refuse to be 'all square' with their neighbour cannot expect to be 'all square' with God.

WEEK 22

## SUNDAY

PSALM 103:1-12 (AV)

Bless the Lord, O my soul:
and all that is within me, bless his holy name.
Bless the Lord, O my soul,
and forget not all his benefits:
Who forgiveth all thine iniquities;
who healeth all thy diseases;
Who redeemeth thy life from destruction;
who crowneth thee with loving kindness and tender mercies;
Who satisfieth thy mouth with food things;
so that thy youth is renewed like the eagle's.
The Lord executeth righteousness and judgement for all who are oppressed.
He made known his ways unto Moses,
his acts unto the children of Israel.
The Lord is merciful and gracious,
slow to anger, and plenteous in mercy.
He will not always chide:
neither will he keep his anger for ever.
He hath not dealt with us after our sins;
nor rewarded us according to our iniquities.
For as the heaven is high above the earth,
so great is his mercy toward them that fear him.
As far as the east is from the west,
so far hath he removed our transgressions from us.

## MONDAY

MATTHEW 9:2-13 (REB)

Some men appeared, bringing to Jesus a paralysed man on a bed. When he saw their faith Jesus said to the man, 'Take heart, my son; your sins are forgiven.' At this some of the scribes said to themselves, 'This man is blaspheming!' Jesus realized what they were thinking, and said, 'Why do you harbour evil thoughts? Is it easier to say, "Your sins are forgiven," or to say, "Stand up and walk"? But to convince you that the Son of Man has authority on earth to forgive sins'—he turned to the paralysed man—'stand up, take your bed, and go home.' And he got up and went off home. The people were filled with awe at the sight, and praised God for granting such authority to men.

As he went on from there Jesus saw a man named Matthew at his seat in the custom-house, and said to him, 'Follow me'; and Matthew rose and followed him.

When Jesus was having a meal in the house, many tax-collectors and sinners were seated with him and his disciples. Noticing this, the Pharisees said to his disciples, 'Why is it that your teacher eats with tax-collectors and sinners?' Hearing this he said, 'It is not the healthy who need a doctor, but the sick. Go and learn what this text means, "I require mercy, not sacrifice." I did not come to call the virtuous, but sinners.'

## TUESDAY

MATTHEW 18:21–35 (NJB)

Then Peter went up to Jesus and said, 'Lord, how often must I forgive my brother if he wrongs me? As often as seven times?' Jesus answered, 'Not seven, I tell you, but seventy-seven times.'

'And so the kingdom of Heaven may be compared to a king who decided to settle his accounts with his servants. When the reckoning began, they brought him a man who owed ten thousand talents; he had no means of paying, so his master gave orders that he should be sold, together with his wife and children and all his possessions, to meet the debt. At this, the servant threw himself down at his masters feet, with the words, "Be patient with me and I will pay the whole sum." And the servant's master felt so sorry for him that he let him go and cancelled the debt. Now as this servant went out, he happened to meet a fellow-servant who owed him one hundred denarii; and he seized him by the throat and began to throttle him, saying, "Pay what you owe me." His fellow-servant fell at his feet and appealed to him, saying, "Be patient with me and I will pay you." But the other would not agree; on the contrary, he had him thrown into prison till he should pay the debt. His fellow-servants were deeply distressed when they saw what had happened, and they went to their master and reported the whole affair to him. Then the master sent for the man and said to him, "You wicked servant, I cancelled all that debt of yours when you appealed to me. Were you not bound, then, to have pity on your fellow-servant just as I had pity on you?" And in his anger the master handed him over to the torturers till he should pay all his debt. And that is how my heavenly Father will deal with you unless you each forgive your brother from your heart.'

## WEDNESDAY

JOHN 8:2–11 (NJB)

At daybreak Jesus appeared in the Temple again; and as all the people came to him, he sat down and began to teach them.

The scribes and Pharisees brought a woman along who had been caught committing adultery; and making her stand there in the middle they said to Jesus, 'Master, this woman was caught in the very act of committing adultery, and in the Law Moses has ordered us to stone women of this kind. What have you got to say?' They asked him this as a test, looking for an accusation to use against him. But Jesus bent down and started writing on the ground with his finger. As they persisted with their question, he straightened up and said, 'Let the one among you who is guiltless be the first to throw a stone at her.' Then he bent down and continued writing on the ground. When they heard this they went away one by one, beginning with the eldest, until the last one had gone and Jesus was left alone with the woman, who remained in the middle. Jesus again straightened up and said, 'Woman, where are they? Has no one condemned you?' 'No one, sir,' she replied. 'Neither do I condemn you,' said Jesus. 'Go away, and from this moment sin no more.'

## THURSDAY

LUKE 23:38–43 (RSV)

There was also an inscription over Jesus, 'This is the King of the Jews.'

One of the criminals who were hanged railed at him, saying, 'Are you not the Christ? Save yourself and us!' But the other rebuked him, saying, 'Do you not fear God, since you are under the same sentence of condemnation? And we indeed justly; for we are receiving the due reward of our deeds; but this man has done nothing wrong.' And he said, 'Jesus, remember me when you come into your kingdom.' And he said to him, 'Truly, I say to you, today you will be with me in Paradise.'

## FRIDAY

ACTS 13:32–43 (RSV)

Paul continued, 'And we bring you the good news that what God promised to the fathers, this he has fulfilled to us their children by raising Jesus; as also it is written in the second psalm,

"Thou are my Son,
today I have begotten thee."

And as for the fact that he raised him from the dead, no more to return to corruption, he spoke in this way,

"I will give you the holy and sure
blessings of David."

Therefore he says also in another psalm,

"Thou wilt not let thy Holy One see
corruption."

For David, after he had served the counsel of God in his own generation, fell asleep, and was laid with his fathers, and saw corruption; but he whom God raised up saw no corruption. Let it be known to you therefore, brethren, that through this man forgiveness of sins is proclaimed to you, and by him every one that believes is freed from everything from which you could not be freed by the law of Moses. Beware, therefore, lest there come upon you what is said in the prophets:

"Behold, you scoffers, and wonder,
and perish;
for I do a deed in your days,
a deed you will never believe, if one
declares it to you."'

As they went out, the people begged that these things might be told them the next sabbath. And when the meeting of the synagogue broke up, many Jews and devout converts to Judaism followed Paul and Barnabas, who spoke to them and urged them to continue in the grace of God.

## SATURDAY

PHILEMON 1–3, 10–21 (NIV)

Paul, a prisoner of Christ Jesus, and Timothy our brother,

To Philemon our dear friend and fellow-worker, to Apphia our sister, to Archippus our fellow-soldier and to the church that meets in your home:

Grace to you and peace from God our Father and the Lord Jesus Christ.

I appeal to you for my son Onesimus,

who became my son while I was in chains. Formerly he was useful to you, but now he has become useful both to you and to me.

I am sending him—who is my very heart—back to you. I would have liked to keep him with me so that he could take your place in helping me while I am in chains for the gospel. But I did not want to do anything without your consent, so that any favour you do will be spontaneous and not forced. Perhaps the reason he was separated from you for a little while was that you might have him back for good—no longer as a slave, but better than a slave, as a dear brother. He is very dear to me but even dearer to you, both as a man and as a brother in the Lord.

So if you consider me a partner, welcome him as you would welcome me. If he has done you any wrong or owes you anything, charge it to me. I, Paul, am writing this with my own hand. I will pay it back—not to mention that you owe me your very self. I do wish, brother, that I may have some benefit from you in the Lord; refresh my heart in Christ. Confident of your obedience, I write to you, knowing that you will do even more than I ask.

WEEK 23

# THE UNFAILING GIFT

With the experience of a marriage and family broken and mended, Hosea the prophet was well equipped to convey the agonizing love of a parent for a wayward child (Sunday). All love begins with God, and another parent features in the well-known story of the 'prodigal' son in Monday's reading. We cannot 'freeze' that parable half way. The elder brother is important—he needs as much sensitivity as the younger, for love is not complete until it is shared by all.

Jesus not only repeated the Old Testament commands to love God and our neighbour, but he added that of loving our enemies also. The mark of his followers should be that they 'love one another' (Tuesday).

The apostles Paul and John (Wednesday and Friday) both point to the self-offering of Christ in his death on the cross as the supreme expression of God's love. We cannot truly grasp that 'God is love' without it. Thursday shows part of the context of the well-known passage from Paul's letter to the Corinthians. Paul aims to build up unity in a congregation too easily split by differences in public worship.

Saturday takes us back to Paul's letter to the Romans, for the magnificent conclusion to one of the greatest chapters in the whole Bible. Love may lead us through a catalogue of all-but-intolerable trials, but love will end as it began—in the eternal, unflinching purpose of a self-giving Father.

# Love

It is not exaggerating to say that love is a description of the whole Christian life.

◆ **First comes God's love for us**. In the Old Testament, God loves Israel and rescues her from slavery. Though this love may involve discipline and judgment, yet he has sworn never to give her up: 'Israel' is engraved on the palms of his hands. The people of Israel, for their part, are commanded to love God with all their powers, along with their brother-Israelites and the foreigners among them.

In the New Testament the fundamental fact is that God is Love, and that there is a richness of love within God. Jesus is the Father's 'beloved Son' and the Son loves the Father. Out of that love flows the divine love for mankind, which shows itself in the coming of Jesus and particularly in his death. 'God commends his love in that while we were still sinners Christ died for us.' 'God loved the world so much that he gave his only son.' The cross is an expression of God's love; in no way is it the action of a vindictive deity.

The life, death and resurrection of Jesus are part of one loving rescue operation. In fact, the apostle Paul speaks of Jesus loving us in a once-for-all, unrepeatable way. He is 'the Son of God who *loved* me (once, on a definite occasion) and gave himself for me.' In one of the great passages of triumph in the Bible, in Romans chapter 8 verses 37–39, Paul exults in the fact that nothing in all creation can separate him from the love of God in Christ.

◆ **Next comes our love for God**. The New Testament says rather less about this, perhaps simply because God's love comes first. But Jesus endorses the great commandment, 'You shall love the Lord your God . . .' And in John's Gospel he emphasizes that we show our love for God by obeying him. The Christian is called to a single-minded love that will cling to God in the face of the attractions of the world or even family ties. And Jesus restores Peter precisely by pressing the question whether he loves him 'more than these' (the other disciples).

◆ **Then there follows our love for other people**. Perhaps the most striking aspect of the Bible's teaching on love is that it is presented as a command. It is not primarily a matter of feeling or liking or talking. It has to do with the will. If love is commanded, then to love our brethren or our neighbour or even our enemy is not something which is up for negotiation. If it is commanded then it is possible.

This is likely to make most people feel inadequate. But the Bible stresses that our love for our fellows is in the way of a *response*. It is a response to the love of Jesus; we love because he first loved us. It is a response to the Spirit within us: he sheds the love of God abroad in our hearts. It is a response to our being united to Christ as branches are connected to the stem of a vine. Love is his fruit.

WEEK
23

Love is the mark of the church. The world is to know the disciples of Jesus not by their zeal or doctrinal purity but by the love they have for one another. Love has to be incarnated. Christian living is not a matter of working out an ethical system. There is always a specific person, here in front of you, in a concrete situation.

Love is the greatest of gifts. Paul sets love against cleverness, or even knowledge, if by that is meant something secret which only the select few can grasp. Love builds up where knowledge can puff up. Love is a matter of action. It shows itself in a thousand different forms—in hospitality, in greeting, in not being snobbish, in not keeping a score of wrongs, in weeping with those who weep, in encouraging, in giving up your 'rights', in speaking out, in working together, in seeking reconciliation. It is the 'more excellent way'.

## SUNDAY

HOSEA 11:1–4, 8–9 (RSV)

When Israel was a child, I loved him,
and out of Egypt I called my son.
The more I called them,
the more they went from me;
they kept sacrificing to the Baals,
and burning incense to idols.

Yet it was I who taught Ephraim to walk,
I took them up in my arms;
but they did not know that I healed them.
I led them with cords of compassion,
with the bands of love,
and I became to them as one
who eases the yoke on their jaws,
and I bent down to them and fed them.

How can I give you up, O Ephraim!
How can I hand you over, O Israel!
How can I make you like Admah!
How can I treat you like Zeboiim!
My heart recoils within me,
my compassion grows warm and tender.
I will not execute my fierce anger,
I will not again destroy Ephraim;
for I am God and not man,
the Holy One in your midst,
and I will not come to destroy.

## MONDAY

LUKE 15:11–32 (NIV)

Jesus continued: 'There was a man who had two sons. The younger one said to his father, "Father, give me my share of the estate." So he divided his property between them.

'Not long after that, the younger son got together all he had, set off for a distant country and there squandered his wealth in wild living. After he had spent everything, there was a severe famine in that whole country, and he began to be in need. So he went and hired himself to a citizen of that country, who sent him to his fields to feed pigs. He longed to fill his stomach with the pods that the pigs were eating, but no-one gave him anything.

'When he came to his senses, he said, "How many of my father's hired men have food to spare, and here I am starving to death! I will set out and go back to my father and say to him: Father, I have sinned against you. I am no longer worthy to be called your son; make me like one of your hired men." So he got up and went to his father.

'But while he was still a long way off, his father saw him and was filled with compassion for him; he ran to his son, threw his arms around him and kissed him.

'The son said to him "Father, I have sinned against heaven and against you. I am no longer worthy to be called your son."

'But the father said to his servants, "Quick! Bring the best robe and put it on him. Put a ring on his finger and sandals on his feet. Bring the fatted calf and kill it. Let's have a feast and celebrate. For this son of mine was dead and is alive again; he was lost and is found." So they began to celebrate.

'Meanwhile, the older son was in the field. When he came near the house, he heard music and dancing. So he called one of the servants and asked him what was going on. "Your brother has come," he replied, "and your father has killed the fattened calf because he has him back safe and sound."

'The older brother became angry and refused to go in. So his father went out and pleaded with him. But he answered his father, "Look! All these years I've been slaving for you and never disobeyed your orders. Yet you never gave me even a young goat so I could celebrate with my friends. But when this son of yours who has squandered your property with prostitutes comes home, you kill the fattened calf for him!"

' "My son," the father said, "you are always with me, and everything I have is yours. But we had to celebrate and be glad, because this brother of yours was dead and is alive again; he was lost and is found." '

## TUESDAY

JOHN 15:9–17 (NJB)

Jesus said to his disciples, 'I have loved you just as the Father has loved me. Remain in my love. If you keep my commandments you will remain in my love, just as I have kept my Father's commandments and remain in his love. I have told you this so that my own joy may be in you and your joy be complete. This is my commandment: love one another as I have loved you. No one can have greater love than to lay down his life for his friends. You are my friends, if you do what I command you. I shall no longer call you servants, because a servant does not know his master's business; I call you friends, because I have made known to you everything I have learnt from my Father. You did not choose me, no, I chose you; and I commissioned you to go out and to bear fruit, fruit that will last; so that the Father will give you anything you ask him in my name. My command to you is to love one another.'

## WEDNESDAY

ROMANS 5:1–8 (AV)

Therefore being justified by faith, we have peace with God through our Lord Jesus Christ: By whom also we have access by faith into this grace wherein we stand, and rejoice in hope of the glory of God. And not only so, but we glory in tribulations also: knowing that tribulation worketh patience; And patience, experience; and experience, hope: And hope maketh not ashamed; because the love of God is shed abroad in our hearts by the Holy Ghost which is given unto us. For when we were yet without strength, in due time Christ died for the ungodly. For scarcely for a righteous man will one die: yet peradventure for a good man some would even dare to die. But God commendeth his love toward us, in that, while we were yet sinners, Christ died for us.

## THURSDAY

1 CORINTHIANS 12:27–14:1 (RSV)

Now you are the body of Christ and individually members of it. And God has appointed in the church first apostles, second prophets, third teachers, then workers of miracles, then healers, helpers, administrators, speakers in various kinds of tongues. Are all apostles? Are all prophets? Are all teachers? Do all work miracles? Do all possess gifts of healing? Do all speak with tongues? Do all interpret? But earnestly desire the higher gifts.

And I will show you a still more excellent way.

If I speak in the tongues of men and of angels, but have not love, I am a noisy gong or a clanging cymbal. And if I have prophetic powers, and understand all mysteries and all knowledge, and if I have all faith, so as to remove mountains, but have not love, I am nothing. If I give away all I have, and if I deliver my body to be burned, but have not love, I gain nothing.

Love is patient and kind; love is not jealous or boastful; it is not arrogant or rude. Love does not insist on its own way; it is not irritable or resentful; it does not rejoice at wrong, but rejoices in the right. Love bears all things, believes all things, hopes all things, endures all things.

Love never ends; as for prophecies, they will pass away; as for tongues, they will cease; as for knowledge, it will pass away. For our knowledge is imperfect and our prophecy is imperfect; but when the perfect comes, the imperfect will pass away. When I was a child, I spoke like a child, I thought like a child, I reasoned like a child; when I became a man, I gave up childish ways. For now we see in a mirror dimly, but then face to face. Now I know in part; then I shall understand fully, even as I have been fully understood. So faith, hope, love abide, these three; but the greatest of these is love.

Make love your aim, and earnestly desire the spiritual gifts, especially that you may prophesy.

## FRIDAY

1 JOHN 4:7–21 (NIV)

Dear friends, let us love one another, for love comes from God. Everyone who loves has been born of God and knows God. Whoever does not love does not know God, because God is love. This is how God showed his love among us: He sent his one and only Son into the world that we might live through him. This is love: not that we loved God, but that he loved us and sent his Son as an atoning sacrifice for our sins. Dear friends, since God so loved us, we also ought to love one another. No-one has ever seen God; but if we love each other, God lives in us and his love is made complete in us.

We know that we live in him and he in us, because he has given us of his Spirit. And we have seen and testify that the Father has sent his Son to be the Saviour of the world. If anyone acknowledges that Jesus is the Son of God, God lives in him and he in God. And so we know and rely on the love God has for us.

God is love. Whoever lives in love

lives in God, and God in him. In this way, love is made complete among us so that we will have confidence on the day of judgment, because in this world we are like him. There is no fear in love. But perfect love drives out fear, because fear has to do with punishment. The man who fears is not made perfect in love.

We love because he first loved us. If anyone says, 'I love God,' yet hates his brother, he is a liar. For anyone who does not love his brother, whom he has seen, cannot love God, whom he has not seen. And he has given us this command: Whoever loves God must also love his brother.

## SATURDAY

ROMANS 8:28–39 (AV)

And we know that all things work together for good to them that love God, to them who are the called according to his purpose. For whom he did foreknow, he also did predestinate to be conformed to the image of his Son, that he might be the firstborn among many brethren. Moreover whom he did predestinate, them he also called: and whom he called, them he also glorified.

What shall we then say to these things? If God be for us, who can be against us? He that spared not his own Son, but delivered him up for us all, how shall he not with him also freely give us all things? Who shall lay any thing to the charge of God's elect? It is God that justifieth. Who is he that condemneth? It is Christ that died, yea rather, that is risen again, who is even at the right hand of God, who also maketh intercession for us. Who shall separate us from the love of Christ? shall tribulation, or distress, or persecution, or famine, or nakedness, or peril, or sword? As it is written, For thy sake we are killed all the day long; we are accounted as sheep for the slaughter. Nay, in all these things we are more than conquerors through him that loved us. For I am persuaded, that neither death, nor life, nor angels, nor principalities, nor powers, nor things present, nor things to come, nor height, nor depth, nor any other creature, shall be able to separate us from the love of God, which is Christ Jesus our Lord.

# SING A NEW SONG!

WEEK 24

The Bible rings with the sound of people worshipping God. Worship occurs as human beings offer their daily lives to God and, in the more specialized meaning, as God's people meet to sing and express that offering together.

So this week we join God's worshippers at some of the celebrations which characterize the praises of God's people. We start with one special offering on an Egyptian night of both terror and expectation—the Passover (Sunday). Some of our most precious worship comes from times of great danger.

The next reading finds God's people on the far side of the Red Sea. Now their worship is less tense and more exuberant. This song of God's victory has become a prototype for many thanksgivings for even greater deliverances (Monday).

We could call the Psalms Israel's hymnbook. Indeed, many of our own hymns and songs are based on psalms. Psalm 84 (Tuesday) finds that delight in God himself can equip us for journeys through barren places.

The two letters quoted on Wednesday find Paul pleading for a life of worship, as well as encouraging and guiding Christians in specific occasions of praise and learning. On Thursday we find him trying to regulate where this had got out of hand in the Corinthian church. He reminds them that it is important to build up and strengthen the church, and that love holds everything together.

Friday's letter to the Hebrews lifts the veil on the eternal dimension of worship while exorting Christians to stir one another up. And Saturday brings us through heaven's open door, where all creation's praises are heard and where the slain Lamb of God is the central focus of 'wonder, love and praise'.

WEEK 24

# Worship

To worship means 'to give God honour' and acknowledge his worth. When we worship, then, we are more or less saying to God: 'Thank you for all you have done for us and given us. Help us to put you first in our daily lives.'

The first Christians were Jews and used to worshipping the God of all creation. But so great was the impact of Jesus Christ on their lives that he turned upside down their understanding of worship, so that he himself became the centre of their worship, along with the Father and the Spirit. Prayer was offered in the name of Jesus and hymns sung in his honour. For example, the famous description of Christ in Paul's letter to the Philippians was almost certainly an early Christian hymn and one well known to Paul's readers. At their baptism, Christians declared 'Jesus is Lord' and so made clear the centrality of Jesus in worship.

The focal point of worship in the New Testament is the Lord's Supper or 'Eucharist' ('thanksgiving meal').

Worship is our response to what God has done and continues to do. But we must work out in our own culture just how worship is to be carried out, applying principles of New Testament insight.

◆ **Is worship to be formal or informal?** The church of the New Testament had no developed forms of ministry or worship. To judge from Paul's first letter to the Corinthian church, worship was largely improvised with a great deal of freedom of expression and with a vivid awareness of the presence of the Spirit in power. Paul's letter shows that he was not altogether happy with complete spontaneity which, instead of leading to real 'Spirit-freedom', resulted in bondage for many. He gently suggests some controls so that all the Christians might feel equally at home.

The Bible gives no norms for worship, which varied according to place and culture. And so surely we should be extremely careful about expressing judgments as to whether any particular style of worship is 'right' or 'wrong'. In our own day some prefer their worship to be offered with full and rich ceremonial—with choirs, processions, vestments and with other ritual forms. Others, however, like it plain with the minimum of fuss, with lots of participation, hearty singing and, perhaps, even with the raising of hands in adoration. Both styles are correct according to the needs of the worshippers, realizing that temperament and culture are important factors to be considered. Some cultures will want it 'high and hazy', other cultures 'low and lazy'. What is important is that our worship should be relevant to the congregation and its culture—otherwise it will not be authentic.

◆ **What importance have buildings?** Christianity began as a non-religious type of faith. Because Jesus had brought a complete salvation and opened the door to the Father, Christians had no need for the temple, a sacrificing priesthood or even religious buildings! Because the first Christians did not conform to contemporary religious ideas they were called 'atheists'! It is a sad irony today that people outside the church identify a congregation by a building rather than by a people.

Now buildings clearly help. To have a base, a home which the family may adapt to express a living faith and where others can be brought in is, of course, nothing but gain. But buildings can also become snares and hindrances. We may end up caring more for the building than the gospel and more for our traditions than the Lord of the traditions. We are called not to be museum-tenders but a people willing to share our faith in a living Lord.

◆ **What makes living worship?** Just as there are no hard and fast laws about the structure of worship, so there are no laws as to what must be included. Certain elements, however, stand out in New Testament church life and demand attention. The first Christians worshipped with grateful and joyful hearts. No one could accuse them of dullness! Paul writes: 'Sing psalms, hymns and sacred songs; sing to God with thanksgiving in your hearts.' Should not joy and praise be a fixed feature in our worship too?

Then again, receiving instruction in the faith appears to have been another important ingredient. This would account for the emphasis placed on teachers and prophets in the early church. Their role was to build up the congregation through their ministry. So today, a church which neglects instruction and sound learning will produce immature and weak Christians. Another element would have been prayers of intercession and confession.

But without any question, the pinnacle of praise and adoration would have been when the New Testament Christians broke bread together and celebrated their 'Eucharist'.

Let us note, finally, a refreshingly relaxed and unfussed air about the New Testament approach to worship. It was their love-response to Jesus, and love cannot be bound with rules and regulations.

WEEK 24

## SUNDAY

EXODUS 12:1–11, 14, 25–27 (REB)

The Lord said to Moses and Aaron in Egypt: 'This month is to be for you the first of the months; you are to make it the first month of the year. Say to the whole community of Israel: On the tenth day of this month let each man procure a lamb or kid for his family, one for each household, but if a household is too small for one lamb or kid, then, taking into account the number of persons, the man and his nearest neighbour may take one between them. They are to share the cost according to the amount each person eats. Your animal, taken either from the sheep or the goats, must be without blemish, a yearling male. Have it in safe keeping until the fourteenth day of this month, and then all the assembled community of Israel must slaughter the victims between dusk and dark. They must take some of the blood and smear it on the two doorposts and on the lintel of the houses in which they eat the victims. On that night they must eat the flesh roasted on the fire; they must eat it with unleavened bread and bitter herbs. You are not to eat any of it raw or even boiled in water, but roasted: head, shins, and entrails. You are not to leave any of it till morning; anything left over until morning must be destroyed by fire.

This is the way in which you are to eat it: have your belt fastened, sandals on your feet, and your staff in your hand, and you must eat in urgent haste. It is the Lord's Passover.'

'You are to keep this day as a day of remembrance, and make it a pilgrim-feast, a festival of the Lord; generation after generation you are to observe it as a statute for all time.'

'When you enter the land which the Lord will give you as he promised, you are to observe this rite. When your children ask you, "What is the meaning of this rite?" you must say, "It is the Lord's Passover, for he passed over the houses of the Israelites in Egypt when he struck the Egyptians and spared our houses." ' The people bowed low in worship.

## MONDAY

EXODUS 14:29–15:3, 15:20–21 (REB)

Meanwhile the Israelites had passed along the dry ground through the sea, with the water forming a wall for them to right and to left. That day the Lord saved Israel from the power of Egypt. When the Israelites saw the Egyptians lying dead on the seashore, and saw the great power which the Lord had put forth against Egypt, the people were in awe of the Lord and put their faith in him and in Moses his servant.

Then Moses and the Israelites sang this song to the Lord:

'I shall sing to the Lord, for he has
risen up in triumph;
horse and rider he has hurled
into the sea.
The Lord is my refuge and my
defence;
he has shown himself my
deliverer.
He is my God, and I shall glorify him;

my father's God, and I shall exalt
him.
The Lord is a warrior; the Lord is his
name.'

The prophetess Miriam, Aaron's sister, took up her tambourine, and all the women followed her, dancing to the sound of tambourines; and Miriam sang them this refrain:

'Sing to the Lord, for he has risen up
in triumph:
horse and rider he has hurled
into the sea.'

## TUESDAY

PSALM 84:1–12 (RSV)

How lovely is thy dwelling place,
O Lord of hosts!
My soul longs, yea, faints for the
courts of the Lord;
my heart and flesh sing for joy to
the living God.

Even the sparrow finds a home,
and the swallow a nest for
herself,
where she may lay her young,
at thy altars, O Lord of hosts,
my King and my God.
Blessed are those who dwell in thy
house,
ever singing thy praise!

Blessed are the men whose strength
is in thee,
in whose heart are the highways
to Zion.
As they go through the valley of
Baca
they make it a place of springs;
the early rain also covers it with
pools.
They go from strength to strength;
the God of gods will be seen in
Zion.

O Lord God of hosts, hear my
prayer;
give ear, O God of Jacob!
Behold our shield, O God;
look upon the face of thine anointed!

For a day in thy courts is better
than a thousand elsewhere.
I would rather be a doorkeeper in
the house of God
than dwell in the tents of wickedness.
For the Lord God is a sun and
shield;
he bestows favour and honour.
No good thing does the Lord withhold
from those who walk uprightly.
O Lord of hosts,
blessed is the man who trusts in
thee!

## WEDNESDAY

ROMANS 12:1–3 (REB)

Therefore, my friends, I implore you by God's mercy to offer your very selves to him: a living sacrifice, dedicated and fit for his acceptance, the worship offered by mind and heart. Conform no longer to the pattern of this present world, but be transformed by the renewal of your minds. Then you will be able to discern the will of God, and to know what is good, acceptable, and perfect.

By authority of the grace God has

given me I say to everyone among you: do not think too highly of yourself, but form a sober estimate based on the measure of faith that God has dealt to each of you.

COLOSSIANS 3:12–17 (REB)

Put on, then, garments that suit God's chosen and beloved people: compassion, kindness, humility, gentleness, patience. Be tolerant with one another and forgiving, if any of you has cause for complaint: you must forgive as the Lord forgave you. Finally, to bind everything together and complete the whole, there must be love. Let Christ's peace be arbiter in your decisions, the peace to which you were called as members of a single body. Always be thankful. Let the gospel of Christ dwell among you in all its richness; teach and instruct one another with all the wisdom it gives you. With psalms and hymns and spiritual songs, sing from the heart in gratitude to God. Let every word and action, everything you do, be in the name of the Lord Jesus, and give thanks through him to God the Father.

## THURSDAY

1 CORINTHIANS 14:13–19, 23–26 (NIV)

For this reason the man who speaks in a tongue should pray that he may interpret what he says. For if I pray in a tongue, my spirit prays, but my mind is unfruitful. So what shall I do? I will pray with my spirit, but I will also pray with my mind. If you are praising God with your spirit, how can one who finds himself among those who do not understand say 'Amen' to your thanksgiving, since he does not know what you are saying? You may be giving thanks well enough, but the other man is not edified.

I thank God that I speak in tongues more than all of you. But in the church I would rather speak five intelligible words to instruct others than ten thousand words in a tongue.

So if the whole church comes together and everyone speaks in tongues, and some who do not understand or some unbelievers come in, will they not say you are out of your mind? But if an unbeliever or someone who does not understand comes in while everybody is prophesying, he will be convinced by all that he is a sinner and will be judged by all, and the secrets of his heart will be laid bare. So he will fall down and worship God, exclaiming, 'God is really among you!'

What then shall we say, brothers? When you come together, everyone has a hymn, or a word of instruction, a revelation, a tongue or an interpretation. All of these must be done for the strengthening of the church.

## FRIDAY

HEBREWS 10:19–25, 12:25–29 (RSV)

Therefore, brethren, since we have confidence to enter the sanctuary by the blood of Jesus, by the new and living way which he opened for us through the curtain, that is, through his flesh, and since we have a great priest over the house of God, let us draw near with a true heart in full assurance of faith, with our hearts sprinkled clean from an evil conscience and our bodies washed with pure water. Let us hold fast the confession of our hope without wavering, for he who promised is faithful; and let us consider how to stir up one another to love and good works, not neglecting to meet together, as is the habit of some, but encouraging one another, and all the more as you see the Day drawing near.

See that you do not refuse him who is speaking. For if they did not escape when they refused him who warned them on earth, much less shall we escape if we reject him who warns from heaven. His voice then shook the earth; but now he has promised, 'Yet once more I will shake not only the earth but also the heaven.' This phrase, 'Yet once more,' indicates the removal of what is shaken, as of what has been made, in order that what cannot be shaken may remain. Therefore let us be grateful for receiving a kingdom that cannot be shaken, and thus let us offer to God acceptable worship, with reverence and awe; for our God is a consuming fire.

## SATURDAY

REVELATION 5:6–14 (AV)

And I beheld, and, lo, in the midst of the throne and of the four beasts, and in the midst of the elders, stood a Lamb as it had been slain, having seven horns and seven eyes, which are the seven Spirits of God sent forth into all the earth. And he came and took the book out of the right hand of him that sat upon the throne. And when he had taken the book, the four beasts and four and twenty elders fell down before the Lamb, having every one of them harps, and golden vials full of odours, which are the prayers of saints. And they sung a new song, saying, Thou art worthy to take the book, and to open the seals thereof: for thou wast slain, and hast redeemed us to God by thy blood out of every kindred, and tongue, and people, and nation; And hast made us unto our God kings and priests: and we shall reign on the earth.

And I beheld, and I heard the voice of many angels round about the throne and the beasts and the elders: and the number of them was ten thousand times ten thousand, and thousands of thousands; Saying with a loud voice, Worthy is the Lamb that was slain to receive power, and riches, and wisdom, and strength, and honour, and glory, and blessing. And every creature which is in heaven, and on the earth, and under the earth, and such as are in the sea, and all that are in them, heard I saying, Blessing, and honour, and glory, and power, be unto him that sitteth upon the throne, and unto the Lamb for ever and ever. And the four beasts said, Amen. And the four and twenty elders fell down and worshipped him that liveth for ever and ever.

# THE PROPHETS

The last great section of the Old Testament is known as The Prophets. The section consists of seventeen books, sixteen of which are called by the name of the prophet whose words they contain (the exception is Lamentations). Isaiah, Jeremiah, Ezekiel and Daniel are known as 'major prophets', and the other twelve named books as the 'minor prophets'.

There had been prophets in Israel since early times, Moses being the first and greatest. Then, through the period of the judges and early kings, prophets appear regularly in the story.

Apart from Moses, we know little of what these prophets taught. But during the eighth century first Amos and then Hosea delivered messages which were written down in books which survived. For more than 300 years a succession of such prophets appeared, covering the whole period up to the people's exile in Babylon, and on through that exile into the years after the Jews had returned home.

These prophets fall into seven groups, according to their setting in the history of Israel and Judah, and of their enemies, first Assyria then Babylon. (*See the panels round the map.*)

The Old Testament prophets certainly made accurate predictions—particularly about the coming Messiah. But the heart of the prophets' message was about the present, not the future. Their task was to call the nation back to God's ways and to faith in him alone. So it is important for us to understand a prophet's own times in order to grasp his meaning clearly. Once this is done, the message of the Old Testament prophets speaks powerfully to every age and culture.

**AMOS** and **HOSEA** condemned the sins of Israel, the northern kingdom, in the years before Samaria fell to the Assyrians (in 722BC).

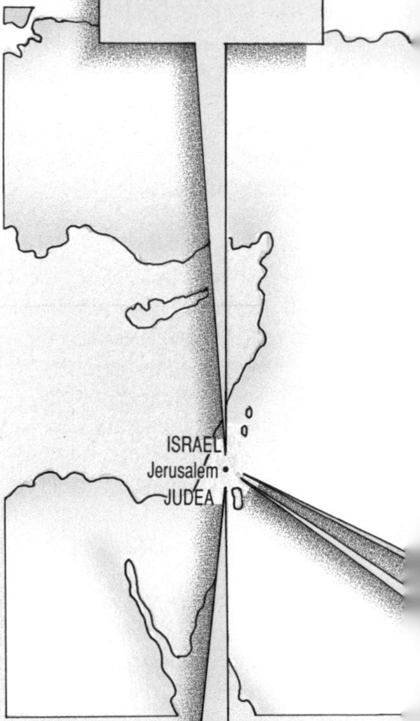

**OBADIAH** foretold doom for the Edomites after they took advantage at the time of Jerusalem's fall to Babylon (586BC).
The book of **LAMENTATIONS** records the suffering of the people left behind when many were taken into exile.

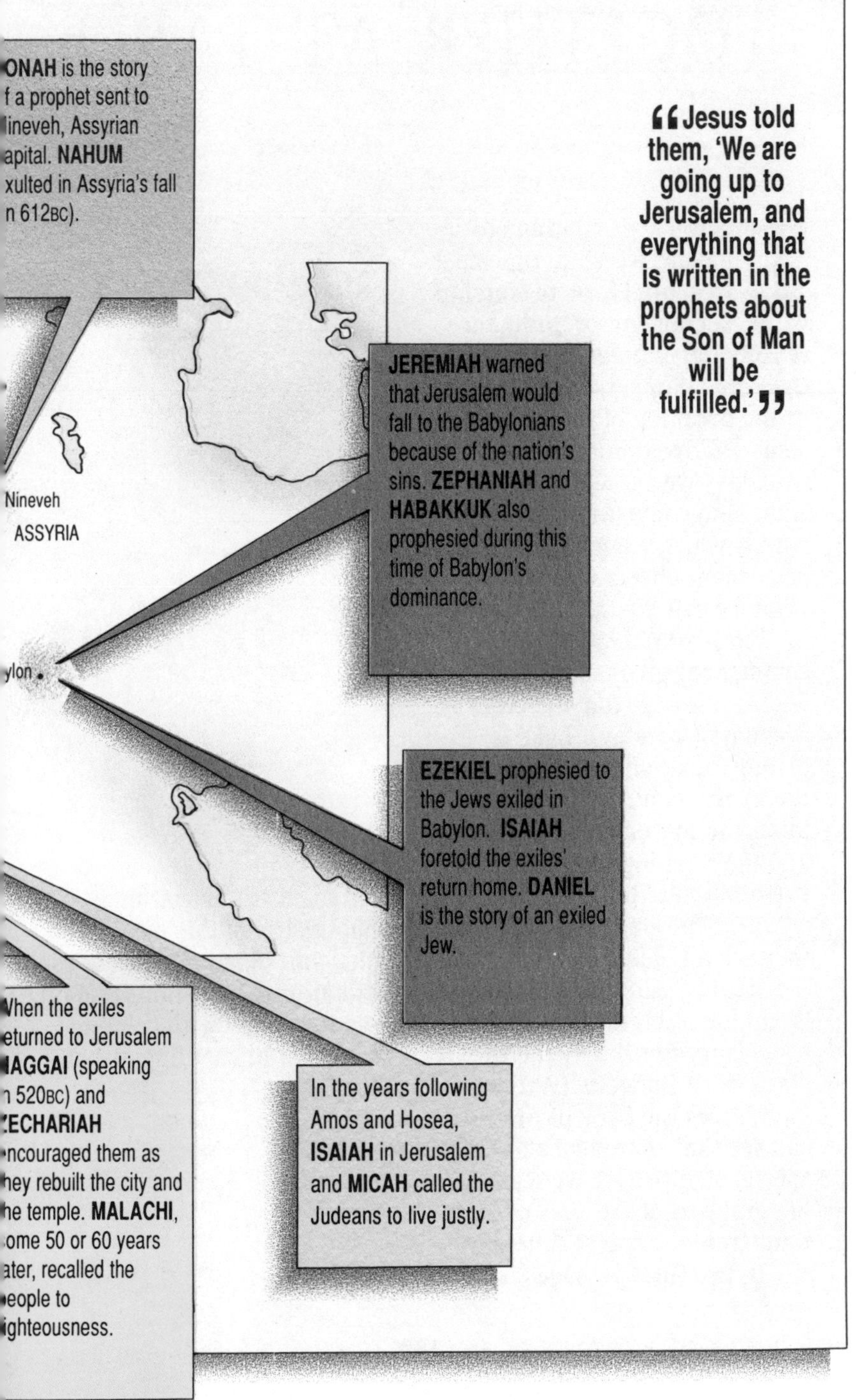
ONAH is the story
f a prophet sent to
ineveh, Assyrian
apital. NAHUM
xulted in Assyria's fall
n 612BC).
JEREMIAH warned
that Jerusalem would
fall to the Babylonians
because of the nation's
sins. ZEPHANIAH and
HABAKKUK also
prophesied during this
time of Babylon's
dominance.
Nineveh
ASSYRIA
ylon
EZEKIEL prophesied to
the Jews exiled in
Babylon. ISAIAH
foretold the exiles'
return home. DANIEL
is the story of an exiled
Jew.
Vhen the exiles
eturned to Jerusalem
IAGGAI (speaking
n 520BC) and
ECHARIAH
ncouraged them as
hey rebuilt the city and
he temple. MALACHI,
ome 50 or 60 years
ater, recalled the
eople to
ighteousness.
In the years following
Amos and Hosea,
ISAIAH in Jerusalem
and MICAH called the
Judeans to live justly.

**“Jesus told them, ‘We are going up to Jerusalem, and everything that is written in the prophets about the Son of Man will be fulfilled.’ ”**

WEEK 25

# TOGETHER AT TABLE

This week we continue to look at worship. One most treasured form of worship is the 'sacrament' or 'ordinance' of Holy Communion—otherwise the Lord's Supper, the Eucharist or the Breaking of Bread. When Jesus fed five thousand people (Sunday) we get a glimpse of what is to come. But the commands which made this meal a permanent observance came at what we call the Last Supper.

John (who omits the commands) gives some powerful details missing from the other accounts (Monday). Luke is among those who tell the story of the upper room, the friends at table, the shared bread and cup—and the startling words of explanation of Jesus' simple actions (Tuesday). From now on they are a reminder of his death.

It is at the following Sunday's 'breaking of bread' that the risen Jesus is recognized by the two disciples at Emmaus (Wednesday). From the book of Acts, we can see that shared meals with a special significance were an integral part of the lives of Christians from the start (Thursday).

In two final passages, Paul gives some strong warnings about misuse of this meal, since formal participation alone does not guarantee salvation (Friday), while treating it with contempt comes near to ensuring disaster (Saturday).

WEEK 25

# Breaking Bread

The central act of Christian worship is known by several titles—Communion; Lord's Supper; Eucharist (which means 'thanksgiving'); Mass (the Roman Catholic term). Whatever the name, it began as a meal, and that is easy to forget when all you receive is a piece of bread and a sip of wine. The modern communion probably started as believers ate together in each other's homes. Later it may have become formalized and linked with a 'love feast' and later still separated off as a distinct ritual. Whatever its origins, however, it will have carried more or less the same meanings for those who took part.

◆ **It was a meal of open invitation**. The original Eucharist was the last supper. Quite literally, it was the *last* supper of all the suppers and feasts which Jesus had held during his ministry. No one had been excluded from those meals. 'This man welcomes sinners and eats with them.' The Eucharist was the meal of a community where there was 'neither Jew nor Greek, male nor female, slave nor free'.

◆ **It was a meal of fellowship with Jesus himself**. The first Christians would certainly have been conscious of the presence of Jesus with them, however they expressed it. 'He was known to them in the breaking of the bread.' John tells the story of the feeding of the five thousand in a way which calls the Eucharist to mind. Those who took part were 'feeding on Jesus, the living bread'.

◆ **The Eucharist pointed people back to the death of Jesus**. It was not so much bread and wine which were important as bread broken like Christ's body on the cross and wine poured out like his blood. 'Do this,' was Jesus' command, 'to remember me.' The last supper was a Passover meal, and in the early days at least Christians would be reminded that both meals speak of being freed from slavery. Here was a new agreement with God, sealed and delivered in Jesus' blood.

◆ **The Eucharist was a meal of reconciliation and unity**. 'All of us, though many, are one body, for we all share the same loaf.' Those whom Christ invited to his feast should love one another and care for one another. The behaviour of the rich at Corinth was a scandalous denial of this. They ate their own food and got drunk while poorer Christians went hungry. But in doing this they despised the body of Christ. Again, Peter's refusal to eat with Gentiles at Antioch was seen, correctly, as a total contradiction of the fact that Jesus had broken down all social and racial barriers.

◆ **Those who took part in the Lord's supper declared themselves Christ's men and women**. This is why Paul roundly asserts, 'You cannot drink the cup of the Lord *and* the cup of demons.' In some ways the Eucharist was much more than a symbol. Some Corinthian Christians ate food which had been blessed in the pagan temple, but this was an act of idolatry if you took seriously the idea of sitting down to eat with Jesus.

- **The Eucharist looked forward to the coming of Jesus in triumph**. Jews would have been used to the idea of the messianic banquet—the great feast at the end of the age where the Messiah would be host. Many of Jesus' parables pick up this theme of a celebration meal. So, according to Paul, every Eucharist 'preaches the Lord's death *until he comes*'. It is 'the marriage supper of the Lamb'. Whenever Christians take communion they anticipate that glorious day.

## SUNDAY

MARK 6:34–43 (REB)

When Jesus came ashore and saw a large crowd, his heart went out to them, because they were like sheep without a shepherd; and he began to teach them many things. It was already getting late, and his disciples came to him and said, 'This is a remote place and it is already very late; send the people off to the farms and villages round about, to buy themselves something to eat.' 'Give them something to eat yourselves,' he answered. They replied, 'Are we to go and spend two hundred denarii to provide them with food?' 'How many loaves have you?' he asked. 'Go and see.' They found out and told him, 'Five, and two fish.' He ordered them to make the people sit down in groups on the green grass, and they sat down in rows, in companies of fifty and a hundred. Then, taking the five loaves and the two fish, he looked up to heaven, said the blessing, broke the loaves, and gave them to the disciples to distribute. He also divided the two fish among them. They all ate and were satisfied; and twelve baskets were filled with what was left of the bread and the fish.

## MONDAY

JOHN 13:2–16 (NJB)

They were at supper, and the devil had already put it into the mind of Judas Iscariot son of Simon, to betray him. Jesus knew that the Father had put everything into his hands, and that he had come from God and was returning to God, and he got up from table, removed his outer garments and, taking a towel, wrapped it round his waist; he then poured water into a basin and began to wash the disciples' feet and to wipe them with the towel he was wearing.

He came to Simon Peter, who said to him, 'Lord, are you going to wash my feet?' Jesus answered, 'At the moment you do not know what I am doing, but later you will understand.' 'Never!' said Peter, 'You shall never wash my feet.' Jesus replied, 'If I do not wash you, you can have no share with me.' Simon Peter said, 'Well then, Lord, not only my feet, but my hands and head as well!' Jesus said, 'No one who has had a bath needs washing, such a person is clean all over. You too are clean, though not all of you are.' He knew who was going to betray him, and that was why he said, 'though not all of you are.'

When he had washed their feet and put on his outer garments again he went back to the table. 'Do you understand', he said, 'what I have done to you? You call me Master and Lord, and rightly; so I am. If I then, the Lord and Master, have washed your feet, you must wash each other's feet. I have given you an example so that you may copy what I have done to you. 'In all truth I tell you, no servant is greater than his master, no messenger is greater than the one who sent him.'

## TUESDAY

LUKE 22:7–23 (RSV)

Then came the day of Unleavened Bread, on which the passover lamb had to be sacrificed. So Jesus sent Peter and John, saying, 'Go and prepare the passover for us, that we may eat it.' They said to him, 'Where will you have us prepare it?' He said to them, 'Behold, when you have entered the city, a man carrying a jar of water will meet you; follow him into the house which he enters, and tell the householder, "The Teacher says to you, Where is the guest room, where I am to eat the passover with my disciples?" And he will show you a large upper room furnished; there make ready.' And they went, and found it as he had told them; and they prepared the passover.

And when the hour came, he sat at table, and the apostles with him. And he said to them, 'I have earnestly desired to eat this passover with you before I suffer; for I tell you I shall not eat it until it is fulfilled in the kingdom of God.' And he took a cup, and when he had given thanks he said, 'Take this, and divide it among yourselves; for I tell you that from now on I shall not drink of the fruit of the vine until the kingdom of God comes.' And he took bread, and when he had given thanks he broke it and gave it to them, saying, 'This is my body which is given for you. Do this in remembrance of me.' And likewise the cup after supper, saying, 'This cup which is poured out for you is the new covenant in my blood. But behold the hand of him who betrays me is with me on the table. For the Son of man goes as it has been determined; but woe to that man by whom he is betrayed!' And they began to question one another, which of them it was that would do this.

## WEDNESDAY

LUKE 24:25–35 (RSV)

And Jesus said to them, 'O foolish men, and slow of heart to believe all that the prophets have spoken! Was it not necessary that the Christ should suffer these things and enter into his glory?' And beginning with Moses and all the prophets, he interpreted to them in all the scriptures the things concerning himself.

So they drew near to the village to which they were going. He appeared to be going further, but they constrained him, saying, 'Stay with us, for it is toward evening and the day is now far spent.' So he went in to stay with them. When he was at table with them, he took the bread and blessed, and broke it, and gave it to them. And their eyes were opened and they recognized him; and he vanished out of their sight. They said to each other, 'Did not our hearts burn within us when he talked to us on the road, while he opened to us the scriptures?' And they rose that same hour and returned to Jerusalem; and they found the eleven gathered together and those who were with them, who said, 'The Lord has risen indeed, and has appeared to Simon!' Then they told what had happened on the road, and how he was known to them in the breaking of the bread.

## THURSDAY

ACTS 2:42–47 (AV)

And they continued steadfastly in the apostles' doctrine and fellowship, and in breaking of bread, and in prayers. And fear came upon every soul: and many wonders and signs were done by the apostles. And all that believed were together, and had all things in common; And sold their possessions and goods, and parted them to all men, as every man had need. And they, continuing daily with one accord in the temple, and breaking bread from house to house, did eat their meat with gladness and singleness of heart, praising God, and having favour with all the people. And the Lord added to the church daily such as should be saved.

## FRIDAY

1 CORINTHIANS 10:1–5, 11–17 (NIV)

For I do not want you to be ignorant of the fact, brothers, that our forefathers were all under the cloud and that they all passed through the sea. They were all baptized into Moses in the cloud and in the sea. They all ate the same spiritual food and drank the same spiritual drink; for they drank from the spiritual rock that accompanied them, and that rock was Christ. Nevertheless, God was not pleased with most of them; their bodies were scattered over the desert.

These things happened to them as examples and were written down as warnings for us, on whom the fulfilment of the ages has come. So, if you think you are standing firm, be careful that you don't fall! No temptation has seized you except what is common to man. And God is faithful; he will not let you be tempted beyond what you can bear. But when you are tempted, he will also provide a way out so that you can stand up under it.

Therefore, my dear friends, flee from idolatry. I speak to sensible people; judge for yourselves what I say. Is not the cup of thanksgiving for which we give thanks a participation in the blood of Christ? And is not the bread that we break a participation in the body of Christ? Because there is one loaf, we, who are many, are one body, for we all partake of the one loaf.

## SATURDAY

1 CORINTHIANS 11:17–22, 27–34 (NIV)

In the following directives I have no praise for you, for your meetings do more harm than good. In the first place, I hear that when you come together as a church, there are divisions among you, and to some extent I believe it. No doubt there have to be differences among you to show which of you have God's approval. When you come together, it is not the Lord's Supper you eat, for as you eat, each of you goes ahead without waiting for anybody else. One remains hungry, another gets drunk. Don't you have homes to eat and drink in? Or do you despise the church of God and humiliate those who have nothing? What shall I say to you? Shall I praise you for this? Certainly not!

Therefore, whoever eats the bread or drinks the cup of the Lord in an unworthy manner will be guilty of sinning against the body and blood of the Lord. A man ought to examine himself before he eats of the bread and drinks of the cup. For anyone who eats and drinks without recognizing the body of the Lord eats and drinks judgment on himself. That is why many among you are weak and sick, and a number of you have fallen asleep. But if we judged ourselves, we would not come under judgment. When we are judged by the Lord, we are being disciplined so that we will not be condemned with the world.

So then, my brothers, when you come together to eat, wait for each other. If anyone is hungry, he should eat at home, so that when you meet together it may not result in judgment.

# THE UNFORGETTABLE MORNING

WEEK 26

The first Christians were witnesses to Jesus' resurrection. On this truth their faith rested; and they argued their case from their own first-hand experience. Indeed, part of their testimony went back to Jesus' words at the start of his ministry, when he hinted at what was to come (Sunday), although at that time his followers were unable to grasp the truth.

The raising of Lazarus was sensational enough (Monday) but the words Jesus spoke preceding it are even more far-reaching: 'I am the resurrection and the life'.

Tuesday's reading from Mark's Gospel brings us what may well be the first written account of the Sunday morning after the Friday of Jesus' death—ending suddenly and with understandable fear. John's careful description of events (Wednesday and Thursday), like the other reports, highlights the role of women as witnesses. As evidence given by a woman was not considered valid at that time, a Jewish author with a point to prove would hardly invent this scene.

Later, the apostle Paul sets out not simply the evidence but what it means and where it leads us (Friday). John in Revelation (Saturday) encounters the risen Lord in his vision, and passes on Jesus' messages to the churches, of which Smyrna's is the most full of joy and praise.

WEEK 26

# Raised from Death

The ancient Easter greeting puts it in a nutshell: 'The Lord is risen'; 'He is risen indeed.' Without the fact of the resurrection, the cross would have been an unmitigated disaster. If Christ did not rise from death, then the Christian faith is vain and Jesus becomes one more might-have-been.

The resurrection stories stress the importance of witnesses. The disciples saw an empty tomb, a stone rolled aside, graveclothes. They also met Jesus—in an upper room, by the lakeside, on the road, in a garden. The narratives do not seem to make any distinction between the two sets of experiences. The resurrection is presented as a fact, as something which happened, independently of anyone's inner feelings. Does this mean the tomb was empty? No one supposed that an empty tomb proved the resurrection, of course. And 'resurrection' involves more than a dead body come back to life. But matter still matters. 'Resurrection' in a New Testament sense will not allow the bones of Jesus to be in the tomb at the same time as the disciples were experiencing the 'resurrection appearances'.

In fact you can see the Gospel writers struggling with this problem. They are sure that they have met the same Jesus whom they knew before his death. He is not a ghost, his body bears the marks of crucifixion, he even eats broiled fish and cooks breakfast. But they are equally sure that he is not just the same Jesus, a kind of super-Lazarus, come back to life but doomed to die again in time. Sometimes they seem not to be able to recognize him until the penny drops; he stands in their midst although the doors have been locked. We are meant to conclude that Jesus has passed beyond death, into another kind of existence in which his body has been transformed.

This gives us a clue to the meaning of the resurrection. For the first-century Jew, resurrection could only mean the end of the age and the dawning of a new world. Resurrections do not happen inside history; they put an end to history. And Christians realized that something literally epoch-making had occurred. From now on, time could be split in two, with Jesus at the mid-point.

The resurrection has something to say, therefore, about the past, the present and the future.

- **Looking back, the resurrection set the seal on the ministry of Jesus**. His life was given an authoritative interpretation. People might ask, 'Did he teach the truth? Was he who he said he was?' The resurrection answered the questions with a resounding 'yes'. Above everything else it forced the inquirer to make sense of a death which otherwise was no more than another Roman execution.
- **The resurrection affects the present also, because the Christ who rose is still alive today**. Christians are risen with Christ. Many of the resurrection stories have a meaning for now as well as for then. Of course, they are about the first disciples. But they are also about Christians today, who can

still walk with Christ on the road to Emmaus, know him in the breaking of bread, be addressed in their grief (as Mary was), in their doubt (like Thomas) or their remorse (like Peter by the lakeside). The resurrection is the guarantee that nothing can separate us from his love.

◆ **And the resurrection looks on into the future, as Paul shows in his idea of the 'firstfruits'.** Jesus is the first of a great harvest. Because Jesus conquered death everyone in Christ will be made alive. This truth underpinned Paul's life-work. No one could say to him, 'Life is pointless. We are all doomed to die. Whatever you do will be lost and utterly forgotten.' Paul would have retorted that because Jesus Christ had risen, and because Christians would one day rise, nothing done 'in the Lord' could ever be in vain.

WEEK 26

## SUNDAY

JOHN 2:13–22 (REB)

As it was near the time of the Jewish Passover, Jesus went up to Jerusalem. In the temple precincts he found the dealers in cattle, sheep, and pigeons, and the money-changers seated at their tables. He made a whip of cords and drove them out of the temple, sheep, cattle, and all. He upset the tables of the money-changers, scattering their coins. Then he turned on the dealers in pigeons: 'Take them out of here,' he said; 'do not turn my Father's house into a market.' His disciples recalled the words of scripture: 'Zeal for your house will consume me.' The Jews challenged Jesus: 'What sign can you show to justify your action?' 'Destroy this temple,' Jesus replied, 'and in three days I will raise it up again.' The Jews said, 'It has taken forty-six years to build this temple. Are you going to raise it up again in three days?' But the temple he was speaking of was his body. After his resurrection his disciples recalled what he had said, and they believed the scripture and the words that Jesus had spoken.

## MONDAY

JOHN 11:21–27, 38–44 (REB)

Martha said to Jesus, 'Lord, if you had been here my brother would not have died. Even now I know that God will grant you whatever you ask of him.' Jesus said, 'Your brother will rise again.' 'I know that he will rise again', said Martha, 'at the resurrection on the last day.' Jesus said, 'I am the resurrection and the life. Whoever has faith in me shall live, even though he dies; and no one who lives and has faith in me shall ever die. Do you believe this? 'I do, Lord,' she answered; 'I believe that you are the Messiah, the Son of God who was to come into the world.'

Jesus, again deeply moved, went to the tomb. It was a cave, with a stone placed against it. Jesus said, 'Take away the stone.' Martha, the dead man's sister, said to him, 'Sir, by now there will be a stench; he has been there four days.' Jesus said, 'Did I not tell you that if you have faith you will see the glory of God?' Then they removed the stone.

Jesus looked upwards and said, 'Father, I thank you for hearing me. I know that you always hear me, but I have spoken for the sake of the people standing round, that they may believe it was you who sent me.' Then he raised his voice in a great cry: 'Lazarus, come out.' The dead man came out, his hands and feet bound with linen bandages, his face wrapped in a cloth. Jesus said, 'Loose him; let him go.'

## TUESDAY

MARK 16:1–8 (NIV)

When the Sabbath was over, Mary Magdalene, Mary the mother of James, and Salome bought spices so that they might go to anoint Jesus' body. Very early on the first day of the week, just after sunrise, they were on their way to the tomb and they asked each other, 'Who will roll the stone away from the entrance of the tomb?'

But when they looked up, they saw that the stone, which was very large, had been rolled away. As they entered the tomb, they saw a young man dressed in a white robe sitting on the right side, and they were alarmed.

'Don't be alarmed,' he said. 'You are looking for Jesus the Nazarene, who was crucified. He has risen! He is not here. See the place where they laid him. But go, tell his disciples and Peter, "He is going ahead of you into Galilee. There you will see him, just as he told you."'

Trembling and bewildered, the women went out and fled from the tomb. They said nothing to anyone, because they were afraid.

## WEDNESDAY

JOHN 20:1–9 (RSV)

Now on the first day of the week Mary Magdalene came to the tomb early, while it was still dark, and saw that the stone had been taken away from the tomb. So she ran, and went to Simon Peter and the other disciple, the one whom Jesus loved, and said to them, 'They have taken the Lord out of the tomb, and we do not know where they have laid him.' Peter then came out with the other disciple, and they went toward the tomb. They both ran, but the other disciple outran Peter and reached the tomb first; and stooping to look in, he saw the linen cloths lying there, but he did not go in. Then Simon Peter came, following him, and went into the tomb; he saw the linen cloths lying, and the napkin, which had been on his head, not lying with the linen cloths but rolled up in a place by itself. Then the other disciple, who reached the tomb first, also went in, and he saw and believed; for as yet they did not know the scripture, that he must rise from the dead.

## THURSDAY

JOHN 20:10–23 (RSV)

Then the disciples went back to their homes.

But Mary stood weeping outside the tomb, and as she wept she stooped to look into the tomb; and she saw two angels in white, sitting where the body of Jesus had lain, one at the head and one at the feet. They said to her, 'Woman, why are you weeping?' She said to them, 'Because they have taken away my Lord, and I do not know where they have lain him.' Saying this, she turned round and saw Jesus standing, but she did not know it was Jesus. Jesus said to her, 'Woman, why are you weeping? Whom do you seek?' Supposing him to be the gardener, she said to him, 'Sir, if you have carried him away, tell me where you have laid him, and I will take him away.' Jesus said to her, 'Mary.' She turned and said to him in Hebrew, 'Rabboni!' (which means Teacher). Jesus said to her, 'Do not hold me, for I have not yet ascended to the Father; but go to my brethren and say to them, I am ascending to my Father and your Father, to my God and your God.' Mary Magdalene went and said to the disciples, 'I have see the Lord'; and she told them that he had said these things to her.

On the evening of that day, the first day of the week, the doors being shut where the disciples were, for fear of the Jews, Jesus came and stood among them and said to them, 'Peace be with you.' When he had said this, he showed them his hands and his side. Then the disciples were glad when they saw the Lord. Jesus said to them again, 'Peace be with you. As the Father has sent me, even so I send you.' And when he had said this, he breathed on them, and said to them, 'Receive the Holy Spirit. If you forgive the sins of any, they are forgiven; if you retain the sins of any, they are retained.'

## FRIDAY

1 CORINTHIANS 15:1–8, 12–20 (AV)

Moreover, brethren, I declare unto you the gospel which I preached unto you, which also ye have received, and wherein ye stand; By which also ye are saved, if ye keep in memory what I preached unto you, unless ye have believed in vain. For I delivered unto you first of all that which I also received, how that Christ died for our sins according to the scriptures; And that he was buried, and that he rose again the third day according to the scriptures: And that he was seen of Cephas, then of the twelve: After that, he was seen of above five hundred brethren at once; of whom the greater part remain unto this present, but some are fallen asleep. After that, he was seen of James; then of all the apostles. And last of all he was seen of me also, as of one born out of due time.

Now if Christ be preached that he rose from the dead, how say some among you that there is no resurrection of the dead? But if there be no resurrection of the dead, then is Christ not risen: And if Christ be not risen, then is our preaching in vain, and your faith is also vain. Yea, and we are found false witnesses of God; because we have testified of God that he raised up Christ: whom he raised not up, if so be that the dead rise not. For if the dead rise not, then is not Christ raised: And if Christ be not raised, your faith is vain; ye are yet in your sins. Then they also which are fallen asleep in Christ are perished. If in this life only we have hope in Christ, we are of all men most miserable. But now is Christ risen from the dead, and become the firstfruits of them that slept.

## SATURDAY

REVELATION 1:12–20, 2:8–11 (NJB)

I turned round to see who was speaking to me, and when I turned I saw seven golden lamp-stands and, in the middle of them, one like a Son of man, dressed in a long robe tied at the waist with a belt of gold. His head and his hair were white with the whiteness of wool, like snow, his eyes like a burning flame, his feet like burnished bronze when it has been refined in a furnace, and his voice like the sound of the ocean. In his right hand he was holding seven stars, out of his mouth came a sharp sword, double-edged, and his face was like the sun shining with all its force.

When I saw him, I fell at his feet as though dead, but he laid his right hand on me and said, 'Do not be afraid; it is I, the First and the Last; I am the Living One, I was dead and look—I am alive for ever and ever, and I hold the keys of death and of Hades. Now write down all that you see of present happenings and what is still to come. The secret of the seven stars you have seen in my right hand, and of the seven golden lamp-stands, is this: the seven stars are the angels of the seven churches, and the seven lamp-stands are the seven churches themselves.'

Write to the angel of the church in Smyrna and say, 'Here is the message of the First and the Last, who was dead and has come to life again: I know your hardships and your poverty, and—though you are rich—the slander of the people who falsely claim to be Jews but are really members of the synagogue of Satan. Do not be afraid of the sufferings that are coming to you. Look, the devil will send some of you to prison to put you to the test, and you must face hardship for ten days. Even if you have to die, keep faithful, and I will give you the crown of life for your prize. Let anyone who can hear, listen to what the Spirit is saying to the churches: for those who prove victorious will come to no harm from the second death.'

WEEK 27

# CORONATION DAY

Jesus' entry into this world, and his exit from it—the ascension—have a powerful significance. But this significance would hardly have been apparent to anyone joining the very few people present on either occasion. This week we look at some of the Bible passages relating to Jesus' ascension.

The two Psalms which start this week (Sunday and Monday) may seem remote from the quiet hilltop of 'Ascension Day'. But Psalm 24 vividly presents the arrival of the King of glory, and Psalm 68 celebrates God's triumph in words specifically applied to Jesus by the New Testament.

We read in John's Gospel (Tuesday), how Jesus prepares his disciples for his departure, and the ending of Mark's Gospel, though it may not be part of the original gospel text, reflects early traditions about the actual event.

Luke's account of the ascension, recorded in Acts (Thursday), is the classic account, and what comes over strongly is the promised arrival of the Holy Spirit, and the world-wide, missionary commitment which will follow.

Extracts from three New Testament letters on Friday and Saturday all interpret the physical departure of Christ, drawing out its consequences for our forgiveness, faith, prayer and worship.

# The Ascension

When Jesus, his resurrection appearances complete, 'ascended' out of his disciples' sight, he 'returned home' to his Father. One of the greatest spectacles of the ancient world was when a general who had won a major victory returned home with the spoils of war, his defeated enemies trailing behind. Ringing in his ears would be the praises of his people. Paul wrote of Jesus' ascension: 'When he ascended on high he led captivity captive and gave gifts to men.' Jesus returned home in triumph, sin and death conquered through his death and resurrection.

The ascension, then, was a most important event, full of meaning for us today. **It reminds us that Jesus is our risen Lord, our reigning King, and our eternal High Priest.**

- **Risen Lord.** Peter on the Day of Pentecost preaches, 'This Jesus . . . God has made Lord and Christ.' That is, the resurrection has vindicated the claims Jesus made to be Son of God. He is head of his people, and he pours out the gifts of his Spirit on them. In the verse already quoted—adapting a sentence from the Psalms—Paul makes the moment of Jesus' ascension the point when the church was ready to receive the Spirit, when he 'gave gifts to men'. Risen and ascended, Jesus now makes available to us his power and victory.
- **Reigning King.** The day of his ascension was Jesus' coronation day. As victor over the powers of evil, he returned to his Father, and now he shares the throne of God. All authority is given to him in heaven and earth. He reigns as King over all those who now call him Lord, and one day he will reign over the whole of creation when he comes in power and glory. But he does not reign alone. To quote the apostle Paul again, 'We have been raised with Christ.'
- **Eternal High Priest.** It is in the letter to the Hebrews that the theme of Jesus as high priest is most clearly expressed. In the Old Testament the high priest came before God bearing the blood of a sacrifice, thus claiming God's forgiveness for the people. Jesus came before his Father claiming the sacrifice of his own life, a sacrifice which need never be repeated. Because of what he achieved, we can 'enter with boldness into the holy place'. Jesus Christ is now our High Priest, our Mediator with God. Through him we offer our sacrifices of praise and thanksgiving to God, and through him we receive God's salvation and blessing.

We can see, then, that the doctrine of the ascension carries deep significance for Christians which affects our daily living. It tells us that Jesus is Lord of our lives. But it also brings it home to us that he is our eternal High Priest whose gift of life is full, free and final.

No wonder the New Testament Christians lived such triumphant lives. They were aware that Christ's victory was their victory, and they lived as though it was!

WEEK 27

## SUNDAY

PSALM 24:1–10 (NIV)

The earth is the Lord's, and everything in it,
the world, and all who live in it;
for he founded it upon the seas
and established it upon the waters.

Who may ascend the hill of the Lord?
Who may stand in his holy place?
He who has clean hands and a pure heart,
who does not lift up his soul to an idol
or swear by what is false.
He will receive blessing from the Lord
and vindication from God his Saviour.
Such is the generation of those who seek him,
who seek your face, O God of Jacob.

Lift up your heads, O you gates;
be lifted up, you ancient doors,
that the King of glory may come in.
Who is this King of glory?
The Lord strong and mighty,
the Lord mighty in battle.
Lift up your heads, O you gates;
lift them up, you ancient doors,
that the King of glory may come in.
Who is he, this King of glory?
The Lord Almighty—
he is the King of glory.

## MONDAY

PSALM 68:1–4, 18–21, 32–35 (NIV)

May God arise, may his enemies be scattered;
may his foes flee before him.
As smoke is blown away by the wind,
may you blow them away;
as wax melts before the fire,
may the wicked perish before God.
But may the righteous be glad
and rejoice before God;
may they be happy and joyful.

Sing to God, sing praise to his name,
extol him who rides on the clouds—
his name is the Lord—
and rejoice before him.

When you ascended on high,
you led captives in your train;
you received gifts from men,
even from the rebellious—
that you, O Lord God, might dwell there.

Praise be to the Lord, to God our Saviour,
who daily bears our burdens.
Our God is a God who saves;
from the Sovereign Lord comes escape from death.

Surely God will crush the heads of his enemies,
the hairy crowns of those who go on in their sins.

Sing to God, O kingdoms of the earth,
sing praise to the Lord,
to him who rides the ancient skies above,
who thunders with mighty voice.

Proclaim the power of God,
whose majesty is over Israel,
whose power is in the skies.
You are awesome, O God, in your sanctuary;
the God of Israel gives power and strength to his people.

Praise be to God!

## TUESDAY

JOHN 14:1–6, 16:25–28 (AV)

Jesus said, 'Let not your heart be troubled: ye believe in God, believe also in me. In my Father's house are many mansions: if it were not so, I would have told you. I go to prepare a place for you. And if I go and prepare a place for you, I will come again, and receive you unto myself; that where I am, there ye may be also. And whither I go ye know, and the way ye know.' Thomas saith unto him, 'Lord, we know not whither thou goest; and how can we know the way?' Jesus saith unto him, 'I am the way, the truth, and the life; no man cometh unto the Father, but by me.'

'These things have I spoken unto you in proverbs: but the time cometh, when I shall no more speak unto you in proverbs, but I shall shew you plainly of the Father. At that day ye shall ask in my name: and I say not unto you, that I will pray the Father for you: For the Father himself loveth you, because ye have loved me, and have believed that I came out from God. I came forth from the Father, and am come into the world: again, I leave the world, and go to the Father.'

## WEDNESDAY

MARK 16:12–20 (AV)

After that Jesus appeared in another form unto two of them, as they walked, and went into the country. And they went and told it unto the residue: neither believed they them.

Afterwards he appeared unto the eleven as they sat at meat, and upbraided them with their unbelief and hardness of heart, because they believed not them which had seen him after he was risen. And he said unto them, Go ye into all the world, and preach the gospel to every creature. He that believeth and is baptized shall be saved; but he that believeth not shall be damned. And these signs shall follow them that believe; In my name shall they cast out devils; they shall speak with new tongues; They shall take up serpents; and if they drink any deadly thing, it shall not hurt them; they shall lay hands on the sick, and they shall recover.

So then after the Lord had spoken unto them, he was received up into heaven, and sat on the right hand of God. And they went forth, and preached every where, the Lord working with them, and confirming the word with signs following. Amen.

## THURSDAY

ACTS 1:1–11 (RSV)

In the first book, O Theophilus, I have dealt with all that Jesus began to do and teach, until the day when he was taken up, after he had given commandment through the Holy Spirit to the apostles whom he had chosen. To them he presented himself alive after his passion by many proofs, appearing to them during forty days, and speaking of the kingdom of God. And while staying with them he charged them not to depart from Jerusalem, but to wait for the promise of the Father, which, he said, 'you heard from me, for John baptized with water, but before many days you shall be baptized with the Holy Spirit.'

So when they had come together, they asked him, 'Lord, will you at this time restore the kingdom to Israel?' He said to them, 'It is not for you to know times or seasons which the Father has fixed by his own authority. But you shall receive power when the Holy Spirit has come upon you; and you shall be my witnesses in Jerusalem and in all Judea and Samaria and to the end of the earth.' And when he had said this, as they were looking on, he was lifted up, and a cloud took him out of their sight. And while they were gazing into heaven as he went, behold, two men stood by them in white robes, and said, 'Men of Galilee, why do you stand looking into heaven? This Jesus, who was taken up from you into heaven, will come in the same way as you saw him go into heaven.'

## FRIDAY

EPHESIANS 1:15–23 (NJB)

That is why I, having once heard about your faith in the Lord Jesus, and your love for all God's holy people, have never failed to thank God for you and to remember you in my prayers. May the God of our Lord Jesus Christ, the Father of glory, give you a spirit of wisdom and perception of what is revealed, to bring you to full knowledge of him. May he enlighten the eyes of your mind so that you can see what hope his call holds for you, how rich is the glory of the heritage he offers among his holy people, and how extraordinarily great is the power that he has exercised for us believers; this accords with the strength of his power at work in Christ, the power which he exercised in raising him from the dead and enthroning him at his right hand, in heaven, far above every principality, ruling force, power or sovereignty, or any other name that can be named, not only in this age but also in the age to come. He has put all things under his feet, and made him, as he is above all things, the head of the Church; which is his Body, the fullness of him who is filled, all in all.

COLOSSIANS 3:1–3 (NJB)

Since you have been raised up to be with Christ, you must look for the things that are above, where Christ is, sitting at God's right hand. Let your thoughts be on things above, not on the things that are on the earth, because you have died, and now the life you have is hidden with Christ in God. But when Christ is revealed—and he is your life—you, too, will be revealed with him in glory.

## SATURDAY

HEBREWS 4:12–16, 7:23–8:2 (NJB)

The word of God is something alive and active: it cuts more incisively than any two-edged sword: it can seek out the place where soul is divided from spirit, or joints from marrow; it can pass judgement on secret emotions and thoughts. No created thing is hidden from him; everything is uncovered and stretched fully open to the eyes of the one to whom we must give account of ourselves.

Since in Jesus, the Son of God, we have the supreme high priest who has gone through to the highest heaven, we must hold firm to our profession of faith. For the high priest we have is not incapable of feeling our weakness with us, but has been put to the test in exactly the same way as ourselves, apart from sin. Let us, then, have no fear in approaching the throne of grace to receive mercy and to find grace when we are in need of help.

The former priests were many in number, because death put an end to each one of them; but this one, because he remains for ever, has a perpetual priesthood. It follows, then, that his power to save those who come to God through him is absolute, since he lives for ever to intercede for them.

Such is the high priest that met our need, holy, innocent and uncontaminated, set apart from sinners, and raised up above the heavens; he has no need to offer sacrifices every day, as the high priests do, first for their own sins and only then for those of the people; this he did once and for all by offering himself. The Law appoints high priests who are men subject to weakness; but the promise on oath, which came after the Law, appointed the Son who is made perfect for ever.

The principal point of all that we have said is that we have a high priest of exactly this kind. He has taken his seat at the right of the throne of divine Majesty in the heavens, and he is the minister of the sanctuary and of the true Tent which the Lord, and not any man, set up.

WEEK 28

# SENT LIKE THE SON

This week we look at the theme of mission. God is a 'sending' God and our first reading looks at the pictures Isaiah uses to underline his conviction that Israel's task is to bring good news to the world. An arrow, a light, a herald, a watchman—God's people have a part to play in taking the good news to the world.

The story of Jonah tells of a one-man mission to Nineveh, a great Gentile city (Monday). While these extracts omit the famous episode of the 'great fish', they show how much greater is God's concern for people than Jonah's.

For Tuesday's reading, Luke describes how Jesus presents his own manifesto of good news, quoting another of Isaiah's prophecies. The initial response at Nazareth soon turned from favour to outrage. In turn, Jesus warned his disciples that they could expect no better treatment (Wednesday); and among his final reminders and promises we hear again that disciples must make other disciples (Thursday).

Friday's extracts from the Acts of the Apostles show us Paul commissioned to travel with Barnabas, then guided with Luke the writer into Europe (Macedonia) and eventually reaching Rome. Earlier he had written to the Christians in Rome about God's call to mission (Saturday), and as Paul quotes Isaiah, we end the week where we started, as prophecy finds fulfilment.

# Mission

David Livingstone, the famous Scottish missionary-explorer of the last century, was once asked why he chose to be a missionary. 'God had only one Son,' he said, 'and he was a missionary.' It was that fact that made him choose his career.

Mission in fact starts and ends with God. The Bible makes it clear that he is a 'sending' God. He loves his world so much that in spite of our sin and weakness he sent his messengers, he sent his prophets, and finally he sent his Son to establish his kingdom. The entire activity of God in creation and salvation has a mission aspect to it because God's concern flows from his love. He loves us too much to leave us where we are.

Three important truths about mission need to be understood:

- **Mission is God's work.** It is a mistake to begin with the church. Mission springs from the love of the Father, is given practical expression in the work of the Son and is made effective through the ministry of the Holy Spirit. It is God's outgoing love for the whole of creation, God's work in God's world.

- **Mission is God's care for the whole of life.** The good news which Christ came to share embraces the whole of reality and takes in not only preaching good news to those who are in spiritual need (evangelism) but also caring for the poor, the needy and oppressed. Mission which stops at the doors of the church is defective, because God's mission is world-centred and not merely church-centred. Indeed the Bible's order of things has God moving out to the world before he moves out to the church.

- **Mission is God's people caring for God's world.** Because God cares, we care. Because his love has been poured into our hearts, it overflows into his world. Pentecost is the great symbol of this. The gift of the Holy Spirit not only created the church, it made all Christians missionaries and we are all involved in the task of mission.

One way we do this is by simply *being who we are*. The key word is 'presence'. Just as Jesus brought in the kingdom by living among people and showing the compassion of God, so the Christian, by being with others, can bring the presence of Jesus and show his love and goodness.

Another way is by *sharing what we have*. Someone once defined evangelism as 'one beggar telling another beggar where to find bread'. In the task of evangelism we simply share what Jesus Christ means to us and has done for us. It may not be our gift to preach or explain the intellectual dimensions of the Christian faith, but every Christian can tell his or her own story of what God has done and is continuing to do.

And yet another way is by *serving others*. Just as Jesus came to serve, so the Christian gospel becomes good news for people when it is expressed not only in words but also in loving action and service.

'Go into the world and preach the gospel,' said Jesus, and this is still the church's charter. This makes missionary congregations of Christian churches—being, sharing and serving. A church begins to grow when it turns its attention outwards to the world. But that movement away from its own life and concerns may be the pathway into pain, challenge and crisis because it is the movement of the cross. But remember mission ends with God as well as beginning with him. And so we have every confidence that God's purposes are being worked out.

## SUNDAY

ISAIAH 49:1–6, 52:7–10 (REB)

Listen to me, you coasts and islands,
pay heed, you peoples far distant:
the Lord called me before I was born,
he named me from my mother's womb.
He made my tongue a sharp sword
and hid me under the shelter of his hand;
he made me into a polished arrow,
in his quiver he concealed me.
He said to me, 'Israel, you are my servant
through whom I shall win glory.'
Once I said, 'I have toiled in vain;
I have spent my strength for nothing, and to no purpose.'
Yet my cause is with the Lord
and my reward with my God.
The Lord had formed me in the womb to be his servant,
to bring Jacob back to him
that Israel should be gathered to him,
so that I might rise to honour in the Lord's sight
and my God might be my strength.
And now the Lord has said to me:
'It is too slight a task for you, as my servant,
to restore the tribes of Jacob,
to bring back the survivors of Israel:
I shall appoint you a light to the nations
so that my salvation may reach earth's farthest bounds.'

How beautiful on the mountains are
the feet of the herald,
the bringer of good news,
announcing deliverance,
proclaiming to Zion, 'Your God has become king.'
Your watchmen raise their voices
and shout together in joy;
for with their own eyes they see
the Lord return to Zion.
Break forth together into shouts of joy,
you ruins of Jerusalem;
for the Lord has comforted his people,
he has redeemed Jerusalem.
The Lord has bared his holy arm
in the sight of all nations,
and the whole world from end to end
shall see the deliverance
wrought by our God.

## MONDAY

JONAH 1:1–3, 3:1–5, 3:10–4:4, 4:11 (REB)

The word of the Lord came to Jonah son of Amittai: 'Go to the great city of Nineveh; go and denounce it, for I am confronted by its wickedness.' But to escape from the Lord Jonah set out for Tarshish. He went down to Joppa, where he found a ship bound for Tarshish. He paid the fare and went on board to travel with it to Tarshish out of the reach of the Lord.

A second time the word of the Lord came to Jonah: 'Go to the great city of Nineveh; go and denounce it in the words I give you.' Jonah obeyed and went at once to Nineveh. It was a vast city, three days' journey across, and Jonah began by going a day's journey into it. Then he proclaimed: 'In forty days Nineveh will be overthrown!'

The people of Nineveh took to heart this warning from God; they declared a public fast, and high and low alike put on sackcloth.

When God saw what they did and how they gave up their wicked ways, he relented and did not inflict on them the punishment he had threatened.

This greatly displeased Jonah. In anger he prayed to the Lord: 'It is just as I feared, Lord, when I was still in my own country, and it was to forestall this that I tried to escape to Tarshish. I knew that you are a gracious and compassionate God, long-suffering, ever constant, always ready to relent and not to inflict punishment. Now take away my life, Lord: I should be better dead than alive.' 'Are you right to be angry?' said the Lord.

'And should not I be sorry about the great city of Nineveh, with its hundred and twenty thousand people who cannot tell their right hand from their left, as well as cattle with number?'

## TUESDAY

LUKE 4:14–22 (RSV)

And Jesus returned in the power of the Spirit into Galilee, and a report concerning him went out through all the surrounding country. And he taught in their synagogues, being glorified by all.

And he came to Nazareth, where he had been brought up; and he went to the synagogue, as his custom was on the sabbath day. And he stood up to read; and there was given to him the book of the prophet Isaiah. He opened the book and found the place where it was written,

'The Spirit of the Lord is upon me,
because he has anointed me to preach good news to the poor.
He has sent me to proclaim release to the captives
and recovering of sight to the blind,
to set at liberty those who are oppressed,
to proclaim the acceptable year of the Lord.'

And he closed the book, and gave it back to the attendant, and sat down; and the eyes of all in the synagogue were fixed on him. And he began to say to them, 'Today the scripture has been fulfilled in your hearing.' And all spoke well of him, and wondered at the gracious words which proceeded out of his mouth; and they said, 'Is not this Joseph's son?'

## WEDNESDAY

MATTHEW 10:1, 5–20 (NIV)

Jesus called his twelve disciples to him and gave them authority to drive out evil spirits and to cure every kind of disease and sickness.

These twelve Jesus sent out with the following instructions: 'Do not go among the Gentiles or enter any town of the Samaritans. Go rather to the lost sheep of Israel. As you go, preach this message: "The kingdom of heaven is near." Heal the sick, raise the dead, cleanse those who have leprosy, drive out demons. Freely you have received, freely give. Do not take along any gold or silver or copper in your belts; take no bag for the journey, or extra tunic, or sandals or a staff; for the worker is worth his keep.

'Whatever town or village you enter, search for some worthy person there and stay at his house until you leave. As you enter the home, give it your greeting. If the home is deserving, let your peace rest on it; if it is not, let your peace return to you. If anyone will not welcome you or listen to your words, shake the dust off your feet when you leave that home or town. I tell you the truth, it will be more bearable for Sodom and Gomorrah on the day of judgment than for that town.

'I am sending you out like sheep among wolves. Therefore be as shrewd as snakes and as innocent as doves. But be on your guard against men; they will hand you over to the local councils and flog you in their synagogues. On my account you will be brought before governors and kings as witnesses to them and to the Gentiles. But when they arrest you, do not worry about what to say or how to say it. At that time you will be given what to say, for it will not be you speaking, but the Spirit of your Father speaking through you.'

## THURSDAY

MATTHEW 28:16–20 (NIV)

Then the eleven disciples went to Galilee, to the mountain where Jesus had told them to go. When they saw him, they worshipped him; but some doubted. Then Jesus came to them and said, 'All authority in heaven and on earth has been given to me. Therefore go and make disciples of all nations, baptizing them in the name of the Father and of the Son and of the Holy Spirit, and teaching them to obey everything I have commanded you. And surely I will be with you always, to the very end of the age.'

## FRIDAY

ACTS 13:1–5, 16:6–10, 28:11–16, 30–31 (NJB)

In the church at Antioch the following were prophets and teachers: Barnabas, Simeon called Niger, and Lucius of Cyrene, Manaen, who had been brought up with Herod the tetrarch, and Saul. One day while they were offering worship to the Lord and keeping a fast, the Holy Spirit said, 'I want Barnabas and Saul set apart for the work to which I have called them. So it was that after fasting and prayer they laid their hands on them and sent them off.

So these two, sent on their mission by the Holy Spirit, went down to Seleucia and from there set sail for Cyprus. They landed at Salamis and proclaimed the word of God in the synagogues of the Jews; John acted as their assistant.

Paul and Silas travelled through Phrygia and the Galatian country, because they had been told by the Holy Spirit not to preach the word in Asia.

When they reached the frontier of Mysia they tried to go into Bithynia, but as the Spirit of Jesus would not allow them, they went through Mysia and came down to Troas.

One night Paul had a vision: a Macedonian appeared and kept urging him in these words, 'Come across to Macedonia and help us.' Once he had seen this vision we lost no time in arranging a passage to Macedonia, convinced that God had called us to bring them the good news.

At the end of three months we set sail in a ship that had wintered in the island; she came from Alexandria and her figurehead was the Twins. We put in at Syracuse and spent three days there; from there we followed the coast up to Rhegium. After one day there a south wind sprang up and on the second day we made Puteoli, where we found some brothers and had the great encouragement of staying a week with them. And so we came to Rome.

When the brothers there heard about us they came to meet us, as far as the Forum of Appius and the Three Taverns. When Paul saw them he thanked God and took courage. On our arrival in Rome Paul was allowed to stay in lodgings of his own with the soldier who guarded him.

He spent the whole of the two years in his own rented lodging. He welcomed all who came to visit him, proclaiming the kingdom of God and teaching the truth about the Lord Jesus Christ with complete fearlessness and without any hindrance from anyone.

# SATURDAY

ROMANS 10:5–15 (AV)

For Moses describeth the righteousness which is of the law, That the man which doeth those things shall live by them. But the righteousness which is of faith speaketh on this wise, Say not in thine heart, Who shall ascend into heaven? (that is, to bring Christ down from above:) Or, Who shall descend into the deep? (that is, to bring up Christ again from the dead.) But what saith it? The word is nigh thee, even in thy mouth, and in thy heart: that is, the word of faith, which we preach; That if thou shalt confess with thy mouth the Lord Jesus, and shalt believe in thine heart that God hath raised him from the dead, thou shalt be saved. For with the heart man believeth unto righteousness; and with the mouth confession is made unto salvation. For the scripture saith, Whosoever believeth on him shall not be ashamed. For there is no difference between the Jew and the Greek: for the same Lord over all is rich unto all that call upon him. For whosoever shall call upon the name of the Lord shall be saved.

How then shall they call on him in whom they have not believed? and how shall they believe in him of whom they have not heard? and how shall they hear without a preacher? And how shall they preach, except they be sent? As it is written, How beautiful are the feet of them that preach the gospel of peace, and bring glad tidings of good things!

# THE RHYTHM OF LIFE

WEEK 29

These days with increasing leisure, earlier retirement and the problems brought about by unemployment, it is important to understand what God has to say about work and rest.

The first two readings this week speak of work and rest in the sublime words of the Bible's opening chapters. First we see God at work and at rest, then we see the first work that 'the man' was given to do in caring for a rich creation.

Tuesday's Psalm, too, sets human labour in the context of the work of God, while some pithy verses from Proverbs (Wednesday) have a clear message for the sluggard—and others! Centuries later, a paragraph from one of Paul's letters (Saturday) suggests that not all had heeded such warnings!

The book of Ecclesiastes has a well-known passage about the

right 'time' for human activities. While presenting only part of the truth about life 'under the sun', its many reflections on toil speak to our contemporary world with some force (Thursday). In this week's one gospel extract (Thursday) we find Jesus again at work, teaching about what he and his Father are doing together.

WEEK 29

# Work and Rest

For some people a job is no more than a nasty interruption of their social life; they cannot wait for Friday night. The Bible's view of work will seem peculiar to them, for the Bible approves of work. God himself is a worker. In the beginning God made the heavens and the earth and he takes pleasure in what he has made. And Jesus spent a good proportion of his life working as a carpenter.

Working, then, is part of what it means to be made in God's image; God works and he gives us the privilege of working. If this is the true perspective on work, then certain important things follow:

- **It is through our work that we can glorify God**. 'Whatever your hand finds to do, do it with all your might.' 'Do everything in the name of the Lord Jesus.'
- **Work is also one way in which we can co-operate with God in his rule over creation**. The earliest picture of the relationship between God and humanity is Adam and Eve in a garden—an image of God's life-giving power ('I give you . . . every seed-bearing plant') coupled with human responsibility ('till the ground . . . subdue the earth'). It is a partnership. God does not do it all himself, nor can we act as if we own the place. Stewardship is the key idea. A steward is in total charge of a project, but he knows that one day he will be called to give an account of how he has discharged his responsibilities.
- **Our work plays its part in fulfilling our humanity**. It is not good for someone to be idle, and unemployment can be a very reducing experience. The Bible has a high regard for skilled craftsmen, the sort of people who use their talents to make music or build and beautify the temple. 'There is nothing better for a man than to enjoy his work,' says the writer of Ecclesiastes.
- **And work, of course, is a way of serving others**. 'Work,' writes the apostle Paul, 'so that you may have something to share with those in need.'

This is the ideal. However, the Bible is nothing if not realistic. Work is not always fulfilling and deeply satisfying. Like everything else it has become contaminated by human sin. This is expressed vividly in the Adam and Eve story as God's curse on the ground. What should be joyful labour becomes painful drudgery and toil. So work, like many of God's good gifts, can become a means of exploiting people or even enslaving them. It can be perverted into a way of satisfying greed or hunger for power. In the end something which was meant to fulfil our humanity can degenerate into trudging round a soul-destroying treadmill.

Work was not the whole story even from the very beginning, however. In a profound insight, the creation story pictures God resting from his labours on the seventh day. Life is meant to have a rhythm of work and rest, of creation and re-creation. So we are given the sabbath. Far from preventing people enjoying themselves, the sabbath was to ensure that people *did* enjoy themselves. It was a day of joy and delight. Even the animals and the soil were given a holiday.

People were not created slaves. It is right that we should serve God in our work but we should also enjoy him in our worship. God did not make people to wander in a wilderness of restlessness. It is good to work hard, but it is also good to discover a still point for our lives by taking time out to rest in God. Only then do we live out the truth to which the rhythm of work and sabbath point.

WEEK 29

## SUNDAY

GENESIS 1:31–2:4A (RSV)

And God saw everything that he had made, and behold, it was very good. And there was evening and there was morning, a sixth day. Thus the heavens and the earth were finished, and all the host of them. And on the seventh day God finished his work which he had done, and he rested on the seventh day from all his work which he had done. So God blessed the seventh day and hallowed it, because on it God rested from all his work which he had done in creation. These are the generations of the heavens and the earth when they were created.

## MONDAY

GENESIS 2:4B–15 (RSV)

In the day that the Lord God made the earth and the heavens, when no plant of the field was yet in the earth and no herb of the field had yet sprung up—for the Lord God had not caused it to rain upon the earth, and there was no man to till the ground; but a mist went up from the earth and watered the whole face of the ground—then the Lord God formed man of dust from the ground, and breathed into his nostrils the breath of life; and man became a living being. And the Lord God planted a garden in Eden, in the east; and there he put the man whom he had formed. And out of the ground the Lord God made to grow every tree that is pleasant to the sight and good for food, the tree of life also in the midst of the garden, and the tree of the knowledge of good and evil. A river flowed out of Eden to water the garden, and there it divided and became four rivers. The name of the first is Pishon; it is the one which flows around the whole land of Havilah, where there is gold; and the gold of that land is good; bdellium and onyx stone are there. The name of the second river is Gihon; it is the one which flows around the whole land of Cush. And the name of the third river is Tigris, which flows east of Assyria. And the fourth river is the Euphrates. The Lord God took the man and put him in the garden of Eden to till it and keep it.

## TUESDAY

PSALM 104:13–24 (NIV)

He waters the mountains from his
upper chambers;
the earth is satisfied by the fruit
of his work.
He makes grass grow for the cattle,
and plants for man to cultivate—
bringing forth food from the
earth:
wine that gladdens the heart of man,
oil to make his face shine,
and bread that sustains his
heart.
The trees of the Lord are well
watered,
the cedars of Lebanon that he
planted.
There the birds make their nests;
the stork has its home in the pine
trees.

The high mountains belong to the wild goats;
the crags are a refuge for the conies.

The moon marks off the seasons,
and the sun knows when to go down.
You bring darkness, it becomes night,
and all the beasts of the forest prowl.
The lions roar for their prey
and seek their food from God.
The sun rises, and they steal away;
they return and lie down in their dens.
Then man goes out to his work,
to his labour until evening.

How many are your works, O Lord!
In wisdom you made them all;
the earth is full of your creatures.

## WEDNESDAY

PROVERBS 6:6–11, 20:4–13 (REB)

Go to the ant, you sluggard,
observe her ways and gain wisdom.
She has no prince, no governor or ruler
but in summer she gathers in her store of food
and lays in her supplies at harvest.
How long, you sluggard, will you lie abed?
When will you rouse yourself from sleep?
A little sleep, a little slumber,
a little folding of the hands in rest—
and poverty will come on you like a footpad,
want will assail you like a hardened ruffian.

The lazy man who does not plough in autumn
looks for a crop at harvest and gets nothing.
Counsel in another's heart is like deep water,
but a discerning person will draw it up.
Many assert their loyalty,
but where will you find one to keep faith?
If someone leads a good and upright life,
happy are his children after him!
A king seated on his throne in judgment
has an eye to sift out all that is evil.
Who can say, 'I have a clear conscience;
I am purged from my sin'?
A double standard in weights and measures
is an abomination to the Lord.
By his actions a child reveals himself,
whether or not his conduct is innocent and upright.
An attentive ear, an observant eye,
the Lord made them both.
Love sleep, and you will know poverty;
keep awake, and you will eat your fill.

## THURSDAY

ECCLESIASTES 3:1–14 (AV)

To everything there is a season, and a time to every purpose under the heaven: A time to be born, and a time to die; a time to plant, and a time to pluck up that which is planted; A time to kill, and a time to heal; a time to break down, and a time to build up; A time to weep, and a time to laugh; a time to mourn, and a time to dance; A time to cast away stones, and a time to gather stones together; a time to embrace, and a time to refrain from embracing; A time to get, and a time to lose; a time to keep, and a time to cast away; A time to rend, and a time to sew; a time to keep silence, and a time to speak; A time to love, and a time to hate; a time of war, and a time of peace.

What profit hath he that worketh in that wherein he laboureth? I have seen travail, which God hath given to the sons of men to be exercised in it. He hath made every thing beautiful in his time: also he hath set the world in their heart, so that no man can find out the work that God maketh from the beginning to the end. I know that there is no good in them, but for a man to rejoice, and to do good in his life. And also that every man should eat and drink, and enjoy the good of all his labour, it is the gift of God. I know that, whatsoever God doeth, it shall be for-ever: nothing can be put to it, nor any thing taken from it: and God doeth it, that men should fear before him.

## FRIDAY

JOHN 9:1–7, 13–16 (NJB)

As Jesus went along, he saw a man who had been blind from birth. His disciples asked him, 'Rabbi, who sinned, this man or his parents, that he should have been born blind?' 'Neither he nor his parents sinned,' Jesus answered, 'he was born blind so the works of God might be revealed in him. As long as the day lasts we must carry out the work of the one who sent me; the night will soon be here when no one can work. As long as I am in the world I am the light of the world.'

Having said this, he spat on the ground, made a paste with the spittle, put this over the eyes of the blind man, and said to him, 'Go and wash in the Pool of Siloam' (the name means 'one who has been sent'). So he went off and washed and came back able to see.

They brought to the Pharisees the man who had been blind. It had been a Sabbath day when Jesus made the paste and opened the man's eyes, so when the Pharisees asked him how he had gained his sight, he said, 'He put a paste on my eyes, and I washed, and I can see.' Then some of the Pharisees said, 'That man cannot be from God: he does not keep the Sabbath.' Others said, 'How can a sinner produce signs like this?' And there was division among them.

# SATURDAY

2 THESSALONIANS 3:6–13 (REB)

These are our instructions to you, friends, in the name of our Lord Jesus Christ: hold aloof from every Christian who falls into idle habits, and disregards the tradition you received from us. You yourselves know how you ought to follow our example: you never saw us idling; we did not accept free hospitality from anyone; night and day in toil and drudgery we worked for a living, rather than be a burden to any of you—not because we do not have the right to maintenance, but to set an example for you to follow. Already during our stay with you we laid down this rule: anyone who will not work shall not eat. We mention this because we hear that some of you are idling their time away, minding everybody's business but their own. We instruct and urge such people in the name of the Lord Jesus Christ to settle down to work and earn a living.

My friends, you must never tire of doing right.

# THE WORLD OF THE NEW TESTAMENT

Three great cultures form the backdrop against which the New Testament is played out: the Roman, the Greek and the Jewish. Religious tendencies such as the Gnostics and the mystery religions arose in different regions at different times.

## PHARISEES

These were teachers of the Jewish Law, who tried to apply the Law to every daily circumstance. This made them highly punctilious and legalistic. Jesus confronted Pharisees repeatedly. Paul was trained as a Pharisee.

**"(The Pharisees were) a certain sect who prided themselves in the exact skill they had in the law of their fathers, and made people believe they were highly favoured by God."**

Josephus, *Antiquities of the Jews*

## SADDUCEES

Members of aristocratic Jewish families, the Sadducees controlled the office of high priest. Their great religious concerns were the temple and the priesthood. It was Sadducees who condemned Jesus and handed him over to Pilate.

**"The Sadducees say that we are to consider obligatory those observances which are in the written word, but are not to observe what are derived from the traditions of the fathers."**

Josephus, *Antiquities of the Jews*

## THE ROMAN EMPIRE

All the cities and territories mentioned in the New Testament were part of the Roman empire, under some form of Roman government and subject to Roman taxes. Rome's civil and military administration was a strong factor in everyone's lives.

## SSENES

e great Essene ntre was the mmunity of Qumran, the Dead Sea, here the famous rolls were recently und. Essenes lieved they were ing in the last days. ey practised a orously disciplined ay of life.

## GREEK CULTURE

The culture of the Roman empire was dominated by Greek influence—it was a 'hellenistic' culture. Greek education, philosophy, drama and music were an inescapable influence.

## LANGUAGES

**Hebrew**, the language of the Jewish Bible, was familiar to all Jews. But **Aramaic** was the language of everyday conversation in Palestine. Throughout the Roman empire, **Greek** was the common language, and the New Testament was written in Greek. **Latin** was the native language of the Romans themselves, spoken in Jerusalem by the occupying forces.

**“Paul said, ‘Men of Athens! I see that in every way you are very religious. For as I walked round and observed your objects of worship, I even found an altar with this inscription: To an unknown god.’”**

Acts chapter 17

**“Whenever we rucify the guilty, the most crowded roads are chosen, where the most people can see nd be moved by this fear.”**

Quintilian, *Declamationes*

## THE GNOSTICS

This term describes a variety of religious movements stressing a secret knowledge (Greek, *gnosis*) as the root to salvation. Gnostics believed the spiritual and material worlds were in sharp conflict. Some heresies opposed in New Testament letters were of a gnostic kind.

## MYSTERY RELIGIONS

Being 'initiated into the mysteries' was a prestigious practice in the empire. Some mystery cults, such as the cult of Eleusis, originated with the ancient Greeks. Others, such as the cult of Mithras, spread from further east. Christians had to show that salvation through Christ was different from salvation through mysteries.

WEEK 30

# THE MYSTERIOUS DIFFERENCE

The very first chapter of the Bible tells us that God created us 'male and female'. The first archetypal story of this week's readings is both foundational and full of mystery. This story underlines the human need of partnership, the insufficiency of animals as companions, and the creation of woman from man which will lead to the birth of all subsequent humans from women. The first 'love song'—for it is in poetic form—is followed by the text forming the basis of marriage, as understood throughout the Bible.

The pastoral story of Ruth and Boaz from a later age (Monday) contains much beauty and sensitivity, but also more than a hint of relationships which have been spoiled—between rich and poor, Jew and Gentile, male and female. Tuesday's Psalm delights in a royal partnership and also provides a prelude to the Song of Songs (Thursday) which overlaps in turn with next week's theme. Proverbs (Wednesday) concludes with an impressive portrait of feminine expertise within both family and community.

The New Testament passages (Friday and Saturday) reflect the need for healthy relationships between the sexes in the church and outside it; some roles are still distinct, but John's final paragraph where he refers to 'the man who does the will of God' is certainly inclusive.

WEEK 30

# Male and Female

Probably the greatest social revolution of our time has been the emancipation of women. Until this century women were limited to their three traditional strongholds: children, kitchen and church. Outside these areas women could not move without being frowned on. But now women have greater freedom and opportunity in practically every society and this has been of benefit to us all.

But there have been harmful side effects. Some feminists reject the traditional roles of women completely. Some even consider men their bitter foe. And women seem now to be at even greater risk on the streets of our cities, from violent, embittered men.

Against this background, what is the Bible's teaching about male/female relationships?

- **We were created equal.** In God's sight, men and women have equal honour and standing. Both sexes were made in the 'image of God' and destined for an eternal relationship with our Father. This is the divine charter for human freedom and dignity.

- **We were created to be together.** The creation story tells us that a man and a woman were not created to be separate and isolated but to be together, two beings absolutely essential and necessary to one another. Apart from one another male and female cannot *be*. We need each other not only to survive but to be truly ourselves.

- **We were created to be different.** The desire for equality may so easily blur the significantly different things we contribute to the human family. Women and men are not the same—and the differences are far more than sexual. They include the way we perceive life, our attitudes to others, the nature of our gifts and our consciousness of sinfulness. Such differences, falsely perceived, can become points of division and bitterness. But when accepted rightly, as part of the way we complement one another, they lead to enrichment and strength.

Christians make a very important contribution to society by working out the Bible's teaching. Take, for example, the way men and women unintentionally threaten one another. Women feel hedged about by age-old traditions and attitudes, which can still make them feel oppressed in church and society. Men can find women's emancipation deeply threatening. 'Brains rather than brawn' is the currency of a modern society, and so some men feel undervalued, their strength no longer needed.

How can Christians help to confront these feelings, remove the threat and make accepting relationships possible? Even in highly developed societies women sometimes complain that they are not valued as persons by men but as sex objects, particularly at work. Directly contrary to this, the Christian message is of human dignity, treating the person of the opposite sex as a sacred person made by God for God.

WEEK 30

## SUNDAY

GENESIS 2:18–25 (RSV)

Then the Lord God said, 'It is not good that man should be alone; I will make a helper fit for him.' So out of the ground the Lord God formed every beast of the field and every bird of the air, and brought them to the man to see what he would call them; and whatever the man called every living creature, that was its name. The man gave names to all cattle, and to the birds of the air, and to every beast of the field; but for the man there was not found a helper fit for him. So the Lord God caused a deep sleep to fall upon the man, and while he slept took one of his ribs and closed up its place with flesh; and the rib which the Lord God had taken from the man he made into a woman and brought her to the man. Then the man said,

'This at last is bone of my bones
  and flesh of my flesh;
she shall be called Woman,
  because she was taken out of
  Man.'

Therefore a man leaves his father and his mother and cleaves to his wife, and they become one flesh. And the man and his wife were both naked, and were not ashamed.

## MONDAY

RUTH 2:2–13 (REB)

One day Ruth the Moabite asked Naomi, 'May I go to the harvest fields and glean behind anyone who will allow me?' 'Yes, go, my daughter,' she replied. So Ruth went gleaning in the fields behind the reapers. As it happened, she was in that strip of the fields which belonged to Boaz of Elimelech's family, and there was Boaz himself coming out from Bethlehem. He greeted the reapers, 'The Lord be with you!' and they responded, 'The Lord bless you!' 'Whose girl is this?' he asked the servant in charge of the reapers. The servant answered, 'She is a Moabite girl who has come back with Naomi from Moab. She asked if she might glean, gathering among the sheaves behind the reapers. She came and has been on her feet from morning till now; she has hardly had a moment's rest in the shelter.'

Boaz said to Ruth, 'Listen, my daughter: do not go to glean in any other field. Do not look any farther, but stay close to my servant-girls. Watch where the men reap, and follow the gleaners; I have told the men not to molest you. Any time you are thirsty, go and drink from the jars they have filled.' She bowed to the ground and said, 'Why are you so kind as to take notice of me, when I am just a foreigner?' Boaz answered, 'I have been told the whole story of what you have done for your mother-in-law since the death of your husband, how you left father and mother and homeland and came among a people you did not know before. The Lord reward you for what you have done; may you be richly repaid by the Lord the God of Israel, under whose wings you have come for refuge.' She said: 'I hope you will continue to be pleased with me, sir, for you have eased my mind by speaking kindly to me, though I am not one of your slavegirls.'

## TUESDAY

PSALM 45:1–4, 10–15 (RSV)

My heart overflows with a goodly theme;
I address my verses to the king:
my tongue is like the pen of a ready scribe.

You are the fairest of the sons of men;
grace is poured upon your lips;
therefore God has blessed you for ever.
Gird your sword upon your thigh, O mighty one,
in your glory and majesty!

In your majesty ride forth victoriously
for the cause of truth and to defend the right;
let your right hand teach you dread deeds!

Hear, O daughter, consider, and incline your ear;
forget your people and your father's house;
and the king will desire your beauty.
Since he is your lord, bow to him;
the people of Tyre will sue your favour with gifts,
the richest of the people with all kinds of wealth.

The princess is decked in her chamber with gold-woven robes;
in many-coloured robes she is led to the king,
with her virgin companions, her escort, in her train.
With joy and gladness they are led along
as they enter the palace of the king.

## WEDNESDAY

PROVERBS 31:10–23, 28–31 (NIV)

A wife of noble character who can find?
She is worth far more than rubies.
Her husband has full confidence in her
and lacks nothing of value.
she brings him good, not harm,
all the days of her life.
She selects wool and flax
and works with eager hands.
She is like the merchant ships,
bringing her food from afar.
She gets up while it is still dark;
she provides food for her family
and portions for her servant girls.
She considers a field and buys it;
out of her earnings she plants a vineyard.
She sets about her work vigorously;
her arms are strong for her tasks.
She sees that her trading is profitable,
and her lamp does not go out at night.
In her hand she holds the distaff
and grasps the spindle with her fingers.
She opens her arms to the poor
and extends her hands to the needy.
When it snows, she has no fear for her household;
for all of them are clothed in scarlet.
She makes coverings for her bed;
she is clothed in fine linen and purple.
Her husband is respected at the city gate,

where he takes his seat among
the elders of the land.

Her children arise and call her
blessed;
her husband also, and he praises
her:
'Many women do noble things,
but you surpass them all.'
Charm is deceptive, and beauty is
fleeting;
but a woman who fears the Lord
is to be praised.
Give her the reward she has earned,
and let her works bring her
praise at the city gate.

## THURSDAY

SONG OF SONGS 2:1–13 (RSV)

I am a rose of Sharon,
a lily of the valleys.
As a lily among brambles,
so is my love among maidens.
As an apple tree among the trees of
the wood,
so is my beloved among young
men.
With great delight I sat in his
shadow,
and his fruit was sweet to my
taste.
He brought me to the banqueting
house,
and his banner over me was love.
Sustain me with raisins,
refresh me with apples;
for I am sick with love.
O that his left hand were under my
head,
and that his right hand embraced
me!
I adjure you, O daughters of
Jerusalem,
by the gazelles or the hinds of
the field,
that you stir not up nor awaken love
until it please.
The voice of my beloved!
Behold, he comes,
leaping upon the mountains,
bounding over the hills.
My beloved is like a gazelle,
or a young stag.
Behold, there he stands
behind our wall,
gazing in at the windows,
looking through the lattice.
My beloved speaks and says to me:
'Arise, my love, my fair one,
and come away;
for lo, the winter is past,
the rain is over and gone.
The flowers appear on the earth,
and the time of singing has
come,
and the voice of the turtledove
is heard in our land.
The fig tree puts forth its figs,
and the vines are in blossom;
they give forth fragrance.
Arise, my love, my fair one,
and come away.
O my dove, in the clefts of the rock,
in the covert of the cliff,
let me see your face,
let me hear your voice,
for your voice is sweet,
and your face is comely.
Catch us the foxes,
the little foxes,
that spoil the vineyards,
for our vineyards are in blossom.'

## FRIDAY

1 TIMOTHY 5:1–10 (NJB)

Never speak sharply to a man older than yourself, but appeal to him as you would to your own father; treat younger men as brothers, older women as mothers and young women as sisters with all propriety.

Be considerate to widows—if they really are widowed. If a widow has children or grandchildren, they are to learn first of all to do their duty to their own families and repay their debt to their parents, because this is what pleases God. But a woman who is really widowed and left on her own has set her hope on God and perseveres night and day in petitions and prayer. The one who thinks only of pleasure is already dead while she is still alive: instruct them in this, too, so that their lives may be blameless. Anyone who does not look after his own relations, especially if they are living with him, has rejected the faith and is worse than an unbeliever.

Enrolment as a widow is permissible only for a woman at least sixty years old who has had only one husband. She must be a woman known for her good works—whether she has brought up her children, been hospitable to strangers and washed the feet of God's holy people, helped people in hardship or been active in all kinds of good work.

## SATURDAY

1 JOHN 2:12–17 (NIV)

I write to you, dear children, because your sins have been forgiven on account of his name. I write to you, fathers, because you have known him who is from the beginning. I write to you, young men, because you have overcome the evil one. I write to you, dear children, because you have known the Father. I write to you, fathers, because you have known him who is from the beginning. I write to you, young men, because you are strong, and the word of God lives in you, and you have overcome the evil one.

Do not love the world or anything in the world. If anyone loves the world, the love of the Father is not in him. For everything in the world—the cravings of sinful man, the lust of his eves and the boasting of what he has and does—comes not from the Father but from the world. The world and its desires pass away, but the man who does the will of God lives for ever.

WEEK 31

# TWO'S COMPANY

Last week's theme, 'male and female', was not confined to sexuality. This week we see how sexual relationships are portrayed in the Bible. The story of Jacob's love for Rachel has some qualities of a modern love-story—including romance, suspense, villainy and comedy (Sunday)!

Two further readings from the Song of Songs (Monday and Tuesday) convey something of both the drama and the sensuous beauty of this book, even in translation. Traditional interpretations of the Song of Songs have often been mystical and allegorical, but a sexual and very human relationship forms the basis of its vivid scenes and warm language.

Wednesday's reading is from Proverbs, with its timeless picture of the misuse of sexuality and the deadly deceits of lust. Hosea, by contrast, tells of a restored relationship, linking the loving repair of a broken marriage with the renewed fellowship between God and the people (Thursday).

Two New Testament letters complete the week, in which Paul addresses particular questions raised at Corinth and tackles the more general need for holy living required at Thessalonica (Friday and Saturday). Both extracts combine pastoral realism with the high standards called for among Christians, and made possible by Christ.

# Sexuality

'If it's fun, stop it.' Many people assume that this is the kind of thing the Bible says about sex. In fact, what it teaches about this aspect of our humanity is positive, perceptive and profoundly realistic.

- **Sexuality is part of our wholeness**. It is in the union of male and female that the 'one flesh' is to be found. God created humankind 'in his own image', but the image consists of 'male and female taken together' not in either to the exclusion of the other. So Paul grasps the liberating truth that the man's body belongs to the woman and the woman's body to the man. The image of God can only be expressed in partnership and co - operation with another.
- **The act of sex is also a great mystery**. It is one of the most profound ways of knowing another person. Indeed to 'know' is often a way of speaking of sexual intercourse. The love of God for Israel is pictured as a marriage. The church is the bride of Christ. Paul argues that you 'cannot' join your body to that of a prostitute without damaging the intimate relationship which the Christian has with Christ. Sex ought never to be seen as a purely physical release. It always has profound effects on our personalities.
- **Erotic love is one of God's gracious gifts to humanity**. The Song of Songs is a hymn in praise of erotic love. It is not, as some Christians have tried to argue, primarily an allegory of God's love for the soul. The song rejoices in sexuality without shame or guilt, in a way which, at times, has been too uninhibited for the church's taste. But Christians ought not to be more 'pure' or 'spiritual' than God himself!
- **Along with this high view of sex goes a realistic understanding of its dangerous power**. Sex is always on the point of claiming godlike power over us and reducing us to slavery. This was literally so in some of the pagan cults of Bible times, which depersonalized people through cult prostitution. And it is so today in the pornography industry. But Jesus alone is Lord, not the gods and goddesses of sex.

  The Bible's teaching on the single state is entirely in keeping with this. Sexual experience is a grace but it is not the only way to wholeness.

  People may choose to remain unmarried with no personal loss (and indeed there may be gain to themselves and their service of Christ). The incarnation shows that we do not need to be sexually active to find perfect love, maturity and fulfilment. Jesus was not less 'whole' because he never married.

It is because of the intimate connexion between sex and personality that the Bible hedges the act with so many rules. Sexuality must be expressed in its proper setting—that of husband and wife within marriage. Because sex is so close to the divine and to the demonic, so beautiful yet so dangerous, it must be as carefully insulated as any radioactive material. Hence the prohibitions on everything that deviates from the 'marriage' model: rape, prostitution, homosexuality, adultery, bestiality. Such acts are condemned as sin. Yet Jesus offered the sexual sinner not rejection, but love, forgiveness and acceptance. The Samaritan woman, the adulteress and the prostitutes were called to turn from their sin and follow him.

## SUNDAY

GENESIS 29:9–20 (RSV)

While Jacob was still speaking with the shepherds, Rachel came with her father's sheep; for she kept them. Now when Jacob saw Rachel the daughter of Laban his mother's brother, and the sheep of Laban his mother's brother, Jacob went up and rolled the stone from the well's mouth, and watered the flock of Laban his mother's brother. Then Jacob kissed Rachel, and wept aloud. And Jacob told Rachel that he was her father's kinsman, and that he was Rebekah's son; and she ran and told her father.

When Laban heard the tidings of Jacob his sister's son, he ran to meet him, and embraced him and kissed him, and brought him to his house. Jacob told Laban all these things, and Laban said to him, 'Surely you are my bone and my flesh!' And he stayed with him a month.

Then Laban said to Jacob, 'Because you are my kinsman, should you therefore serve me for nothing? Tell me, what shall your wages be?' Now Laban had two daughters; the name of the older was Leah, and the name of the younger was Rachel. Leah's eyes were weak, but Rachel was beautiful and lovely. Jacob loved Rachel; and he said, 'I will serve you seven years for your younger daughter Rachel.' Laban said, 'It is better that I give her to you than that I should give her to any other man; stay with me.' So Jacob served seven years for Rachel, and they seemed to him but a few days because of the love he had for her.

## MONDAY

SONG OF SONGS 5:1–16 (RSV)

I come to my garden, my sister, my
  bride,
I gather my myrrh with my spice,
I eat my honeycomb with my honey,
I drink my wine with my milk.

Eat, O friends, and drink:
  drink deeply, O lovers!

I slept, but my heart was awake.
Hark! my beloved is knocking.
'Open to me, my sister, my love,
  my dove, my perfect one;
for my head is wet with dew,
  my locks with the drops of the
  night.'
I had put off my garment,
  how could I put it on?
I had bathed my feet,
  how could I soil them?
My beloved put his hand to the
  latch,
  and my heart was thrilled within
  me.
I arose to open to my beloved,
  and my hands dripped with
  myrrh,
my fingers with liquid myrrh,
  upon the handles of the bolt.
I open to my beloved,
  but my beloved had turned and
  gone.
My soul failed me when he spoke.
I sought him, but found him not;
  I called him, but he gave me no
  answer.
The watchman found me,
  as they went about in the city;
they beat me, they wounded me,
  they took away my mantle,
  those watchmen of the walls.
I adjure you, O daughters of

Jerusalem,
if you find my beloved,
that you tell him
I am sick with love.

What is your beloved more than
another beloved,
O fairest among women?
What is your beloved more than
another beloved,
that you thus adjure us?

My beloved is all radiant and ruddy,
distinguished among ten
thousand.
His head is the finest gold;
his locks are wavy,
black as a raven.
His eyes are like doves
beside springs of water,
bathed in milk,
fitly set.
His cheeks are like beds of spices,
yielding fragrance.
His lips are lilies,
distilling liquid myrrh.
His arms are rounded gold,
set with jewels.
His body is ivory work,
encrusted with sapphires.
His legs are alabaster columns,
set upon bases of gold.
His appearance is like Lebanon,
choice as the cedars.
His speech is most sweet,
and he is altogether desirable.
This is my beloved and this is my
friend.
O daughters of Jerusalem.

# TUESDAY

SONG OF SONGS 7:1–9 (RSV)

How graceful are your feet in
sandals,
O queenly maiden!
Your rounded thighs are like jewels,
the work of a master hand.
Your navel is a rounded bowl
than never lacks mixed wine.
Your belly is a heap of wheat,
encircled with lilies.
Your two breasts are like two fawns,
twins of a gazelle.
Your neck is like an ivory tower.
Your eyes are pools in Heshbon,
by the gate of Bathrabbim.
Your nose is like a tower of
Lebanon,
overlooking Damascus.
Your head crowns you like Carmel,
and your flowing locks are like
purple;
a king is held captive in the
tresses.

How fair and pleasant you are,
O loved one, delectable maiden!
You are stately as a palm tree,
and your breasts are like its
clusters.
I say I will climb the palm tree
and lay hold of its branches.
Oh, may your breasts be like clusters of the vine,
and the scent of your breath like
apples,
and your kisses like the best wine
that goes down smoothly,
gliding over lips and teeth.

## WEDNESDAY

PROVERBS 7:6–23 (REB)

I glanced out of the window of my house,
I looked down through the lattice,
and I saw among the simpletons,
among the young men there I noticed
a lad devoid of all sense.
He was passing along the street at her corner,
stepping out in the direction of her house
at twilight, as the day faded,
at dusk as the night grew dark,
and there a woman came to meet him.
She was dressed like a prostitute, full of wiles,
flighty and inconstant,
a woman never content to stay at home,
lying in wait by every corner,
now in the street, now in the public squares.
She caught hold of him and kissed him;
brazenly she accosted him and said,
'I had a sacrifice, an offering, to make
and I have paid my vows today;
so I came out to meet you,
to look for you, and now I have found you.
I have spread coverings on my couch,
coloured linen from Egypt.
I have perfumed my bed
with myrrh, aloes, and cassia.
Come! Let us drown ourselves in pleasure,
let us abandon ourselves to a night of love;
for my husband is not at home.
He has gone away on a long journey,
taking a bag of silver with him;
he will not be home until full moon.'
Persuasively she cajoled him,
coaxing him with seductive words.
He followed her, the simple fool,
like an ox on its way to be slaughtered,
like an antelope bounding into the noose,
like a bird hurrying into the trap;
he did not know he was risking his life
until the arrow pierced his vitals.

## THURSDAY

HOSEA 2:14–20 (NIV)

'Therefore I am now going to allure her;
I will lead her into the desert
and speak tenderly to her.
There I will give her back her vineyards,
and will make the Valley of Achor a door of hope.
There she will sing as in the days of her youth,
as in the day she came up out of Egypt.

'In that day,' declares the Lord,
'you will call me "my husband";
you will no longer call me "my master".
I will remove the names of the Baals

from her lips;
no longer will their names be invoked.
In that day I will make a covenant for them
with the beasts of the field and the birds of the air
and the creatures that move along the ground.
Bow and sword and battle
I will abolish from the land,
so that all may lie down in safety.
I will betroth you to me for ever;
I will betroth you in righteousness and justice,
in love and compassion.
I will betroth you in faithfulness,
and you will acknowledge the Lord.'

## FRIDAY

1 CORINTHIANS 7:1–9 (NJB)

Now for the questions about which you wrote. Yes, it is a good thing for a man not to touch a woman; yet to avoid immorality every man should have his own wife and every woman her own husband. The husband must give to his wife what she has a right to expect, and so too the wife to her husband. The wife does not have authority over her own body, but the husband does; and in the same way the husband does not have authority over his own body, but the wife does. You must not deprive each other, except by mutual consent for a limited time, to leave yourselves free for prayer, and to come together again afterwards; otherwise Satan may take advantage of any lack of self-control to put you to the test. I am telling you then as a concession, not an order. I should still like everyone to be as I am myself; but everyone has his own gift from God, one this kind and the next something different.

To the unmarried and to widows I say: it is good for them to stay as they are, like me. But if they cannot exercise self-control, let them marry, since it is better to be married than to be burnt up.

## SATURDAY

1 THESSALONIANS 4:1–8 (NJB)

Finally, brothers, we urge you and appeal to you in the Lord Jesus; we instructed you how to live in the way that pleases God, and you are so living; but make more progress still. You are well aware of the instructions we gave you on the authority of the Lord Jesus.

God wills you all to be holy. He wants you to keep away from sexual immorality, and each one of you to know how to control his body in a way that is holy and honourable, not giving way to selfish lust like the nations who do not acknowledge God. He wants nobody at all ever to sin by taking advantage of a brother in these matters; the Lord always pays back sins of that sort, as we told you before emphatically. God called us to be holy, not to be immoral; in other words, anyone who rejects this is rejecting not human authority, but God, who gives you his Holy Spirit.

# HOME, SWEET HOME?

WEEK 32

This week's readings touch on some of the delights and disasters, potential and actual, of family life —whether 'nuclear' or extended.

The lovely story of Isaac and Rebekah (Sunday) sees a new home and family established but gives no hint of troubles to come. Their son Jacob (referred to as Israel here) was to preside over a desperately divided household (Monday). Here we read of Jacob's providential reuniting and reconciliation with his son Joseph in Egypt.

Ruth's story (Tuesday) concludes with one of the Bible's briefest but most significant family trees; genealogies were of great importance in Hebrew culture.

A 'family' Psalm (Wednesday) is followed by a selection of home truths from Proverbs (Thursday), delivered with characteristically brief and contrasted cameos drawn from life.

Friday brings us to the gospels, where in spite of (or because of?) the over-riding claims of God's kingdom, Jesus strongly affirms husbands and wives, marriage and children (Friday). And the apostle Paul has advice for family relationships, referring all to Christ as he writes to fellow-Christians (Saturday).

# Marriage and the Family

'Marriage,' goes the saying, 'is the nursery of heaven.' At least it is meant to be, although no one imagines that all marriages are perfect. Like every other human relationship marriage can be undermined by weakness, sin and selfishness. And if anyone is going to have an enduring relationship of love with another human being, it needs to be worked at and begun afresh every day.

Despite the ever-increasing numbers of broken marriages, marriage is still the basic social unit in practically every society, and this was certainly God's intention from the beginning. He created humankind in his image as male and female, and it was his will that they should find fulfilment in one another. Paul even uses the loving and holy relationship between Christ and his church as a model for marriage as it should be. And Jesus treated marriage as a lifelong obligation which no one should sever. Divorce is always a terrible break in God's purposes, brought about through human weakness and sin.

What does the Bible teach about a good marriage and wholesome family life?

- **Faithfulness and trust.** In marriage there is only one person we can give ourselves to intimately, and that is our partner. A 'holy' marriage is one in which the other person is sacred and all other men and women are 'out of bounds'. The problem today is that this clear boundary is so often transgressed, sometimes even by Christians. The main cause, as we know so well, is the power of sexual desire, to which none of us is too holy to be impervious. A couple who want to be faithful will keep the lines of communication open, building trust and helping each other to steer clear of situations which could become too difficult to handle.
- **A disciplined framework.** Love between the sexes is the seed-bed in which true love is propagated for the entire family. That love will express itself in a loving framework of life in which children will grow up to be mature adults themselves. The Bible has some down-to-earth things to say to us. Disciplining children is not always wrong: indeed, punishment appropriate to the misdeed will be necessary at times, so that children are brought up to heed what is right. Punishment which flows from love will never be harsh or cruel. Just because we are parents does not mean that we own our children: they belong to the Lord first. So Paul calls us to work at our family relationships—children to obey, and parents not to provoke or discourage.
- **Companionship.** The good marriage and happy home is where our best friends are. In that context it should be natural to play, pray, laugh and have fun together—simply enjoying being with members of our own family. So marriage and the family, when they function at their best, can give us a foretaste of what heaven is like and of the divine family of which God the Father is the head.

## SUNDAY

GENESIS 24:50–67 (RSV)

Then Laban and Bethuel answered, 'The thing comes from the Lord; we cannot speak to you bad or good. Behold, Rebekah is before you, take her and go, and let her be the wife of your master's son, as the Lord has spoken.'

When Abraham's servant heard their words, he bowed himself to the earth before the Lord. And the servant brought forth jewelry of silver and of gold, and raiment, and gave them to Rebekah; he also gave to her brother and to her mother costly ornaments. And he and the men who were with him ate and drank, and they spent the night there. When they arose in the morning, he said, 'Send me back to my master.' Her brother and her mother said, 'Let the maiden remain with us a while, at least ten days; after that she may go.' But he said to them, 'Do not delay me, since the Lord has prospered my way; let me go that I may go to my master.' They said, 'We will call the maiden, and ask her.' And they called Rebekah, and said to her, 'Will you go with this man?' She said, 'I will go.' So they sent away Rebekah their sister and her nurse, and Abraham's servant and his men. And they blessed Rebekah, and said to her, 'Our sister, be the mother of thousands of ten thousands; and may your descendants possess the gate of those who hate them!' Then Rebekah and her maids arose, and rode upon the camels and followed the man; thus the servant took Rebekah, and went his way.

Now Isaac had come from Beerlahairoi, and was dwelling in the Negeb. And Isaac went out to meditate in the field in the evening; and he lifted up his eyes and looked, and behold, there were camels coming. And Rebekah lifted up her eyes, and when she saw Isaac, she alighted from the camel, and said to the servant, 'Who is the man yonder, walking in the field to meet us?' The servant said, 'It is my master.' So she took her veil and covered herself. And the servant told Isaac all the things that he had done. Then Isaac brought her into the tent, and took Rebekah, and she became his wife; and he loved her. So Isaac was comforted after his mother's death.

## MONDAY

GENESIS 46:6–7, 26–30 (RSV)

They also took their cattle and their goods, which they had gained in the land of Canaan, and came into Egypt, Jacob and all his offspring with him, his sons, and his sons' sons with him, his daughters, and his sons' daughters; all his offspring he brought with him into Egypt.

All the persons belonging to Jacob who came into Egypt, who were his own offspring, not including Jacob's sons' wives, were sixty-six persons in all; and the sons of Joseph, who were born to him in Egypt, were two; all the persons of the house of Jacob, that came into Egypt, were seventy.

He sent Judah before him to Joseph, to appear before him in Goshen; and they came to the land of Goshen. Then Joseph made ready his chariot and went up to meet Israel his father in

Goshen; and he presented himself to him, and fell on his neck, and wept on his neck a good while. Israel said to Joseph, 'Now let me die, since I have seen your face and know that you are still alive.'

## TUESDAY

RUTH 3:1–6, 4:13–22 (REB)

One day Naomi, Ruth's mother-in-law, said to her, 'My daughter, I want to see you settled happily. Now there is our kinsman Boaz, whose girls you have been with. Tonight he will be winnowing barley at the threshing-floor. Bathe and anoint yourself with perfumed oil, then get dressed and go down to the threshing-floor; but do not make yourself known to the man until he has finished eating and drinking. When he lies down make sure you know the place where he is. Then go in, turn back the covering at his feet and lie down. He will tell you what to do.' 'I will do everything you say,' replied Ruth.

She went down to the threshing-floor and did exactly as her mother-in-law had told her.

So Boaz took Ruth and she became his wife. When they had come together the Lord caused her to conceive, and she gave birth to a son. The women said to Naomi, 'Blessed be the Lord, who has not left you this day without next-of-kin. May the name of your dead son be kept alive in Israel! The child will give you renewed life and be your support and stay in your old age, for your devoted daughter-in-law, who has proved better to you than seven sons, has borne him.' Naomi took the child and laid him in her own lap, and she became his foster-mother. Her women neighbours gave him a name: 'Naomi has a son; we shall call him Obed,' they said. He became the father of Jesse, David's father.

This is the genealogy of Perez: Perez was the father of Hezron, Hezron of Ram, Ram of Amminadab, Amminadab of Nahshon, Nahshon of Salmon, Salmon of Boaz, Boaz of Obed, Obed of Jesse, and Jesse of David.

## WEDNESDAY

PSALM 128 (NIV)

Blessed are all who fear the Lord,
who walk in his ways.
You will eat the fruit of your labour;
blessings and prosperity will be yours.
Your wife will be like a fruitful vine
within your house;
your sons will be like olive shoots
round your table.
Thus is the man blessed
who fears the Lord.

May the Lord bless you from Zion
all the days of your life;
may you see the prosperity of Jerusalem,
and may you live to see your children's children.

Peace be upon Israel.

# THURSDAY

PROVERBS 1:8–9, 13:24, 15:16,17,20, 17:6, 22:6, 23:13–14, 23:22 (NIV)

Listen, my son, to your father's
instruction
and do not forsake your mother's
teaching.
They will be a garland to grace your
head
and a chain to adorn your neck.

He who spares the rod hates his
son,
but he who loves him is careful to
discipline him.

Better a little with the fear of the
Lord
than great wealth with turmoil.

Better a meal of vegetables where
there is love
than a fattened calf with hatred.

A wise son brings joy to his father,
but a foolish man despises his
mother.

Children's children are a crown to
the aged,
and parents are the pride of their
children.

Train a child in the way he should
go,
and when he is old he will not
turn from it.

Do not withhold discipline from child;
if you punish him with the rod,
he will not die.
Punish him with the rod
and save his soul from death.

Listen to your father, who gave you
life,
and do not despise your mother
when she is old.

# FRIDAY

MARK 10:1–16 (NJB)

After leaving there, Jesus came into the territory of Judaea and Transjordan. And again crowds gathered round him, and again he taught them, as his custom was. Some Pharisees approached him and asked, 'Is it lawful for a man to divorce his wife?' They were putting him to the test. He answered them, 'What did Moses command you?' They replied, 'Moses allowed us to draw up a writ of dismissal in cases of divorce.' Then Jesus said to them, 'It was because you were so hard hearted that he wrote this commandment for you. But from the beginning of creation he made them male and female. This is why a man leaves his father and mother, and the two become one flesh. They are no longer two, therefore, but one flesh. So then, what God has united, human beings must not divide. Back in the house the disciples questioned him about this, and he said to them, 'Whoever divorces his wife and marries another is guilty of adultery against her. And if a woman divorces her husband and marries another she is guilty of adultery too.'

People were bringing little children to him, for him to touch them. The disciples scolded them, but when Jesus saw this he was indignant and said to them, 'Let the little children come to me; do not stop them; for it is to such as these that the kingdom of God belongs. In truth I tell you, anyone who does not welcome the kingdom of God like a little child will never enter it.' Then he embraced them, laid his hands on them and gave them his blessing.

# SATURDAY

EPHESIANS 5:21–25, 5:33–6:4 (NIV)

Submit to one another out of reverence for Christ.

Wives, submit to your husbands as to the Lord. For the husband is the head of the wife and Christ is the head of the church, his body, of which he is the Saviour. Now as the church submits to Christ, so also wives should submit to their husbands in everything.

Husbands, love your wives, just as Christ loved the church and gave himself up for her.

Each one of you also must love his wife as he loves himself, and the wife must respect her husband.

Children, obey your parents in the Lord, for this is right. 'Honour your father and mother'—which is the first commandment with a promise—'that it may go well with you and that you may enjoy long life on the earth.'

Fathers, do not exasperate your children; instead, bring them up in the training and instruction of the Lord.

WEEK 33

# FRIENDS IN NEED

Relatives are given to us; friends are those we choose; but neighbours can be anywhere! The law of Moses has much to say about good-neighbourly relationships. Exodus (Sunday) shows that honesty and goodness, even when inconvenient, are part of what it means to be in covenant with God. The laws in Leviticus, too, interweave godliness and true worship with holiness in everyday living, finance included (Monday).

The wit and wisdom of Proverbs follow on Tuesday, on one of this book's favourite themes: neighbourliness. In a quite different style, Zechariah's prophecy suggests that among the ingredients for a peaceful city are security for the young and the old, and justice for all (Wednesday).

The lawyer who tempts Jesus (or tests him—Thursday) gets for his reward the famous story of the Good Samaritan—Samaritans being traditional enemies of Jews. Jesus challenges him, and us, to look for the qualities of a neighbour not in others but in ourselves: I am to be the neighbour, wherever I am needed.

Finally, from the New Testament, the letters of Paul (Friday) and James (Saturday) concur in giving neighbourliness a solid grounding in God's concern and care for us. It is totally inconsistent with our calling to steal, get drunk or allow class distinction in church.

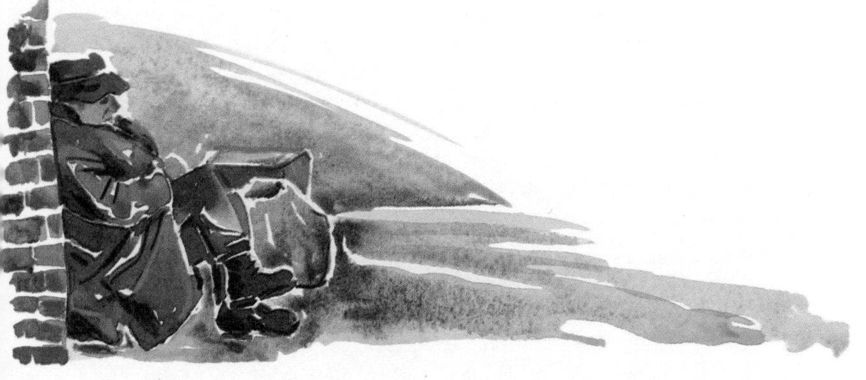

WEEK 33

# The Neighbour

The Old Testament laws include many about 'the neighbour'. The neighbour is the person next door or along the street, the brother-Israelite, the fellow-citizen or, at a pinch, the visitor who has settled down with you for a while.

Such a person has to be respected as you would respect yourself. He must be loved in the day-to-day details of life. You are not to steal his wife, life, property or children. You are not to defraud him in trade, withhold his wages, oppress him with exorbitant rates of interest, curse him if he is deaf or trip him up if blind. You are not secretly to shift his boundary stone to gain extra land, nor give false evidence against him in court, nor even covet anything that rightfully belongs to him.

The neighbour laws were just one of the ways in which Israel was to be 'holy' like her God. The community flourished when each person loved his neighbour as himself. When everyone was set against his neighbour, it signalled the breakdown of society.

The laws on neighbours were well known. The issue in Jesus' day was about who was to count as a neighbour. Where to draw the line was a matter of intense debate. Most agreed the term included the fellow-countryman and the convert. Some argued that personal enemies did not count, and others taught that you had a duty to push 'heretics, informers and renegades' *into* the ditch, not pull them out. Pharisees, not surprisingly, excluded non-Pharisees. No one dreamed that Gentiles could ever be neighbours, of course. And there was a saying that 'a piece of bread given by a Samaritan is more unclean than swine's flesh'. Everyone continued to define the exclusion zone.

'Who is my neighbour?' a scribe once asked Jesus. This assumes that you have got to draw the line somewhere. In fact, Jesus refused to answer the question in those terms. Instead he told a story, the Good Samaritan, which was deeply offensive to the hearers, since relations with the Samaritans at that time were particularly bad. The word 'Samaritan' was an obscene insult. The scribe, not wishing to soil his lips, could only manage 'the one who showed mercy' as a description of the neighbour. But this half-breed heretic was a true neighbour according to and even beyond the Law. He had compassion on a man who would have shrunk from his touch had he not been half-dead. The neighbours by race, blood, culture and religion proved false. The 'open cheque' the Samaritan gave to the innkeeper showed that he had never learned to draw a limit to compassion or neighbourliness.

The church picked up her Master's teaching. All the Law is summed up in the command to love our neighbour. Even the riff-raff can love their neighbours and hate their enemies. But what James called 'the royal law' helps me see that my enemy *is* my neighbour.

## SUNDAY

EXODUS 23:1–9 (NIV)

Do not spread false reports. Do not help a wicked man by being a malicious witness.

Do not follow the crowd in doing wrong. When you give testimony in a lawsuit, do not pervert justice by siding with the crowd, and do not show favouritism to a poor man in his lawsuit.

If you come across your enemy's ox or donkey wandering off, be sure to take it back to him. If you see the donkey of someone who hates you fallen down under its load, do not leave it there; be sure you help him with it.

Do not deny justice to your poor people in their lawsuits. Have nothing to do with a false charge and do not put an innocent or honest person to death, for I will not acquit the guilty.

Do not accept a bribe, for a bribe blinds those who see and twists the words of the righteous.

Do not oppress an alien; you yourselves know how it feels to be aliens, because you were aliens in Egypt.

## MONDAY

LEVITICUS 19:1–10, 13–18 (NIV)

The Lord said to Moses, 'Speak to the entire assembly of Israel and say to them: "Be holy because I, the Lord your God, am holy.

' "Each of you must respect his mother and father, and you must observe my Sabbaths. I am the Lord your God.

' "Do not turn to idols or make gods of cast metal for yourselves. I am the Lord your God.

' "When you sacrifice a fellowship offering to the Lord, sacrifice it in such a way that it will be accepted on your behalf. It shall be eaten on the day you sacrifice it or on the next day; anything left over until the third day must be burned up. If any of it is eaten on the third day, it is impure and will not be accepted. Whoever eats it will be held responsible because he has desecrated what is holy to the Lord; that person must be cut off from his people.

' "When you reap the harvest of your land, do not reap to the very edges of your field or gather the gleanings of your harvest. Do not go over your vineyard a second time or pick up the grapes that have fallen. Leave them for the poor and the alien. I am the Lord your God." '

' "Do not defraud your neighbour or rob him.

' "Do not hold back the wages of a hired man overnight.

' "Do not curse the deaf or put a stumbling-block in front of the blind, but fear your God. I am the Lord.

' "Do not pervert justice; do not show partiality to the poor or favouritism to the great, but judge your neighbour fairly.

' "Do not go about spreading slander among your people.

' "Do not do anything that endangers your neighbour's life. I am the Lord.

' "Do not hate your brother in your heart. Rebuke your neighbour frankly so that you will not share in his guilt.

' "Do not seek revenge or bear a grudge against one of your people, but love your neighbour as yourself. I am the Lord."'

## TUESDAY

PROVERBS 25:8–20 (NJB)

What your eyes have witnessed
do not produce too quickly at the trial,
for what are you to do at the end
should your neighbour confute you?

Have the quarrel out with your neighbour
but do not disclose another's secret,
for fear your listener put you to shame,
and the loss of repute be irremediable.

Like apples of gold inlaid with silver
is a word that is aptly spoken.
A golden ring, an ornament of finest gold,
is a wise rebuke to an attentive ear.

The coolness of snow in harvest time,
such is a trustworthy messenger to those who send him:
he revives the soul of his master.

Clouds and wind, but no rain:
such is anyone whose promises are princely but never kept.

With patience a judge may be cajoled:
a soft tongue breaks bones.

Eat to your satisfaction what honey you may find,
but not to excess or you will bring it up again.

Do not set foot too often in your neighbour's house,
for fear he tire of you and come to hate you.

A mace, a sword, a piercing arrow,
such is anyone who bears false witness against a companion.

Decaying tooth, lame foot,
such is the fickle when trusted in time of trouble:
as well take off your coat in bitter weather.

You are pouring vinegar on a wound
when you sing songs to a sorrowing heart.

## WEDNESDAY

ZECHARIAH 8:3–6, 14–17 (RSV)

Thus says the Lord: I will return to Zion, and will dwell in the midst of Jerusalem, and Jerusalem shall be called the faithful city, and the mountain of the Lord of hosts, the holy mountain. Thus says the Lord of hosts: Old men and old women shall again sit in the streets of Jerusalem, each with staff in hand for very age. And the streets of the city shall be full of boys and girls playing in its streets. Thus says the Lord of hosts: If it is marvellous in the sight of the remnant of this people in these days, should it also be marvellous in my sight, says the Lord of hosts?

For thus says the Lord of hosts: 'As I purposed to do evil to you, when your fathers provoked me to wrath, and I did not relent, says the Lord of hosts, so again have I purposed in these days to do good to Jerusalem and to the house of Judah; fear not. These are the things that you shall do: Speak the truth to one another, render in your gates judgments that are true and make for peace, do not devise evil in your hearts against one another, and love no false oath, for all these things I hate, says the Lord.'

## THURSDAY

LUKE 10:25–37 (AV)

And behold, a certain lawyer stood up, and tempted Jesus, saying, Master, what shall I do to inherit eternal life? He said unto him, What is written in the law? how readest thou? And he answering said, Thou shalt love the Lord thy God with all thy heart, and with all thy soul, and with all thy strength, and with all thy mind: and thy neighbour as thyself. And he said unto him, Thou hast answered right: this do, and thou shalt live. But he, willing to justify himself, said unto Jesus, And who is my neighbour?

And Jesus answering said, A certain man went down from Jerusalem to Jericho, and fell among thieves which stripped him of his raiment, and wounded him, and departed, leaving him half dead. And by chance there came down a certain priest that way: and when he saw him, he passed by on the other side. And likewise a Levite, when he was at the place, came and looked on him, and passed by on the other side. But a certain Samaritan, as he journeyed, came where he was: and when he saw him, he had compassion on him, And went to him, and bound up his wounds, pouring in oil and wine, and set him on his own beast, and brought him to an inn, and took care of him. And on the morrow when he departed, he took out two pence, and gave them to the host, and said unto him, Take care of him; and whatsoever thou spendest more, when I come again, I will repay thee.

Which now of these three, thinkest thou, was neighbour unto him that fell among the thieves? And he said, He that shewed mercy on him. Then said Jesus unto him, Go, and do thou likewise.

## FRIDAY

ROMANS 13:8–24 (REB)

Leave no debt outstanding, but remember the debt of love you owe one another. He who loves his neighbour has met every requirement of the law. The commandments, 'You shall not commit adultery, you shall not commit murder, you shall not steal, you shall not covet,' and any other commandment there may be, are all summed up in the one rule, 'Love your neighbour as yourself.' Love cannot wrong a neighbour; therefore love is the fulfilment of the law.

Always remember that this is the hour of crisis: it is high time for you to wake out of sleep, for deliverance is nearer to us now than it was when first we believed. It is far on in the night; day is near. Let us therefore throw off the deeds of darkness and put on the armour of light. Let us behave with decency as befits the day: no drunken orgies, no debauchery or vice, no quarrels or jealousies! Let Christ Jesus himself be the armour that you wear; give your unspiritual nature no opportunity to satisfy its desires.

## SATURDAY

JAMES 2:1–9 (NIV)

My brothers, as believers in our glorious Lord Jesus Christ, don't show favouritism. Suppose a man comes into your meeting wearing a gold ring and fine clothes, and a poor man in shabby clothes also comes in. If you show special attention to the man wearing fine clothes and say, 'Here's a good seat for you,' but say to the poor man, 'You stand there,' or 'Sit on the floor by my feet,' have you not discriminated among yourselves and become judges with evil thoughts?

Listen, my dear brothers: Has not God chosen those who are poor in the eyes of the world to be rich in faith and to inherit the kingdom he promised those who love him? But you have insulted the poor. Is it not the rich who are exploiting you? Are they not the ones who are dragging you into court? Are they not the ones who are slandering the noble name of him to whom you belong?

If you really keep the royal law found in Scripture, 'Love your neighbour as yourself,' you are doing right. But if you show favouritism, you sin and are convicted by the law as lawbreakers.

# TEARS AND TORMENTS

WEEK 34

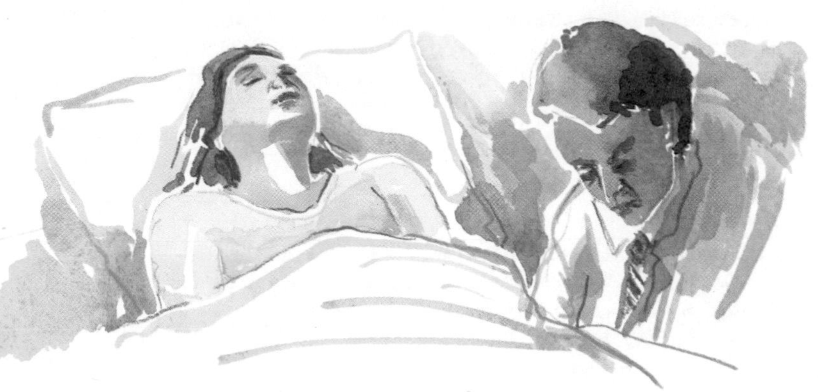

These days, through the media, we are more than ever aware of a suffering world. The Bible also presents the world's suffering, sometimes in horrific detail—though for different reasons. It brings no neat answers, but many of its characters cry out 'Why?'.

One of them is Job, whose book probes this heart-rending mystery in a formal drama which is also profoundly personal. Sunday's reading brings us to the peak of his torments after the deprivation and bereavements of the opening chapter.

We have met Ecclesiastes, 'the preacher', before; here too is a realistic account (Monday) of the tear-filled human condition. And the Lamentations are rooted in one unforgettable historical event; Jerusalem is conquered and in ruins, and most of her population taken into exile (Tuesday).

All this is known to Jesus, who himself (Wednesday) has an agony of God-forsakenness to face. He foresees every detail, and his friends can hardly believe it.

But later the suffering of Christians takes on a new meaning, even a new joy, from the cross of Christ. Both Peter (Saturday) and Paul (Friday) experienced this through their own tortures. And in Romans, Paul's horizon is the whole pain-wracked creation (Thursday); he lives, writes and endures in the clear hope of a pain-free future almost beyond words in its glory.

WEEK 34

# Suffering

Suffering is the greatest barrier that stops people believing in a loving heavenly Father.' Those who have suffered or have watched others suffer understand this fully. There can be few who have not asked, 'Why doesn't God do something?'

Although the Bible does not give a direct, intellectual answer to the question of suffering, yet it is possible to draw out some of its insights. First, some suffering comes because human beings have free wills. God has given to mankind a delegated freedom. Adam may choose either to till the garden or to take of the forbidden fruit. The rulers of this world are free to 'crucify the Lord of glory'. In the story, the prodigal son is free to squander his inheritance in a far country. This is a real freedom. And some kinds of suffering—from war, for instance, or from injustice—are the result of human abuse of this freedom to choose.

The second insight, perhaps more difficult to understand, is that this world is a fallen world. There are some mysterious verses in Paul's letter to the Romans where the apostle suggests that the creation is 'frustrated', 'in bondage to decay'. Sin affects the created world. 'Thorns and briars' grow in the 'Garden of the Lord'. It is just possible to see from this how some pain, suffering, disease or natural disaster might be explained. The creation is no longer as it should be; it is somehow spoiled through sin.

Thirdly, we ought not to soften the biblical truth that, in a moral universe, suffering is sometimes the result of sin. This world is a stable world, regular and predictable. It is this which makes real choices possible. But its very regularity means that the fire which warms may also burn and that a sinful life may carry its own retribution within it.

All this is on a mental level, and so of little comfort to those who are actually suffering or watching others suffer. For them the Bible has a different word, which speaks to our faith.

- **Christ has died, so he understands our pain**. It is easy to forget that at the heart of Christianity is a crucified God. God does not watch his suffering world with detachment. He comes into people's pain; agonizes and bleeds with them.
- **Christ is risen, so no one suffers alone**. If Jesus is alive then something good can be brought out of suffering. Even for Jesus there were some things that could only be learned through suffering. Paul discovered that God's grace was enough for him only through being tormented by a thorn in the flesh. Christians are called to believe, sometimes in the teeth of the evidence, that God can transform every situation.
- **Christ will come again, so suffering cannot be the last word**. One day the universe will be redeemed, the lame man leap, the dumb sing. The New Testament ends with the vision of a day when 'God will wipe every tear from their eyes' and 'there will be no more death or mourning or crying or pain'.

## SUNDAY

JOB 2:1–3:4 (RSV)

Again there was a day when the sons of God came to present themselves before the Lord, and Satan also came among them to present himself before the Lord. And the Lord said to Satan, 'Whence have you come?' Satan answered the Lord, 'From going to and fro on the earth, and from walking up and down on it.' And the Lord said to Satan, 'Have you considered my servant Job, that there is none like him on the earth, a blameless and upright man, who fears God and turns away from evil? He still holds fast his integrity, although you moved me against him, to destroy him without cause.' Then Satan answered the Lord, 'Skin for skin! All that a man has he will give for his life. But put forth thy hand now, and touch his bone and his flesh, and he will curse thee to thy face.' And the Lord said to Satan, 'Behold, he is in your power; only spare his life.'

So Satan went forth from the presence of the Lord, and afflicted Job with loathsome sores from the sole of his foot to the crown of his head. And he took a potsherd with which to scrape himself, and sat among the ashes.

Then his wife said to him, 'Do you still hold fast your integrity? Curse God, and die.' But he said to her, 'You speak as one of the foolish women would speak. Shall we receive good at the hand of God, and shall we not receive evil?' In all this Job did not sin with his lips.

Now when Job's three friends heard of all this evil that had come upon him, they came each from his own place, Eliphaz the Temanite, Bildad the Shuhite, and Zophar the Naamathite. They made an appointment together to come to condole with him and comfort him. And when they saw him from afar, they did not recognize him; and they raised their voices and wept; and they rent their robes and sprinkled dust upon their heads toward heaven. And they sat with him on the ground seven days and seven nights, and no one spoke a word to him, for they saw that his suffering was very great.

After this Job opened his mouth and cursed the day of his birth. And Job said: 'Let the day perish wherein I was born, and the night which said, "A man-child is conceived." Let that day be darkness! May God above not seek it, nor light shine upon it.'

## MONDAY

ECCLESIASTES 4:1–8 (AV)

So I returned, and considered all the oppressions that are done under the sun: and behold the tears of such as were oppressed, and they had no comforter; and on the side of their oppressors there was power; but they had no comforter. Wherefore I praised the dead which are already dead more than the living which are yet alive. Yea, better is he than both they, which hath not yet been, who hath not seen the evil work that is done under the sun.

Again, I considered all travail, and every right work, that for this a man is envied of his neighbour. This is also vanity and vexation of spirit. The fool foldeth his hands together, and eateth his own flesh. Better is an handful with quietness, than both the hands full with travail and vexation of spirit.

Then I returned, and I saw vanity under the sun. There is one alone, and there is not a second; yea, he hath neither child nor brother: yet is there no end of all his labour; neither is his eye satisfied with riches; neither saith he, For whom do I labour, and bereave my soul of good? This is also vanity, yea, it is a sore travail.

## TUESDAY

LAMENTATIONS 1:1–4, 12–16, 2:10–16 (RSV)

How lonely sits the city
  that was full of people!
How like a widow has she become,
  she that was great among the nations!
She that was a princess among the cities
  has become a vassal.

She weeps bitterly in the night,
  tears on her cheeks;
among all her lovers
  she has none to comfort her;
all her friends have dealt treacherously with her,
  they have become her enemies.

Judah has gone into exile because of affliction
  and hard servitude;
she dwells now among the nations,
  but finds no resting place;
her pursuers have all overtaken her
  in the midst of her distress.

The roads to Zion mourn,
  for none come to the appointed feasts;
all her gates are desolate,
  her priests groan;
her maidens have been dragged away,
  and she herself suffers bitterly.

'Is it nothing to your, all you who pass by?
  Look and see
if there is any sorrow like my sorrow
  which was brought upon me,
which the Lord inflicted
  on the day of his fierce anger.

'From on high he sent fire;
  into my bones he made it descend;
he spread a net for my feet;
  he turned me back;
he has left me stunned,
  faint all the day long.

'My transgressions were bound into a yoke;
  by his hand they were fastened together;
they were set upon my neck;
  he caused my strength to fail;
the Lord gave me into the hands
  of those I cannot withstand.

'The Lord flouted all my mighty men
  in the midst of me;
he summoned an assembly against me
  to crush my young men;
the Lord has trodden as in a wine press
  the virgin daughter of Judah.

'For these things I weep;
  my eyes flow with tears;
for a comforter is far from me,
  one to revive my courage;

my children are desolate,
for the enemy has prevailed.'

The elders of the daughter of Zion
sit on the ground in silence;
they have cast dust on their heads
and put on sackcloth;
the maidens of Jerusalem
have bowed their heads to the ground.

My eyes are spent with weeping;
my soul is in tumult;
my heart is poured out in grief
because of the destruction of the daughter of my people,
because infants and babes faint
in the streets of the city.

They cry to their mothers,
'Where is bread and wine?'
as they faint like wounded men
in the streets of the city,
as their life is poured out
on their mothers' bosom.

What can I say for you, to what compare you,
O daughter of Jerusalem?
What can I liken to you, that I may comfort you,
O virgin daughter of Zion?
For vast as the sea is your ruin;
who can restore you?

Your prophets have seen for you
false and deceptive visions;
they have not exposed your iniquity
to restore your fortunes,
but have seen for you oracles
false and misleading.

All who pass along the way
clap their hands at you;
they hiss and wag their heads
at the daughter of Jerusalem;
'Is this the city which was called
the perfection of beauty,
the joy of all the earth?'

All your enemies
rail against you;
they hiss, they gnash their teeth,
they cry: 'We have destroyed her!
Ah, this is the day we longed for;
now we have it; we see it!'

## WEDNESDAY

MARK 10:32–34, 15:33–39 (REB)

They were on the road going up to Jerusalem, and Jesus was leading the way; and the disciples were filled with awe, while those who followed behind were afraid. Once again he took the Twelve aside and began to tell them what was to happen to him. 'We are now going up to Jerusalem,' he said, 'and the Son of Man will be handed over to the chief priests and the scribes; they will condemn him to death and hand him over to the Gentiles. He will be mocked and spat upon, and flogged and killed; and three days afterwards, he will rise again.'

At midday a darkness fell over the whole land, which lasted till three in the afternoon; and at three Jesus cried aloud, 'Eloï, Eloï, lema sabachthani?' which means, 'My God, my God, why have you forsaken me?' Hearing this, some of the bystanders said, 'Listen! He is calling Elijah.' Someone ran and soaked a sponge in sour wine and held it to his lips on the end of a stick. 'Let us see', he said, 'if Elijah will come to take him down.' Then Jesus gave a loud cry and died; and the curtain of the temple was torn in two from top to bottom. When the centurion who was standing opposite him saw how he died, he said, 'This man must have been a son of God.'

## THURSDAY

ROMANS 8:18–25 (NIV)

I consider that our present sufferings are not worth comparing with the glory that will be revealed in us. The creation waits in eager expectation for the sons of God to be revealed. For the creation was subjected to frustration, not by its own choice, but by the will of the one who subjected it, in hope that the creation itself will be liberated from its bondage to decay and brought into the glorious freedom of the children of God.

We know that the whole creation has been groaning as in the pains of childbirth right up to the present time. Not only so, but we ourselves, who have the firstfruits of the Spirit, groan inwardly as we wait eagerly for our adoption as sons, the redemption of our bodies. For in this hope we were saved. But hope that is seen is no hope at all. Who hopes for what he already has? But if we hope for what we do not yet have, we wait for it patiently.

## FRIDAY

2 CORINTHIANS 1:3–11 (NIV)

Praise be to the God and Father of our Lord Jesus Christ, the Father of compassion and the God of all comfort, who comforts us in all our troubles, so that we can comfort those in any trouble with the comfort we ourselves have received from God. For just as the sufferings of Christ flow over into our lives, so also through Christ our comfort overflows. If we are distressed, it is for your comfort and salvation; if we are comforted, it is for your comfort, which produces in you patient endurance of the same sufferings we suffer. And our hope for you is firm, because we know that just as you share in our sufferings, so also you share in our comfort.

We do not want you to be uninformed, brothers, about the hardships we suffered in the province of Asia. We were under great pressure, far beyond our ability to endure, so that we despaired even of life. Indeed, in our hearts we felt the sentence of death. But this happened that we might not rely on ourselves but on God, who raises the dead. He has delivered us from such a deadly peril, and he will deliver us. On him we have set our hope that he will continue to deliver us, as you help us by your prayers. Then many will give thanks on our behalf for the gracious favour granted us in answer to the prayers of many.

## SATURDAY

1 PETER 4:12–19 (NJB)

My dear friends, do not be taken aback at the testing by fire which is taking place among you, as though something strange were happening to you; but in so far as you share in the sufferings of Christ, be glad, so that you may enjoy a much greater gladness when his glory is revealed. If you are insulted for bearing Christ's name, blessed are you, for on you rests the Spirit of God, the Spirit of glory. None of you should ever deserve to suffer for being a murderer, a thief, a criminal or an informer; but if any of you should suffer for being a Christian, then there must be no shame but thanksgiving to God for bearing this name. The time has come for the judgment to begin at the household of God; and if it begins with us, what will be the end for those who refuse to believe God's gospel? If it is hard for the upright to be saved, what will happen to the wicked and to sinners? So even those whom God allows to suffer should commit themselves to a Creator who is trustworthy, and go on doing good.

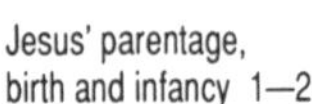

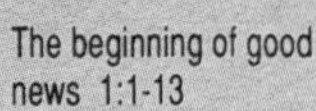

## MATTHEW
## Five great speeches

Jesus' parentage, birth and infancy 1—2

Baptism, temptation; the ministry begins 3—4

First great speech: the Sermon on the Mount 5—7

Scenes from Jesus' work in Galilee 8—9

Second great speech: Jesus sends the twelve out to preach 10

Questions and conflict 11—12

Third great speech: parables of the kingdom 13

Miracles and teaching 14—16:12

Jesus recognized as Christ; predictions of suffering; the transfiguration 16:13—17

Fourth great speech: the life of a disciple 18

Teaching 19—20

In Jerusalem 21—23

Fifth great speech: future perils and parables of judgment 24—25

The anointing, the last supper, Gethsemane, the trials 26—27:26

Jesus is crucified and buried 27:27-66

The resurrection; the great commission 28

## MARK
## Fast-moving snapshots

The beginning of good news 1:1-13

Jesus' power and authority 1:14—3:12

Jesus commissions the twelve; conflict 3:13-35

Parables and miracles 4—5

Sorrow and misunderstanding; then light begins to dawn 6—8:26

Peter declares that Jesus is Christ: the turning-point 8:27—9:1

Transfiguration, a miracle, teaching 9:2-10

Jesus enters Jerusalem; the temple; parables and questions 11—12

What will happen before the end? 13

The anointing; the last supper; Gethsemane; the two trials 14—15:20

Jesus is crucified and buried 15:21-47

The resurrection 16:1-8

(16:9-20 was not part of the original text)

## LUKE
## A great journey

Jesus' birth and childhood 1—2

Baptism and temptation; the ministry begins 3—4

Disciples are called; healings; conflict begins 5—6:11

Jesus chooses twelve 6:12-19

The sermon on the plain 6:20-49

The compassion of Jesus 7

Parables, miracles, teaching 8—9:50

The journey to Jerusalem: parables, warnings, teaching on discipleship 9:51—19:27

Journey's end: Jerusalem and opposition 19:28—21:4

Signs of the last days 21:5-38

Last supper; Gethsemane; the two trials 22—23:25

Jesus is crucified and buried 23:26-56

The resurrection 24

## JOHN
## Seven signs

Jesus, the Word of God 1:1-18

John the Baptist and the first disciples 1:19-51

First sign: water into wine 2:1-12

Jesus in the temple; Nicodemus; Jesus and John 2:13—3

The woman of Samaria 4:1-41

The second and third signs 4:42—5:9

Disputes with religious leaders 5:10-47

Fourth and fifth signs; Jesus the bread of life 6

In Jerusalem for the Feast of Tabernacles 7—8

Sixth sign: a man born blind 9

The good shepherd 10:1-21

Disputes, and seventh sign: Lazarus raised 10:22—11

Jesus anointed; the entry into Jerusalem 1

The footwashing; Jesus teaches his disciples 13—16

Jesus prays to his Father 17

Arrest, trial, crucifixion and burial 18—19

The empty tomb; an appearance to Mary Magdalene 20

The risen Jesus and his disciples at the lakeside 21

## HE FOUR GOSPELS

### OUR DISTINCT PORTRAITS

e can be very thankful that there are *four* spels, not just one. This way we have a more nprehensive picture of Jesus. Each of the r portraits has something special and portant to bring to the whole.

**Matthew** is the most Jewish Gospel, essing Old Testament prophecies fulfilled in sus. Another focus is on Jesus the teacher: e great sermons interrupt the action in this spel.

**Mark** is the great story-teller. The Gospel is short, fast-moving and action-packed—a series of snapshots.

**Luke**, who also wrote the Acts of the Apostles, is above all a historian. He sets down 'the full truth', drawing on first-hand sources. His Gospel is written specifically for non-Jewish people.

**John** is very different in style from the others. The writer's declared aim is to call people to believe in Jesus as 'the Messiah, the Son of God'.

### EY TO OLOUR HADING

Birth and infancy

Baptism and emptation

Teaching and healing

Last week in Jerusalem

### HOW THE GOSPELS CAME TO US

For thirty years after Jesus died and rose, the apostles declared the good news about him by word of mouth. Meanwhile written records of his sayings and actions were being collected. Eventually those records and word-of-mouth memories about Jesus were brought together to make the four Gospels. These became an essential back-up to the apostles' preaching, steadily increasing in importance as time passed and eyewitnesses of Jesus' life became fewer.

The first three Gospels have quite a lot of material in common, while John's Gospel is quite distinct.

Mark is thought to have been written first, as some of Mark's stories and sayings were used by Matthew and Luke. Early traditions say that a source for Mark's account was the apostle Peter.

Matthew and Luke, as well as using Mark as a source, may have had another common source of stories and sayings. These are the only two Gospels to cover Jesus' birth and infancy.

John describes Jesus' life and teaching from quite a different standpoint, mainly based in Jerusalem rather than Galilee, and using longer discourses rather than short sayings. This Gospel used to be thought of as later, but since the sources are obviously different, this need not be so. Matthew, Luke and John may have been written at any time between about AD65 and AD80, with Mark rather earlier.

WEEK 35

# FACING THE LAST ENEMY

Different cultures cope with death in varied ways. The Old Testament is quite literally 'down to earth'; the death that spreads from Adam to all his descendants never loses its sting, even in days of prosperity and peace. In the first reading (Sunday), Jacob's word to Pharaoh and to his family as he faces death reflect this sorrow. Joseph follows his father, with the added confidence that God will one day resurrect the nation.

Monday's reading concerns David, the future king of Israel. He was not one to hide his emotions, and the deaths together of Saul, his king and enemy, and Jonathan, his prince and friend, evoke this noble lament. Later in the book of Samuel, the dying of David's child brings him to lie all night upon the floor; the death itself brings a kind of release (Tuesday). Elsewhere, the demise of the elderly is characteristically, rhythmically mourned in the haunting homily at the end of Ecclesiastes (Wednesday). Jesus faced the death of friends before his own; he treats death as an enemy. Thursday's extract from John's Gospel (Thursday) shows him confronting the love and the anger of the bereaved, when Lazarus dies.

The friends of Stephen, the first Christian martyr, can share his faith that Jesus will receive him, but need also the healing process of mourning (Friday). Saul (Paul) who was there that day, writes years later of his own imminent 'departure', in closing the last letter we have from his hand (Saturday).

# Dying and Death

'Death, where is your sting? Death, where is your victory?' For Paul death was only a comma and not a full stop. In Old Testament times things were very different; death was a disaster and a curse. In the garden of Eden God warned Adam that eating the forbidden fruit would bring death into the world. The serpent denied this—'you will not surely die'. But the serpent lied. Although physical death did not come until later, the first act of rebellion brought alienation from God. The reward of disobedience was personal decay; a kind of dying began right then, though this only became apparent in the presence of God.

Physical death was the sign that all was not well with humanity. The Bible views it bleakly. Whatever the state of the dead in Sheol, the land of the grave, it was too thin an existence to be called living. Death marked the end of human life and achievement. In the grave 'there was neither working nor planning nor knowledge nor wisdom', according to the preacher in Ecclesiastes. Death also raised the question of the meaning of life. If good and bad, poor and rich, weak and strong all ended up in the same place, then it looked as if time and chance were the only realities. And as Job saw clearly, death challenged God's running of the world. If the wicked prospered in life and died at a ripe old age, how could you say that God was just? It is true that by the time of Jesus some Jews had begun to believe in an afterlife, where rewards and punishments could redress the imbalances of this life. But still for most people death was the great threat hanging over humanity; 'all their lives were held in slavery through their fear of death'.

But the death and resurrection of Jesus has changed the whole picture. He 'tasted death for everyone' and opened up a way through death into a new kind of life. He is 'the resurrection and the life'—a claim made good by the raising of Lazarus. Those who put their trust in him have already escaped spiritual death; they have crossed over from death to life. If the sting of death is sin then Christ's forgiveness draws that sting. Suddenly Christians are able to speak with confidence about the future. Paul can assert that dying is gain since it will mean a closer relationship with Jesus. Life has a purpose and a direction which is not negated by death. Serving God and working for the kingdom is not wasted effort. Even martyrdom is transformed into 'dying in the Lord' and is a prelude to glory. Stephen is stoned to death but is described as 'falling asleep'. Neither death nor life can separate the Christian from the love of God in Christ.

## SUNDAY

GENESIS 47:7–10, 49:28–33, 50:22–26 (RSV)

Then Joseph brought in Jacob his father, and set him before Pharaoh, and Jacob blessed Pharaoh. And Pharaoh said to Jacob, 'How many are the days of the years of your life?' And Jacob said to Pharaoh, 'The days of the years of my sojourning are a hundred and thirty years; few and evil have been the days of the years of my life, and they have not attained to the days of the years of the life of my fathers in the days of their sojourning.' And Jacob blessed Pharaoh, and went out from the presence of Pharaoh.

All these are the twelve tribes of Israel; and this is what their father said to them as he blessed them, blessing each with the blessing suitable to him. Then he charged them, and said to them, 'I am to be gathered to my people; bury me with my fathers in the cave that is in the field of Ephron the Hittite, in the cave that is in the field at Machpelah, to the east of Mamre, in the land of Canaan, which Abraham bought with the field from Ephron the Hittite to possess as a burying place. There they buried Abraham and Sarah his wife; there they buried Isaac and Rebekah his wife; and there I buried Leah—the field and the cave that is in it were purchased form the Hittites.' When Jacob finished charging his sons, he drew up his feet into the bed, and breathed his last, and was gathered to his people.

So Joseph dwelt in Egypt, he and his father's house; and Joseph lived a hundred and ten years. And Joseph saw Ephraim's children of the third generation; the children also of Machir the son of Manasseh were born upon Joseph's knees. And Joseph said to his brothers, 'I am about to die; but God will visit you, and bring you up out of this land to the land which he swore to Abraham, to Isaac, and to Jacob.' Then Joseph took an oath of the sons of Israel, saying, 'God will visit you, and you shall carry up my bones from here.' So Joseph died, being a hundred and ten years old; and they embalmed him, and he was put in a coffin in Egypt.

## MONDAY

2 SAMUEL 1:17–27 (AV)

And David lamented with this lamentation over Saul and over Jonathan his son:

The beauty of Israel is slain upon thy high places: how are the mighty fallen! Tell it not in Gath, publish it not in the streets of Askelon; lest the daughters of the Philistines rejoice, lest the daughters of the uncircumcised triumph. Ye mountains of Gilboa, let there be no dew, neither let there be rain, upon you, nor fields of offerings: for there the shield of the mighty is vilely cast away, the shield of Saul, as though he had not been anointed with oil.

From the blood of the slain, from the the fat of the mighty, the bow of Jonathan turned not back, and the sword of Saul returned not empty. Saul and Jonathan were lovely and pleasant in their lives, and in their death they were not divided: they were swifter than eagles, they were stronger than lions.

Ye daughters of Israel, weep over Saul, who clothed you in scarlet, with other delights, who put on ornaments of gold upon your apparel. How are the mighty fallen in the midst of battle!

O Jonathan, thou wast slain in thine high places. I am distressed for thee, my brother Jonathan: very pleasant hast thou been unto me: thy love to me was wonderful, passing the love of women. How are the mighty fallen, and the weapons of war perished!

## TUESDAY

2 SAMUEL 12:15–23 (RSV)

And the Lord struck the child that Uriah's wife bore to David, and it became sick. David therefore besought God for the child; and David fasted, and went in and lay all night upon the ground. And the elders of his house stood beside him, to raise him from the ground; but he would not, nor did he eat food with them.

On the seventh day the child died. And the servants of David feared to tell him that the child was dead; for they said, 'Behold, while the child was yet alive, we spoke to him, and he did not listen to us; how then can we say to him the child is dead? He may do himself some harm.'

But when David saw that his servants were whispering together, David perceived that the child was dead; and David said to his servants, 'Is the child dead?' They said, 'He is dead.'

Then David arose from the earth, and washed, and anointed himself, and changed his clothes; and he went into the house of the Lord, and worshipped; he then went to his own house; and when he asked, they set food before him, and he ate.

Then his servants said to him, 'What is this thing that you have done? You fasted and wept for the child while it was alive; but when the child died, you arose and ate food.' He said, 'While the child was still alive, I fasted and wept; for I said, "Who knows whether the Lord will be gracious to me, that the child may live?" But now he is dead; why should I fast? Can I bring him back again? I shall go to him, but he will not return to me.'

## WEDNESDAY

ECCLESIASTES 12:1–8 (AV)

Remember now thy Creator in the days of thy youth, while the evil days come not, nor the years draw nigh, when thou shalt say, I have no pleasure in them; While the sun, or the light, or the moon, or the stars, be not darkened, nor the clouds return after the rain.

In the day when the keepers of the house shall tremble, and the strong men shall bow themselves, and the grinders cease because they are few, and those that look out of the windows be darkened, And the doors shall be shut in the streets, when the sound of the grinding is low, and he shall rise up at the voice of the bird, and all the daughters of musick shall be brought low; Also when they shall be afraid of that which is high, and fears shall be in the way, and the almond tree shall flourish, and the grasshopper shall be a burden, and desire shall fail: because man goeth to his long home, and the mourners go about the streets: Or ever the silver cord be loosed, or the golden bowl be broken, or the pitcher be broken at the fountain, or the wheel broken at the cistern.

Then shall the dust return to the earth as it was: and the spirit shall return unto God who gave it.

Vanity of vanities, saith the preacher; all is vanity.

## THURSDAY

JOHN 11:1–21 (REB)

There was a man named Lazarus who had fallen ill. His home was at Bethany, the village of Mary and her sister Martha. This Mary, whose brother Lazarus had fallen ill, was the woman who had anointed the Lord with ointment and wiped his feet with her hair. The sisters sent a message to him: 'Sir, you should know that your friend lies ill.' When Jesus heard this he said, 'This illness is not to end in death; through it God's glory is to be revealed and the Son of God glorified.' Therefore, though he loved Martha and her sister and Lazarus, he stayed where he was for two days after hearing of Lazarus's illness.

He then said to his disciples, 'Let us go back to Judaea.' 'Rabbi,' his disciples said, 'it is not long since the Jews there were wanting to stone you. Are you going there again?' Jesus replied, 'Are there not twelve hours of daylight? Anyone can walk in the daytime without stumbling, because he has this world's light to see by. But if he walks after nightfall he stumbles, because the light fails him.'

After saying this he added, 'Our friend Lazarus had fallen asleep, but I shall go and wake him.' The disciples said, 'Master, if he is sleeping he will recover.' Jesus had been speaking of Lazarus's death, but they thought that he meant natural sleep. Then Jesus told them plainly: 'Lazarus is dead. I am glad for your sake that I was not there; for it will lead you to believe. But let us go to him.' Thomas, called 'the Twin', said to his fellow disciples, 'Let us also go and die with him.'

On his arrival Jesus found that Lazarus had already been four days in the tomb. Bethany was just under two miles from Jerusalem, and many of the Jews had come from the city to visit Martha and Mary and condole with them about their brother. As soon as Martha heard that Jesus was on his way, she went to meet him, and left Mary sitting at home.

Martha said to Jesus, 'Lord, if you had been here my brother would not have died.'

## FRIDAY

ACTS 7:54–8:2 (REB)

This touched them on the raw, and they ground their teeth with fury. But Stephen, filled with the Holy Spirit, and gazing intently up to heaven, saw the glory of God, and Jesus standing at God's right hand. 'Look!' he said. 'I see the heavens opened and the Son of Man standing at the right hand of God.' At this they gave a great shout, and stopped their ears; they made a concerted rush at him, threw him out of the city, and set about stoning him. The witnesses laid their coats at the feet of a young man named Saul. As they stoned him Stephen called out, 'Lord Jesus, receive my spirit.' He fell on his knees and cried aloud, 'Lord, do not hold this sin against them,' and with that he died. Saul was among those who approved of his execution.

That day was the beginning of a time of violent persecution for the church in Jerusalem; and all except the apostles were scattered over the country districts of Judaea and Samaria. Stephen was given burial by devout men, who made a great lamentation for him.

## SATURDAY

2 TIMOTHY 4:6–18 (NIV)

For I am already being poured out like a drink offering, and the time has come for my departure. I have fought the good fight, I have finished the race, I have kept the faith. Now there is in store for me the crown of righteousness, which the Lord, the righteous Judge, will award to me on that day—and not only to me, but also to all who have longed for his appearing.

Do your best to come to me quickly, for Demas, because he loved this world, has deserted me and has gone to Thessalonica. Crescens has gone to Galatia, and Titus to Dalmatia. Only Luke is with me. Get Mark and bring him with you, because he is helpful to me in my ministry. I sent Tychicus to Ephesus. When you come, bring the cloak that I left with Carpus at Troas, and my scrolls, especially the parchments.

Alexander the metalworker did me a great deal of harm. The Lord will repay him for what he has done. You too should be on your guard against him, because he strongly opposed our message.

At my first defence, no-one came to my support, but everyone deserted me. May it not be held against them. But the Lord stood at my side and gave me strength, so that through me the message might be fully proclaimed and all the Gentiles might hear it. And I was delivered from the lion's mouth. The Lord will rescue me from every evil attack and will bring me safely to his heavenly kingdom. To him be glory for ever and ever. Amen.

WEEK 36

# GOD'S GOOD EARTH

Human beings may be late arrivals on this planet, but from the day the earth appeared it has been designated our home. Sunday's reading takes us back again to the primeval creation, to a world lit only by the radiant lamps of God's sky.

On Monday we hear the law of God. Here, God's people are instructed to take meticulous care for the earth's rhythms and cycles of growth. Then we read how on the verge of the 'promised land', Moses reminds Israel of their humiliating past and their God-given future, in the country they were so soon to be given (Tuesday).

The Psalms (Wednesday) are filled with the praise of the Lord for the earth's fruitfulness. The emphasis is distinct from surrounding nature-religions, for this is also praise for the word and law of God.

Two portions of Jeremiah's long book show this dogged prophet's realism and faith. We see that, even in exile, God's people are to respect their temporary home (Thursday). And when they are hopelessly besieged and militarily powerless, they are to hold on to God's promise that the land will again be theirs (Friday).

The book of Revelation strikes a different note (Saturday). In preparation for new heavens and earth, the good land that God prepared and we polluted must itself submit to the judgment of its Creator.

# The Land

Most people want a place of their own; it is a natural human longing. To say, 'That's my house' or 'That's my land' gives great pleasure, and many more would love to be able to say it. It was this desire that drove the American settlers out into the wilderness to claim the land, to build their farms and houses and to start a new life in a new world. In a very similar way, the Hebrews set out from Egypt to settle down in a 'land of promise'. But there was one significant difference: the Hebrews believed that their land was given to them by God.

Three great themes are at the heart of the Bible idea of 'land':

◆ **God promised Israel a land** where they could find peace and prosperity. 'Go from your country,' said God to Abraham, 'to the land which I will show you.' God's call to Abraham to leave his security in one land and to seek for another was the dream which shaped Israel as a people. This explains why they considered it right to drive out other occupants of the land; all others were exercising 'squatters' rights', while they alone were the rightful inheritors.

◆ **The land represented God's presence.** In the Old Testament we find that as God's people settled down in the land so the land itself, and important elements within it, became symbols of God's presence. So to this day three major religions call the land of Israel 'the Holy Land'. Jerusalem (Zion), its most sacred city and, for the Jew, the temple as the place where the Ark of the Covenant once resided, symbolize God's personal presence.

Taken on their own, these two themes could lead people to conclude that the land was theirs for ever and they could do whatever they liked with it. And we find this attitude coming out from time to time in the Old Testament when people forgot the third very crucial element:

◆ **The land really belongs to God;** the people's task was to be wise and careful stewards. So we find in the book of Deuteronomy many instructions to take care of the land, not to waste or exhaust it. Every seventh year the land should lie fallow to regain its strength. The lesson is drummed in. Because God has given it to you to enjoy, out of gratitude to him you should be generous to others. Let some of your produce go to the foreigner, the fatherless and the widow. Share your wealth with the poor and the foreigner because 'you were once poor and a stranger'.

Every third year, one tenth of all produce had to be set aside as a contribution to the needy. God even declares: 'There will be no poor among you.' And every seventh year, slaves should be given the option of freedom and a generous token of the wealth of the land they had helped to produce. God's ownership of the land was symbolically recognized each year through the offering of the 'first fruits', presented in the temple to the Lord.

We can see at once one very important difference between the Christian and the Jew. For the Jews the land is an essential feature of their faith, but for the Christian what counts is possessing God and being a citizen of heaven. Still there is a belief common to both: whatever patch of land we enjoy, together with the material blessings that go with it, is not to be used selfishly but for God and his people.

This is why Christians should be among those who want the poor to share the riches of this world, why we will be generous and sacrificial in our giving to the needy, and why we will care for the land and use it for God's glory and his people.

## SUNDAY

GENESIS 1:9–19 (AV)

And God said, Let the waters under the heaven be gathered together unto one place, and let the dry land appear: and it was so. And God called the dry land Earth; and the gathering together of the waters he called Seas: and God saw that it was good. And God said, Let the earth bring forth grass, the herb yielding seed, and the fruit tree yielding fruit after his kind, whose seed is in itself, upon the earth: and it was so. And the earth brought forth grass, and herb yielding seed after his kind, and the tree yielding fruit, whose seed was in itself, after his kind: and God saw that it was good. And the evening and the morning were the third day.

And God said, Let there be lights in the firmament of the heaven to divide the day from the night; and let them be for signs, and for seasons, and for days and years: And let them be for lights in the firmament of the heaven to give light upon the earth: and it was so. And God made two great lights; the greater light to rule the day, and the lesser light to rule the night: he made the stars also. And God set them in the firmament of the heaven to give light upon the earth, And to rule over the day and over the night, and to divide the light from the darkness: and God saw that it was good. And the evening and the morning were the fourth day.

## MONDAY

LEVITICUS 25:1–13 (RSV)

The Lord said to Moses on Mount Sinai, 'Say to the people of Israel, When you come into the land which I give you, the land shall keep a sabbath to the Lord. Six years you shall sow your field, and six years you shall prune your vineyard, and gather in its fruits; but in the seventh year there shall be a sabbath of solemn rest for the land, a sabbath to the Lord; you shall not sow your field or prune your vineyard. What grows of itself in your harvest you shall not reap, and the grapes of your undressed vine you shall not gather; it shall be a year of solemn rest for the land. The sabbath of the land shall provide food for you, for yourself and for your male and female slaves and for your hired servant and the sojourner who lives with you; for your cattle also and for the beasts that are in your land all its yield shall be for food.

'And you shall count seven weeks of years, seven times seven years, so that the time of the seven weeks of years shall be to you forty-nine years. Then you shall send abroad the loud trumpet on the tenth day of the seventh month; on the day of atonement you shall send abroad the trumpet throughout all your land. And you shall hallow the fiftieth year, and proclaim liberty throughout the land to all its inhabitants; it shall be a jubilee for you, when each of you shall return to his property and each of you shall return to his family. A jubilee shall that fiftieth year be to you; in it you shall neither sow, nor reap what grows of itself, nor gather the grapes from the undressed vines. For it is a jubilee; it shall be holy to you; you shall eat what it yields out of the field.

In this year of jubilee each of you shall return to his own property.'

## TUESDAY

DEUTERONOMY 8:6–18 (NIV)

Observe the commands of the Lord your God, walking in his ways and revering him. For the Lord your God is bringing you into a good land—a land with streams and pools of water, with springs flowing in the valleys and hills; a land with wheat and barley, vines and fig trees, pomegranates, olive oil and honey; a land where bread will not be scarce and you will lack nothing; a land where the rocks are iron and you can dig copper out of the hills.

When you have eaten and are satisfied, praise the Lord your God for the good land he has given you. Be careful that you do not forget the Lord your God, failing to observe his commands, his laws and his decrees that I am giving you this day. Otherwise, when you eat and are satisfied, when you build fine houses and settle down, and when your herds and flocks grow large and your silver and gold increase and all you have is multiplied, then your heart will become proud and you will forget the Lord your God, who brought you out of Egypt, out of the land of slavery. He led you through the vast and dreadful desert, that thirsty and waterless land, with its venomous snakes and scorpions. He brought you water out of hard rock. He gave you manna to eat in the desert, something your fathers had never known, to humble and to test you so that in the end it might go well with you. You may say to yourself, 'My power and the strength of my hands have produced this wealth for me.' But remember the Lord your God, for it is he who gives you the ability to produce wealth, and so confirms his covenant, which he swore to your forefathers, as it is today.

## WEDNESDAY

PSALM 147:7–20 (NIV)

Sing to the Lord with thanksgiving;
make music to our God on the harp.
He covers the sky with clouds:
he supplies the earth with rain
and makes grass grow on the hills.
He provides food for the cattle
and for the young ravens when they call.

His pleasure is not in the strength of the horse,
nor his delight in the legs of a man;
the Lord delights in those who fear him,
who put their hope in his unfailing love.

Extol the Lord, O Jerusalem;
praise your God, O Zion,
for he strengthens the bars of your gates
and blesses your people within you.

He grants peace to your borders
and satisfies you with the finest
of wheat.

He sends his command to the earth;
his word runs swiftly.
He spreads the snow like wool
and scatters the frost like ashes.
He hurls down his hail like pebbles.
Who can withstand his icy blast?
He sends his sword and melts them;
he stirs up his breezes, and the
waters flow.

He has revealed his word to Jacob,
his laws and decrees to Israel.
He has done this for no other
nation;
they do not know his laws.

Praise the Lord.

## THURSDAY

JEREMIAH 29:1, 4–7 (REB)

Jeremiah sent a letter from Jerusalem to the elders who were left among the exiles, to the priests, prophets, and all the people whom Nebuchadnezzar had deported from Jerusalem to Babylon.

These are the words of the Lord of Hosts the God of Israel: To all the exiles whom I deported from Jerusalem to Babylon: Build houses and live in them; plant gardens and eat the produce; marry wives and rear families; choose wives for your sons and give your daughters to husbands, so that they may bear sons and daughters. Increase there and do not dwindle away. Seek the welfare of any city to which I have exiled you, and pray to the Lord for it; on its welfare your welfare will depend.

## FRIDAY

JEREMIAH 32:3–15 (REB)

King Zedekiah had imprisoned Jeremiah after demanding what he meant by this prophecy: 'These are the words of the Lord: I shall give this city into the power of the king of Babylon, and he will capture it. Nor will King Zedekiah of Judah escape from the Chaldaeans; he will be surrendered to the king of Babylon and will speak with him face to face and see him with his own eyes. Zedekiah will be taken to Babylon and will remain there until the day I visit him, says the Lord. However much you fight against the Chaldaeans you will have no success.'

Jeremiah said: this word of the Lord came to me: Hanamel son of your uncle Shallum is coming to you; he will say, 'Buy my field at Anathoth; as next-of-kin you have the right of redemption to buy it.' Just as the Lord had foretold, my cousin Hanamel came to me in the court of the guardhouse and said, 'Buy my field at Anathoth in Benjamin. You have the right of redemption and possession as next-of-kin, so buy it for yourself.'

I recognized that this instruction came from the Lord, so I bought the field at Anathoth from my cousin Hanamel and weighed out the price for him, seventeen shekels of silver. I signed and sealed the deed, had it witnessed, and then weighed the money on the scales. I took my copies of the deed of purchase, both the sealed and the unsealed copies, and handed them over to Baruch son of Neriah, son of Mahseiah, in the presence of Hanamel my cousin and the witnesses whose names were subscribed on the deed of purchase, and of the Judaeans sitting in the court of the guardhouse. In their presence I gave my instructions to Baruch: These are the words of the Lord of Hosts the God of Israel: Take these copies of the deed of purchase, both the sealed and the unsealed copies, and deposit them in an earthenware jar so that they may be preserved for a long time to come. For these are the words of the Lord of Hosts the God of Israel: Houses, fields, and vineyards will again be bought and sold in this land.

## SATURDAY

REVELATION 8:6–13 (NJB)

The seven angels that had the seven trumpets now made ready to sound them. The first blew his trumpet and, with that, hail and fire, mixed with blood, were hurled on the earth: a third of the earth was burnt up, and a third of all trees, and every blade of grass was burnt. The second angel blew his trumpet, and it was as though a great mountain blazing with fire was hurled into the sea: a third of the sea turned into blood, a third of all living things in the sea were killed, and a third of all ships were destroyed. The third angel blew his trumpet, and a huge star fell from the sky, burning like a ball of fire, and it fell on a third of all rivers and on the springs of water; this was the star called Wormwood, and a third of all water turned to wormwood, so that many people died; the water had become so bitter. The fourth angel blew his trumpet, and a third of the sun and a third of the moon and a third of the stars were blasted, so that the light went out of a third of them and the day lost a third of its illumination, and likewise the night.

In my vision, I heard an eagle, calling aloud as it flew high overhead, 'Disaster, disaster, disaster, on all the people on earth at the sound of the other three trumpets which the three angels have yet to blow!'

# FOUR-LEGGED FRIENDS

In the Bible animals and birds are shown to be vital to our well-being. Indeed, we learn year by year more of nature's interdependence, in the life of both city and countryside.

We read right at the very beginning of the Bible that God 'blessed' the living creatures (Sunday). And when judgment comes in the flood, Noah's mandate is to conserve all of them, male and female, clean and unclean. Two of the feathered, two-legged variety become his messengers as the waters subside (Monday).

The laws about clean and unclean creatures are (among other things) a zoologist's delight; not all the named species are easily identifiable today, but the principle of making distinctions lay close to the heart of Israel's ritual (Tuesday).

Balaam's donkey (Wednesday) is altogether different. Like a later relative on Palm Sunday, this large-eared servant has something to tell us, who use her name so unkindly, just as she had a message for her original master.

For some of the poetry of the animal world we turn to Job (Thursday) and Proverbs (Friday). Here are writers with a naturalist's eye for detail within the differing contexts of their books.

The vision of all sorts of animals which Peter has on a rooftop in Jaffa (Saturday) is crucial. It teaches him that his sensitivities about the Gentiles are now out of date. The old ritual distinctions of the law have been dissolved by the gospel.

WEEK 37

# The Animals

The Animal Rights movement has made the place of animals in the world a matter of intense debate. In the Bible, animals in all their variety are clearly part of God's creation. The book of Job describes with loving attention to detail the ox, the war horse, the lioness, the mountain goat, the wild donkey, the ostrich, the 'behemoth' (hippopotamus) and 'leviathan' (crocodile). But it is significant that the purpose of this catalogue is to demonstrate the absolute power of God and the smallness of humanity. If animals have rights it is only because God made them, determines their behaviour and, as Jesus said about the sparrow, watches over them constantly.

Within this system human beings have an important place. Male and female together are the crown of God's creation. He has made them, as the psalmist said, 'a little lower than the angels', but has given them the right to have dominion over the animal kingdom, putting 'all sheep and oxen under their feet'. Dominion is not a licence to abuse animals, treating them with cruelty and acting as if we owned them. People are God's stewards, looking after his creation responsibly and always liable to be called to account for the way in which they have discharged their role. Animals are a part of the 'life of faith', which in the Old Testament is spelled out down to the tiniest practical detail. As an illustration of this principle the Law commands that animals are to enjoy the same sabbath freedom from work as their owners.

Animals also had a symbolic function in the Old Testament. First they were at the centre of the sacrificial system. The Israelites could 'see' their sin being lifted and transferred to the sacrificial animal. And as its blood was shed they learned a profound truth about 'atonement', being made at one with God. Atonement was costly and involved the death of a victim. Both Paul and the writer to the Hebrews could use this picture to explain the meaning of Jesus' death.

Second, animals were involved in the food laws. Some were categorized as clean (cows, sheep), others as unclean and not to be eaten (pigs, rabbits). It is impossible now to give a satisfactory explanation for this demarcation and in any case the great vision Peter saw at Joppa marked the end of the food taboos for Christians. But every time a Jew ate a meal he was reminded of the need to be obedient to God's way. He was part of a separate nation, which showed its loyalty to God in every detail of its life; a nation called to be holy even in the kitchen.

It is clear that animals are an indispensable part of God's plan. They were present in Eden before the fall. Their place in the ark showed that they could not be jettisoned when a new world was beginning. And Isaiah's vision of the wolf lying down with the lamb, the cow feeding with the bear and the little child leading them points towards a future when the whole created universe will be a unity again.

## SUNDAY

GENESIS 1:20–25 (AV)

And God said, Let the waters bring forth abundantly the moving creature that hath life, and fowl that may fly above the earth in the open firmament of heaven. And God created great whales, and every living creature that moveth, which the waters brought forth abundantly, after their kind, and every winged fowl after his kind: and God saw that it was good. And God blessed them, saying, Be fruitful, and multiply, and fill the waters in the seas, and let fowl multiply in the earth. And the evening and the morning were the fifth day.

And God said, Let the earth bring forth the living creature after his kind, cattle, and creeping thing, and beast of the earth after his kind: and it was so. And God made the beast of the earth after his kind, and cattle after their kind, and every thing that creepeth upon the earth after his kind: and God saw that it was good.

## MONDAY

GENESIS 8:6–20 (RSV)

At the end of forty days Noah opened the window of the ark which he had made, and sent forth a raven; and it went to and fro until the waters were dried up from the earth. Then he sent forth a dove from him, to see if the waters had subsided from the face of the ground; but the dove found no place to set her foot, and she returned to him to the ark, for the waters were still on the face of the whole earth. So he put forth his hand and took her and brought her into the ark with him. He waited another seven days, and again he sent forth the dove out of the ark; and the dove came back to him in the evening, and lo, in her mouth a freshly plucked olive leaf; so Noah knew that the waters had subsided from the earth. Then he waited another seven days, and sent forth the dove; and she did not return to him any more.

In the six hundred and first year, in the first month, the first day of the month, the waters were dried from off the earth; and Noah removed the covering of the ark, and looked, and behold, the face of the ground was dry. In the second month, on the twenty-seventh day of the month, the earth was dry. Then God said to Noah, 'Go forth from the ark, you and your wife, and your sons and your sons' wives with you. Bring forth with you every living thing that is with you of all flesh—birds and animals and every creeping thing that creeps on the earth—that they may breed abundantly on the earth, and be fruitful and multiply upon the earth.' So Noah went forth, and his sons and his wife and his sons' wives with him. And every beast, every creeping thing, and every bird, everything that moves upon the earth, went forth by families out of the ark.

Then Noah built an altar to the Lord, and took of every clean animal and of every clean bird, and offered burnt offerings on the altar.

## TUESDAY

LEVITICUS 11:13–23, 29–30, 46–47 (RSV)

The Lord said to Moses and Aaron, 'And these you shall have in abomination among the birds, they shall not be eaten, they are an abomination: the eagle, the vulture, the osprey, the kite, the falcon according to its kind, every raven according to its kind, the ostrich, the nighthawk, the sea gull, the hawk according to its kind, the owl, the cormorant, the ibis, the water hen, the pelican, the carrion vulture, the stork, the heron according to its kind, the hoopoe, and the bat.

'All winged insects that go upon all fours are an abomination to you. Yet among the winged insects that go on all fours you may eat those which have legs above their feet, with which to leap on the earth. Of them you may eat: the locust according to its kind, the bald locust according to its kind, the cricket according to its kind, and the grasshopper according to its kind. But all other winged insects which have four feet are an abomination to you.'

'And these are unclean to you among the swarming things that swarm upon the earth: the weasel, the mouse, the great lizard according to its kind, the gecko, the land crocodile, the lizard, the sand lizard, and the chameleon.'

This is the law pertaining to beast and bird and every living creature that moves through the waters and every creature that swarms upon the earth, to make a distinction between the unclean and the clean and between the living creature that may be eaten and the living creature that may not be eaten.

## WEDNESDAY

NUMBERS 22:21–33 (NIV)

Balaam got up in the morning, saddled his donkey and went with the princes of Moab. But God was very angry when he went, and the angel of the Lord stood in the road to oppose him. Balaam was riding on his donkey, and his two servants were with him. When the donkey saw the angel of the Lord standing in the road with a drawn sword in his hand, she turned off the road into a field. Balaam beat her to get her back on the road.

Then the angel of the Lord stood in a narrow path between two vineyards, with walls on both sides. When the donkey saw the angel of the Lord, she pressed close to the wall, crushing Balaam's foot against it. So he beat her again.

Then the angel of the Lord moved on ahead and stood in a narrow place where there was no room to turn, either to the right or to the left. When the donkey saw the angel of the Lord, she lay down under Balaam, and he was angry and beat her with his staff. Then the Lord opened the donkey's mouth, and she said to Balaam, 'What have I done to you to make you beat me these three times?'

Balaam answered the donkey, 'You have made a fool of me! If I had a sword in my hand, I would kill you right now.'

The donkey said to Balaam, 'Am I

not your own donkey, which you have always ridden, to this day? Have I been in the habit of doing this to you?'

'No,' he said.

Then the Lord opened Balaam's eyes, and he saw the angel of the Lord standing in the road with his sword drawn. So he bowed low and fell face down.

The angel of the Lord asked him, 'Why have you beaten your donkey these three times? I have come here to oppose you because your path is a reckless one before me. The donkey saw me and turned away from me these three times. If she had not turned away, I would certainly have killed you by now, but I would have spared her.'

## THURSDAY

JOB 39:1–18 (NIV)

Do you know when the mountain goats give birth?
Do you watch when the doe bears her fawn?
Do you count the months till they bear?
Do you know the time they give birth?
They crouch down and bring forth their young;
their labour pains are ended.
Their young thrive and grow strong in the wilds;
they leave and do not return.

Who let the wild donkey go free?
Who untied his ropes?
I gave him the wasteland as his home,
the salt flats as his habitat.
He laughs at the commotion in the town;
he does not hear a driver's shout.
He ranges the hills from his pasture
and searches for any green thing.

Will the wild ox consent to serve you?
Will he stay by your manger at night?
Can you hold him to the furrow with a harness?
Will he till the valleys behind you?
Will you rely on him for his great strength?
Will you leave your heavy work to him?
Can you trust him to bring in your grain
and gather it to your threshing-floor?

The wings of the ostrich flap joyfully,
but they cannot compare with the pinions and feathers of the stork.
She lays her eggs on the ground and lets them warm in the sand,
unmindful that a foot may crush them,
that some wild animal may trample them.
She treats her young harshly, as if they were not hers;
she cares not that her labour was in vain,
for God did not endow her with wisdom
or give her a share of good sense.
Yet when she spreads her feathers to run,
she laughs at horse and rider.

## FRIDAY

PROVERBS 30:24–31 (REB)

Four things there are which are smallest on earth
yet wise beyond the wisest:
ants, a folk with no strength,
yet they prepare their store of food in the summer;
rock-badgers, a feeble folk,
yet they make their homes among the rocks;
locusts, which have no king,
yet they all sally forth in formation;
the lizard, which can be grasped in the hand,
yet is found in the palaces of kings.

Three things there are which are stately in their stride,
four which are stately as they move:
the lion, mighty among beasts,
which will not turn tail for anyone;
the strutting cock, the he-goat,
and a king going forth at the head of his army.

## SATURDAY

ACTS 10:9–18 (NJB)

Next day, while they were still on their journey and had only a short distance to go before reaching the town, Peter went to the housetop at about the sixth hour to say his prayers. He felt hungry and was looking forward to his meal, but before it was ready he fell into a trance and saw heaven thrown open and something like a big sheet being let down to earth by its four corners; it contained every kind of animal, reptile and bird. A voice then said to him, 'Now, Peter; kill and eat!' But Peter answered, 'Certainly not, Lord; I have never yet eaten anything profane or unclean.' Again, a second time, the voice spoke to him, 'What God has made clean, you have no right to call profane.' This was repeated three times, and then suddenly the container was drawn up to heaven again.

Peter was still at a loss over the meaning of the vision he had seen, when the men sent by Cornelius arrived. They had asked where Simon's house was and they were now standing at the door, calling out to know if the Simon known as Peter was lodging there.

# RENDERING TO CAESAR

Christian ambivalence towards political power goes back to the Bible itself. Our first reading describes how the people of Israel demanded a king 'like all the other nations'. Samuel, the judge and prophet, knew that it would have devastating consequences. But, in the providence of God, the kingship was used for better things than their small ambitions imagined (Sunday).

Tuesday's gospel extracts find Jesus silencing the Pharisees on the issue of Roman taxes. Those who admit to using Caesar's coinage are soon to be found taunting Pilate with risking the loss of Caesar's friendship. Far from parcelling out power between God and Caesar, Jesus teaches that even the power of Rome is not absolute . . . it derives from God.

The Acts of the Apostles portrays several confrontations between church and state. Even when Christians had no political clout, they believed in using the law where they could and breaking it only when they must (Wednesday).

Paul and Peter continue to address this question of our response to political power (Thursday and Friday). Tax-man, magistrate and king all serve God; we obey them while we can. But should there come a time when kings become beasts, whose particular prey is the church (Saturday), we must ask for grace, not for rebellion but for faithful endurance.

WEEK 38

# The State

'You would have no power at all over me if it were not given you from above.' On trial for his life and in the presence of the representative of the most powerful state on earth, Jesus sets the whole issue of government and authority in perspective. 'The authorities that exist have been established by God,' wrote the apostle Paul, but real power belongs to God alone.

God, then, is of higher power and authority than any state. How does this truth affect us as we live under the authority of governments which range, today as in Bible days, from the benevolent to the oppressive?

◆ **The Bible teaches that every state will be called to account by God**. It was his laws which defined Israel's existence and ruled her national life. But this meant that the nation could be attacked by the prophets whenever she fell short of her calling.

But God is not a local deity. States which knew next to nothing about his Law were condemned for war atrocities—not against Israel or Judah, but against other heathen nations. There could hardly be a more dramatic illustration of the truth that power is delegated by the God of the whole earth. Similarly, God is prepared to use foreign states and rulers for his own purpose, for punishing his people or for liberating them. Always, however, the State is subject to God's power. The taunt songs against Nineveh and Babylon are some of the most terrifying pieces of literature in the Old Testament.

◆ **Christians are to have respect for government**. In the New Testament, the State still exercises power by God's permission and, for the most part, exercises it responsibly. Paul is impressed by a framework of law and order which allows right to be rewarded and wrong punished. The author of Acts is careful to point out how the Roman authorities were just men and sympathetic to the Christian cause. Peter argues, 'Who is going to harm you if you are eager to do good?' And so the Christians are told to be subject to the State, to respect and pray for its leaders, pay its taxes and make use of its amenities in the service of the gospel. Jesus did not accept the way of violent resistance and even suggested that there were many duties which were owed to Caesar (by which he meant State authority).

◆ **And yet, because they are 'a colony of heaven', Christians' primary loyalty is to God alone**. With a cool realism the Bible perceives that power corrupts and that any state can start to demand what belongs exclusively to God. Rulers can strut and posture as if they were divine; they can oppress the innocent, crush the weak, stifle the voice of protest and persecute the church. It was a king misnamed 'the Great' who slaughtered the children of Bethlehem, and 'the rulers of this age' who crucified the Lord of glory. At such a terrible time Christians are called to obey God rather than men, to bear witness to their faith, to endure to the end and, if necessary, seal their witness with their blood.

This is not the end of the matter, however. The New Testament contains its own taunt song, in the Book of Revelation, written when the Roman State had begun a cruel persecution of the Christians. The writer sees a terrible vision of the fall of the latter-day Babylon. The powers of the evil state are crushed in the end. Jesus alone is King of kings and Lord of lords.

WEEK 38

## SUNDAY

1 SAMUEL 8:4–20 (REB)

So all the elders of Israel met, and came to Samuel at Ramah. They said to him, 'You are now old and your sons do not follow your ways; appoint us a king to rule us, like all the other nations.' But their request for a king displeased Samuel. He prayed to the Lord, and the Lord told him, 'Listen to the people and all that they are saying; they have not rejected you, it is I whom they have rejected, I whom they will not have to be their king. They are now doing to you just what they have done to me since I brought them up from Egypt: they have forsaken me and worshipped other gods. Hear what they have to say now, but give them a solemn warning and tell them what sort of king will rule them.'

Samuel reported to the people who were asking him for a king all that the Lord had said to him. 'This will be the sort of king who will bear rule over you,' he said. 'He will take your sons and make them serve in his chariots and with his cavalry, and they will run before his chariot. Some he will appoint officers over units of a thousand and units of fifty. Others will plough his fields and reap his harvest; others again will make weapons of war and equipment for the chariots. He will take your daughters for perfumers, cooks, and bakers. He will seize the best of your fields, vineyards, and olive groves, and give them to his courtiers. He will take a tenth of your grain and your vintage to give his eunuchs and courtiers. Your slaves, both men and women, and the best of your cattle and your donkeys he will take for his own use. He will take a tenth of your flocks, and you yourselves will become his slaves. There will come a day when you will cry out against the king whom you have chosen; but the Lord will not answer you on that day.'

The people, however, refused to listen to Samuel. 'No,' they said, 'we must have a king over us; then we shall be like other nations, with a king to rule us, to lead us out to war and fight our battles.'

## MONDAY

ISAIAH 10:5–14 (NIV)

'Woe to the Assyrian, the rod of my
  anger,
  in whose hand is the club of my
  wrath!
I send him against a godless nation,
  I despatch him against a people
  who anger me,
to seize loot and snatch plunder,
  and to trample them down like
  mud in the streets.
But this is not what he intends,
  this is not what he has in mind;
his purpose is to destroy,
  to put an end to many nations.
'Are not my commanders all kings?'
  he says.
  'Has not Calno fared like
  Carchemish?
Is not Hamath like Arpad,
  and Samaria like Damascus?
As my hand seized the kingdoms of
  the idols,
  kingdoms whose images excelled
  those of Jerusalem and Samaria—

shall I not deal with Jerusalem and
her images
as I dealt with Samaria and her
idols?'
When the Lord has finished all his work against Mount Zion and Jerusalem, he will say, 'I will punish the king of Assyria for the wilful pride of his heart and the haughty look in his eyes. For he says:
"By the strength of my hand I have
done this,
and by my wisdom, because I
have understanding.
I removed the boundaries of
nations,
I plundered their treasures;
like a mighty one I subdued their
kings.
As one reaches into a nest,
so my hand reached for the
wealth of the nations;
as men gather abandoned eggs,
so I gathered all the countries;
not one flapped a wing,
or opened its mouth to chirp." '

## TUESDAY

MATTHEW 22:15–22 (RSV)

Then the Pharisees went and took counsel how to entangle Jesus in his talk. And they sent their disciples to him, along with the Herodians, saying, 'Teacher, we know that you are true, and teach the way of God truthfully, and care for no man; for you do not regard the position of men. Tell us, then, what you think. Is it lawful to pay taxes to Caesar, or not?' But Jesus, aware of their malice, said, 'Why put me to the test, you hypocrites? Show me the money for the tax.' And they brought him a coin. And Jesus said to them, 'Whose likeness and inscription is this?' They said, 'Caesar's.' Then he said to them, 'Render therefore to Caesar the things that are Caesar's, and to God the things that are God's.' When they heard it, they marvelled; and they left him and went away.

JOHN 19:9–12 (RSV)

Pilate entered the praetorium again and said to Jesus, 'Where are you from?' But Jesus gave no answer. Pilate therefore said to him, 'You will not speak to me? Do you not know that I have power to release you, and power to crucify you?' Jesus answered him, 'You would have no power over me unless it had been given you from above; therefore he who delivered me to you has the greater sin.'

Upon this Pilate sought to release him, but the Jews cried out, 'If you release this man, you are not Caesar's friend; every one who makes himself a king sets himself against Caesar.'

## WEDNESDAY

ACTS 4:18–20, 16:35–40, 25:7–12 (AV)

And they called them, and commanded them not to speak at all nor teach in the name of Jesus. But Peter and John answered and said unto them, Whether it be right in the sight of God to hearken unto you more than unto God, judge ye. For we cannot but speak the things which we have seen and heard.

And when it was the day, the magistrates sent the serjeants, saying, Let those men go. And the keeper of the prison told this saying to Paul, The magistrates have sent to let you go: now therefore depart, and go in peace. But Paul said unto them, They have beaten us openly uncondemned, being Romans, and have cast us into prison; and now do they thrust us out privily? nay verily; but let them come themselves and fetch us out. And the serjeants told these words unto the magistrates: and they feared, when they heard that they were Romans. And the serjeants told these words unto the magistrates: and they feared, when they heard that they were Romans. And they came and besought them, and brought them out, and desired them to depart out of the city. And they went out of the prison, and entered into the house of Lydia: and when they had seen the brethren, they comforted them, and departed.

And when Festus was come, the Jews laid many and grievous complaints against Paul, which they could not prove. While he answered for himself, Neither against the law of the Jews, neither against the temple, nor yet against Caesar, have I offended any thing at all. But Festus, willing to do the Jews a pleasure, answered Paul, and said, Wilt thou go up to Jerusalem, and there be judged of these things before me? Then said Paul, I stand at Caesar's judgment seat, where I ought to be judged: to the Jews have I done no wrong, as thou very well knowest. For if I be an offender, or have committed any thing worthy of death, I refuse not to die: but if there be none of these things whereof these accuse me, no man may deliver me unto them, I appeal unto Caesar. Then Festus, when he had conferred with the council, answered, Hast thou appealed unto Caesar? unto Caesar shalt thou go.

## THURSDAY

ROMANS 13:1–7 (NJB)

Everyone is to obey the governing authorities, because there is no authority except from God and so whatever authorities exist have been appointed by God. So anyone who disobeys an authority is rebelling against God's ordinance; and rebels must expect to receive the condemnation they deserve. Magistrates bring fear not to those who do good, but to those who do evil. So if you want to live with no fear of authority, live honestly and you will have approval; it is there to serve God for you and for your good. But if you do what is wrong, then you may well be afraid; because it is not for nothing that the symbol of authority is a sword: it is there to serve God, too, as his avenger, to bring retribution to wrongdoers. You must be obedient, therefore, not only because of this retribution, but also for conscience's sake. And this is why you should pay taxes, too, because the authorities are all serving God as his agents, even while they are busily occupied with that particular task. Pay to each one what is due to each: taxes to the one to whom tax is due, tolls to the one to whom tolls are due, respect to the one to whom respect is due, honour to the one to whom honour is due.

## FRIDAY

1 PETER 2:11–17 (NIV)

Dear friends, I urge you, as aliens and strangers in the world, to abstain from sinful desires, which war against your soul. Live such good lives among the pagans that, though they accuse you of doing wrong, they may see your good deeds and glorify God on the day he visits us.

Submit yourselves for the Lord's sake to every authority instituted among men: whether to the king, as the supreme authority, or to governors, who are sent by him to commend those who do right. For it is God's will that by doing good you should silence the ignorant talk of foolish men. Live as free men, but do not use your freedom as a cover-up for evil; live as servants of God. Show proper respect to everyone: Love the brotherhood of believers, fear God, honour the king.

## SATURDAY

REVELATION 13:1–10 (REB)

Then I saw a beast rising out of the sea. It had ten horns and seven heads; on the horns were ten diadems, and on each head was a blasphemous name. The beast I saw resembled a leopard, but its feet were like a bear's and its mouth like a lion's. The dragon conferred on it his own power, his throne, and great authority.

One of the heads seemed to have been given a death blow, yet its mortal wound was healed. The whole world went after the beast in wondering admiration, and worshipped the dragon because he had conferred his authority on the beast; they worshipped the beast also. 'Who is like the beast?' they said. 'Who can fight against it?'

The beast was allowed to mouth bombast and blasphemy, and was granted permission to continue for forty-two months. It uttered blasphemies against God, reviling his name and his dwelling-place, that is, those who dwell in heaven. It was also allowed to wage war on God's people and to defeat them, and it was granted authority over every tribe, nation, language, and race. All the inhabitants of the earth will worship it, all whose names have not been written in the book of life of the Lamb, slain since the foundation of the world.

You have ears, so hear! Whoever is to be made prisoner, to prison he shall go; whoever is to be slain by the sword, by the sword he must be slain. This calls for the endurance and faithfulness of God's people.

# GALILEE AND JERUSALEM

Jesus grew up in Galilee, and much of his teaching was given there. He visited Jerusalem for festivals, and there he spent that last tragic week. The provinces of Galilee and Judea were separated by seventy miles of non-Jewish territory. The drama of Jesus' life and ministry was played out against this twofold background.

Galilee was more fertile than the area of Jerusalem and Judea. Farming and fishing were major occupations. But the region also had major towns, and was generally more prosperous than the south.

It was under different government to Jerusalem. And though it was predominantly Jewish, its population was much more international, perhaps owing to its position on major trade routes. It was often known as `Galilee of the Gentiles'.

"You will find that a prophet does not come out of Galilee."

**John 7:52**

**1 Nazareth** Here Jesus was brought up. Its people rejected his preaching.

**2 Tiberias** Founded by Herod Antipas as his capital.

**3 Capernaum** The centre for Jesus' ministry in Galilee. Peter's house was here.

**4 Sepphoris** A Greek city, the administrative capital. It boasted a large Greek theatre.

**5 Cana** The scene of Jesus' first miracle.

**6 Chorazin** On a hill above the Sea of Galilee. Jesus taught here.

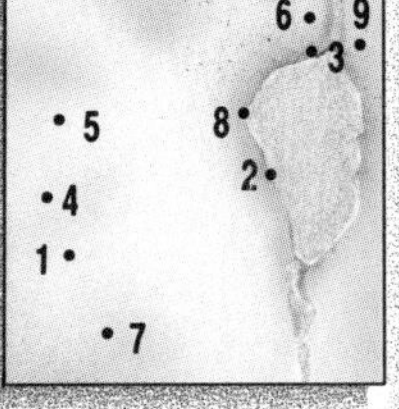


**7 Nain** Jesus restored the son of a Nain widow to life.

**8 Magdala** A major fishing harbour, home of Mary Magdalene.

**9 Bethsaida** A fishing town, birthplace of several disciples.

> “O Jerusalem, Jerusalem, you who kill the prophets.”
>
> **Luke 13:34**

> “When Jesus entered Jerusalem, the whole city was stirred and asked, ‘Who is this?’ The crowds answered, ‘This is Jesus, the prophet from Nazareth in Galilee.’”
>
> **Matthew 21:10–11**

Jerusalem was (and is) the historic holy city of the Jews. It was the city God had promised. All Jews looked to it as the focal point of their faith.

There was the temple, and Jews congregated there for the major annual festivals. Perhaps because of this, the people of Jerusalem were much stronger on law-observance than the Galileans.

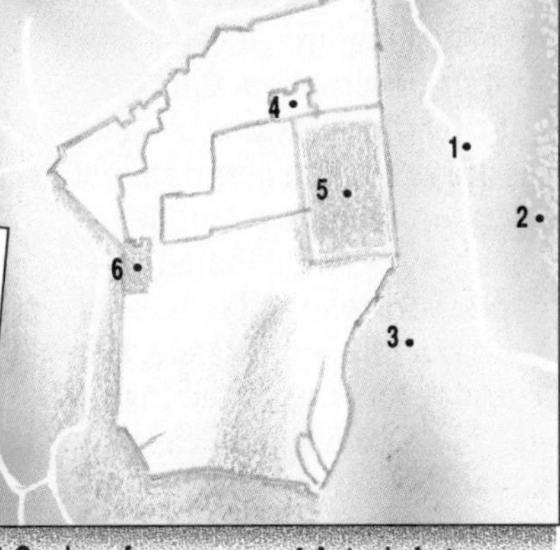


**1 Garden of Gethsemane** Across the Kidron valley and below the Mount of Olives. Here Jesus was arrested.

**2 Mount of Olives** The top of the mount looks across to the temple. Jesus approached Jerusalem this way on his final visit.

**3 Kidron valley** To the east of Jerusalem, below the temple.

**4 Antonia fortress** The base for the Roman garrison.

**5 The Temple** Built by Herod to replace two earlier buildings. This was the centre for Jewish worship and sacrifices.

**6 Herod's Palace** After Herod, the Roman governors used this, and Jesus stood before Pilate here.

WEEK 39

# SWORD AND SCALES

A modern Lord Chief Justice declared of every citizen, 'Be he never so high, the law is above him'. In the Bible, the foundations of justice are laid in such legislation as we find in our first extract, from Deuteronomy (Sunday). Here Moses speaks of God's demands, both in broad terms and in detailed cases, underlining the rights of the widow and orphan, the poor and the alien (or stranger).

The long line of Old Testament prophets thundered out their declarations of God's justice to each generation and on every occasion. On Monday Isaiah's anger is kindled by oppressors who hide their crimes behind a religious facade. On Tuesday he berates the ingratitude of those who had every advantage but whose personal and social greed would bring God's judgment.

Amos castigates not only the surrounding nations but his own people (Wednesday). Micah too exposes the kind of corruption and cruelty which, many centuries later, have an ominously up-to-date sound (Thursday).

Jesus both stands in this prophetic tradition and goes beyond it (Friday). He too speaks fearlessly of God's justice in the nation's capital. He addresses the very people who should observe it best—the scribes and Pharisees—and with a sense of coming catastrophe. Later, James is another who insists by letter (Saturday) that God is not mocked, and that time is short.

# Justice

When we look around it seems all too obvious that we live in a very unjust world. *It seems unfair* that the resources of this globe are controlled by one third of the population while the remaining two thirds live on or below the poverty line. *It seems unfair* that in most societies, East and West, there will be found the rich who own a great deal of the resources and control their distribution. *It seems unfair* that the unjust often go unpunished while the honest and deserving are harshly treated.

But this dismal picture is inevitable only when God is left out of our reckoning. In the Bible he is the source of justice. One of the best of the many good things he has given us is a clear moral framework. If we want to use this framework to find the way of justice, we have to focus on two qualities — holiness and love.

◆ **True holiness is based on God's holy law.** 'Justice' is really a translation of the word 'righteousness'. This is a quality of life God wants from us all as we keep his commandments. But this is easier said than done. Sin is so deeply rooted in us all that we are quite unable to live this kind of life. Only by claiming in faith the forgiveness and new life which God offers us in Jesus Christ can we ever find God's righteousness.

God's law, then, cannot itself make us righteous. But still, as forgiven people, we make it our aim to live as God requires and to honour his way of living. So God's people will keep his laws and those of their society. We will honour the just claims made on us by others and try to live as honest, reliable and just people.

◆ **True justice is based on God's holy love.** Christian love is not a mawkish thing but a fierce commitment to God and his world. It is a love which does more than feel sorry for the needy; it tries to do something for them. When William Wilberforce started his campaign for the abolition of slavery he was not guided by sentimentalism but by clear Christian principles of justice gleaned from the character of God's love. He knew that the gospel values every person—black and white, male and female—as of equal worth before God. He believed with all his heart that it was morally wrong for one human being to be owned by another, and he felt the scandal of one person being free to live with dignity while the other had a full human existence shut off from him. Love broke from Wilberforce as a cry for justice—a cry that spanned his whole life.

True Christianity refuses to be confined within the narrow area of life we call 'religious'. It is a way of life which spills over into our everyday experience, our social life and our political aspirations. If it is a living faith, Christianity will stand at the crossroads of human life and call people to a just God who wants everyone without exception to enjoy his bounty.

## SUNDAY

DEUTERONOMY 24:10–22 (REB)

When you make any loan to anyone, do not enter his house to take a pledge from him. Wait outside, and the person whose creditor you are must bring the pledge out to you. If he is a poor man, do not sleep in the cloak he has pledged. Return it to him at sunset so that he may sleep in it and bless you; then it will be counted to your credit in the sight of the Lord your God.

You must not keep back the wages of a man who is poor and needy, whether a fellow-countryman or an alien living in your country in one of your settlements. Pay him his wages on the same day before sunset, for he is poor and he relies on them: otherwise he may appeal to the Lord against you, and you will be guilty of sin.

Parents are not to be put to death for their children, nor children for their parents; each one may be put to death only for his own sin.

You must not deprive aliens and the fatherless of justice or take a widow's cloak in pledge. Bear in mind that you were slaves in Egypt and the Lord your God redeemed you from there; that is why I command you to do this.

When you reap the harvest in your field and overlook a sheaf, do not go back to pick it up; it is to be left for the alien, the fatherless, and the widow, so that the Lord your God may bless you in all that you undertake.

When you beat your olive trees, do not strip them afterwards: what is left is for the alien, the fatherless, and the widow.

When you gather the grapes from your vineyard, do not glean afterwards; what is left is for the alien, the fatherless, and the widow. Keep in mind that you were slaves in Egypt; that is why I command you to do this.

## MONDAY

ISAIAH 1:2–6, 10–20 (RSV)

Hear, O heavens, and give ear, O
  earth;
  for the Lord has spoken:
'Sons have I reared and brought up,
  but they have rebelled against
  me.
The ox knows its owner,
  and the ass its master's crib;
but Israel does not know,
  my people does not understand.'

Ah, sinful nation,
  a people laden with iniquity,
offspring of evildoers,
  sons who deal corruptly!
They have forsaken the Lord,
  they have despised the Holy One
  of Israel,
  they are utterly estranged.

Why will you still be smitten,
  that you continue to rebel?
The whole head is sick,
  and the whole heart is faint.
From the sole of the foot even to the
  head,
  there is no soundness in it,
but bruises and sores
  and bleeding wounds;
they are not pressed out, or bound
  up,
  or softened with oil.

Hear the word of the Lord,

you rulers of Sodom!
Give ear to the teaching of our God,
you people of Gomorrah!
'What to me is the multitude of your sacrifices?'
says the Lord;
'I have had enough of burnt offerings of rams
and the fat of fed beasts;
I do not delight in the blood of bulls,
or of lambs, or of he-goats.

'When you come to appear before me,
who requires of you
this trampling of my courts?
Bring no more vain offerings;
incense is an abomination to me.
New moon and sabbath and the calling of assemblies—
I cannot endure iniquity and solemn assembly.
Your new moons and your appointed feasts
my soul hates;
they have become a burden to me,
I am weary of bearing them.
When you spread forth your hands,
I will hide my eyes from you;
even though you make many prayers,
I will not listen;
your hands are full of blood.
Wash yourselves; make yourselves clean;
remove the evil of your doings
from before my eyes;
cease to do evil,
learn to do good;
seek justice,
correct oppression;
defend the fatherless,
plead for the widow.

'Come now, let us reason together,'
says the Lord:
'though your sins are like scarlet,
they shall be as white as snow;
though they are red like crimson,
they shall become like wool.
If you are willing and obedient,
you shall eat the good of the land;
But if you refuse and rebel,
you shall be devoured by the sword;
for the mouth of the Lord has spoken.'

## TUESDAY

ISAIAH 5:1–12 (RSV)

Let me sing for my beloved
a love song concerning his vineyard:
My beloved had a vineyard
on a very fertile hill.
He digged it and cleared it of stones,
and planted it with choice vines;
he built a watchtower in the midst of it,
and hewed out a wine vat in it;
and he looked for it to yield grapes,
but it yielded wild grapes.

And now, O inhabitants of Jerusalem and men of Judah,
judge, I pray you, between me
and my vineyard.
What more was there to do for my vineyard,
that I have not done in it?
When I looked for it to yield grapes,
why did it yield wild grapes?

And now I will tell you
what I will do to my vineyard.
I will remove its hedge,

and it shall be devoured;
I will break down its wall,
and it shall be trampled down.
I will make it a waste;
it shall not be pruned or hoed,
and briers and thorns shall grow up;
I will also command the clouds
that they rain no rain upon it.

For the vineyard of the Lord of hosts
is the house of Israel,
and the men of Judah
are his pleasant planting;
and he looked for justice,
but behold, bloodshed;
for righteousness,
but behold, a cry!

Woe to those who join house to house,
who add field to field,
until there is no more room,
and you are made to dwell alone
in the midst of the land.
The Lord of hosts has sworn in my hearing:
'Surely many houses shall be desolate,
large and beautiful houses,
without inhabitant.
For ten acres of vineyard shall yield
but one bath,
and a homer of seed shall yield
but an ephah.'

Woe to those who rise early in the morning,
that they may run after strong drink,
who tarry late into the evening
till wine inflames them!
They have lyre and harp,
timbrel and flute and wine at their feasts;
but they do not regard the deeds of the Lord,
or see the work of his hands.

## WEDNESDAY

AMOS 1:9–12, 2:6–8 (NIV)

This is what the Lord says:
'For three sins of Tyre,
even for four, I will not turn back my wrath.
Because she sold whole communities of captives to Edom,
disregarding a treaty of brotherhood,
I will send fire upon the walls of Tyre
that will consume her fortresses.'

This is what the Lord says:
'For the sins of Edom,
even for four, I will not turn back my wrath.
Because he pursued his brother with a sword,
stifling all compassion,
because his anger raged continually
and his fury flamed unchecked,
I will send fire upon Teman
that will consume the fortresses of Bozrah.'

This is what the Lord says:
'For three sins of Israel,
even for four, I will not turn back my wrath.
They sell the righteous for silver,
and the needy for a pair of sandals.
They trample on the heads of the poor
as upon the dust of the ground

and deny justice to the oppressed.
Father and son use the same girl
and so profane my holy name.
They lie down beside every altar
on garments taken in pledge.
In the house of their God
they drink wine taken as fines.'

## THURSDAY

MICAH 2:1–3, 3:1–4, 7:1–4 (NIV)

Woe to those who plan iniquity,
to those who plot evil on their beds!
At morning's light they carry it out
because it is in their power to do it.
They covet fields and seize them,
and houses, and take them.
They defraud a man of his home,
a fellow-man of his inheritance.

Therefore, the Lord says:
'I am planning disaster against this people,
from which you cannot save yourselves.
You will no longer walk proudly,
for it will be a time of calamity.'

Then I said,
'Listen, you leaders of Jacob,
you rulers of the house of Israel.
Should you not know justice,
you who hate good and love evil;
who tear the skin from my people
and the flesh from their bones;
who eat my people's flesh,
strip off their skin
and break their bones in pieces;
who chop them up like meat for the pan,
like flesh for the pot?'

Then they will cry out to the Lord,
but he will not answer them.
At that time he will hide his face from them
because of the evil they have done.

What misery is mine!
I am like one who gathers summer fruit
at the gleaning of the vineyard;
there is no cluster of grapes to eat,
none of the early figs that I crave.
The godly have been swept from the land;
not one upright man remains.
All men lie in wait to shed blood;
each hunts his brother with a net.
Both hands are skilled in doing evil;
the ruler demands gifts,
the judge accepts bribes,
the powerful dictate what they desire—
they all conspire together.
The best of them is like a brier,
the most upright worse than a thorn hedge.
The day of your watchmen has come,
the day God visits you.
Now is the time of their confusion.

## FRIDAY

MATTHEW 23:1–4, 23–24, 33–39 (RSV)

Then said Jesus to the crowds and to his disciples, 'The scribes and the

Pharisees sit on Moses' seat; so practise and observe whatever they tell you, but not what they do; for they preach, but do not practise. They bind heavy burdens, hard to bear, and lay them on men's shoulders; but they themselves will not move them with their finger.'

'Woe to you, scribes and Pharisees, hypocrites! for you tithe mint and dill and cumin, and have neglected the weighter matters of the law, justice and mercy and faith; these you ought to have done, without neglecting the others. You blind guides, straining out a gnat and swallowing a camel!'

'You serpents, you brood of vipers, how are you to escape being sentenced to hell? Therefore I send you prophets and wise men and scribes, some of whom you will kill and crucify, and some you will scourge in your synagogues and persecute from town to town, that upon you may come all the righteous blood shed on earth, from the blood of innocent Abel to the blood of Zechariah the son of Barachiah, whom you murdered between the sanctuary and the altar. Truly, I say to you, all this will come upon this generation.

'O Jerusalem, Jerusalem, killing the prophets and stoning those who are sent to you! How often would I have gathered your children together as a hen gathers her brood under her wings, and you would not! Behold, your house is forsaken and desolate.

For I tell you, you will not see me again, until you say, "Blessed is he who comes in the name of the Lord." '

## SATURDAY

JAMES 5:1–9 (AV)

Go to now, ye rich men, weep and howl for your miseries that shall come upon you. Your riches are corrupted, and your garments are motheaten. Your gold and silver is cankered; and the rust of them shall be a witness against you, and shall eat your flesh as it were fire. Ye have heaped treasure together for the last days. Behold, the hire of the labourers who have reaped down your fields, which is of you kept back by fraud, crieth: and the cries of them which have reaped are entered into the ears of the Lord of sabaoth. Ye have lived in pleasure on the earth, and been wanton; ye have nourished your hearts, as in a day of slaughter. Ye have condemned and killed the just; and he doth not resist you.

Be patient therefore, brethren, unto the coming of the Lord. Behold, the husbandman waiteth for the precious fruit of the earth, and hath long patience for it, until he receive the early and latter rain. Be ye also patient; stablish your hearts: for the coming of the Lord draweth nigh. Grudge not one against another, brethren, lest ye be condemned: behold, the judge standeth before the door.

WEEK 40

# THE WOUNDS OF THE WORLD

One of the most agonizing aspects of the Bible lies before us this week—what could be our approach to war and peace? Much of Israel's early history is concerned with the conquest of the 'promised land'. Joshua's book (Sunday) presents a military leader embarked on a holy crusade against peoples so decadent and corrupted that only complete purging will suffice to make clean the land.

Monday's reading in the book of Judges follows up the story of conquest with its own graphic accounts of cruelty, folly and bloodshed, often beyond any pretence at control (Monday). Abner's later heartcry 'Must the sword devour for ever?' might be written over so many of these wars, and shines like a beacon in hope of better things (Tuesday).

The words of Chronicles (Wednesday) refer to the failure by the great king David to keep the peace, while Jeremiah heroically witnesses to the fact that military force is often worse than useless (Thursday). If such truths seem obvious to us, our bloody century is hardly in a position to judge theirs. At least Psalm and prophet (Friday) both testify to the God who ends wars, destroys weapons, and loves peace with justice.

Finally, James writes (Saturday) in the tone of one who can hardly conceive how Christians fail to grasp the way of faith and the way of Christ.

WEEK 40

# War and Peace

Did you know that at this present moment at least twenty wars are being fought around the world? Peace seems to be the exception, not war. In spite of our many achievements, mankind cannot find the answer to conflict. We may be able to split the atom but we do not know how to bring together bitterly divided people.

The Christian approach to war and peace is found in the character of God. The Bible describes him as the 'God of peace'. But it also calls him a 'Warrior'. How do we reconcile these two apparent opposites?

The answer is found when we identify the enemy with which God is at war—all forms of injustice, wrongdoing and sin. Instead of keeping himself immune from conflict, God is deeply immersed in battle against the forces of evil. The ministry of Jesus illustrates this. In his works he was in conflict with the various disorders which imprison people; in his words he battled with sin, especially the hypocrisy and practical godlessness of religious people. The final showdown came in his death when he met the full fury of evil and 'made peace through the blood of his cross'. His first words to his disciples after his resurrection were 'Peace be with you', signalling that his victory had brought harmony and reconciliation between God and humankind.

What does this imply for Christians today?

- **We are involved in God's war.** Followers of Christ are part of God's army fighting against all that opposes his rule. There will only ever be real peace when sin is defeated—sin in human relationships, sin in social life and sin in political structures. Just as Jesus was not slow to speak out against all that oppressed people, so his followers should not be afraid to oppose sin in whatever guise it comes.
- **We are peacemakers.** The Christian fights best when he or she announces peace, not war. And to drive home this point, Jesus gave the radical teaching that when we are struck on one cheek we should offer the other to the smiter! By this he meant that a positive approach to peace, which was certainly not cowardice or passive submission, was ten times better than violence.
- **We use the weapons of peace,** as Jesus did: clear teaching which confronts hypocrisy and wrongdoing; a willingness to speak to our 'enemies' and address them with love, understanding and respect; a desire to negotiate rather than drive people away. The Old Testament prophesied that one day only 'peace-weapons' will remain, when swords are beaten into ploughshares.
- **Violence will always be the last resort.** Christians are divided over the question whether violence is ever justified. There are those who say that Christians should be pacifists, and this tradition is long and honourable. However, I am convinced that when evil comes in its starkest forms which

will not listen to the voice of reason, which refuse to negotiate, and which trample down the innocent and defenceless, then there may be cause for citizens to defend themselves and the values which they believe in passionately. This argument is usually called the 'Just War' theory. It asserts that war is only ever justified when four conditions are met. The cause must be just; war must be absolutely the last resort, when all other avenues to avoid conflict have failed; conflict must not involve non-combatants; war should be limited in its scope, avoiding unnecessary loss of life and destruction. It is a large question whether these last two conditions can ever be met in modern, especially nuclear, warfare.

But the Christian's primary commitment is, of course, to peace, and it should be our earnest desire to play a full part in God's battle against the visible and invisible forces which tear this planet apart. The good news is that God is going to have the last word. Sin, death and evil will be defeated and God's reign of peace in all its fulness will one day be a reality. That's worth working for!

## SUNDAY

JOSHUA 5:13–6:10 (RSV)

When Joshua was by Jericho, he lifted up his eyes and looked, and behold, a man stood before him with his drawn sword in his hand; and Joshua went to him and said to him, 'Are you for us, or for our adversaries?' And he said, 'No; but as commander of the army of the Lord I have now come.' And Joshua fell on his face to the earth, and worshipped, and said to him, 'What does my lord bid his servant?' And the commander of the Lord's army said to Joshua. 'Put off your shoes from your feet; for the place where you stand is holy.' And Joshua did so.

Now Jericho was shut up from within and from without because of the people of Israel; none went out, and none came in. And the Lord said to Joshua, 'See, I have given into your hand Jericho, with its king and mighty men of valour. You shall march around the city, all the men of war going around the city once. Thus shall you do for six days. And seven priests shall bear seven trumpets of rams' horns before the ark; and on the seventh day you shall march around the city seven times, the priests blowing the trumpets. And when they make a long blast with the ram's horn, as soon as you hear the sound of the trumpet, then all the people shall shout with a great shout; and the wall of the city will fall down flat, and the people shall go up every man straight before him.' So Joshua the son of Nun called the priests and said to them, 'Take up the ark of the covenant, and let seven priests bear seven trumpets of rams' horns before the ark of the Lord.' And he said to the people, 'Go forward; march around the city, and let the armed men pass on before the ark of the Lord.'

And as Joshua had commanded the people, the seven priests bearing the seven trumpets of rams' horns before the Lord went forward, blowing the trumpets, with the ark of the covenant of the Lord following them. And the armed men went before the priests who blew the trumpets, and the rear guard came after the ark, while the trumpets blew continually. But Joshua commanded the people, 'You shall not shout or let your voice be heard, neither shall any word go out of your mouth, until the day I bid you shout; then you shall shout.'

## MONDAY

JUDGES 9:42–55, 21:25 (RSV)

On the following day the men went out into the fields. And Abimelech was told. He took his men and divided them into three companies, and laid wait in the fields; and he looked and saw the men coming out of the city, and he rose against them and slew them. Abimelech and the company that was with him rushed forward and stood at the entrance of the gate of the city, while the two companies rushed upon all who were in the fields and slew against them. And Abimelech fought against the city all that day; he took the city, and killed the people that were in it; and he razed the city and sowed it with salt.

When all the people of the Tower of Shechem heard of it, they entered the stronghold of the house of Elberith. Abimelech was told that all the people of the Tower of Shechem were gathered together. And Abimelech went up to Mount Zalmon, he and all the men that were with him; and Abimelech took an axe in his hand, and cut down a bundle of brushwood, and took it up and laid it on his shoulder. And he said to the men that were with him, 'What you have seen me do, make haste to do, as I have done.' So every one of the people cut down his bundle and following Abimelech put it against the stronghold, and they set the stronghold on fire over them, so that all the people of the Tower of Shechem also died, about a thousand men and women.

Then Abimelech went to Thebez, and encamped against Thebez, and took it. But there was a strong tower within the city, and all the people of the city fled to it, all the men and women, and shut themselves in; and they went to the roof of the tower. And Abimelech came to the tower, and fought against it, and drew near to the door of the tower to burn it with fire. And a certain woman threw an upper millstone upon Abimelech's head, and crushed his skull. Then he called hastily to the young man his armour-bearer, and said to him, 'Draw your sword and kill me, lest men say of me, "A woman killed him."' And his young man thrust him through, and he died. And when the men of Israel saw that Abimelech was dead, they departed every man to his home.

In those days there was no king in Israel; every man did what was right in his own eyes.

# TUESDAY

2 SAMUEL 2:17–28 (NIV)

The battle that day was very fierce, and Abner and the men of Israel were defeated by David's men.

The three sons of Zeruiah were there: Joab, Abishai and Asahel. Now Asahel was as fleet-footed as a wild gazelle. He chased Abner, turning neither to the right nor to the left as he pursued him. Abner looked behind him and asked, 'Is that you, Asahel?'

'It is,' he answered.

Then Abner said to him, 'Turn aside to the right or to the left; take on one of the young men and strip him of his weapons.' But Asahel would not stop chasing him.

Again Abner warned Asahel, 'Stop chasing me! Why should I strike you down? How could I look your brother Joab in the face?'

But Asahel refused to give up the pursuit; so Abner thrust the butt of his spear into Asahel's stomach, and the spear came out through his back. He fell there and died on the spot. And every man stopped when he came to the place where Asahel had fallen and died.

But Joab and Abishai pursued Abner, and as the sun was setting, they came to the hill of Ammah, near Giah on the way to the wasteland of Gibeon. Then the men of Benjamin rallied behind Abner. They formed themselves into a group and took their stand on top of a hill.

Abner called out to Joab, 'Must the sword devour for ever? Don't you realize that this will end in bitterness? How long before you order your men to stop pursuing their brothers?'

Joab answered, 'As surely as God lives, if you had not spoken, the men would have continued the pursuit of their brothers until morning.'

So Joab blew the trumpet, and all the men came to a halt; they no longer pursued Israel, not did they fight any more.

## WEDNESDAY

1 CHRONICLES 22:6–13 (NIV)

Then David called for his son Solomon and charged him to build a house for the Lord, the God of Israel. David said to Solomon: 'My son, I had it in my heart to build a house for the Name of the Lord my God. But this word of the Lord came to me: "You have shed much blood and have fought many wars. You are not to build a house for my Name, because you have shed much blood on the earth in my sight. But you will have a son who will be a man of peace and rest, and I will give him rest from all his enemies on every side. His name will be Solomon, and I will grant Israel peace and quiet during his reign. He is the one who will build a house for my Name. He will be my son, and I will be his father. And I will establish the throne of his kingdom over Israel for ever.'

'Now, my son, the Lord be with you, and may you have success and build the house of the Lord your God, as he said you would. May the Lord give you discretion and understanding when he puts you in command over Israel, so that you may keep the law of the Lord your God. Then you will have success if you are careful to observe the decrees and laws that the Lord gave to Moses for Israel. Be strong and courageous. Do not be afraid or discouraged.

## THURSDAY

JEREMIAH 38:1–13 (REB)

Shephatiah son of Mattan, Gedaliah son of Pashhur, Jucal son of Shelemiah, and Pashhur son of Malchiah heard how Jeremiah was addressing all the people; he was saying: These are the words of the Lord: Whoever remains in the city will die by the sword, famine, or pestilence, but whoever surrenders to the Chaldaeans will survive; he will escape with his life. These are the words of the Lord: This city will assuredly be delivered into the power of the king of Babylon's army, and be captured. The officers said to the king, 'This man ought to be put to death. By talking in this way he is demoralizing the soldiers left in the city and indeed the rest of the people. It is not the people's welfare he seeks but their ruin.' King Zedekiah said, 'He is in your hands; the king is powerless against you.' So they took Jeremiah and put him into the cistern in the court of the guardhouse, letting him down with ropes. There was no water in the cistern, only mud, and Jeremiah sank in the mud.

Ebedmelech the Cushite, a eunuch, who was in the palace, heard that they had put Jeremiah into a cistern and he went to tell the king, who was seated at the Benjamin Gate. 'Your majesty,' he said, 'these men have acted viciously in their treatment of the prophet Jeremiah. They have thrown him into a cistern, and he will die of hunger where he is, for there is no more bread in the city.' The king instructed Ebedmelech the Cushite to take three men with him and hoist Jeremiah out of the cistern before he perished. Ebedmelech went to the palace with the men and took some tattered, cast-off clothes from a storeroom and lowered them with ropes to Jeremiah in the cistern. He called to Jeremiah, 'Put these old clothes under your armpits to pad the ropes.' Jeremiah did so, and they pulled him up out of the cistern with the ropes. Jeremiah remained in the court of the guardhouse.

## FRIDAY

PSALM 46:1, 8–11 (AV)

God is our refuge and strength,
 a very present help in trouble.

Come, behold the works of the Lord,
 what desolations he hath made
 in the earth.
He maketh wars to cease unto the
 end on the earth;
 he breaketh the bow, and cutteth
 the spear in sunder;
 he burneth the chariot in the fire.
Be still, and know that I am God:
 I will be exalted among the heathen, I will be exalted in the
 earth.
The Lord of hosts is with us;
 the God of Jacob is our refuge.

MICAH 4:1–4 (AV)

But in the last days it shall come to pass, that the mountain of the house of the Lord shall be established in the top of the mountains, and it shall be exalted above the hills; and people shall flow unto it. And many nations shall come, and say, Come, and let us go up to the mountain of the Lord, and to the house of the God of Jacob; and he will teach us of his ways, and we will walk in his paths: for the law shall go forth of Zion, and the word of the Lord from Jerusalem.

And he shall judge among many people, and rebuke strong nations afar off; and they shall beat their swords into ploughshares, and their spears into pruninghooks: nation shall not lift up a sword against nation, neither shall they learn war any more. But they shall sit every man under his vine and under his fig tree; and none shall make them afraid: for the mouth of the Lord of hosts hath spoken it.

## SATURDAY

JAMES 4:1–12 (NJB)

Where do these wars and battles between yourselves first start? Is it not precisely in the desires fighting inside your own selves? You want something and you lack it; so you kill. You have an ambition that you cannot satisfy; so you fight to get your way by force. It is because you do not pray that you do not receive; when you do pray and do not receive, it is because you prayed wrongly, wanting to indulge your passions.

Adulterers! Do you not realize that love for the world is hatred for God? Anyone who chooses the world for a friend is constituted an enemy of God. Can you not see the point of the saying in scripture, 'The longing of the spirit he sent to dwell in us is a jealous longing'? But he has given us an even greater grace, as scripture says: God opposes the proud but he accords his favour to the humble. Give in to God, then; resist the devil, and he will run away from you. The nearer you go to God, the nearer God will come to you. Clean your hands, you sinners, and clear your minds, you waverers. Appreciate your wretchedness, and weep for it in misery. Your laughter must be turned to grief, your happiness to gloom. Humble yourselves before the Lord and he will lift you up.

Brothers, do not slander one another. Anyone who slanders a brother, or condemns one, is speaking against the Law and condemning the Law. But if you condemn the Law, you have ceased to be subject to it and become a judge over it.

There is only one lawgiver and he is the only judge and has the power to save or to destroy. Who are you to give a verdict on your neighbour?

# THE POWER OF THE PURSE

Today more than ever, it seems, everything and almost everyone has a price-tag. We are always talking, and thinking, about money. So, with a different perspective, does the Bible. But we can rarely bring ourselves to believe what it says.

In four readings from the gospels, Jesus teaches about money. First our charitable giving must be secret. He reminds us that our real treasure is invisible (Sunday). What matters is not what we give, but what we keep. There is no fool like a rich fool (Monday). Tuesday's reading concerns our attitude to our money. And Wednesday's looks at the hidden motives we have in relation to money. Dishonesty can even reach the inner circle of disciples. Jesus' teaching often arises from particular incidents or conversations; it is given to crowds, smaller groups, or individual enquirers, and sometimes he takes the initiative himself.

For the first Christians, the handling of their money was openly discussed. Paul's second Corinthian letter spells out some principles of 'giving' from a situation of inter-church relief (Thursday), while he instructs Timothy, another church leader, also to approach this subject directly and without apology (Friday).

Saturday's reading combines a Psalm about integrity with the promise from the letter to Hebrew Christians that God's reliability can remove covetousness and promote contentment—indeed, it must!

WEEK 41

# Money

We all need money and most people want a good income to enjoy a decent standard of living. But money in itself is not real wealth. Money is important to us because of the things it can be exchanged for—such as food, clothing and other possessions. There is very little in the way of material things that money cannot buy. And it can also give us power—power to control our own lives, and, when there is a lot of it, power over other people.

Because of the power of money there are some who regard it as evil. There is an old saying: 'Money is the root of all evil.' But this is simply not true. The Bible never condemns money. Some of its great characters—Abraham, Joseph, Job, Joseph of Arimathea—were wealthy people. What the Bible does say is that 'the *love* of money is the root of all evils'. Money itself is neutral, but selfishness and greed can make money a source of evil, with inordinate wealth for some at the expense of crippling poverty for others.

This is not all there is to be said, however. From a Christian perspective, money can be a potent force for good as well as for evil. What is a mature Christian attitude towards it?

- ◆ **God expects us to share our wealth and possessions.** On the whole Christianity has an excellent track record on this issue. Of course there are many Christians who have abused their wealth, but many more have given away their wealth to the poor or have diverted much of it to charitable ends. In our own day it is more crucial than ever that we share our resources with those in need. True treasure, said Jesus, is stored up in heaven and not laid up in banks or building societies. It is the wealth of love, generosity and compassion which endures for ever. Christians should be known for their radical self-giving as Jesus is remembered for his.

  The Bible lays down one very clear starting-point for our giving and this is known as the 'tithe' (or tenth part). It ought to be our aim to set aside a tenth of our gross pay for God's work. This is where sacrificial giving starts.

- ◆ **The wealth of society should be distributed evenly.** We are not supporting any particular socialist philosophy because some of these systems can be as cruel, heartless and impersonal as the capitalism they are keen to replace. A society which embraces a Christian attitude to life will want to uphold the right of every citizen to a dignified, full existence with adequate medical care, education and housing for all. Such a society will divert resources so that those in need can break out of the poverty trap.

The love of money may be a source of evil. But money can also be a tool with great potential for doing God's work. Let us use it well.

## SUNDAY

MATTHEW 6:1–4, 19–21 (RSV)

Jesus said 'Beware of practising your piety before men in order to be seen by them; for then you will have no reward from your Father who is in heaven. Thus, when you give alms, sound no trumpet before you, as the hypocrites do in the synagogues and in the streets, that they may be praised by men. Truly, I say to you, they have received their reward. But when you give alms, do not let your left hand know what your right hand is doing, so that your alms may be in secret; and your father who sees in secret will reward you.'

Do not lay up for yourselves treasures on earth, where moth and rust consume and where thieves break in and steal, but lay up for yourselves treasures in heaven, where neither moth nor rust consumes and where thieves do not break in and steal. For where your treasure is, there will your heart be also.

## MONDAY

MARK 12:41–44 (REB)

As Jesus was sitting opposite the temple treasury, he watched the people dropping their money into the chest. Many rich people were putting in large amounts. Presently there came a poor widow who dropped in two tiny coins, together worth a penny. He called his disciples to him and said, 'Truly I tell you: this poor widow has given more than all those giving to the treasury; for the others who have given had more than enough, but she, with less than enough, has given all that she had to live on.'

LUKE 12:13–21 (REB)

Someone in the crowd said to Jesus, 'Teacher, tell my brother to divide the family property with me.' He said to the man, 'Who set me over you to judge or arbitrate?' Then to the people he said, 'Beware! Be on your guard against greed of every kind, for even when someone has more than enough, his possessions do not give him life.' And he told them this parable: 'There was a rich man whose land yielded a good harvest. He debated with himself: "What am I to do? I have not the space to store my produce. This is what I will do," said he: "I will pull down my barns and build them bigger. I will collect in them all my grain and other goods, and I will say to myself, 'You have plenty of good things laid by, enough for many years to come: take life easy, eat, drink, and enjoy yourself.'" ' But God said to him, "You fool, this very night you must surrender your life; and the money you have made, who will get it now?" That is how it is with the man who piles up treasure for himself and remains a pauper in the sight of God.'

## TUESDAY

LUKE 18:18–27 (REB)

One of the rulers put this question to him: 'Good Teacher, what must I do to win eternal life?' Jesus said to him, 'Why do you call me good? No one is good except God alone. You know the commandments: "Do not commit adultery; do not murder; do not steal; do not give false evidence; honour your father and mother." ' The man answered, 'I have kept all these since I was a boy.' On hearing this Jesus said, 'There is still one thing you lack: sell everything you have and give to the poor, and you will have treasure in heaven; then come and follow me.' When he heard this his heart sank, for he was a very rich man. When Jesus saw it he said, 'How hard it is for the wealthy to enter the kingdom of God! It is easier for a camel to go through the eye of a needle than for a rich man to enter the kingdom of God.' Those who heard asked, 'Then who can be saved?' He answered, 'What is impossible for men is possible for God.'

## WEDNESDAY

JOHN 12:1–8 (NJB)

Six days before the Passover, Jesus went to Bethany, where Lazarus was, whom he had raised from the dead. They gave a dinner for him there; Martha waited on them and Lazarus was among those at table. Mary brought in a pound of very costly ointment, pure nard, and with it anointed the feet of Jesus, wiping them with her hair; the house was filled with the scent of the ointment. Then Judas Iscariot—one of his disciples, the man who was to betray him—said, 'Why was this ointment not sold for three hundred denarii and the money given to the poor?' He said this, not because he cared about the poor, but because he was a thief; he was in charge of the common fund and used to help himself to the contents. So Jesus said, 'Leave her alone; let her keep it for the day of my burial. You have the poor with you always, you will not always have me.'

## THURSDAY

2 CORINTHIANS 8:1–9, 9:6–11 (RSV)

We want you to know, brethren, about the grace of God which has been shown in the churches of Macedonia, for in a severe test of affliction, their abundance of joy and their extreme poverty have overflowed in a wealth of liberality on their part. For they gave according to their means, as I can testify, and beyond their means, of their own free will, begging us earnestly for the favour of taking part in the relief of the saints—and this, not as we expected, but first they gave themselves to the Lord and to us by the will of God. Accordingly we have urged Titus that as he had already made a beginning, he should also complete among you this gracious work. Now as you excel in everything—in faith, in utterance, in knowledge, in all earnestness, and in your love for us—see that you excel in this gracious work also.

I say this not as a command, but to prove by the earnestness of others that your love also is genuine. For you know the grace of our Lord Jesus Christ, that though he was rich, yet for your sake he became poor, so that by his poverty you might become rich.

The point is this: he who sows sparingly will also reap sparingly, and he who sows bountifully will also reap bountifully. Each one must do as he has made up his mind, not reluctantly or under compulsion, for God loves a cheerful giver. And God is able to provide you with every blessing in abundance, so that you may always have enough of everything and may provide in abundance for every good work. As it is written,

'He scatters abroad, he gives to the
    poor;
    his righteousness endures for
    ever.'

He who supplies seed to the sower and bread for food will supply and multiply your resources and increase the harvest of your righteousness. You will be enriched in every way for great generosity, which through us will produce thanksgiving to God.

## FRIDAY

1 TIMOTHY 6:3–10, 17–19 (NIV)

If anyone teaches false doctrines and does not agree to the sound instruction of our Lord Jesus Christ and to godly teaching, he is conceited and understands nothing. He has an unhealthy interest in controversies and arguments that result in envy, quarrelling, malicious talk, evil suspicions and constant friction between men of corrupt mind, who have been robbed of the truth and who think that godliness is a means to financial gain.

But godliness with contentment is great gain. For we brought nothing into the world, and we can take nothing out of it. But if we have food and clothing, we will be content with that. People who want to get rich fall into temptation and a trap and into many foolish and harmful desires that plunge men into ruin and destruction. For the love of money is a root of all kinds of evil. Some people, eager for money, have wandered from the faith and pierced themselves with many griefs.

Command those who are rich in this present world not to be arrogant nor to put their hope in wealth, which is so uncertain, but to put their hope in God, who richly provides us with everything for our enjoyment. Command them to do good, to be rich in good deeds, and to be generous and willing to share. In this way they will lay up treasure for themselves as a firm foundation for the coming age, so that they may take hold of the life that is truly life.

## SATURDAY

PSALM 15 (NIV)

Lord, who may dwell in your
    sanctuary?
    Who may live on your holy hill?

He whose walk is blameless
    and who does what is righteous,
who speaks the truth from his heart
    and has no slander on his
    tongue,
who does his neighbour no wrong

and casts no slur on his fellow
man,
who despises a vile man
but honours those who fear the
Lord,
who keeps his oath
even when it hurts,
who lends his money without usury
and does not accept a bribe
against the innocent.

He who does these things
will never be shaken.

HEBREWS 13:1–8 (NIV)

Keep on loving each other as brothers. Do not forget to entertain strangers, for by so doing some people have entertained angels without knowing it. Remember those in prison as if you were their fellow prisoners, and those who are ill-treated as if you yourselves were suffering.

Marriage should be honoured by all, and the marriage bed kept pure, for God will judge the adulterer and all the sexually immoral. Keep your lives free from the love of money and be content with what you have, because God has said,

'Never will I leave you;
never will I forsake you.'

So we say with confidence,

'The Lord is my helper; I will not be
afraid.
What can man do to me?'

Remember your leaders, who spoke the word of God to you. Consider the outcome of their way of life and imitate their faith. Jesus Christ is the same yesterday and today and for ever.

# THE WEEK STARTS HERE!

'Keep Sunday Special' is a slogan that stirs passions wherever vested interests are threatened. The whole idea of 'the week' as distinct from the given measures of time in days, months and years, has deep roots in Israel's faith. And the Psalm which starts this week (on Sunday, its first day) celebrates 'the day which the Lord has made' in close connection with the prophecy of resurrection when it refers to the once-rejected stone becoming the cornerstone.

Like the other gospel-writers, Luke's account of Easter marks the day as if starting a week, or an age, of new things (Monday). John adds the story of the 'Sunday after Easter' for Thomas's encounter with the risen Christ (Tuesday).

Wednesday's reading finds one early group of Christians meeting, on the 'first day of the week', while Friday's clearly reflects that the keeping of Sunday was significant in the church at Corinth.

The passage from Paul's letter to the Romans (Thursday) discusses the question of special days in the life of the church. On Saturday we read in Revelation, the last book of the Bible, that John encountered the risen Lord in a vision 'on the Lord's day'.

WEEK 42

# Sunday

Sunday is the Christian's holy day. There may not seem anything startling about that fact, but the shift from the seventh day of the week (the sabbath) to the first (the Lord's day) marked a total revolution in the thinking of the early Christians. The first followers of Jesus were mainly Jews. Christianity began in Palestine. Keeping the sabbath holy was one of the most important signs of belonging to the people of God. How was it that such a momentous change could take place?

The answer lies in the resurrection of Christ. All the Gospels insist that it was 'on the first day of the week' that the women came to Jesus' tomb and found it empty. It was on the first day that Jesus appeared to his disciples. And it was on the first day, one week later, that he revealed himself to Thomas. From the very beginning Sunday was linked in the disciples' minds with the day Christ was raised from death.

It seems likely that the change from sabbath to Sunday happened almost at once. It never surfaced as a point of controversy between Jewish and Gentile Christians; it seems to have been common practice in the church as a whole. When Paul went to Troas the church met for worship on the first day of the week. When he wrote to the Christians at Corinth he suggested that Sunday was a good day to put money aside for the work of the gospel. From the first it looks as though Sunday was a day for worship and for meeting other Christians.

Later generations brought the sabbath into Sunday and made it a day full of 'thou shalt nots'. But such legalism was never a part of the early church. Paul was tolerant of Jewish Christians who wanted to keep the sabbath but insisted that this could not be a matter of law. Present-day Christians may well want to take time out from their work to celebrate Jesus Christ as their Lord, but the New Testament gives no support to Bertrand Russell's acid comment, 'The Bible says you must not work on Saturday, which Christians take to mean you must not play on Sunday.'

How, then, should Christians use Sunday today? On this day Jesus rose from the dead and was declared to be Lord. It marked the beginning of a new age. In fact, later generations of Christians often referred to it as 'the eighth day' because it signalled the creation of a new world; it was one better than the sabbath. John called the day on which he received his vision of the risen Christ 'the Lord's Day'. This description was probably a sideswipe at the monthly Emperor's Day. For John the 'Lord of all' was Jesus, not the Roman emperor Domitian.

All this suggests that Sunday is the special day for celebrating the great fact that 'Jesus is Lord' and demonstrating that the new age has dawned. Of course Christians should live in perpetual celebration of this, but Sunday serves as a reminder, helping keep our celebration alive for the rest of the week.

# SUNDAY

PSALM 118:1–4, 16–26, 28–29 (AV)

O Give thanks unto the Lord;
for he is good: because his mercy endureth for ever.
Let Israel now say,
that his mercy endureth for ever.
Let the house of Aaron now say,
that his mercy endureth for ever.
Let them now that fear the Lord say,
that his mercy endureth forever.

The right hand of the Lord is exalted:
the right hand of the Lord doeth valiantly.
I shall not die,
but live, and declare the works of the Lord.
The Lord hath chastened me sore:
but he hath not given me over unto death.
Open to me the gates of righteousness:
I will go into them, and I will praise the Lord:
This gate of the Lord,
into which the righteous shall enter.
I will praise thee:
for thou hast heard me, and art become my salvation.
The stone which the builders refused
is become the head stone of the corner.
This is the Lord's doing;
it is marvellous in our eyes.
This is the day which the Lord hath made;
we will rejoice and be glad in it.
Save now, I beseech thee, O Lord:
O Lord, I beseech thee, send now prosperity.
Blessed be he that cometh in the name of the Lord:
we have blessed you out of the house of the Lord.

Thou art my God, and I will praise thee:
thou are my God, I will exalt thee.
O give thanks unto the Lord;
for he is good: for his mercy endureth for ever.

# MONDAY

LUKE 24:1–8 (NIV)

On the first day of the week, very early in the morning, the women took their spices they had prepared and went to the tomb. They found the stone rolled away from the tomb, but when they entered, they did not find the body of the Lord Jesus. While they were wondering about this, suddenly two men in clothes that gleamed like lightning stood beside them. In their fright the women bowed down with their faces to the ground, but the men said to them, 'Why do you look for the living among the dead? He is not here; he has risen! Remember how he told you, while he was with you in Galilee: "The Son of Man must be delivered into the hands of sinful men, be crucified and on the third day be raised again." ' Then they remembered his words.

## TUESDAY

JOHN 20:24–31 (NIV)

Now Thomas (called Didymus), one of the Twelve, was not with the disciples when Jesus came. When the other disciples told him that they had seen the Lord, he declared, 'Unless I see the nail marks in his hands and put my finger where the nails were, and put my hand into his side, I will not believe it.'

A week later his disciples were in the house again, and Thomas was with them. Though the doors were locked, Jesus came and stood among them, and said, 'Peace be with you!' Then he said to Thomas, 'Put your finger here; see my hands. Reach out your hand and put it in my side. Stop doubting and believe.'

Thomas answered, 'My Lord and my God!'

Then Jesus told him, 'Because you have seen me, you have believed; blessed are those who have not seen and yet have believed.'

Jesus did many other miraculous signs in the presence of his disciples, which are not recorded in this book. But these are written that you may believe that Jesus is the Christ, the Son of God, and that by believing you may have life in his name.

## WEDNESDAY

ACTS 20:6–12 (NIV)

But we sailed from Philippi after the Feast of the Unleavened Bread, and five days later joined the others at Troas, where we stayed seven days.

On the first day of the week we came together to break bread. Paul spoke to the people and, because he intended to leave the next day, kept on talking until midnight. There were many lamps in the upstairs room where we were meeting. Seated in a window was a young man named Eutychus, who was sinking into a deep sleep as Paul talked on and on. When he was sound asleep, he fell to the ground from the third storey and was picked up dead. Paul went down, threw himself on the young man and put his arms around him. 'Don't be alarmed,' he said. 'He's alive!' Then he went upstairs again and broke bread and ate. After talking until daylight, he left. The people took the young man home alive and were greatly comforted.

## THURSDAY

ROMANS 14:5–12 (NJB)

One person thinks that some days are holier than others, and another thinks them all equal. Let each of them be fully convinced in his own mind. The one who makes special observance of a particular day observes it in honour of the Lord. So the one who eats freely, eats in honour of the Lord, making his thanksgiving to God; and the one who does not, abstains from eating in honour of the Lord and makes his thanksgiving to God. For none of us lives for himself and none of us dies for himself; while we are alive, we are living for the Lord, and when we die, we die for the Lord: and so, alive or dead, we belong to the Lord. It was for this purpose that Christ both died and came to life again: so that he might be Lord of both the dead and the living. Why, then, does one of you make himself judge over his brother, and why does another among you despise his brother? All of us will have to stand in front of the judgment-seat of God: as scripture says: By my own life says the Lord, every knee shall bow before me, every tongue shall give glory to God. It is to God, then, that each of us will have to give an account of himself.

## FRIDAY

1 CORINTHIANS 16:1–9 (REB)

Now about the collection in aid of God's people: you should follow the instructions I gave to our churches in Galatia. Every Sunday each of you is to put aside and keep by him whatever he can afford, so that there need be no collecting when I come. When I arrive, I will give letters of introduction to persons approved by you, and send them to carry your gift to Jerusalem. If it seems right for me to go as well, they can travel with me.

I shall come to Corinth after passing through Macedonia—for I am travelling by way of Macedonia—and I may stay some time with you, perhaps even the whole winter; and then you can help me on my way wherever I go next. I do not want this to be a flying visit; I hope to spend some time with you, if the Lord permits. But I shall remain at Ephesus until Pentecost, for a great opportunity has opened for effective work, and there is much opposition.

## SATURDAY

REVELATION 1:1–11 (RSV)

The revelation of Jesus Christ, which God gave him to show to his servants what must soon take place; and he made it known by sending his angel to his servant John, who bore witness to the word of God and to the testimony of Jesus Christ, even to all that he saw. Blessed is he who reads aloud the words of the prophecy, and blessed are those who hear, and who keep what is written therein; for the time is near.

John to the seven churches that are in Asia:

Grace to you and peace from him who is and who was and who is to come, and from the seven spirits who are before his throne, and from Jesus Christ the faithful witness, the first-born of the dead, and the ruler of kings on earth.

To him who loves us and has freed us from our sins by his blood and made us a kingdom, priests to his God and Father, to him be glory and dominion for ever and ever. Amen. Behold, he is coming with the clouds, and every eye will see him, every one who pierced him; and all tribes of the earth will wail on account of him. Even so. Amen.

'I am the Alpha and the Omega,' says the Lord God, who is and who was and who is to come, the Almighty.

I John, your brother, who share with you in Jesus the tribulation and the kingdom and the patient endurance, was on the island called Patmos on account of the word of God and testimony of Jesus. I was in the Spirit on the Lord's day, and I heard behind me a loud voice like a trumpet saying,

'Write what you see in a book and send it to the seven churches, to Ephesus and to Smyrna and to Pergamum and to Thyatira and to Sardis and to Philadelphia and to Laodicea.'

# TAKING THE PLUNGE

WEEK 43

Christian baptism is the New Testament sign of initiation into the church. Although Christians have differed in the emphasis placed on this ceremony of water, most would agree that even before Christ there were signs of what was to come. In the New Testament, Paul says that the Israelites were figuratively 'baptized into Moses' and Sunday's reading from Joshua refers to the past life of God's people 'on the other side of the flood'. Joshua's challenge to commitment has a call to decisive dedication.

We read too of the baptism of Jesus—unexpected because apparently unnecessary. John's baptism was 'for repentance'. Monday's reading records baptisms by Jesus' disciples, as well as his reference to the 'living water' he will give.

After Jesus' death and resurrection and on the day of Pentecost, baptism appears as a ready-made initiation offered to new believers. Later, Peter refers to it very positively in his first letter (Tuesday).

On the next three days we look at selections from Acts. These show the baptism of an Ethiopian by Philip the evangelist (Wednesday); of more Gentiles by Peter (Thursday); and of Lydia at Philippi and some former disciples of John the Baptist, by Paul (Friday).

On Saturday, in three extracts from Paul's letters, he urges three sets of readers to live up to their status as people who are resurrected, believing, and united in Christ.

WEEK
43

# Baptism

When a new Christian in New Testament times went down into the water of baptism, what was at stake was total commitment. This commitment was being displayed in three different ways, and it presents a challenge to us today.

- ◆ **In baptism God commits himself totally to us.** Baptism declares God's love and grace which is expressed supremely in Jesus' life and death. His death was in fact his baptism, which opened the way of life and peace to us. Baptism declares to us that we are forgiven, that we are now God's children and that his Spirit is given to all who follow him. Baptism, therefore, says as much about God as about us; it speaks of his sacrificial love, that he will never forsake us and never let us go.
- ◆ **In baptism we commit ourselves totally to him.** In the service of baptism the new Christian is actually stating two things. First, that he or she repents of a sinful past life and is willing to renounce it. Second, that the new owner of his or her life is now Jesus Christ. Paul links together Jesus' death and resurrection and our baptism. The new Christian, by going under the waters of baptism, enters into the death of Jesus and rises from it to share in the resurrection. Jesus' death was his baptism for us; our baptism is a death to the old life. For the New Testament Christian this was no game or play with words. To say 'Jesus is Lord', as each did at baptism, amounted to saying that from now on Jesus Christ came before everything else. They were prepared to face insults, ignominy and perhaps even death because of the love of their Lord.
- ◆ **In baptism the church gives itself totally to us.** Baptism is not a private and personal agreement between God and us. It takes place within the family of the church, and without that family we cannot survive as Christians. We need its fellowship, its life and its help. Through his church God's grace comes to us in innumerable ways, leading us into deeper faith and commitment and on into greater maturity. When we talk about the 'sacrament' of baptism we are speaking of two things which are going on at the same time. The outward part includes such things as water, Bible readings, the minister and the congregation. The inner part is what God is doing in the sacrament through his Spirit. That part, like the seed sown in the ground, only becomes visible much later on. The classic picture of baptism is as 'new birth', and this is a reality to Christians because they are aware that through the Holy Spirit they now look at life quite differently, and belong now to a new group of people.

How far is this New Testament pattern recognizable in our practice of baptism today? This is a question to be asked both of churches that baptize infants and of those that baptize only adults. God wants not half-hearted believers, but men and women who are wholehearted and reckless in their love for him. Do our baptismal disciplines express this element of commitment? Many churches are guilty sometimes of dropping standards in their obsession to make 'more' disciples. But those who have not counted the cost will quickly fall away.

We should question as well whether our church is taking its responsibility seriously to love and care for new Christians. Just as we would question the love of a mother and father who did not bother about their children, so with a church which allows people to drift away from its fellowship and is not a welcoming and accepting family. Such a church is not worthy of the trust which God has placed in it.

WEEK 43

## SUNDAY

JOSHUA 24:14–15 (AV)

Now therefore fear the Lord, and serve him in sincerity and in truth: and put away the gods which your fathers served on the other side of the flood, and in Egypt; and serve ye the Lord. And if it seem evil unto you to serve the Lord, choose you this day whom ye will serve; whether the gods which your fathers served that were on the other side of the flood, or the gods of the Amorites, in whose land ye dwell: but as for me and my house, we will serve the Lord.

MATTHEW 3:13–17 (AV)

Then cometh Jesus from Galilee to Jordan unto John, to be baptized of him. But John forbad him, saying, I have need to be baptized of thee, and comest thou to me? And Jesus answering said unto him, Suffer it to be so now: for thus it becometh us to fulfil all righteousness. Then he suffered him. And Jesus, when he was baptized, went up straightway out of the water: and, lo, the heavens were opened unto him, and he was the Spirit of God descending like a dove, and saw lighting upon him: And lo a voice from heaven, saying, This is my beloved Son, in whom I am well pleased.

## MONDAY

JOHN 4:1–10 (NIV)

The Pharisees heard that Jesus was gaining and baptizing more disciples than John, although in fact it was not Jesus who baptized, but his disciples. When the Lord learned of this, he left Judea and went back once more to Galilee.

Now he had to go through Samaria. So he came to a town in Samaria called Sychar, near the plot of ground Jacob had given to his son Joseph. Jacob's well was there, and Jesus, tired as he was from the journey, sat down by the well. It was about the sixth hour.

When a Samaritan woman came to draw water, Jesus said to her, 'Will you give me a drink?' (His disciples had gone into the town to buy food.)

The Samaritan woman said to him, 'You are a Jew and I am a Samaritan woman. How can you ask me for a drink?' (For Jews do not associate with Samaritans.)

Jesus answered her, 'If you knew the gift of God and who it is that asks you for a drink, you would have asked him and he would have given you living water.'

## TUESDAY

ACTS 2:37–41 (RSV)

Now when they heard this they were cut to the heart, and said to Peter and the rest of the apostles, 'Brethren, what shall we do?' And Peter said to them, 'Repent, and be baptized every one of you in the name of Jesus Christ for the forgiveness of your sins; and you shall receive the gift of the Holy Spirit. For the promise is to you and to your children and to all that are far off, every one whom the Lord our God calls to him.' And he testified with many other words and exhorted them, saying, 'Save yourselves from this crooked generation.' So those who received his word were baptized, and there were added that day about three thousand souls.

1 PETER 3:18–23 (RSV)

For Christ also died for sins once for all, the righteous for the unrighteous, that he might bring us to God, being put to death in the flesh but made alive in the spirit; in which he went and preached to the spirits in prison, who formerly did not obey, when God's patience waited in the days of Noah, during the building of the ark, in which a few, that is, eight persons, were saved through water. Baptism, which corresponds to this, now saves you, not as a removal of dirt form the body but as an appeal to God for a clear conscience, through the resurrection of Jesus Christ, who has gone into heaven and is at the right hand of God, with angels, authorities, and powers subject to him.

## WEDNESDAY

ACTS 8:26–39 (RSV)

But an angel of the Lord said to Philip, 'Rise and go toward the south to the road that goes down from Jerusalem to Gaza.' This is a desert road. And he rose and went. And behold, an Ethiopian, a eunuch, a minister of Candace, queen of the Ethiopians, in charge of all her treasure, had come to Jerusalem to worship and was returning; seated in his chariot, he was reading the prophet Isaiah. And the Spirit said to Philip, 'Go up, and join this chariot.' So Philip ran to him, and heard him reading Isaiah the prophet, and asked, 'Do you understand what you are reading?' And he said, 'How can I, unless some one guides me?' And he invited Philip to come up and sit with him. Now the passage of the scripture which he was reading was this:

'As a sheep led to the slaughter
  or a lamb before its shearer is dumb,
  so he opens not his mouth.
In his humiliation justice was denied him.
  Who can describe his generation?
For his life is taken up from the earth.'

And the eunuch said to Philip, 'About whom, pray, does the prophet say this, about himself or about some one else?' Then Philip opened his mouth, and beginning with this scripture he told him the good news of Jesus. And as they went along the road they came to some water, and the eunuch said, 'See, here is water! What is to prevent my being baptized?' And he commanded the chariot to stop, and they both went down into the water, Philip and the eunuch, and he baptized him. And when they came up out of the water, the Spirit of the Lord caught up Philip; and the eunuch saw him no more, and went on his way rejoicing.

## THURSDAY

ACTS 10:36–48 (RSV)

Peter continued 'You know the word which he sent to Israel, preaching good news of peace by Jesus Christ (he is Lord of all), the word which was proclaimed throughout all Judea, beginning from Galilee after the baptism which John preached: how God anointed Jesus of Nazareth with the Holy Spirit and with power; how he went about doing good and healing all that were oppressed by the devil, for God was with him. And we are witnesses to all that he did both in the country of the Jews and in Jerusalem. They put him to death by hanging him on a tree; but God raised him on the third day and made him manifest; not to all the people but to us who were chosen by God as witnesses, who ate and drank with him after he rose from the dead. And he commanded us to preach to the people, and to testify that he is the one ordained by God to be the judge of the living and the dead. To him all the prophets bear witness that every one who believes in him receives forgiveness of sins through his name.'

While Peter was still saying this, the Holy Spirit fell on all who heard the word. And the believers from among the circumcised who came with Peter were amazed, because the gift of the Holy Spirit had been poured out even on the Gentiles. For they heard them speaking in tongues and extolling God. Then Peter declared, 'Can any one forbid water for baptizing these people who have received the Holy Spirit just as we have?' And he commanded them to be baptized in the name of Jesus Christ. Then they asked him to remain for some days.

## FRIDAY

ACTS 16:11–15, 19:1–7 (RSV)

Setting sail therefore from Troas, we made a direct voyage to Samothrace, and the following day to Neapolis, and from there to Philippi, which is the leading city of the district of Macedonia, and a Roman colony. We remained in this city some days; and on the sabbath day we went outside the gate to the riverside, where we supposed there was a place of prayer; and we sat down and spoke to the women who had come together. One who heard us was a woman named Lydia, from the city of Thyatira, a seller of purple goods, who was a worshipper of God. The Lord opened her heart to give heed to what was said by Paul. And when she was baptized, with her household, she besought us, saying, 'If you have judged me to be faithful to the Lord, come to my house and stay.' And she prevailed upon us.

When Apollas was at Corinth, Paul passed through the upper country and came to Ephesus. There he found some disciples. And he said to them, 'Did you receive the Holy Spirit when you believed?' And they said, 'No, we have never even heard that there is a Holy Spirit.' And he said, 'Into what then were you baptized?' They said, 'Into John's baptism.' And Paul said, 'John baptized with the baptism of repentance, telling the people to believe in the one who was to come after him, that is,

Jesus.' On hearing this, they were baptized in the name of the Lord Jesus. And when Paul had laid his hands upon them, the Holy Spirit came on them; and they spoke with tongues and prophesied. There were about twelve of them in all.

## SATURDAY

ROMANS 6:1–4 (NJB)

What should we say then? Should we remain in sin so that grace may be given the more fully? Out of the question! We have died to sin; how could we go on living in it? You cannot have forgotten that all of us, when we were baptized into Christ Jesus, were baptized into his death. So by our baptism into his death we were buried with him, so that as Christ was raised from the dead by the Father's glorious power, we too should begin living a new life.

1 CORINTHIANS 1:10–17 (NJB)

Brothers, I urge you, in the name of our Lord Jesus Christ, not to have factions among yourselves but all to be in agreement in what you profess; so that you are perfectly united in your beliefs and judgments. From what Chloe's people have been telling me about you, brothers, it is clear that there are serious differences among you. What I mean is this: every one of you is declaring, 'I belong to Paul,' or 'I belong to Apollos' or 'I belong to Cephas,' or 'I belong to Christ.' Has Christ been split up? Was it Paul that was crucified for you, or was it in Paul's name that you were baptized? I am thankful I did not baptize any of you, except Crispus and Gaius, so that no one can say that you were baptized in my name. Yes, I did baptize the family of Stephanas, too; but besides these I do not think I baptized anyone.

After all, Christ sent me not to baptize, but to preach the gospel; and not by means of wisdom of language, wise words which would make the cross of Christ pointless.

GALATIANS 3:26–28 (NJB)

All of you are the children of God, through faith, in Christ Jesus, since every one of you that has been baptized has been clothed in Christ. There can be neither Jew nor Greek, there can be neither slave nor freeman, there can be neither male nor female—for you are all one in Christ Jesus.

# LETTERS FROM PAUL

Of the twenty-one letters in the New Testament, thirteen are thought to have been written by Paul the apostle. They give a penetrating insight into the faith and life of the churches in the first years of their existence.

Paul encountered the risen Jesus on the Damascus road, and his life was turned round. He became the key figure in the spread of Christianity to the west, and was foremost in thinking out what the good news of Jesus meant to people of the different cultures of the Roman empire.

He undertook three 'missionary journeys', to found Christian churches and to establish their faith and life. His letters are to the Christians of the churches he founded, and to particular

### 1 Thessalonians

**(50-51)**

The tone is of tremendous encouragement. Paul is encouraged by the faith of these new Christians, and wants to encourage them still further.

### 2 Thessalonians

**(51-52)**

The Thessalonian Christians misunderstood what Paul wrote in his first letter about Christ's second coming. This letter informs them more fully about the future.

### Galatians

**(54-57)**

Written to oppose a damaging error—that to be saved a person must keep the whole law of Moses. No, writes Paul. Salvation is through faith in Jesus alone.

### Romans

**(54-57)**

A reasoned statement of the whole Christian gospel. We are saved, not by good works, but through the grace of Jesus who died and rose for us.

### 1 Corinthians

**(54-57)**

Paul was saddened to hear of division and immorality among the Corinthian Christians. He writes to tell them how Christians should live and love one another.

### 2 Corinthians

**(56-58)**

Here Paul's heart is revealed. He shows d personal concern for churches, whom he h been called to serve.

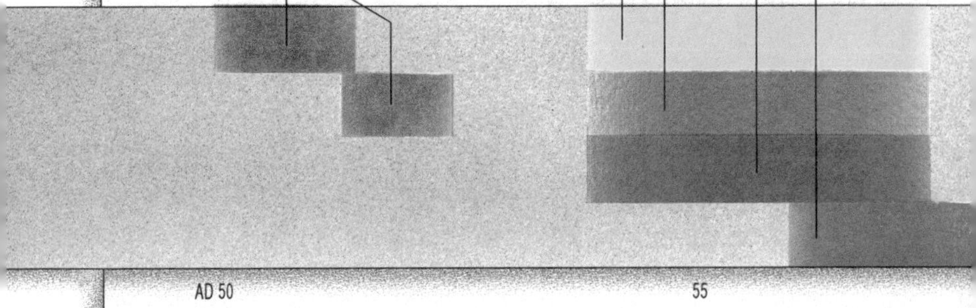

AD 50 55

leaders. Generally the letters begin with a statement of the beliefs they share, then move on to details of practical life for churches and for individual Christians. The background to all this can be read in Acts chapters 9 to 28. The dates given are probable.

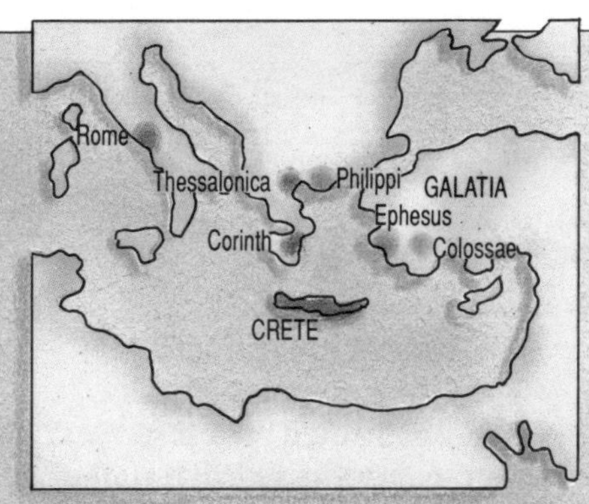


**Philippians**
**(early 60s)**
Full of love and deep joy. Writing from prison, Paul is not phased by his approaching death.

**Philemon**
**(early 60s)**
Asks Philemon to receive back an escaped slave, Onesimus, whom Paul has led to Christ.

**Titus**
**(perhaps 63-64)**
Written to the leader of the church in Crete. Much would depend on the leaders of these young churches.

**Colossians**
**(early 60s)**
Written from prison to Christians Paul never met. Focuses on the supremacy of Jesus Christ.

**1 Timothy**
**(perhaps 63-64)**
The once-shy Timothy is now leader of the Ephesian church. Paul encourages and advises him.

**2 Timothy**
**(perhaps 64)**
Expecting death very soon, Paul encourages Timothy to persevere in his ministry, using his own life as an example.

**Ephesians**
**(early 60s)**
The theme is God's plan 'to bring all creation together...with Christ as head'. Another 'prison letter'.

60 65

WEEK 44

# LIFE-LONG LEARNERS

Disciples are learners. The first disciples of Jesus embarked on a three-year programme of practical training which began with their response to his personal summons, and led on and up to Jesus' death at Calvary.

John's account of the beginnings, starting with John the Baptist, reads like that of an eyewitness (Sunday). Mark's version of a landmark in Simon Peter's learning was probably passed on to him from Peter's own recollection (Monday). Both episodes set the role and authority of Jesus at the centre.

Tuesday's reading only confirms what Jesus' closest friends must have realized already; following Jesus was never going to be easy (Tuesday). Words from the later New Testament letters chosen for the rest of this week show how the Christian struggle was perceived by some of their leaders.

Paul's battle-cry (Wednesday) comes near the end of a letter largely taken up with seeing the church family as a body. We do not fight alone, nor with this world's weapons. On Thursday, the letter to the Hebrews describes the Christian life as running a race—it is a life of discipline. Lastly, it is left to Peter to point to self-control, motivated by Christ, as part of a disciple's witness, a safeguard against disaster, and a key to the eternal future (Friday and Saturday). But Christ's pain, and our own, are never far from his thoughts.

WEEK 44

# Discipleship

'Disciple' is a 'Gospels' word. Apart from a few references in Acts, the rest of the New Testament prefers to describe the Christian in other terms. But 'disciple' is a good word; it has a simplicity and a concreteness about it. What does it mean?

- **To be a disciple is to follow Jesus**. Discipleship begins with a call—'Come to me', 'Follow me'—and to be a Christian is to walk behind Jesus, as Bartimaeus, a blind man whom he healed, followed Jesus 'in the way'. In fact, 'The Way' briefly became a way of describing the Christian community. Jesus leads, whether to the other side of the lake, to Jerusalem or to Galilee, and the call to disciples is 'to follow in his steps', even if this means taking up our own cross behind him.
- **Following Jesus involves breaking with the past**. The Galilean fishermen left nets and family; Levi had to walk away from the tax office. The rich young ruler was unwilling to make this break. Jesus referred to this as 'hating your life' and 'forsaking all' for his sake. Many in the crowds found the cost too high and 'walked no more with him'.
- **The word 'disciple' literally means a learner**, and this highlights a third aspect of the Christian life. Disciples have not left school. Jesus invited men and women to 'take on his yoke and learn from him'. In this he was just like the rabbis who taught their students a whole-life package. The twelve are chosen 'to be *with* him'. He offers 'to *make* them fishers of men'. By watching, listening and living with Jesus the disciples learned the secret of the kingdom at a level much deeper than words. They saw Jesus praying, arguing, healing, teaching. Some saw him transfigured or in agony. To be a disciple is to learn from Jesus by sharing every part of his life.

One difficult lesson to learn was that life was to be shared with other disciples as well. The circle round Jesus became a new community, replacing the ties of kinship or status. Jesus' family are those who hear the word of God and obey it. When Peter complained bitterly that he had given up everything to follow Jesus, he was promised a new home and family. The distinguishing mark of this new community was to be its mutual love.

This was no closed community, however. Anyone could join. Though Jesus often taught his followers in secret, yet this was only a prelude to sending them out to preach, teach, heal and exorcize. There was a rhythm of learning and doing. In this way they continued his work. Jesus had promised to make his disciples 'fishers of men'. Once he sent out twelve of them, once seventy, and these missions clearly prefigured the great commission, which he gave right at the end, to them and to every Christian to bear witness and 'make disciples of all nations'.

One final theme emerges from the Gospels—that of weakness and failure. The disciples are typically shown as faithless, dull and uncomprehending.

They cannot grasp the truth about Christ's passion, they reject the women who bring children to Jesus, they dispute about who is the greatest, fail to stay awake with Jesus in his agony and at his arrest run for their lives. Some, like Nicodemus, try to be secret followers 'for fear of the Jews'. Judas betrays; Peter, despite his boasts, denies. The churches for whom the Gospels were first written would have read these passages as a call to be faithful and as an illustration of Jesus' warning: 'without me you can do nothing.'

## SUNDAY

JOHN 1:35–46 (NJB)

The next day as John stood there again with two of his disciples, Jesus went past, and John looked towards him and said, 'Look, there is the lamb of God.' And the two disciples heard what he said and followed Jesus. Jesus turned round, saw them following and said, 'What do you want?' They answered, 'Rabbi'—which means Teacher—'where do you live?' He replied, 'Come and see;' so they went and saw where he lived, and stayed with him that day. It was about the tenth hour.

One of these two who became followers of Jesus after hearing what John had said was Andrew, the brother of Simon Peter. The first thing Andrew did was to find his brother and say to him, 'We have found the Messiah'—which means the Christ—and he took Simon to Jesus. Jesus looked at him and said, 'You are Simon son of John; you are to be called Cephas'—which means Rock.

The next day, after Jesus had decided to leave for Galilee, he met Philip and said, 'Follow me.' Philip came from the same town, Bethsaida, as Andrew and Peter. Philip found Nathanael and said to him, 'We have found him of whom Moses in the Law and the prophets wrote, Jesus son of Joseph, from Nazareth.' Nathanael said to him, 'From Nazareth? Can anything good come from that place?' Philip replied, 'Come and see.'

## MONDAY

MARK 8:31–38 (REB)

Jesus began to teach them that the Son of Man had to endure great suffering, and to be rejected by the elders, chief priests, and scribes; to be put to death, and to rise again three days afterwards. He spoke about it plainly. At this Peter took hold of him and began to rebuke him. But Jesus, turning and looking at his disciples, rebuked Peter. 'Out of my sight, Satan!' he said. 'You think as men think, not as God thinks.'

Then he called the people to him, as well as his disciples, and said to them, 'Anyone who wants to be a follower of mine must renounce self; he must take up his cross and follow me. Whoever wants to save his life will lose it, but whoever loses his life for my sake and for the gospel's will save it. What does anyone gain by winning the whole world at the cost of his life? What can he give to buy his life back? If anyone is ashamed of me and my words in this wicked and godless age, the Son of Man will be ashamed of him, when he comes in the glory of his Father with the holy angels.'

## TUESDAY

LUKE 9:51–62 (REB)

As the time approached when he was to be taken up to heaven, he set his face resolutely towards Jerusalem, and sent messengers ahead. They set out and went into a Samaritan village to make arrangements for him; but the villagers would not receive him because he was on his way to Jerusalem. When the disciples James and John saw this they said, 'Lord, do you want us to call down fire from heaven to consume them?' But he turned and rebuked them, and they went on to another village.

As they were going along the road a man said to him, 'I will follow you wherever you go.' Jesus answered, 'Foxes have their holes and birds their roosts; but the Son of Man has nowhere to lay his head.' To another he said, 'Follow me,' but the man replied, 'Let me first go and bury my father.' Jesus said, 'Leave the dead to bury their dead; you must go and announce the kingdom of God.' Yet another said, 'I will follow you, sir; but let me first say goodbye to my people at home.' To him Jesus said, 'No one who sets his hand to the plough and then looks back is fit for the kingdom of God.'

## WEDNESDAY

EPHESIANS 6:10–18 (AV)

Finally, my brethren, be strong in the Lord, and in the power of his might. Put on the whole armour of God, that ye may be able to stand against the wiles of the devil. For we wrestle not against flesh and blood, but against principalities, against powers, against the rulers of the darkness of this world, against spiritual wickedness in high places. Wherefore take unto you the whole armour of God, that ye may be able to withstand in the evil day, and having done all, to stand. Stand therefore, having your loins girt about with truth, and having on the breastplate of righteousness; And your feet shod with the preparation of the gospel of peace; Above all, taking the shield of faith, wherewith ye shall be able to quench all the fiery darts of the wicked. And take the helmet of salvation, and the sword of the Spirit, which is the word of God: Praying always with all prayer and supplication in the Spirit, and watching thereunto with all perseverance and supplication for all saints.

## THURSDAY

HEBREWS 12:1–14 (RSV)

Therefore, since we are surrounded by so great a cloud of witnesses, let us also lay aside every weight, and sin which clings so closely, and let us run with perseverance the race that is set before us, looking to Jesus the pioneer and perfecter of our faith, who for the joy that was set before him endured the cross, despising the shame, and is seated on the right hand of the throne of God.

Consider him who endured from sinners such hostility against himself, so that you may not grow weary or fainthearted. In your struggle against sin you have not yet resisted to the point of shedding your blood. And have you forgotten the exhortation which addresses you as sons?—

'My son, do not regard lightly the
    discipline of the Lord,
    nor lose courage when you are
    punished by him.
For the Lord disciplines him whom
    he loves,

and chastises every son whom he
receives.'
It is for discipline that you have to endure. God is treating you as sons; for what son is there whom his father does not discipline? If you are left without discipline, in which all have participated, then you are illegitimate children and not sons. Besides this, we have had earthly fathers to discipline us and we respected them. Shall we not much more be subject to the Father of spirits and live? For they disciplined us for a short time at their pleasure, but he disciplines us for our good, that we may share his holiness. For the moment all discipline seems painful rather than pleasant; later it yields the peaceful fruit of righteousness to those who have been trained by it.

Therefore lift your drooping hands and strengthen your weak knees, and make straight paths for your feet, so that what is lame may not be put out of joint but rather be healed. Strive for peace with all men, and for the holiness without which no one will see the Lord.

## FRIDAY

1 PETER 3:8–18, 4:1–5 (NIV)

Finally, all of you, live in harmony with one another; be sympathetic, love as brothers, be compassionate and humble. Do not repay evil with evil or insult with insult, but with blessing, because to this you were called so that you may inherit a blessing. For,

'Whoever would love life and see
good days
must keep his tongue from evil
and his lips from deceitful
speech.
He must turn from evil and do good;
he must seek peace and pursue
it.
For the eyes of the Lord are on the
righteous
and his ears are attentive to their
prayer,
but the face of the Lord is against
those who do evil.'

Who is going to harm you if you are eager to do good? But even if you should suffer for what is right, you are blessed. 'Do not fear what they fear; do not be frightened.' But in your hearts set apart Christ as Lord. Always be prepared to give an answer to everyone who asks you to give the reason for the hope that you have. But do this with gentleness and respect, keeping a clear conscience, so that those who speak maliciously against your good behaviour in Christ may be ashamed of their slander. It is better, if it is God's will, to suffer for doing good than for doing evil. For Christ died for sins once for all, the righteous and the unrighteous, to bring you to God.

Therefore, since Christ suffered in his body, arm yourselves also with the same attitude, because he who has suffered in his body is done with sin. As a result, he does not live the rest of his earthly life for evil human desires, but rather for the will of God. For you have spent enough time in the past doing what pagans choose to do—living in debauchery, lust, drunkenness, orgies, carousing and detestable idolatry. They think it strange that you do not plunge with them into the same flood of dissipation, and they heap abuse on you. But they will have to give account to him who is ready to judge the living and the dead.

## SATURDAY

2 PETER 1:2–11 (NIV)

Grace and peace be yours in abundance through the knowledge of God and of Jesus our Lord.

His divine power has given us everything we need for life and godliness through our knowledge of him who called us by his own glory and goodness. Through these he has given us his very great and precious promises, so that through them you may participate in the divine nature and escape the corruption in the world caused by evil desires.

For this very reason, make every effort to add to your faith goodness; and to goodness, knowledge; and to knowledge, self-control; and to self-control, perseverance; and to perseverance, godliness; and to godliness, brotherly kindness; and to brotherly kindness, love. For if you possess these qualities in increasing measure, they will keep you from being ineffective and unproductive in your knowledge of our Lord Jesus Christ. But if anyone does not have them, he is nearsighted and blind, and has forgotten that he has been cleansed from his past sins.

Therefore, my brothers, be all the more eager to make your calling and election sure. For if you do these things, you will never fall, and you will receive a rich welcome into the eternal kingdom of our Lord and Saviour Jesus Christ.

WEEK 45

# ONE BODY, MANY PARTS

The apostle Paul described the church (God's people, not a building) as the body of Christ. Drawing partly on Old Testament ideas, partly on the actual words of Jesus, partly on his own experience at conversion, he was strongly moved by this image and loved to spell out its implications.

Paul sets down many of the functions of the differing 'members' (or parts) in writing to the Romans (Sunday), and another, overlapping list to the Corinthians (Monday). But Tuesday's reading puts the principle above the details. The body-metaphor teaches us to despise neither our own contribution nor that of others. If there is to be boasting, it can hardly be about 'gifts', but (he has to point out with wry firmness) about the less welcome presents of weakness and pain (Wednesday).

In Paul's letter to the Ephesians, he returns to the body image to speak of gifts of ministry. These are not given to bestow status or rank, but to help to build up all the people (Thursday). Two further letters also speak of gifts and graces ranging from miracles and wonders (Friday) to hospitality and 'above all . . . love' (Saturday). Crucially, the applause and acclamation are not to be for ourselves.

WEEK 45

# Spiritual Gifts

The first gift the Christian receives is the gift of the Holy Spirit. He comes to every Christian who opens his or her life to Jesus Christ. He works in our lives, deepening our love for Jesus, and honing our abilities and gifts in his service.

The clearest teaching about the gifts of the Holy Spirit is found in 1 Corinthians 12, but there are also lists in Romans 12, Ephesians 4, and 1 Peter 4. The church of Corinth had a problem, one stemming from their very success. To their great joy they found that their faith actually worked! Things started to happen. There were those who discovered that they had gifts of healing, prophecy, teaching, miracle-working, tongues-speaking, leadership and so on. So great was the Spirit's generosity that his 'anointing' came on many in the fellowship. But instead of these wonderful experiences leading to greater service for Christ and deeper humility, those who received gifts used them to boost themselves, with the result that selfishness, pride and envy began to split the fellowship open. Paul has to remind them strongly that gifts are given by God—Father, Son and Spirit—and they do not originate from us. And they are to be used for one another, the limbs and organs in a single body.

Paul makes no tidy classification of the gifts. But for the sake of convenience they can be separated into two kinds:

- **Speaking gifts.** Among other gifts of speech, Paul mentions teaching, speaking in tongues and prophecy, which are gifts fit to be used in the congregation. 'Tongues' is a gift which has perplexed many. It seems to be a special language given to individuals for praise, worship and strengthening. Sometimes it bubbles forth in ecstatic utterances. Paul does not deprecate the gift but he does deplore people using it for their own sake. He therefore instructs that when it is used in the congregation it must be interpreted. 'Prophecy' is not another form of preaching but, more probably, a special message from God about the spiritual needs of the congregation.
- **Action gifts.** Paul mentions a number of gifts which are also channels of the Spirit's power but where the emphasis falls on what is done rather than on what is said: healing, miracle-working, helping others and even administration.

The rich abundance of divine gifts which flowered in such variety in Corinth is testimony to the gracious activity of the Spirit, but it would be unwise to expect their experience to be reproduced in exactly the same form today. 'The Spirit blows where he wills,' and refuses to be confined to what we expect. Yet still he gives gifts which match our needs today.

It is just as important for us as for the Corinthians to heed the controls that Paul set around the use of the gifts in the congregation.

First, they were to be used to build up others. The purpose of spiritual gifts is service. Paul rebukes those 'speakers-in-tongues' whose enthusiasm was hindering the church. We, too, should be cautious of any gift which appears to divide the congregation or exalt the user. We will want to ask: Does this gift build up the life of our church?

Next comes the principle of love. The gifts will pass away when their work is done, but love lasts for ever. What is more, Paul argues, without love to guide and control, spiritual gifts have no more value than the noise of a clanging gong. Alongside his teaching about spiritual gifts, Paul sets a most wonderful passage on the nature of Christian love. Some have suggested that it is modelled on the person and work of Jesus Christ, in whom we find that perfect balance of giftedness and sacrificial love.

And another essential control in the use of gifts is that of order. Paul does not want to freeze out any genuine gift; rather, he wants them to flourish within an ordered spiritual quietness in the fellowship. Speaking in tongues, prophecy and other expressions of the Spirit's activity are still allowed in worship, but Paul brings them under sensible control so that all may benefit.

And what about the church we attend? Our situation may be the opposite of that of the church at Corinth. Instead of the Spirit working in profusion there may be deadness, dull order instead of spontaneity, apathy instead of eager expectancy. The Holy Spirit never gives up on the church, and we should never cease to love, pray and hope that God's gifts may flourish in abundance where we are.

WEEK 45

## SUNDAY

ROMANS 12:4–21 (AV)

For as we have many members in one body, and all members have not the same office: So we, being many, are one body in Christ, and every one members one of another. Having then gifts differing according to the grace that is given to us, whether prophecy, let us prophesy according to the proportion of faith; Or ministry, let us wait on our ministering: or he that teacheth, on teaching; Or he that exhorteth, on exhortation: he that ruleth, with diligence; he that sheweth mercy, with cheerfulness.

Let love be without dissimulation. Abhor that which is evil; cleave to that which is good. Be kindly affectioned one to another with brotherly love; in honour preferring one another; Not slothful in business; fervent in spirit; serving the Lord; Rejoicing in hope; patient in tribulation; continuing instant in prayer; Distributing to the necessity of saints; given to hospitality. Bless them which persecute you: bless, and curse not. Rejoice with them that do rejoice, and weep with them that weep. Be of the same mind one toward another. Mind not high things, but condescend to men of low estate. Be not wise in your own conceits. Recompense to no man evil for evil. Provide things honest in the sight of all men. If it be possible, as much as lieth in you, live peaceably with all men. Dearly beloved, avenge not yourselves, but rather give place unto wrath: for it is written, Vengeance is mine; I will repay, saith the Lord. Therefore if thine enemy hunger, feed him; if he thirst, give him drink: for in so doing thou shalt heap coals of fire on his head. Be not overcome of evil, but overcome evil with good.

## MONDAY

1 CORINTHIANS 12:1–11 (RSV)

Now concerning spiritual gifts, brethren, I do not want you to be uninformed. You know that when you were heathen, you were led astray to dumb idols, however you may have been moved. Therefore I want you to understand that no one speaking by the Spirit of God ever says 'Jesus be cursed!' and no one can say 'Jesus is Lord' except by the Holy Spirit.

Now there are varieties of gifts, but the same Spirit; and there are varieties of service, but the same Lord; and there varieties of working, but it is the same God who inspires them all in every one. To each is given the manifestation of the Spirit for the common good. To one is given through the Spirit the utterance of wisdom, and to another the utterance of knowledge according to the same Spirit, to another faith by the same Spirit, to another gifts of healing by the one Spirit, to another the working of miracles, to another prophecy, to another the ability to distinguish between spirits, to another various kinds of tongues, to another the interpretation of tongues. All these are inspired by one and the same Spirit, who apportions to each one individually as he wills.

## TUESDAY

1 CORINTHIANS 12:12–26 (RSV)

For just as the body is one and has many members, and all the members of the body, though many, are one body, so it is with Christ. For by one Spirit we were all baptized into one body—Jews or Greeks, slaves or free—and all were made to drink of one Spirit.

For the body does not consist of one member but of many. If the foot should say, 'Because I am not a hand, I do not belong to the body,' that would not make it any less a part of the body. And if the ear should say, 'Because I am not an eye, I do not belong to the body,' that would not make it any less a part of the body. If the whole body were an eye, where would be the hearing? If the whole body were an ear, where would be the sense of smell? But as it is, God arranged the organs in the body, each one of them, as he chose. If all were a single organ, where would the body be? As it is, there are many parts, yet one body. The eye cannot say to the hand, 'I have no need of you.' On the contrary, the parts of the body which seem to be weaker are indispensable, and those parts of the body which we think less honourable we invest with greater honour, and our unpresentable parts are treated with greater modesty, which our more presentable parts do not require. But God has so composed the body, giving the greater honour to the inferior part, that there may be no discord in the body, but that the members may have the same care for one another. If one member suffers, all suffer together; if one member is honoured, all rejoice together.

## WEDNESDAY

2 CORINTHIANS 12:1–10 (NIV)

I must go on boasting. Although there is nothing to be gained, I will go on to visions and revelations from the Lord. I know a man in Christ who fourteen years ago was caught up to the third heaven. Whether it was in the body or out of the body I do not know—God knows. And I know that this man—whether in the body or apart from the body I do not know, but God knows—was caught up to paradise. He heard inexpressible things, things that man is not permitted to tell. I will boast about a man like that, but I will not boast about myself, except about my weaknesses. Even if I should choose to boast, I would not be a fool, because I would be speaking the truth. But I refrain, so no-one will think more of me than is warranted by what I do or say.

To keep me from becoming conceited because of these surpassingly great revelations, there was given me a thorn in my flesh, a messenger of Satan, to torment me. Three times I pleaded with the Lord to take it away from me. But he said to me, 'My grace is sufficient for you, for my power is made perfect in weakness.' Therefore I will boast all the more gladly about my weaknesses, in insults, in hardships, in persecutions, in difficulties. For when I am weak, then I am strong.

## THURSDAY

EPHESIANS 4:1–13 (NIV)

As a prisoner for the Lord, then, I

urge you to live a life worthy of the calling you have received. Be completely humble and gentle; be patient, bearing with one another in love. Make every effort to keep the unity of the Spirit through the bond of peace. There is one body and one Spirit—just as you were called to one hope when you were called—one Lord, one faith, one baptism; one God and Father of all, who is over all and through all and in all.

But to each one of us grace has been given as Christ apportioned it. This is why it says: 'When he ascended on high, he led captives in his train and gave gifts to men.' (What does 'he ascended' mean except that he also descended to the lower, earthly regions? He who descended is the very one who ascended higher than all the heavens, in order to fill the whole universe.) It was he who gave some to be apostles, some to be prophets, some to be evangelists, and some to be pastors and teachers, to prepare God's people for works of service, so that the body of Christ may be built up until we all reach unity in the faith and in the knowledge of the Son of God and become mature, attaining to the whole measure of the fulness of Christ.

## FRIDAY

HEBREWS 1:13–2:4 (REB)

To which of the angels has he ever said, 'Sit at my right hand until I make your enemies your footstool'? Are they not all ministering spirits sent out in God's service, for the sake of those destined to receive salvation?

That is why we are bound to pay all the more heed to what we have been told, for fear of drifting from our course. For if God's word spoken through angels had such force that any violation of it, or any disobedience, met with its proper penalty, what escape can there be for us if we ignore so great a deliverance? This deliverance was first announced through the Lord, and those who heard him confirmed it to us, God himself adding his testimony by signs and wonders, by miracles of many kinds, and by gifts of the Holy Spirit distributed at his own will.

## SATURDAY

1 PETER 4:7–11 (NJB)

The end of all things is near, so keep your minds calm and sober for prayer. Above all preserve an intense love for each other, since love covers over many a sin. Welcome each other into your houses without grumbling. Each one of you has received a special grace, so, like good stewards responsible for all these varied graces of God, put it at the service of others. If anyone is a speaker, let it be as the words of God, if anyone serves, let it be as in strength granted by God; so that in everything God may receive the glory, through Jesus Christ, since to him alone belong all glory and power for ever and ever. Amen.

WEEK 46

# LIFESTYLE FOR LEADERS

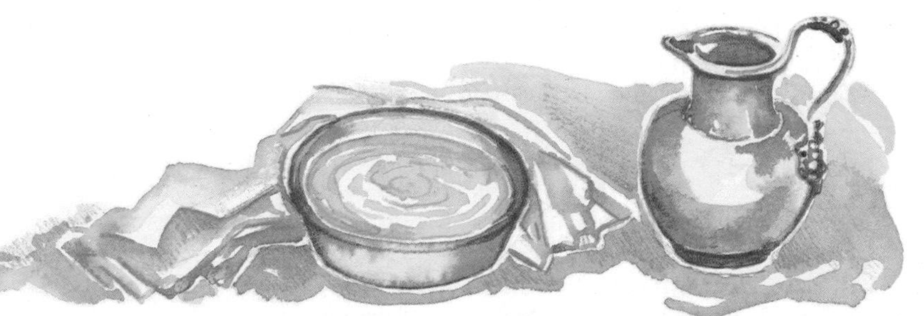

The practices of the established religious leaders of Jesus' day were the subject of a number of uncompromising attacks, recorded in the gospel. Jesus knew that in order to build a new pattern of spiritual leadership, it was necessary first to expose and demolish the old (Sunday).

Not surprisingly, his disciples did not grasp or embrace the new style straightaway. On Monday we see two of them vainly trying to cling to the old system, and even climb up on top of it. But Jesus' way is one of service and sacrifice.

After the resurrection of Jesus, Peter is given a threefold commission (which echoes his triple denial). This is followed up by a specific warning of where his ministry will take him (Tuesday). It is not given even to Peter to know the fate of others.

The words of Paul at Miletus (Wednesday) remind Christians that, although preaching both wins converts and gives offence, words must be backed up by a way of life. Later, he writes to the Christians in Corinth about the paradox that while despair and breakdown are often close (Thursday), that hardly matters so long as Jesus is glorified.

Two final readings, one personal and one general, suggest what we still have much to learn in what we expect from church leaders—and how they are selected, assessed, trained and sustained (Friday and Saturday).

WEEK 46

# Servants of God

We often speak of 'the church's ministry', as if this meant only clergy and full-timers. But 'ministry' simply means 'service'. Ministry begins when people start to follow Jesus Christ. It is the hallmark of discipleship: to be a follower is to serve.

When the first disciples started to follow Jesus he soon got them to work learning and doing. They entered into his ministry of proclaiming the kingdom just as we also, when we serve others, enter into it. At the heart of the New Testament is this conviction that since Pentecost, when the Spirit came on the waiting disciples, all Christians have gifts and talents to offer their Lord and one another. So important is this point that we can put it this way: the church is ministry.

The whole church is to be a 'royal priesthood'. Although there is only one true priest—Jesus Christ, who died a sacrificial death for us all—the church took over Israel's priestly role of representing God to the world. Yet still there are distinctive ministries which God gives to his people within the wider ministry of the church.

The first ministry we see in the New Testament is that of the 'Twelve', probably to be identified with the apostles. Their identity came from having been with Jesus in his earthly life and witnessed his resurrection. After Pentecost, ministry arose very naturally according to what was needed and as the Spirit poured out his varied gifts. Many of the terms used arise from the nature of the task—the teacher, the prophet, the deacon, the healer, the interpreter and even the word 'bishop' which means 'overseer'.

No single authorized order of ministry arose in the New Testament. There seem to have been many different patterns of ministry. It was only after the New Testament period that a threefold order emerged—bishop, presbyter (or 'elder') and deacon.

We need to pick out three essential jobs which Christian ministry at its best will perform:

- **Authority.** It is very important for the sake of the body that we obey those who are set over us in the Lord. Although Paul teaches that every Christian is a 'minister', yet he urges obedience to those ministers who have been given authority and that we should recognize clearly their role to lead and guide the church. This is a very important principle for the church today when there are some who think they have the right to depart from the teaching of their churches and found new ones.
- **Service.** We have no gifts which are just for us. Ministry is never for ourselves but always for others. Jesus showed us the example by taking a towel and washing the feet of others. Whether it is our lot to preach to thousands or to work as a porter in a hospital, all ministry for Jesus is sacrificial. It is often unrewarding and humdrum, and sometimes its consequences can be painful and costly. But for the Christian it is always worthwhile.

◆ **Building up.** Because the church belongs to Jesus Christ, those who have special ministries within the body have a duty to build it up to please him. This happens when there is effective leadership—a growing church will have leaders with vision and clear goals. Gifted teaching also plays an important part, since it is through steady proclamation of the faith that people grow from immaturity to a mature and adult understanding.

But the sacraments also help this process of building up. The first, **baptism**, is a once-for-all sign of new birth. It is an essential mark of belonging to Jesus. Although it has always been normal practice for this sacrament to be administered by a lawfully-appointed minister, in fact any Christian can baptize if given that responsibility. And the second sacrament, **holy communion**, was intended to be taken repeatedly as a sign of nourishment. From earliest times the leader of this 'meal' was someone authorized by the body to celebrate the feast on their behalf. It has been common since about the third century to call this celebrant a 'priest'. This word is not acceptable to all Christians, as to some it seems to imply that Christ's work on the cross was somehow not complete. Others are happy with it as long as it merely indicates that the 'priest' is representing the priesthood of the whole body.

The Bible's teaching reminds us that we are engaged in ministry whatever we do—whether we work in the church or in the world. Ministry does not belong only to a special group but to us all. Nevertheless, God does call people to special functions within the body and we should all be alert to the challenge to take up new tasks for him and to use our talents in his service.

## SUNDAY

MATTHEW 7:13–18, 23:2, 23:5–11 (AV)

Jesus said, 'Enter ye in at the strait gate: for wide is the gate, and broad is the way, that leadeth to destruction, and many there be which go in thereat: Because strait is the gate, and narrow is the way, which leadeth unto life, and few there be that find it.

'Beware of false prophets, which come to you in sheep's clothing, but inwardly they are ravening wolves. Ye shall know them by their fruits. Do men gather grapes of thorns, or figs of thistles? Even so every good tree bringeth forth good fruit; but a corrupt tree bringeth forth evil fruit. A good tree cannot bring forth evil fruit, neither can a corrupt tree bring forth good fruit.'

Jesus said, 'The scribes and the Pharisees sit in Moses' seat.

'But all their works they do for to be seen of men: they make broad their phylacteries, and enlarge the borders of their garments, And love the uppermost rooms at feasts, and the chief seats in the synagogues, And greetings in the markets, and to be called of men, Rabbi, Rabbi. But be not ye called Rabbi: for one is your Master, even Christ; and all ye are brethren. And call no man your father upon the earth: for one is your Father, which is in heaven. Neither be ye called masters: for one is your Master, even Christ. But he that is greatest among you shall be your servant.

## MONDAY

MARK 10:35–45 (NJB)

James and John, the sons of Zebedee, approached him. 'Master,' they said to him, 'We want you to do us a favour.' He said to them, 'What is it you want me to do for you?' They said to him, 'Allow us to sit one at your right hand and the other at your left in your glory.' But Jesus said to them, 'You do not know what you are asking. Can you drink the cup that I shall drink, or be baptized with the baptism with which I shall be baptized?' They replied, 'We can.' Jesus said to them, 'The cup that I shall drink you shall drink, and with the baptism with which I shall be baptized you shall be baptized, but as for seats at my right hand or my left, these are not mine to grant; they belong to those to whom they have been allotted.'

When the other ten heard this they began to feel indignant with James and John, so Jesus called them to him and said to them, 'You know that among the gentiles those they call their rulers lord it over them, and their great men make their authority felt. Among you this is not to happen. No; anyone who wants to become great among you must be your servant, and anyone who wants to be first among you must be slave to all. For the Son of man himself came not to be served but to serve, and to give his life as a ransom for many.'

## TUESDAY

JOHN 21:15–24 (REB)

After breakfast Jesus said to Simon Peter, 'Simon son of John, do you love me more than these others? 'Yes, Lord,' he answered, 'you know that I love you.' 'Then feed my lambs,' he said. A second time he asked, 'Simon son of John, do you love me?' 'Yes, Lord, you know I love you.' 'Then tend my sheep.' A third time he said, 'Simon son of John, do you love me?' Peter was hurt that he asked him a third time, 'Do you love me?' 'Lord,' he said, 'you know everything; you know I love you.' Jesus said, 'Then feed my sheep.

In very truth I tell you: when you were young you fastened your belt about you and walked where you chose; but when you are old you will stretch out your arms, and a stranger will bind you fast, and carry you where you have no wish to go.' He said this to indicate the manner of death by which Peter was to glorify God. Then he added, 'Follow me.'

Peter looked round, and saw the disciple whom Jesus loved following—the one who at supper had leaned back close to him to ask the question, 'Lord, who is it that will betray you?' When he saw him, Peter asked, 'Lord, what about him?' Jesus said, 'If it should be my will that he stay until I come, what is it to you? Follow me,'

That saying of Jesus became current among his followers, and was taken to mean that that disciple would not die. But in fact Jesus did not say he would not die; he only said, 'If it should be my will that he stay until I come, what is it to you.'

It is this same disciple who vouches for what is written here. He it is who wrote it, and we know that his testimony is true.

## WEDNESDAY

ACTS 20:17–35 (NIV)

From Miletus, Paul sent to Ephesus for the elders of the church. When they arrived, he said to them: 'You know how I lived the whole time I was with you, from the first day I came into the province of Asia. I served the Lord with great humility and with tears, although I was severely tested by the plots of the Jews. You know that I have not hesitated to preach anything that would be helpful to you but have taught you publicly and from house to house. I have declared to both Jews and Greeks that they must turn to God in repentance and have faith in our Lord Jesus.

And now, compelled by the Spirit, I am going to Jerusalem, not knowing what will happen to me there. I only know that in every city the Holy Spirit warns me that prison and hardships are facing me. However, I consider my life worth nothing to me, if only I may finish the race and complete the task the Lord Jesus has given me—the task of testifying to the gospel of God's grace.

Now I know that none of you among whom I have gone about preaching the kingdom will ever see me again. Therefore, I declare to you today that I am innocent of the blood of all men. For I have not hesitated to proclaim to you the whole will of God.

Guard yourselves and all the flock of which the Holy Spirit has made you overseers. Be shepherds of the church of God, which he bought with his own blood. I know that after I leave, savage wolves will come in among you and will not spare the flock. Even from your own number men will arise and distort the truth in order to draw away disciples after them. So be on your guard! Remember that for three years I never stopped warning each of you night and day with tears.

Now I commit you to God and to the word of his grace, which can build you up and give you an inheritance among all those who are sanctified. I have not coveted anyone's silver or gold or clothing. You yourselves know that these hands of mine supplied my own needs and the needs of my companions. In everything I did, I showed you that by this kind of hard work we must help the weak, remembering the words the Lord Jesus himself said: "It is more blessed to give than to receive." '

## THURSDAY

2 CORINTHIANS 4:7–18 (NIV)

But we have this treasure in jars of clay to show that this all-surpassing power is from God and not from us. We are hard pressed on every side, but not crushed; perplexed, but not in despair; persecuted, but not abandoned; struck down, but not destroyed. We always carry around in our body the death of Jesus, so that the life of Jesus may also revealed in our body. For we who are alive are always being given over to death for Jesus' sake, so that his life may be revealed in our mortal body. So then, death is at work in us, but life is at work in you.

It is written: 'I believed; therefore I have spoken.' With that same spirit of faith we also believe and therefore speak, because we know that the one who raised the Lord Jesus from the dead will also raise us with Jesus and will present us with you in his presence. All this is for your benefit, so that the grace that is reaching more and more people may cause thanksgiving to overflow to the glory of God.

Therefore we do not lose heart. Though outwardly we are wasting away, yet inwardly we are being renewed day by day. For our light and momentary troubles are achieving for us an eternal glory that far outweighs them all. So we fix our eyes not on what is seen, but on what is unseen. For what is seen is temporary, but what is unseen is eternal.

## FRIDAY

1 TIMOTHY 3:1–10 (RSV)

The saying is sure: If any one aspires to the office of bishop, he desires a noble task. Now a bishop must be above reproach, the husband of one wife, temperate, sensible, dignified, hospitable, an apt teacher, no drunkard, not violent but gentle, not quarrelsome, and no lover of money. He must manage his own household well, keeping his children submissive and respectful in every way; for if a man does not know how to manage his own household, how can he care for God's church? He must not be a recent convert, or he may be puffed up with conceit and fall into the condemnation of the devil; moreover he must be well thought of by outsiders, or he may fall into reproach and the snare of the devil.

Deacons likewise must be serious, not double-tongued, not addicted to much wine, not greedy for gain; they must hold the mystery of the faith with a clear conscience. And let them also be tested first; then if they prove themselves blameless let them serve as deacons.



## SATURDAY

### 1 PETER 5:1–5 (RSV)

So I exhort the elders among you, as a fellow elder and a witness of the sufferings of Christ as well as a partaker in the glory that is to be revealed. Tend the flock of God that is your charge, not by constraint but willingly, not for shameful gain but eagerly, not as domineering over those in your charge but being examples to the flock. And when the chief Shepherd is manifested you will obtain the unfading crown of glory. Likewise you that are younger be subject to the elders. Clothe yourselves, all of you, with humility toward one another, for 'God opposes the proud, but gives grace to the humble.'

## LETTERS FROM CHRISTIAN LEADERS

### HEBREWS

This is the mystery book of the New Testament. No one really knows who wrote it—or who received it, except that they were Jewish Christians. The theme is that Jesus has completed all that the Old Testament began. He is greater than angels or prophets; his death brings salvation in a way Old Testament sacrifices could not.

**“We have confidence to enter...by a new and living way... (so) let us draw near to God.”**

So, however great the pressure, Christians should continue to trust Jesus and not turn back to old ways.

### JAMES

A totally practical letter about the importance of a high standard of conduct. It was probably written by the leader of the Jerusalem church, James the ‘brother of the Lord’.

**“Anyone who listens to the word but does not do what it says is like a man who looks at himself in a mirror ... and immediately forgets.”**

The connecting theme is one of integrity. The Christian should avoid double standards in every area of living. This letter echoes the teaching of the Sermon on the Mount.

### 1 PETER

Peter's letter is full of the joy of belonging to Jesus Christ, which no suffering can shake. Peter is writing to prepare Christians for persecution which is coming. He believes that suffering can be the crucible in which faith is purified. The great example of innocent suffering is Jesus himself.

**“Christ suffered for you, leaving you an example, that you should follow in his steps.”**

### 2 PETER

Concentrate on true knowledge of God, and live as those who long for Christ's return. These are the antidote this letter offers to the corrupting teaching that morality does not matter for Christians.

## 1 JOHN

The three 'letters of John' seem certainly to nave been written by he composer of the ourth Gospel. It is vritten to Christians confused by false eaching. John gives hree vital tests of true aith: real Christians ive open lives, love one another, and

**"Whoever does not love does not know God, because God is love."**

elieve Jesus was God ving as a human eing. The whole letter s woven round these hree ideas.

## 2 & 3 JOHN

These tiny letters, the shortest books in the Bible, are addressed to 'the dear lady and her children', that is, 'the church and her members', and to a church leader, Gaius, who is confronting a petty local dictator.

## JUDE

This brief letter concentrates on strengthening Christians to resist false teachers. It closely parallels a part of 2 Peter, and is full of Old Testament allusions.

**"To the only God our Saviour be glory, majesty, power and authority, through Jesus Christ our Lord."**

WEEK 47

# THE NAME SUPREME

The highest name that the Jewish people could speak was 'Lord'. It was the title given to God. To apply this title to Jesus of Nazareth was an early indication of what his followers thought of him, and his place in their hearts and their worship.

The name 'Redeemer', used of God in the Old Testament, is not directly applied to Christ in the New—though we read that he came 'to redeem' and to bring 'redemption'. But many other divine names and titles in the Bible either point forward to Christ or celebrate his coming.

'Shepherd' is one of the most familiar, claimed by Jesus himself (Wednesday), embraced by his followers (Friday), and first foreshadowed in the Old Testament not only in the Psalms but also by such prophets as Jeremiah and Ezekiel (Sunday). Here prophets also add other 'messianic' titles to direct their hearers forward in hope. The Branch, the King, the Fountain, the Lord our Righteousness—Zechariah (Monday) is later found adding to earlier clusters of names.

In the series of 'I am' sayings in John's Gospel, Jesus claims to be the bread of life (Tuesday), the door (Wednesday) and the true vine (Thursday), among others. The book of Revelation links in with this gospel in adding 'the Word of God', and the final ringing acclamation of 'King of kings and Lord of lords' (Saturday). As these quotations illustrate, each title in its own way reflects the prime work of Jesus the Redeemer, completed at the cross.

# Jesus the Redeemer

WEEK 47

'Redeemer' was a very expressive term in the ancient world. But modern readers 'hear' it as a religious word, although trading stamps and the pawn shop give us a small clue. We may have better luck with the word 'ransom' which, in an age of terrorist activity, is depressingly up to date. 'Ransom' brings the idea of a victim who has fallen into the hands of powerful enemies and a release which involves the payment of a large sum of money.

Similar ideas lay behind the use of 'redeem' in the ancient world. For example, aristocratic Greek or Roman prisoners of war were sometimes 'ransomed' at enormous cost. Again, a slave might buy his freedom by a kind of religious fiction known as 'sacred release', in which he took money along to a temple, where he became part of a sacred story in which the god 'bought him out' or 'redeemed' him.

The Bible is packed with redemption ideas:

◆ **Israel had its next-of-kin redeemers**, near relatives who had the responsibility of looking after members of the family when they fell on bad times. So your redeemer might be called on to buy a field from you if you were getting into debt, buy your freedom if you had got yourself enslaved and marry your wife if you had inconveniently died. There were, in addition, dozens of situations where someone might need to ward off a plague or death sentence by payment of money and so 'redeem himself'. The same themes recur through these examples—a victim, a desperate plight and liberation. But always at a price.

◆ **In the New Testament Jesus is the Redeemer**. The title draws in all the associations already mentioned. Sin is slavery; it is a plight from which people cannot free themselves but it is a plight into which they have deliberately fallen. Their failure to keep God's Law brings his just condemnation on them, so the Law which should be a check-marker for holy living becomes a ghastly reminder of failure. Paul expresses the sense of being a slave and victim in an agonized cry, 'I have the desire to do what is good, but I cannot carry it out . . .' As so often, the Psalmist states the heart of the problem: 'No man can redeem the life of another or give to God a ransom for him. The ransom for a life is costly, no payment is ever enough.'

The good news is that Jesus, as God Incarnate, could find the ransom price. He himself described his death on the cross as giving 'his life as a ransom for many'. It is important not to push the picture beyond its limits. The New Testament never actually says to whom or what the price was paid. But it does make clear that Jesus frees people who are unable to free themselves. And this act of liberation costs God. He never just says of human sin, 'Never mind. Let's pretend it never happened.'

Redemption affects the present and

the future. Here and now a sinner can experience forgiveness of sins, freedom from slavery, and a life with purpose to it. At the end of the age, Christians look for total freedom—from the penalty, power and even the presence of sin.

They expect the 'redemption' even of the created universe. Meanwhile they are called to live life as marked men and women ('sealed', the Bible calls it), who have been 'bought with a price'.

## SUNDAY

JEREMIAH 23:1–6 (NIV)

'Woe to the shepherds who are destroying and scattering the sheep of my pasture!' declares the Lord. Therefore this is what the Lord, the God of Israel, says to the shepherds who tend my people: 'Because you have scattered my flock and driven them away and have not bestowed care on them, I will bestow punishment on you for the evil you have done,' declares the Lord. 'I myself will gather the remnant of my flock out of all the countries where I have driven them and will bring them back to their pasture, where they will be fruitful and increase in number. I will place shepherds over them who will tend them, and they will no longer be afraid or terrified, nor will any be missing,' declares the Lord.

'The days are coming,' declares the Lord, 'when I will raise up to David a righteous Branch, a King who will reign wisely and do what is just and right in the land. In his days Judah will be saved and Israel will live in safety. This is the name by which he will be called: The Lord Our Righteousness.'

EZEKIEL 34:11–16 (NIV)

'For this is what the Sovereign Lord says: I myself will search for my sheep and look after them. As a shepherd looks after his scattered flock when he is with them, so will I look after my sheep. I will rescue them from all the places where they were scattered on a day of clouds and darkness. I will bring them out from the nations and gather them from the countries, and I will bring them into their own land. I will pasture them on the mountains of Israel, in the ravines and in all the settlements in the land. I will tend them in a good pasture, and the mountain heights of Israel will be their grazing land. There they will lie down in good grazing land, and there they will feed in a rich pasture on the mountains of Israel. I myself will tend my sheep and make them lie down, declares the Sovereign Lord. I will search for the lost and bring back the strays. I will bind up the injured and strengthen the weak, but the sleek and the strong I will destroy. I will shepherd the flock with justice.'

## MONDAY

ZECHARIAH 9:9–10, 13:1 (NIV)

Rejoice greatly; O Daughter of Zion!
Shout, daughter of Jerusalem!
See, your king comes to you,
righteous and having salvation,
gentle and riding on a donkey,
on a colt, the foal of a donkey.
I will take away the chariots from Ephraim
and the war-horses from Jerusalem,
and the battle-bow will be broken.
He will proclaim peace to the nations.
His rule will extend from sea to sea
and from the River to the ends of the earth.

'On that day a fountain will be opened to the house of David and the inhabitants of Jerusalem, to cleanse them from sin and impurity.

## TUESDAY

JOHN 6:25–35 (RSV)

When they found Jesus on the other side of the sea, they said to him, 'Rabbi, when did you come here?' Jesus answered them, 'Truly, truly, I say to you, you seek me, not because you saw signs, but because you ate your fill of the loaves. Do not labour for the food which perishes, but for the food which endures to eternal life, which the Son of man will give to you; for on him has God the Father set his seal.' Then they said to him, 'What must we do, to be doing the works of God?' Jesus answered them, 'This is the work of God, that you believe in him whom he has sent.' So they said to him, 'Then what sign do you do, that we may see, and believe you? What work do you perform? Our fathers ate the manna in the wilderness; as it is written, "He gave them bread from heaven to eat." ' Jesus them said to them, 'Truly, truly, I say to you, it was not Moses who gave you the bread from heaven; my Father gives you the true bread from heaven. For the bread of God is that which comes down from heaven, and gives life to the world.' They said to him, 'Lord, give us this bread always.'

Jesus said to them, 'I am the bread of life; he who comes to me shall not hunger, and he who believes in me shall never thirst.'

## WEDNESDAY

JOHN 10:7–18 (RSV)

So Jesus again said to them, 'Truly, truly, I say to you, I am the door of the sheep. All who came before me are thieves and robbers; but the sheep did not heed them. I am the door; if any one enters by me, he will be saved, and will go in and out and find pasture. The thief comes only to steal and kill and destroy; I came that they may have life, and have it abundantly. I am the good shepherd. The good shepherd lays down his life for the sheep. He who is a hireling and not a shepherd, whose own the sheep are not, sees the wolf coming and leaves the sheep and flees; and the wolf snatches them and scatters them. He flees because he is a hireling and cares nothing for the sheep. I am the good shepherd; I know my own and my own know me, as the Father knows me and I know the Father; and I lay down my life for the sheep. And I have other sheep, that are not of this fold; I must bring them also, and they will heed my voice. So there shall be one flock, one shepherd. For this reason the Father loves me, because I lay down my life, that I may take it again. No one takes it from me, but I lay it down of my own accord. I have power to lay it down, and I have power to take it again; this charge I have received from my Father.'

## THURSDAY

JOHN 15:1–11 (RSV)

Jesus said, 'I am the true vine, and my

Father is the vinedresser. Every branch of mine that bears no fruit, he takes away, and every branch that does bear fruit he prunes, that it may bear more fruit. You are already made clean by the word which I have spoken to you. Abide in me, and I in you. As the branch cannot bear fruit by itself, unless it abides in the vine, neither can you, unless you abide in me. I am the vine, you are the branches. He who abides in me, and I in him, he it is that bears much fruit, for apart from me you can do nothing. If a man does not abide in me, he is cast forth as a branch and withers; and the branches are gathered, thrown into the fire and burned. If you abide in me, and my words abide in you, ask whatever you will, and it shall be done for you. By this my Father is glorified, that you bear much fruit, and so prove to be my disciples. As the Father has loved me, so have I loved you; abide in my love. If you keep my commandments, you will abide in my love, just as I have kept my Father's commandments and abide in his love. These things I have spoken to you, that my joy may be in you, and that your joy may be full.'

## FRIDAY

1 PETER 2:19–25 (NIV)

For it is commendable if a man bears up under the pain of unjust suffering because he is conscious of God. But how is it to your credit if you receive a beating for doing wrong and endure it? But if you suffer for doing good and you endure it, this is commendable before God. To this you were called, because Christ suffered for you, leaving you an example, that you should follow in his steps. 'He committed no sin, and no deceit was found in his mouth.' When they hurled their insults at him, he did not retaliate; when he suffered, he made no threats. Instead, he entrusted himself to him who judges justly. He himself bore our sins in his body on the tree, so that we might die to sins and live from righteousness; by his wounds you have been healed. For you were like sheep going astray, but now you have returned to the Shepherd and Overseer of your souls.

## SATURDAY

REVELATION 19:6–16 (AV)

And I heard as it were the voice of a great multitude, and as the voice of many waters, and as the voice of mighty thunderings, saying, Alleluia: for the Lord God omnipotent reigneth. Let us be glad and rejoice, and give honour to him: for the marriage of the Lamb is come, and his wife hath made herself ready. And to her was granted that she should be arrayed in fine linen, clean and white: for the fine linen is the righteousness of saints.

And he saith unto me, Write, Blessed are they which are called unto the marriage supper of the Lamb. And he saith unto me, These are the true sayings of God. And I fell at his feet to worship him. And he said unto me, See thou do it not: I am thy fellowservant, and of thy brethren that have the testimony of Jesus: worship God: for the testimony of Jesus is the spirit of prophecy.

And I saw heaven opened, and behold a white horse; and he that sat upon him was called Faithful and True, and in righteousness he doth judge and make war. His eyes were as a flame of fire, and on his head were many crowns; and he had a name written, that no man knew, but he himself. And he was clothed with a vesture dipped in blood: and his name is called The Word of God. And the armies which were in heaven followed him upon white horses, clothed in fine linen, white and clean. And out of his mouth goeth a sharp sword, that with it he should smite the nations: and he shall rule them with a rod of iron: and he treadeth the winepress of the fierceness and wrath of Almighty God. And he hath on his vesture and on his thigh a name written, King of Kings, and Lord of Lords.

# THY KINGDOM COME

WEEK 48

Very early on in Israel's history, God was known as one who reigns for ever. Later generations often contrasted his perfect kingship (Sunday) with the human rulers they enjoyed or endured. In the book of Daniel, written in a time of national humiliation, he looks forward to an eternal kingdom better than any yet imagined (Monday)

Then came Jesus, preaching the kingdom of God and asserting that where his healing hand was at work, there the kingdom was (Tuesday). If such a 'reign' eludes exact definitions (to judge by many books full of varied views!), it evokes a wealth of description from Jesus himself. It is like the sowing of seed, or the seed itself; like the kneading of bread, the finding of treasure, the purchase of a pearl (Wednesday). It is always on the move; it may be seen (or not), entered (or not), yet it is 'within you' and 'among you' and 'does not come visibly' (Thursday).

So Jesus taught. Paul his apostle follows these lively clues with paragraphs such as the three quoted for Friday—each one correcting a common, fatal mistake before pointing to kingdom blessings.

The book of Revelation closes this week's scene (Saturday) with a fulfilment of every 'kingdom' hint and shadow. One day it will stand unspoiled, unmistakable, unchallenged.

WEEK 48

# The Kingdom of God

Every political organization or social group that wants to change society has its manifesto or programme. Jesus' manifesto was the 'kingdom of God'. He burst on the scene about AD30 exclaiming: 'The time is fulfilled and the kingdom of God is at hand.'

What did he mean by this? In the time of Jesus the Jews looked for God to intervene in many different ways. Some longed for a revolutionary, political leader who would overthrow the power of Rome; some looked for a period of peace and prosperity in which they could live in safety and bring up their children without fear; some longed for God to send his Chosen One to establish a kingdom for the Jews at Jerusalem.

But Jesus' idea of the kingdom was very new and very different:

- **The kingdom was already here.** 'The kingdom of God is among you,' he said; now he had come the kingdom was here. The mighty works he was doing were signs of the breaking in of his kingdom. To follow Jesus, therefore, meant entering his kingdom.
- **The 'kingdom' was the rule of God in human hearts**, rather than a territory with definable borders, as the word means to us. It means people, not property: people who follow and acknowledge him as Lord. The kingdom, then, for Jesus was a spiritual rather than material reality.
- **The kingdom became a living reality through Jesus' death and resurrection.** After Peter made his great confession that Jesus was 'the Christ, the Son of the living God', Jesus spoke less about the kingdom and more about his cross. But these are not two separate ideas. The kingdom only becomes a kingdom for us through what Jesus did on the cross. His death is the key to the kingdom, the door by which we enter.
- **The kingdom in its fulness is yet to come.** It has come in part, but it will only fully come when Jesus Christ returns to reign. In the meantime the church—that part of God's creation which accepts his authority—must continue to preach the message of the kingdom.

It is clear from Jesus' teaching about the kingdom of God (or 'kingdom of heaven' as Matthew calls it) that he was concerned with the quality of human life. We who belong to the kingdom should show it in holy living, by expressing compassion and concern for others, by being 'salt' and 'light' in society. This will involve social and political action, although we must never fall into the trap of assuming that Jesus' kingdom is a blueprint for social change today. It is important to remember that Jesus never tried to give a clear definition of the kingdom. By teaching in parables he was disclosing a revolutionary message 'in code', so that the poor as well as the rich, the slave as well as the free, the Gentile as well as the Jew, might enter.

## SUNDAY

PSALM 98 (REB)

Sing a new song to the Lord,
for he has done marvellous deeds;
his right hand and his holy arm have won him victory.
The Lord has made his victory known;
he has displayed his saving righteousness to all the nations.
He has remembered his love for Jacob,
his faithfulness towards the house of Israel.
All the ends of the earth have seen the victory of our God.

Acclaim the Lord, all the earth;
break into songs of joy, sing psalms.
Sing psalms in the Lord's honour with the lyre,
with the lyre and with resounding music,
with trumpet and echoing horn
acclaim the presence of the Lord our King.
Let the sea resound and everything in it,
the world and those who dwell there.
Let the rivers clap their hands,
let the mountains sing aloud together
before the Lord; for he comes to judge the earth.
He will judge the world with justice
and the peoples with equity.

## MONDAY

DANIEL 2:1–3, 19–23, 44–48 (NIV)

In the second year of his reign, Nebuchadnezzar had dreams; his mind was troubled and he could not sleep. So the king summoned the magicians, enchanters, sorcerers and astrologers to tell him what he had dreamed. When they came in and stood before the king, he said to them, 'I have had a dream that troubles me and I want to know what it means.'

During the night the mystery was revealed to Daniel in a vision. Then Daniel praised the God of heaven and said:

'Praise be to the name of God for ever and ever;
wisdom and power are his.
He changes times and seasons;
he sets up kings and deposes them.
He gives wisdom to the wise
and knowledge to the discerning.
He reveals deep and hidden things;
he knows what lies in darkness,
and light dwells with him.
I thank and praise you, O God of my fathers:
You have given me wisdom and power,
you have made known to me what we asked of you,
you have made known to us the dream of the king.

'In the time of those kings, the God of heaven will set up a kingdom that will never be destroyed, nor will it be left to another people. It will crush all those kingdoms and bring them to an end, but it will itself endure for ever. This is the meaning of the vision of the rock cut out of a mountain, but not by human hands—a rock that broke the iron, the bronze, the clay, the silver and the gold to pieces.

The great God has shown the king what will take place in the future. The dream is true and the interpretation is trustworthy.'

Then King Nebuchadnezzar fell prostrate before Daniel and paid him honour and ordered that an offering and incense be presented to him. The king said to Daniel, 'Surely your God is the God of gods and the Lord of kings and a revealer of mysteries, for you were able to reveal this mystery.'

## TUESDAY

MATTHEW 12:22–28 (RSV)

Then a blind and dumb demoniac was brought to Jesus, and he healed him, so that the dumb man spoke and saw. And all the people were amazed, and said, 'Can this be the Son of David?' But when the Pharisees heard it they said, 'It is only Beelzebul, the prince of demons.' Knowing their thoughts, he said to them, 'Every kingdom divided against itself is laid waste, and no city or house divided against itself will stand; and if Satan casts out Satan, he is divided against himself; how then will his kingdom stand? And if I cast out demons by Beelzebul, by whom do your sons cast them out? Therefore they shall be your judges. But if it is by the Spirit of God that I cast out demons, then the kingdom of God has come upon you.

## WEDNESDAY

MATTHEW 13:24–33, 44–46, 51–52 (RSV)

Another parable Jesus put before them, saying, 'The kingdom of heaven may be compared to a man who sowed good seed in his field; but while men were sleeping, his enemy came and sowed weeds among the wheat, and went away. So when the plants came up and bore grain, then the weeds appeared also. And the servants of the householder came and said to him, "Sir, did you not sow good seed in your field? How then has it weeds?" He said to them, "An enemy has done this." The servants said to him, "Then do you want us to go and gather them?" But he said, "No; lest in gathering the weeds you root up the wheat along with them. Let both grow together until the harvest; and at harvest time I will tell the reapers, Gather the weeds first and bind them in bundles to be burned, but gather the wheat into my barn." '

Another parable he put before them, saying, 'The kingdom of heaven is like a grain of mustard seed which a man took and sowed in his field; it is the smallest of all seeds, but when it has grown it is the greatest of shrubs and becomes a tree, so that the birds of the air come and make nests in its branches.'

He told them another parable. 'The kingdom of heaven is like leaven which a woman took and hid in three measures of flour, till it was all leavened.'

'The kingdom of heaven is like treasure hidden in a field, which a man found and covered up; then in his joy he goes and sells all that he has and buys that field.

Again, the kingdom of heaven is like a merchant in search of fine pearls, who, on finding one pearl of great value, went and sold all that he had and bought it.'

'Have you understood all this?' They said to him, 'Yes.' And he said to them, 'Therefore every scribe who has been trained for the kingdom of heaven is like a householder who brings out of his treasure what is new and what is old.'

## THURSDAY

LUKE 17:20–25 (NIV)

Once, having been asked by the Pharisees when the kingdom of God would come, Jesus replied, 'The kingdom of God does not come visibly, nor will people say, "Here it is," or "There it is," because the kingdom of God is within you.'

Then he said to his disciples, 'The time is coming when you will long to see one of the days of the Son of Man, but you will not see it. Men will tell you, "There he is!" or "Here he is!" Do not go running off after them. For the Son of Man in his day will be like the lightning, which flashes and lights up the sky from one end to the other. But first he must suffer many things and be rejected by this generation.'

JOHN 3:1–8 (NIV)

Now there was a man of the Pharisees named Nicodemus, a member of the Jewish ruling council. He came to Jesus at night and said, 'Rabbi, we know you are a teacher who has come from God. For no-one could perform the miraculous signs you are doing if God were not with him.'

In reply Jesus declared, 'I tell you the truth, unless a man is born again, he cannot see the kingdom of God.'

'How can a man be born when he is old?' Nicodemus asked. 'Surely he cannot enter a second time into his mother's womb to be born!'

Jesus answered, 'I tell you the truth, unless a man is born of water and the Spirit, he cannot enter the kingdom of God. Flesh gives birth to flesh, but the Spirit gives birth to spirit. You should not be surprised at my saying, "You must be born again." The wind blows wherever it pleases. You hear its sound, but you cannot tell where it comes from or where it is going. So it is with everyone born of the Spirit.'

## FRIDAY

ROMANS 14:13–17 (AV)

Let us not therefore judge one another any more: but judge this rather, that no man put a stumbling-block or an occasion to fall in his brother's way. I know, and am persuaded by the Lord Jesus, that there is nothing unclean of itself: but to him that esteemeth any thing to be unclean, to him it is unclean. But if thy brother be grieved with thy meat, now walkest thou not charitably. Destroy not him with thy meat, for whom Christ died. Let not then your good be evil spoken of: For the kingdom of God is not meat and drink; but righteousness, and peace, and joy in the Holy Ghost.

1 CORINTHIANS 4:18–20, 6:7–11 (AV)

Now some are puffed up, as though I would not come to you. But I will come to you shortly, if the Lord will, and will know, not the speech of them which are puffed up, but the power. For the kingdom of God is not in word, but in power.

Now therefore there is utterly a fault among you, because ye go to law one with another. Why do ye not rather take wrong? why do ye not rather suffer yourselves to be defrauded? Nay, ye do wrong, and defraud, and that your brethren. Know ye not that the unrighteous shall not inherit the kingdom of God? Be not deceived: neither fornicators, nor idolaters, nor adulterers, nor effeminate, nor abusers of themselves with mankind, nor thieves, nor covetous, nor drunkards, nor revilers, nor extortioners, shall inherit the kingdom of God. And such were some of you: but ye are washed, but ye are sanctified, but ye are justified in the name of the Lord Jesus, and by the Spirit of our God.

## SATURDAY

REVELATION 11:15–19 (NJB)

Then the seventh angel blew his trumpet, and voices could be heard shouting in heaven, calling, 'The kingdom of the world has become the kingdom of our Lord and his Christ, and he shall reign for ever and ever.' The twenty-four elders, enthroned in the presence of God, prostrated themselves and touched the ground with their foreheads worshipping God with these words, 'We give thanks to you, Almighty Lord God, He who is, He who was, for assuming your great power, and beginning your reign. The nations were in uproar and now the time has come for your retribution, and for the dead to be judged, and for your servants the prophets, for the saints and for those who fear your name, small and great alike, to be rewarded. The time has come to destroy those who are destroying the earth.

Then the sanctuary of God in heaven opened, and the ark of the covenant could be seen inside it. Then came flashes of lightning, peals of thunder and an earthquake, and violent hail.

# THY WILL BE DONE

WEEK 49

Some of the most exalted poetry and prose of the Bible, in turn inspiring some great music, opens to us a unique vision: God is planning a new creation. Jesus' first miracle, when he changes water into wine (Wednesday), perfectly crystallizes the theme. Contrary to some current 'new age' cults, his own unique glory is at the heart of it, and this is grounded in history.

As water is changed into wine, so is the desert turned to a garden, dust into orchard and forest, and disabled, disheartened souls to exuberant, joyful wholeness (Sunday). A further passage in Isaiah extols the undying word of God and the unfailing strength he provides for those who hope in him (Monday). In such prophecies, Isaiah sees nothing less than the new heaven and new earth which appear again in the book of Revelation. A part of this closes the week (Saturday), centred again on God and on the Lamb who is Christ.

The Old Testament prophet Ezekiel details the spiritual transformation which is first required—and provided by God himself (Tuesday). Much later, in the New Testament Paul and Peter pass on their visions of God's worldwide resurrection (Thursday) and judgment (Friday).

WEEK 49

# The New Creation

Anyone who has felt like saying 'Can we start again, please?' knows how appealing is the thought of a new creation. It speaks to just those longings which are most acute: despair at being locked into old patterns of behaviour, weariness of a life that has become meaningless, memories of past sin and failure which drag us down in the present, a profound sense of loss. 'Behold, I am making everything new,' says God in the Revelation vision, and it is like opening the door into another world. It is almost too good to be true.

Nevertheless, this is the Bible's staggering claim. With the coming of Jesus something radically new exploded on the human scene. He said it was like new wine that would burst the old wineskins; like new cloth ripping away from a threadbare garment; like changing water into wine. Crowds accustomed to careful, cautious teaching were transfixed by his freedom and authority. He turned conventional wisdom on its head. After his death and resurrection it became clear that the powers of the world to come had entered this world. Matthew's version of Jesus' suffering and death stresses that something earth-shattering and life-giving has happened. Jesus has opened up 'a new and living way' into the very presence of God.

The rest of the New Testament looks for other pictures—death to life; darkness to light; bondage to freedom. Paul was deeply impressed by the transformation that took place when Christ took hold of someone. 'If anyone is in Christ...' you can almost hear him thinking, 'it can only properly be compared to a totally new creation.' What God did with chaos at the beginning, when he created something 'good' by word and spirit, he does now in the individual.

'New' is the key word of this experience. In baptism new converts broke decisively with the old life. They 'died' in the water and 'rose' in Christ to live in a completely new way. They had a new song to sing and spoke in new tongues. They were free from the old way of trying and failing to keep the Law or just following the 'cravings of the sinful nature'. They were part of a new community, which crossed the boundaries of class, race, sex and which lived by a new commandment of love. All this was such a change that it seemed right to refer to what had happened as putting off 'the old nature' and putting on the new. Christians were people who had been born all over again!

It is easy to give the impression that that was the end of the matter. But although Paul does not dilute his 'new creation' image, he recognizes that the old personality is still alive and active. Part of the point of telling people about the new beginning they had made was that they should then be able to become (in practice) what they were (in Christ). A new act of creation had taken place. Now the new nature was to be renewed daily in the image of its creator. This was the work of the Spirit of God, but the individual still had a part to play. When Paul writes about God's work in the new person, he nearly always follows it by practical and specific advice about how life is to be lived.

'All things new.' The sweep of the Bible story extends from first creation to last. One day God will create a new heaven and earth out of the remnants of the old. The created universe will be liberated from its present state of decay and frustration. Death, crying, mourning and pain will be destroyed. The old order will have passed away. What such a new creation means is beyond imagination, but the writer of Revelation is sure that the most important thing about it is that God will be at its heart. 'Can we start again, please?' 'Even so. Come, Lord Jesus.'

WEEK 49

## SUNDAY

ISAIAH 35:1–10, 65:17–25 (NIV)

The desert and the parched land will be glad;
the wilderness will rejoice and blossom.
Like the crocus, it will burst into bloom;
it will rejoice greatly and shout for joy.
The glory of Lebanon will be given to it,
the splendour of Carmel and Sharon;
they will see the glory of the Lord,
the splendour of our God.

Strengthen the feeble hands,
steady the knees that give way;
say to those with fearful hearts,
'Be strong, do not fear;
your God will come,
he will come with vengeance;
with divine retribution
he will come to save you.'

Then will the eyes of the blind be opened
and the ears of the deaf unstopped.
Then will the lame leap like a deer,
and the tongue of the dumb shout for joy.
Water will gush forth in the wilderness
and streams in the desert.
The burning sand will become a pool,
the thirsty ground bubbling springs.
In the haunts where jackals once lay,
grass and reeds and papyrus will grow.

And a highway will be there;
it will be called the Way of Holiness.
The unclean will not journey on it;
it will be for those who walk in that Way;
wicked fools will not go about on it.
No lion will be there,
nor will any ferocious beast get up on it;
they will not be found there.
But only the redeemed will walk there,
and the ransomed of the Lord will return.
They will enter Zion with singing;
everlasting joy will crown their heads.
Gladness and joy will overtake them,
and sorrow and sighing will flee away.

'Behold, I will create
new heavens and a new earth.
The former things will not be remembered,
nor will they come to mind.
But be glad and rejoice for ever
in what I will create,
for I will create Jerusalem to be a delight
and its people a joy.
I will rejoice over Jerusalem
and take delight in my people;
the sound of weeping and of crying
will be heard in it no more.

'Never again will there be in it
an infant that lives but a few days,
or an old man who does not live out his years;
he who dies at a hundred

will be thought a mere youth;
he who fails to reach a hundred
will be considered accursed.
They will build houses and dwell in them;
they will plant vineyards and eat their fruit.
No longer will they build houses
and others live in them,
or plant and others eat.
For as the days of a tree,
so will be the days of my people;
my chosen ones will long enjoy
the works of their hands.
They will not toil in vain
or bear children doomed to misfortune;
for they will be a people blessed by the Lord,
they and their descendants with them.
Before they call I will answer;
while they are still speaking I will hear.
The wolf and the lamb will feed together,
and the lion will eat straw like the ox,
but dust will be the serpent's food.
They will neither harm nor destroy
in all my holy mountain,' says the Lord.

## MONDAY

ISAIAH 40:1–8, 27–31 (NIV)

Comfort, comfort my people,
says your God.
Speak tenderly to Jerusalem,
and proclaim to her
that her hard service has been completed,
that her sin has been paid for,
that she has received from the Lord's hand
double for all her sins.

A voice of one calling:
'In the desert prepare
the way for the Lord;
make straight in the wilderness
a highway for our God.
Every valley shall be raised up,
every mountain and hill made low;
the rough ground shall become level,
the rugged places a plain.
And the glory of the Lord will be revealed,
and all mankind together will see it.
For the mouth of the Lord has spoken.'

A voice says, 'Cry out.'
And I said, 'What shall I cry?'

'All men are like grass,
and all their glory is like the flowers of the field.
The grass withers and the flowers fall,
because the breath of the Lord blows on them.
Surely the people are grass.
The grass withers and the flowers fall,
but the word of our God stands for ever.'

Why do you say, O Jacob,
and complain, O Israel,
'My way is hidden from the Lord;
my cause is disregarded by my God'?
Do you not know?

Have you not heard?
The Lord is the everlasting God,
the Creator of the ends of the earth.
He will not grow tired or weary,
and his understanding no-one can fathom.
He gives strength to the weary
and increases the power of the weak.
Even youths grow tired and weary,
and young men stumble and fall;
but those who hope in the Lord
will renew their strength.
They will soar on wings like eagles;
they will run and not grow weary,
they will walk and not be faint.

## TUESDAY

EZEKIEL 36:22–36 (REB)

'Therefore tell the Israelites that the Lord God says: It is not for the sake of you Israelites that I am acting, but for the sake of my holy name, which you have profaned among the peoples where you have gone. I shall hallow my great name, which you have profaned among those nations. When they see that I reveal my holiness through you, they will know that I am the Lord, says the Lord God. I shall take you from among the nations, and gather you from every land, and bring you to your homeland. I shall sprinkle pure water over you, and you will be purified from everything that defiles you; I shall purify you from the taint of all your idols. I shall give you a new heart and put a new spirit within you; I shall remove the heart of stone from your body and give you a heart of flesh. I shall put my spirit within you and make you conform to my statutes; you will observe my laws faithfully. Then you will live in the land I gave to your forefathers; you will be my people, and I shall be your God.'

'Having saved you from all that defiles you, I shall command the grain to be plentiful; I shall bring no more famine upon you. I shall make the trees bear abundant fruit and the ground yield heavy crops, so that you will never again have to bear among the nations the reproach of famine. You will recall your wicked conduct and evil deeds, and you will loathe yourselves because of your wrongdoing and your abominations. I assure you it is not for your sake that I am acting, says the Lord God, so feel the shame and disgrace of your ways, people of Israel.

'The Lord God says: When I have cleansed you of all your wrongdoing, I shall resettle the towns, and the ruined places will be rebuilt. The land now desolate will be tilled, instead of lying waste for every passer-by to see. Everyone will say that this land which was waste has become like a garden of Eden, and the towns once ruined, wasted, and shattered will now be fortified and inhabited. The nations still left around you will know that it is I, the Lord, who have rebuilt the shattered towns and replanted the land laid waste; I, the Lord, have spoken and I shall do it.'

## WEDNESDAY

JOHN 2:1–11 (NJB)

On the third day there was a wedding at Cana in Galilee. The mother of Jesus was there, and Jesus and his disciples had also been invited. And they ran out of wine, since the wine provided for the feast had all been used, and the mother of Jesus said to him, 'They have no wine.' Jesus said, 'Woman, what do you want from me? My hour has not come yet.' His mother said to the servants, 'Do whatever he tells you.' There were six stone water jars standing there, meant for the ablutions that are customary among the Jews: each could hold twenty or thirty gallons. Jesus said to the servants, 'Fill the jars with water,' and they filled them to the brim. Then he said to them, 'Draw some out now and take it to the president of the feast.' They did this; the president tasted the water, and it had turned into wine. Having no idea where it came from—though the servants who had drawn the water knew—the president of the feast called the bridegroom and said, 'Everyone serves good wine first and worse wine when the guests are well wined; but you have kept the best wine till now.'

This was the first of Jesus' signs: it was at Cana in Galilee. He revealed his glory, and his disciples believed in him.

## THURSDAY

1 CORINTHIANS 15:50–58 (RSV)

I tell you this, brethren: flesh and blood cannot inherit the kingdom of God, not does the perishable inherit the imperishable.

Lo! I tell you a mystery. We shall not all sleep, but we shall all be changed, in a moment, in the twinkling of an eye, at the last trumpet. For the trumpet will sound, and the dead will be raised imperishable, and we shall be changed. For this perishable nature must put on the imperishable, and this mortal nature must put on immortality. When the perishable puts on the imperishable, and the mortal puts on immortality, then shall come to pass the saying that is written:

'Death is swallowed up in victory.'
'O death, where is thy victory?
O death, where is thy sting?'

The sting of death is sin, and the power of sin is the law. But thanks be to God, who gives us the victory through our Lord Jesus Christ.

Therefore, my beloved brethren, be steadfast, immovable, always abounding in the work of the Lord, knowing that in the Lord your labour is not in vain.

## FRIDAY

2 PETER 3:8–13 (RSV)

But do not ignore this one fact, beloved, that with the Lord one day is as a thousand years, and a thousand years as one day. The Lord is not slow about his promise as some count slowness, but is forbearing toward you, not wishing that any should perish, but that all should reach repentance. But the day of the Lord will come like a thief, and then the heavens will pass away with a loud noise, and the elements will be dissolved with fire, and the earth and the works that are upon it will be burned up.

Since all these things are thus to be dissolved, what sort of persons ought you to be in lives of holiness and godliness, waiting for and hastening the coming of the day of God, because of which the heavens will be kindled and dissolved, and the elements will melt with fire! But according to his promise we wait for new heavens and a new earth in which righteousness dwells.

## SATURDAY

REVELATION 22:1–7 (AV)

And the angel shewed me a pure river of water of life, clear as crystal, proceeding out of the throne of God and of the Lamb. In the midst of the street of it, and on either side of the river, was there the tree of life, which bare twelve manner of fruits, and yielded her fruit every month: and the leaves of the tree were for the healing of the nations.

And there shall be no more curse: but the throne of God and of the Lamb shall be in it: and his servants shall serve him: And they shall see his face; and his name shall be in their foreheads. And there shall be no night there; and they need no candle, neither light of the sun; for the Lord God giveth them light: and they shall reign for ever and ever. And he said unto me, These sayings are faithful and true: and the Lord God of the holy prophets sent his angel to shew unto his servants the things which must shortly be done. Behold, I come quickly: blessed is he that keepeth the sayings of the prophecy of this book.

# FUTURE SHOCK

WEEK 50

This world will never lack prophets, nor prophets an eager audience. Soothsayers are still in business.

But if false prophets and fortune-tellers abound, true prophets of God are neither so numerous nor so popular. Elijah stands at the head of a line of those whose God-given messages often put their own lives at risk (Sunday). In the same tradition, Micaiah's first response to his king's appeal (Monday) seems to have been grimly ironic; when he alone told the truth, a punch in the face was followed by a day or so in prison. But vindication came very soon.

Prophecy often includes foretelling, but is far more than that. Daniel saw into heaven itself during the visions and dreams of his turbulent career at a foreign court (Tuesday). If their meaning sometimes troubled him, it troubled his captors far more.

Earlier than Daniel, Amos describes his job as a prophet with classic simplicity (Wednesday). Later, Jesus salutes John the Baptist as the last of a line of prophets (Thursday)—a latter-day Elijah. But New Testament prophets, men and women, also had words from God requiring interpretation and action (Saturday).

And the great Prophet is Jesus himself (Friday). As he stands and looks at the temple in Jerusalem as the focus of the nation, he forecasts its destruction—and a greater crisis than the world has yet seen.

WEEK
50

# Prophecy

Is your church a prophetic church? Or does that seem a strange question? If so, how far we are from the times of the Bible when prophets and prophecy had great importance.

The word 'prophet' comes from a root which means 'one who speaks for another', and during Old Testament times God raised up many people to speak for him. 'Thus says the Lord' was their favourite cry. What were the characteristics of a prophet?

- **He challenged the people of God**, calling them to live according to the covenant. A strong core of morality runs through prophetic preaching. God wanted his people to honour, love and serve him. The prophet often came with the call to repent.
- **He interpreted national and international events.** In times of calamity and confusion the prophet played a major role in interpreting what God was doing in that situation and how he wanted his people to behave.
- **He foretold the future.** This was not the prophet's central task, and yet many prophets did predict the future with remarkable accuracy. Sometimes they foretold the near future, so that the fulfilment is recorded in the same book of the Bible. Sometimes their predictions did not come true for centuries, as for example prophecies of the coming Messiah.

In Jesus Christ all Old Testament prophecy was fulfilled. He spoke of John the Baptist as the last and greatest of the prophets, the 'forerunner' who brought the whole tradition to its climax in heralding the coming of the Son of God.

Yet despite this fulfilment of prophecy in Christ, we still find prophets working in the early church. They did not come with fresh revelation because all had been fulfilled in Christ. It would appear that these prophets were so open to God and so sensitive to the Spirit that they acted as spiritual guides to the early Christians.

Prophecy, too, was one of Paul's 'gifts of the Spirit'. And many churches today are discovering the importance of the prophetic element. This is excellent as long as certain criteria are kept in mind. All Christian prophecy must be anchored in the Bible. It will reach beyond the merely pietistic and should speak to real needs in the community. There is a strong social and political element in biblical prophecy. The prophet was a man who stood between God and the whole nation and called them back to the Lord.

A church may be prophetic even if it has no 'prophets'. A prophetic church will try to listen to what God is calling them to be, to do and to say in its own context. When faced with social, political and human problems the prophetic church will speak God's word clearly and boldly, standing up for the underprivileged and downtrodden.

## SUNDAY

1 KINGS 17:1–10 (RSV)

Now Elijah the Tishbite, of Tishbe in Gilead, said to Ahab, 'As the Lord the God of Israel lives, before whom I stand, there shall be neither dew nor rain these years, except by my word.' And the word of the Lord came to him, 'Depart from here and turn eastward, and hide yourself by the brook Cherith, that is east of the Jordan. You shall drink from the brook, and I have commanded the ravens to feed you there.' So he went and did according to the word of the Lord; he went and dwelt by the brook Cherith that is east of the Jordan. And the ravens brought him bread and meat in the morning, and bread and meat in the evening; and he drank from the brook. And after a while the brook dried up, because there was no rain in the land.

Then the word of the Lord came to him, 'Arise, go to Zarephath, which belongs to Sidon, and dwell there. Behold, I have commanded a widow there to feed you.' So he arose and went to Zarephath.

## MONDAY

1 KINGS 22:10–18, 24–28 (RSV)

Now the king of Israel and Jehoshaphat the king of Judah were sitting on their thrones, arrayed in their robes, at the threshing floor at the entrance of the gate of Samaria; and all the prophets were prophesying before them. And Zedekiah the son of Chenaanah made for himself horns of iron, and said, 'Thus says the Lord, "With these you shall push the Syrians until they are destroyed." ' And all the prophets prophesied so, and said, 'Go up to Ramoth-gilead and triumph; the Lord will give it into the hand of the king.'

And the messenger who went to summon Micaiah said to him, 'Behold, the words of the prophets with one accord are favourable to the king; let your word be like the word of one of them, and speak favourably.' But Micaiah said, 'As the Lord lives, what the Lord says to me, that I will speak.' And when he had come to the king, the king said to him, 'Micaiah, shall we go to Ramoth-gilead to battle, or shall we forbear?' And he answered him, 'Go up and triumph; the Lord will give it into the hand of the king.' But the king said to him, 'How many times shall I adjure you that you speak to me nothing but the truth in the name of the Lord?' And he said, 'I saw all Israel scattered upon the mountains, as sheep that have no shepherd; and the Lord said, "These have no master; let each return to his home in peace." ' And the king of Israel said to Jehoshaphat, 'Did I not tell you that he would not prophesy good concerning me, but evil?'

Then Zedekiah the son of Chenaanah came near and struck Micaiah on the cheek, and said, 'How did the Spirit of the Lord go from me to speak to you?' And Micaiah said, 'Behold, you shall see on that day when you go into an inner chamber to hide yourself.' And the king of Israel said, 'Seize Micaiah, and take him back to Amon the governor of the city and to Joash the king's son; and say, "Thus says the king, 'Put this fellow in prison, and feed him with scant fare of bread and water, until I come in peace.' " ' And Micaiah said, 'If you return in peace, the Lord has not spoken by me.' And he said, 'Hear, all you peoples!'

## TUESDAY

DANIEL 7:9–14 (NIV)

As I looked,
thrones were set in place,
    and the Ancient of Days took his seat.
His clothing was as white as snow;
    the hair of his head was white like wool.
His throne was flaming with fire,
    and its wheels were all ablaze.
A river of fire was flowing,
    coming out from before him.
Thousands upon thousands attended him;
    ten thousand times ten thousand stood before him.
The court was seated,
    and the books were opened.

Then I continued to watch because of the boastful words the horn was speaking. I kept looking until the beast was slain and its body destroyed and thrown into the blazing fire. (The other beasts had been stripped of their authority, but were allowed to live for a period of time.)

In my vision at night I looked, and there before me was one like a son of man, coming with the clouds of heaven. He approached the Ancient of Days and was led into his presence. He was given authority, glory and sovereign power; all peoples, nations and men of every language worshipped him. His dominion is an everlasting dominion that will not pass away, and his kingdom is one that will never be destroyed.'

## WEDNESDAY

AMOS 3:6–8, 7:10–15 (NIV)

When a trumpet sounds in a city,
    do not the people tremble?
When disaster comes to a city,
    Has not the Lord caused it?

Surely the Sovereign Lord does nothing
    without revealing his plan
    to his servants the prophets.

The lion has roared—
    who will not fear?
The Sovereign Lord has spoken—
    who can but prophesy?

Then Amaziah the priest of Bethel sent a message to Jeroboam king of Israel: 'Amos is raising a conspiracy against you in the very heart of Israel. The land cannot bear all his words. For this is what Amos is saying:

"Jeroboam will die by the sword,
    and Israel will surely go into exile,
    away from their native land." '

Then Amaziah said to Amos, 'Get out, you seer! Go back to the land of Judah. Earn your bread there and do your prophesying there. Don't prophesy any more at Bethel, because this is the king's sanctuary and the temple of the kingdom.'

Amos answered Amaziah, 'I was neither a prophet nor a prophet's son, but I was a shepherd, and I also took care of sycamore fig-trees. But the Lord took me from tending the flock and said to me, "Go, prophesy to my people Israel." '

## THURSDAY

MATTHEW 11:7–15 (REB)

When the messengers were on their way back, Jesus began to speak to the crowds about John: 'What was the spectacle that drew you to the wilderness? A reed swaying in the wind? No? Then what did you go out to see? A man dressed in finery? Fine clothes are to be found in palaces. But why did you go out? To see a prophet? Yes indeed, and far more than a prophet. He is the man of whom scripture says,

Here is my herald, whom I sent
ahead of you,
and he will prepare your way
before you.

'Truly I tell you: among all who have ever been born, no one has been greater than John the Baptist, and yet the least in the kingdom of Heaven is greater than he.

'Since the time of John the Baptist the kingdom of Heaven has been subjected to violence and violent men are taking it by force. For until John, all the prophets and the law foretold things to come; and John is the destined Elijah, if you will but accept it. If you have ears, then hear.'

## FRIDAY

MARK 13:1–8, 32–37 (NJB)

As Jesus was leaving the Temple one of his disciples said to him, 'Master, look at the size of those stones! Look at the size of those buildings!' And Jesus said to him, 'You see these great buildings? Not a single stone will be left on another; everything will be pulled down.'

And while he was sitting on the Mount of Olives, facing the Temple, Peter, James, John and Andrew questioned him when they were by themselves, 'Tell us, when is this going to happen, and what sign will there be that it is all about to take place?'

Then Jesus began to tell them, 'Take care that no one deceives you. Many will come using my name and saying, "I am he," and they will deceive many. When you hear of wars and rumours of wars, do not be alarmed; this is something that must happen, but the end will not be yet. For nation will fight against nation, and kingdom against kingdom. There will be earthquakes in various places; there will be famines. This is the beginning of the birth-pangs.

'But as for that day or hour, nobody knows it, neither the angels in heaven, nor the Son; no-one but the Father.

'Be on your guard, stay awake, because you never know when the time will come. It is like a man travelling abroad: he has gone from his home, and left his servants in charge, each with his own work to do; and he has told the doorkeeper to stay awake. So stay awake, because you do not know when the master of the house is coming, evening, midnight, cockcrow or dawn; if he comes unexpectedly, he must not find you asleep. And what I am saying to you I say to all: Stay awake!'

## SATURDAY

ACTS 11:27–30, 21:7–14 (RSV)

Now in these days prophets came down from Jerusalem to Antioch. And one of them named Agabus stood up and foretold by the Spirit that there would be a great famine over all the world; and this took place in the days of Claudius. And the disciples determined, every one according to his ability, to send relief to the brethren who lived in Judea; and they did so, sending it to the elders by the hand of Barnabas and Saul.

When we had finished the voyage from Tyre, we arrived at Ptolemais; and we greeted the brethren and stayed with them for one day. On the morrow we departed and came to Caesarea; and we entered the house of Philip the evangelist, who was one of the seven, and stayed with him. And he had four unmarried daughters, who prophesied. While we were staying for some days, a prophet named Agabus came down from Judea. And coming to us he took Paul's girdle and bound his own feet and hands, and said, 'Thus says the Holy Spirit, "So shall the Jews at Jerusalem bind the man who owns this girdle and deliver him into the hands of the Gentiles."' When we heard this, we and the people there begged him not to go up to Jerusalem. Then Paul answered, 'What are you doing, weeping and breaking my heart? For I am ready not only to be imprisoned but even to die at Jerusalem for the name of the Lord Jesus.' And when he would not be persuaded, we ceased and said, 'The will of the Lord be done.'

WEEK 51

# UPWARD AND ONWARD

'If only for this life we have hope in Christ,' writes Paul to the Corinthians, 'we are to be pitied more than all men.' Those who call, as they intermittently do, for an entirely thiswordly edition of the Christian faith, are hardly true to their own history, let alone their community's foundation documents. Even among the Psalms there are hints of the immortality that was to come through the gospel (Sunday).

The ultimate redemption promised by Jesus to those who believe him (Monday) is enlarged on in the next four letters quoted. Philippians finds Paul, the untiring traveller and toiler, unashamed of his and their 'homeland' in heaven (Tuesday). The Colossians hear that the Christ who is in them is 'the hope of glory' (Wednesday). The Thessalonians are taught not to be lost in grief, because the parting of death is not final. And John's sense of wonder at what shall be is in a true line with the Psalms which began this week (Friday)—though into clearer light and faith than they.

Saturday's reading leads us to the very gates of the city, where there is yet an eleventh-hour warning (Saturday). John has been excluded and exiled on earth, but nothing can now prevent him and his fellow-believers from accepting the final, eternal invitation of his Saviour.

WEEK 51

# The Christian Hope

'I hope so' often signifies wishful thinking, uncertainty or vague optimism. Biblical hope is quite different. It is founded on the character of God and has the ring of confident expectation. It is the *exact* opposite of hopelessness. Jeremiah bought a field on which was encamped the Babylonian army which was invading his country. His action is typical. 'Destruction cannot be God's last word,' he is saying. 'He will be true to his nature and his promises—in the end. One day life will begin again.' God is very much a God of promises. Abraham is called to go out into the unknown with only the promise of a land, a nation and a blessing to lead him on. But this promise is something to cling onto in the dark times.

Hope turns life into a journey. It is not a recurring cycle but a movement forwards into the future which God has in store. Mere optimism produces false, cheap hopes: 'Zion will never fall'; 'The temple can never be destroyed'; 'The exile will soon be over.' The prophets lashed out at this kind of easy prediction. They set their hopes on the covenant love of God and looked beyond disaster to the fulfilment of his promises. Though their works contain scarcely a hint of a personal life beyond death, yet their confidence issued in beautiful and haunting visions of an ideal king, a new earth, a reign of justice and peace, the unity of all peoples and the city of God at the centre of the world.

For the Christian these visions and promises came true in Jesus. 'Christ is our hope,' Paul writes, and John looks forward to a day when the people of God will see Jesus as he is and be like him. They will live the life of the age to come, in the presence of God. They will know perfect peace and security under the rule of the King of kings. They will be re-united with those who have died. A new heaven and earth will signal the end of sin, suffering and death. God will be all in all.

This hope is grounded on more than feelings.

- **It was the logic of Jesus' life**. He lived as if there were more to come. His actions were pointers to a kingdom that would not pass away.
- As people experienced the love of God through him, they began to realize that **God would not throw on to the scrap heap what had cost him so much to redeem**.
- **Jesus taught that he would come again.** Many of his parables bear this meaning. It would be a coming as Lord and Judge of the whole world.
- **His resurrection was the pattern and guarantee of the resurrection of all who were in him**. He was like the firstfruits of a great harvest to come.
- **The Spirit of God living in their hearts assured the Christians that the promises were genuine**. They had the down-payment.

How ought Christians to respond to this? There have always been those who have tried to conjure timetables out of the Bible texts. This is straining for a certainty which is unobtainable. Being too taken up with the intricacies of prophecy becomes code-cracking and, at its worst, leads to giving up on this world in view of the catastrophe which is always about to happen. But hope for the future can affect the way we live in the present even when the details are unknown.

Those who live by the Christian hope need not be shaken by every latest fad; their lives have direction and purpose built in. They work to change what is, because they measure it by what will be. They need not be anxious or fear death, since hope is an anchor. They know that nothing done for Christ is wasted, so they do not easily fall prey to despair when they seem to be getting nowhere. They sit loose to this world and its values because it is not their ultimate home. And, perhaps most importantly, they strive to live lives of which they will not need to be ashamed when Jesus comes.

WEEK 51

## SUNDAY

PSALM 16:8–11, 73:21–26 (RSV)

I keep the Lord always before me;
because he is at my right hand, I shall not be moved.

Therefore my heart is glad, and my soul rejoices;
my body also dwells secure.
For thou dost not give me up to Sheol,
or let thy godly one see the Pit.

Thou dost show me the path of life;
in thy presence there is fullness of joy,
in thy right hand are pleasures for evermore.

When my soul was embittered,
when I was pricked in heart,
I was stupid and ignorant,
I was like a beast toward thee.
Nevertheless I am continually with thee;
thou dost hold my right hand.
Thou dost guide me with thy counsel,
and afterward thou wilt receive me to glory.
Whom have I in heaven but thee?
And there is nothing upon earth that I desire besides thee.
My flesh and my heart may fail,
but God is the strength of my heart and my portion for ever.

## MONDAY

LUKE 21:8–11, 25–31 (NIV)

Jess said to his disciples, 'Watch out that you are not deceived. For many will come in my name, claiming, "I am he," and "The time is near." Do not follow them. When you hear of wars and revolutions, do not be frightened. These things must happen first, but the end will not come right away.'

Then he said to them: 'Nation will rise against nation, and kingdom against kingdom. There will be great earthquakes, famines and pestilences in various places, and fearful events and great signs from heaven.'

'There will be signs in the sun, moon and stars. On the earth, nations will be in anguish and perplexity at the roaring and tossing of the sea. Men will faint from terror, apprehensive of what is coming on the world, for the heavenly bodies will be shaken. At that time they will see the Son of Man coming in a cloud with power and great glory. When these things begin to take place, stand up and lift your heads, because your redemption is drawing near.'

He told them this parable: 'Look at the fig-tree and all the trees. When they sprout leaves, you can see for yourselves and know that summer is near. Even so, when you see these things happening, you know that the kingdom of God is near.'

## TUESDAY

PHILIPPIANS 3:7–21 (NJB)

But what were once my assets I now through Christ Jesus count as losses. Yes, I will go furthur: because of the supreme advantage of knowing Christ Jesus my Lord, I count everything else as loss. For him I have accepted the loss of all other things, and look on them all as filth if only I can gain Christ and be given a faith in Christ, an uprightness from God, based on faith, that I may come to know him and the power of his resurrection, and partake of his sufferings by being moulded to the pattern of his death, striving towards the goal of resurrection from the dead. Not that I have secured it already, not yet reached my goal, but I am still pursuing it in the attempt to take hold of the prize for which Christ Jesus took hold of me. Brothers, I do not reckon myself as having taken hold of it; I can only say that forgetting all that lies behind me, and straining forward to what lies in front, I am racing towards the finishing-point to win the prize of God's heavenly call in Christ Jesus. So this is the way in which all of us who are mature should be thinking, and if you are still thinking differently in any way, then God has yet to make this matter clear to you. Meanwhile, let us go forward from the point we have each attained.

Brothers, be united in imitating me. Keep your eyes fixed on those who act according to the example you have from me. For there are so many people of whom I have often warned you, and now I warn you again with tears in my eyes, who behave like the enemies of Christ's cross. They are destined to be lost; their god is the stomach; they glory in what they should think shameful, since their minds are set on earthly things. But our homeland is in heaven and it is from there that we are expecting a Saviour, the Lord Jesus Christ, who will transfigure the wretched body of ours into the mould of his glorious body, through the working of the power which he has, even to bring all things under his mastery.

## WEDNESDAY

COLOSSIANS 1:21–27 (REB)

Formerly you yourselves were alienated from God, his enemies in heart and mind, as you evil deeds showed. But now by Christ's death in his body of flesh and blood God has reconciled you to himself, so that he may bring you into his own presence, holy and without blame or blemish. Yet you must persevere in faith, firm on your foundations and never to be dislodged from the hope offered in the gospel you accepted. This is the gospel which has been proclaimed in the whole creation under heaven, the gospel of which I, Paul, became a minister.

It is now my joy to suffer for you; for the sake of Christ's body, the church, I am completing what still remains for Christ to suffer in my own person. I became a servant of the church by virtue of the task assigned to me by God for your benefit: to put God's word into full effect, that secret purpose hidden for long ages and through many generations, but now disclosed to God's people. To them he chose to make known what a wealth of glory is offered to the Gentiles in this secret purpose: Christ in you, the hope of glory.

WEEK 51

## THURSDAY

1 THESSALONIANS 4:13–5:11 (NIV)

Brothers, we do not want you to be ignorant about those who fall asleep, or to grieve like the rest of men, who have no hope. We believe that Jesus died and rose again and so we believe that God will bring with Jesus those who have fallen asleep in him. According to the Lord's own word, we tell you that we who are still alive, who are left till the coming of the Lord, will certainly not precede those who have fallen asleep. For the Lord himself will come down from heaven, with a loud command, with the voice of the archangel and with the trumpet call of God, and the dead in Christ will rise first. After that, we who are still alive and are left will be caught up with them in the clouds to meet the Lord in the air. And so we will be with the Lord for ever. Therefore encourage each other with these words.

Now, brothers, about times and dates we do not need to write to you, for you know very well that the day of the Lord will come like a thief in the night. While people are saying, 'Peace and safety,' destruction will come on them suddenly, as labour pains on a pregnant woman, and they will not escape.

But you, brothers, are not in darkness so that this day should surprise you like a thief. You are all sons of the light and sons of the day. We do not belong to the night or to the darkness. So then, let us not be like others, who are asleep, but let us be alert and self-controlled. For those who sleep, sleep at night, and those who get drunk, get drunk at night. But since we belong to the day, let us be self-controlled, putting on faith and love as a breastplate, and the hope of salvation as a helmet. For God did not appoint us to suffer wrath but to receive salvation through our Lord Jesus Christ. He died for us so that, whether we are awake or asleep, we may live together with him. Therefore encourage one another and build each other up, just as in fact you are doing.

## FRIDAY

1 JOHN 2:28–3:3 (RSV)

And now, little children, abide in him, so that when he appears we may have confidence and not shrink from him in shame at his coming. If you know that he is righteous, you may be sure that every one who does right is born of him.

See what love the Father has given us, that we should be called children of God; and so we are. The reason why the world does not know us is that it did not know him. Beloved, we are God's children now; it does not yet appear what we shall be, but we know that when he appears we shall be like him, for we shall see him as he is. And every one who thus hopes in him purifies himself as he is pure.

## SATURDAY

REVELATION 22:8–15 (AV)

And I John saw these things, and heard them. And when I had heard and seen, I fell down to worship before the feet of the angel which shewed me these things. Then saith he unto me, See thou do it not; for I am thy fellowservant, and of thy brethren the prophets, and of them which keep the sayings of this book: worship God. And he saith unto me, Seal not the sayings of the prophecy of this book: for the time is at hand. He that is unjust, let him be unjust still: and he that is righteous, let him be righteous still: and he that is holy, let him be holy still. And, behold, I come quickly; and my reward is with me, to give every man according as his work shall be. I am Alpha and Omega, the beginning and the end, the first and the last.

Blessed are they that do his commandments, that they may have right to the tree of life, and may enter in through the gates into the city. For without are dogs, and sorcerers, and whoremongers, and murderers, and idolaters, and whosoever loveth and maketh a lie.

# VISIONS OF GLORY: REVELATION

This amazing vision was given to John on the island of Patmos, then passed on to seven churches. Christians were being persecuted under Emperor Domitian (AD81—96), and the message to them was of encouragement.

However much power persecutors might seem t have, their days were numbered. The final picture was of Christ victorious, his people vindicated, and all evil destroyed.

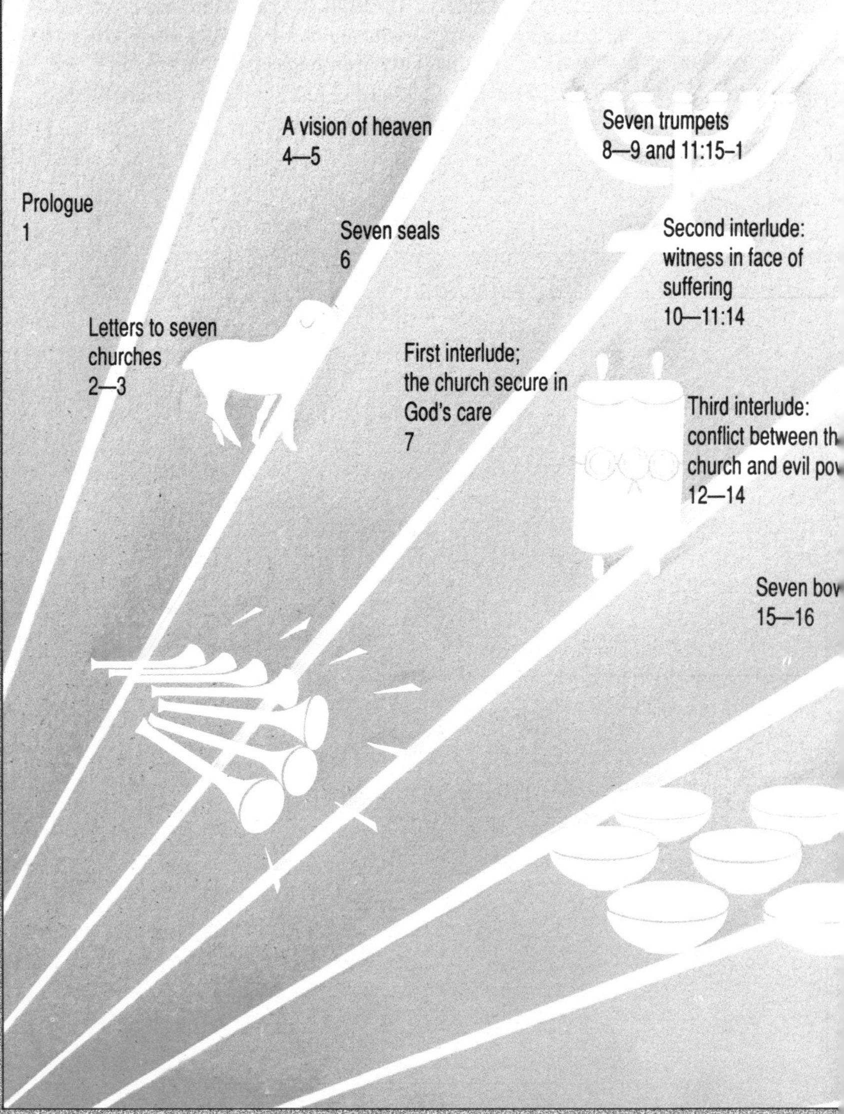

Prologue
1

Letters to seven churches
2—3

A vision of heaven
4—5

Seven seals
6

First interlude; the church secure in God's care
7

Seven trumpets
8—9 and 11:15–1

Second interlude: witness in face of suffering
10—11:14

Third interlude: conflict between th church and evil pov
12—14

Seven bov
15—16

Pergamum
Thyatira
Sardis
Smyrna
Philadelphia
Laodicea
Ephesus
Patmos

## CODE LANGUAGE

Revelation's visionary language represents a special kind of Jewish literature, also to be found in the Old Testament (second half of Daniel, part of Zechariah). These books are often hard to understand, because the original readers would quickly see how the allusions referred to their own hard circumstances, while we may not. But still these strange images retain their power.

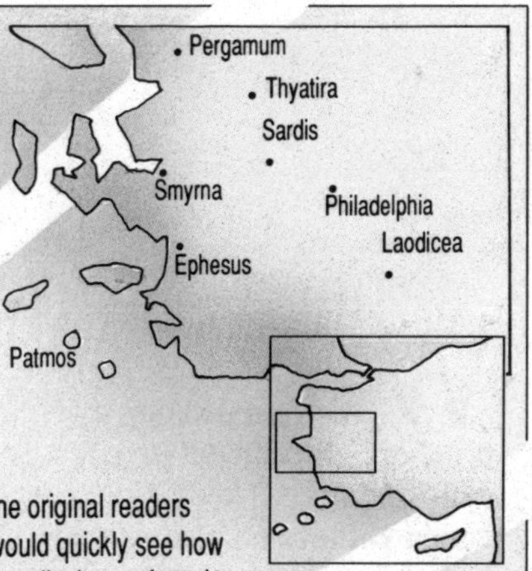

The fall of 'Babylon'
17—19:10

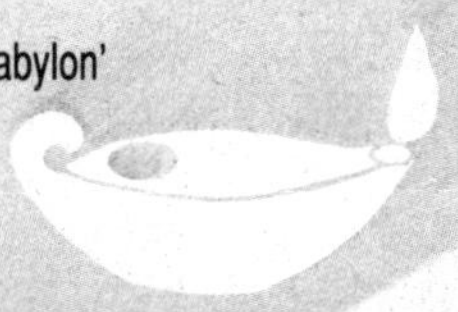

Christ's final coming
19:11–121

Christ's reign and Satan's destruction
20:1–10

The final judgment
20:11–15

New heavens and a new earth
21—22:5

Epilogue
22:6–21

## HAUNTING IMAGES

Certain images crop up repeatedly. Foremost is **the lamb**, a picture of Jesus Christ sacrificed for the world, victor over evil. Another symbol for Jesus is **Alpha and Omega**, first and last letter of the Greek alphabet.

The **lampstands**, in the early chapters, refer to the churches, maintaining Christ's light in the dark world.

**Seven seals, seven bowls and seven trumpets** are a way of describing events leading up to Christ's final coming. They are three ways of picturing the same period of history; evil, war and suffering run through them.

WEEK 52

# THE VISION OF GOD

When God reveals a glimpse of his glory to favoured saints and prophets, the immediate effect is overwhelming. There is no true vision without a voice. Moses, Isaiah and Ezekiel all have experiences almost beyond words, as the first three of our final readings show. But they convey these experiences to us in words, and each time the servant of the Lord also hears the divine revelation in speech that is understood.

To Moses, God shows a presence of sovereign grace (Sunday); to Isaiah, of cleansing holiness (Monday); to Ezekiel, of mysterious glory (Tuesday). To all three God gives through the vision a commitment to speak, serve and lead.

Wednesday's two brief gospel extracts from Matthew and Luke take us into the 'glory' of Jesus as we see his relationship with the Father partly revealed.

Thursday shows us Paul, first overcome in mid-letter with adoration, then concluding another epistle by longing for others to experience the full riches of God the Holy Trinity.

Finally, Saturday combines a small doxology embedded in a small and fierce letter with the last words of the Bible from its last visionary. They are worthy of the first; the Bible's final promise is of Christ's coming, and the last prayer is for his grace for us. Amen!

# God the Trinity

The word 'Trinity', used of God, means that the one God has revealed himself as three persons—Father, Son and Holy Spirit. It is not a biblical word, and it is surprising, if not actually staggering, that the early Christians developed this doctrine. The reasons which led them to do so are to be found in the New Testament—particularly in the way the apostles **met with the living God.**

◆ **A meeting with Jesus Christ.** The first Christians were Jews. Unlike the pagans of their day, they were monotheists, believing firmly in one God who made heaven and earth. Yet we can see in the Gospels the impact the man from Nazareth made on those Jews. His life, his actions and his teaching all conspired to make people ask: 'What kind of man is this? Where does his authority come from?' Then came the time when Peter made his famous declaration: 'You are the Christ (Messiah), the Son of the living God.' Jesus was often evasive about his true nature, preferring the mysterious 'Son of man' description to 'Messiah' and other divine titles. But it dawned on those who surrounded him that the only way to explain this man was by acknowledging that he was in some sense God.

Yet it was the resurrection which brought to a head their thinking about who Jesus was. The sceptical Thomas, after the resurrection, kneels to worship as God the 'man' he had earlier followed: 'My Lord and my God!' Peter preaches on the Day of Pentecost, 'This Jesus, whom you crucified, God has made both Lord and Christ.' From the resurrection on, a new way of understanding Christ developed. Those first Christians were in no doubt whatever that Jesus, their Saviour Jesus, expressed fully and visibly the presence of God himself. Paul, one of the earliest writers, calls him 'Lord', 'image of the invisible God', and 'firstborn of all creation'.

◆ **A meeting with the Holy Spirit.** Jesus told his disciples that after he had gone he would not leave them comfortless; he would send the Holy Spirit to them. They would have learned of the Holy Spirit from the Old Testament: that power of God which came on people for special purposes and then only temporarily. 'He will abide with you for ever,' Jesus told them.

Pentecost was the start of this disturbing encounter with God's Spirit. He came on a bedraggled company of disciples, formed them into a formidable group of God's shock-troopers and made them a loving, caring family. His role was twofold: to direct the attention of people to Jesus as Lord and Saviour, and to come into the lives of those who turned to Jesus through repentance and faith. So to have the Spirit was to be a Christian. The Spirit is given to Christians so that we may know in our own experience the reality of God, and know the salvation offered in Jesus Christ.

◆ **A meeting with Father, Son and Holy Spirit.** The testimony of the New Testament is that those first Christians experienced God in three ways—as Creator, as Saviour and as the one who came into their lives. So there are a large number of references to the three persons in the Godhead. This verse from Paul's letter to the Romans is just an example: 'I urge you, brothers, by our **Lord Jesus Christ** and by the love of the **Spirit**, to join me in my struggles by praying to **God** for me.' The frequency of this threefold pattern indicates how strongly the thinking of the New Testament writers was influenced by their experience of God. They were not writing carefully contrived and thought-out theological books. Rather, from their lived-out experience flowed the excitement of meeting the living God, the one who had revealed himself as Father, Son and Spirit.

It was therefore quite logical and natural that the doctrine of the Trinity—Father, Son and Holy Spirit as separate and equal partners in God's nature—developed in the centuries after the New Testament was written. This is the reason why we recite creeds about the Trinity. And we, like the New Testament Christians, can experience a revolutionary meeting with God the Three-in-One.

## SUNDAY

EXODUS 33:12–23 (REB)

Moses said to the Lord, 'You tell me to lead up this people without letting me know whom you will send with me, even though you have said to me, "I know you by name, and, what is more, you have found favour with me." If I have indeed won your favour, then teach me to know your ways, so that I can know you and continue in favour with you, for this nation is your own people.' The Lord answered, 'I shall go myself and set your mind at rest.' Moses said to him, 'Indeed if you do not go yourself, do not send us up from here; for how can it ever be know that I and your people have found favour with you, except by your going with us? So we shall be distinct, I and your people, from all the peoples on earth.' The Lord said to Moses, 'I shall do what you have asked, because you have found favour with me, and I know you by name.'

But Moses prayed, 'Show me your glory.' The Lord answered, 'I shall make all my goodness pass before you, and I shall pronounce in your hearing the name "Lord". I shall be gracious to whom I shall be gracious, and I shall have compassion on whom I shall have compassion.' But he added, 'My face you cannot see, for no mortal may see me and live.' The Lord said, 'Here is a place beside me. Take your stand on the rock and, when my glory passes by, I shall put you in a crevice of the rock and cover you with my hand until I have passed by. Then I shall take away my hand, and you will see my back, but my face must not be seen.'

## MONDAY

ISAIAH 6:1–8 (AV)

In the year that king Uzziah died I saw also the Lord sitting upon a throne, high and lifted up, and his train filled the temple. Above it stood the seraphims: each one had six wings; with twain he covered his face, and with twain he covered his feet, and with twain he did fly. And one cried unto another, and said, Holy, holy, holy, is the Lord of hosts: the whole earth is full of his glory. And the posts of the door moved at the voice of him that cried, and the house was filled with smoke.

Then said I, Woe is me! for I am undone; because I am a man of unclean lips, and I dwell in the midst of a people of unclean lips: for mine eyes have seen the King, the Lord of hosts. Then flew one of the seraphims unto me, having a live coal in his hand, which he had taken with the tongs from off the altar: And he laid it upon my mouth, and said, Lo, this hath touched thy lips; and thine iniquity is taken away, and thy sin purged. Also I heard the voice of the Lord, saying, Whom shall I send, and who will go for us? Then said I, Here am I; send me.

## TUESDAY

EZEKIEL 1:1–9, 1:22–2:2 (RSV)

In the thirtieth year, in the fourth month, on the fifth day of the month, as I was among the exiles by the river Chebar, the heavens were opened, and I saw visions of God. On the fifth day of the month (it was the fifth year of the exile of King Jehoiachin), the word of the Lord came to Ezekiel the priest, the son of Buzi, in the land of the Chaleans by the river Chebar; and the hand of the Lord was upon him there.

As I looked, behold, a stormy wind came out of the north, and a great cloud, with brightness round about it, and fire flashing forth continually, and in the midst of the fire, as it were gleaming bronze. And from the midst of it came the likeness of four living creatures. And this was their appearance: they had the form of men, but each had four faces, and each of them had four wings. Their legs were straight, and the soles of their feet were like the sole of a calf's foot; and they sparkled like burnished bronze. Under their wings on their four sides they had human hands. And the four had their faces and their wings thus: their wings touched one another; they went every one straight forward, without turning as they went.

Over the heads of the living creatures there was the likeness of a firmament, shining like crystal, spread out above their heads. And under the firmament their wings were stretched out straight, one toward another; and each creature had two wings covering its body. And when they went, I heard the sound of their wings like the sound of many waters, like the thunder of the Almighty, a sound of tumult like the sound of a host; when they stood still, they let down their wings. And there came a voice from above the firmament over their heads; when they stood still, they let down their wings.

And above the firmament over their heads there was the likeness of a throne, in appearance like sapphire; and seated above the likeness of a throne was a likeness as it were of a human form. And upward from what had the appearance of his loins I saw as it were gleaming bronze, like the appearance of fire enclosed round about; and downward from what had the appearance of his loins I saw as it were the appearance of fire, and there was brightness round about him. Like the appearance of the bow that is in the cloud on the day of rain, so was the appearance of the brightness round about.

Such was the appearance of the likeness of the glory of the Lord. And when I saw it, I fell upon my face, and I heard the voice of one speaking.

And he said to me, 'Son of man, stand upon your feet, and I will speak with you.' And when he spoke to me, the Spirit entered into me and set me upon my feet; and I heard him speaking to me.

## WEDNESDAY

MATTHEW 11:25–30 (RSV)

At that time Jesus declared, 'I thank thee, Father, Lord of heaven and earth, that thou hast hidden these things from the wise and understanding and revealed them to babes; yea, Father, for such was thy gracious will. All things have been delivered to me by my Father; and no one knows the Son except the Father, and no one knows the Father except the Son and any one to whom the Son chooses to reveal him. Come to me, all who labour and are heavy laden, and I will give you rest. Take my yoke upon you, and learn from me; for I am gentle and lowly in heart, and you will find rest for your souls. For my yoke is easy, and my burden light.'

LUKE 9:28–36 (RSV)

Now about eight days after these sayings he took with him Peter and John and James, and went up on the mountain to pray. And as he was praying, the appearance of his countenance was altered, and his raiment became dazzling white. And behold, two men talked with him, Moses and Elijah, who appeared in glory and spoke of his departure, which he was to accomplish at Jerusalem. Now Peter and those who were with him were heavy with sleep, and when they wakened they saw his glory and the two men who stood with him. And as the men were parting from him, Peter said to Jesus, 'Master, it is well that we are here; let us make three booths, one for you and one for Moses and one for Elijah'—not knowing what he said. As he said this, a cloud came and overshadowed them; and they were afraid as they entered the cloud, saying, 'This is my Son, my Chosen; listen to him!' And when the voice had spoken, Jesus was found alone. And they kept silence and told no-one in those days anything of what they had seen.

## THURSDAY

ROMANS 11:33–36 (NIV)

Oh, the depth of the riches of the
wisdom and knowledge of God!
How unsearchable his judgments,
and his path beyond tracing out!
'Who has known the mind of the Lord?
Or who has been his counsellor?'
'Who has ever given to God,
that God should repay him?'
For from him and through him
and to him are all things.
To him be the glory for ever!
Amen.

2 CORINTHIANS 13:14 (NIV)

May the grace of the Lord Jesus Christ, and the love of God, and the fellowship of the Holy Spirit be with you all.

## FRIDAY

1 TIMOTHY 6:11–16 (NIV)

But you, man of God, flee from all this, and pursue righteousness, godliness, faith, love, endurance and gentleness. Fight the good fight of the faith. Take hold of the eternal life to which you were called when you made your good confession in the presence of many witnesses. In the sight of God, who gives life to everything, and of Christ Jesus, who while testifying before Pontius Pilate made the good confession, I charge you to keep this commandment without spot or blame until the appearing of our Lord Jesus Christ, which God will bring about in his own time—God, the blessed and only Ruler, the King of kings and Lord of lords, who alone is immortal and who lives in unapproachable light, whom no-one has seen or can see. To him be honour and might for ever. Amen.

## SATURDAY

JUDE 20–25 (AV)

But ye, beloved, building up yourselves on your most holy faith, praying in the Holy Ghost, Keep yourselves in the love of God, looking for the mercy of our Lord Jesus Christ unto eternal life. And of some have compassion, making a difference: And others save with fear, pulling them out of the fire; hating even the garment spotted by the flesh. Now unto him that is able to keep you from falling, and to present you faultless before the presence of his glory with exceeding joy, To the only wise God our Saviour, be glory and majesty, dominion and power, both now and ever. Amen

REVELATION 22:16–21 (AV)

I Jesus have sent mine angel to testify unto you these things in the churches. I am the root and the offspring of David, and the bright and morning star. And the Spirit and the bride say, Come. And let him that heareth say, Come. And let him that is athirst come. And whosoever will, let him take the water of life freely. For I testify unto every man that heareth the words of the prophecy of this book, If any man shall add unto these things, God shall add unto him the plagues that are written in this book: And if any man shall take away from the words of the book of this prophecy, God shall take away his part out of the book of life, and out of the holy city, and from the things which are written in this book. He which testifieth these things saith, Surely I come quickly. Amen. Even so, come, Lord Jesus. The grace of our Lord Jesus Christ be with you all. Amen.

# INDEX TO BIBLE PASSAGES